T0400011

Understanding Insurgent Resilience

This book examines terrorist and insurgent organizations and seeks to understand how such groups persist for so long, while introducing a new strategic doctrine for countering these organizations.

The work discusses whether familial or meritocratic insurgencies are more resilient to counterinsurgency pressures. It argues that it is not the type of organization that determines resilience, but rather the efficiency functions of social capital and trust, which have different natures and forms, within them. It finds that while familial insurgencies can challenge incumbents from the start, they weaken over time, whereas meritocracies will generally strengthen. The book examines four of the most enduring and lethal insurgent organizations: the Haqqani Network in Afghanistan, Lashkar-e-Taiba in Pakistan, Jemaah Islamiyah in Indonesia, and the Abu Sayyaf in the Philippines. The author breaks down each group into its formative strengths and vulnerabilities and presents a bespoke model of strategic counterintelligence that can be used to manipulate, degrade, and destroy each organization.

This book will be of much interest to students of counterinsurgency, terrorism, intelligence, security, and defence studies in general.

Andrew D. Henshaw is an independent adviser to governments on defence and intelligence issues. He has 27 years' experience in military Special Forces and Counterintelligence operations and has a PhD from Macquarie University, Australia.

Cass Military Studies

Countering Insurgencies and Violent Extremism in Asia
Edited by Shanthie Mariet D'Souza

Commercial Insurgencies in the Networked Era
The Revolutionary Armed Forces of Colombia
Oscar Palma

The Politics of Military Families
State, Work Organizations, and the Rise of the Negotiation Household
Edited by René Moelker, Manon Andres, and Nina Rones

Organisational Learning and the Modern Army
A New Model for Lessons-Learned Processes
Tom Dyson

Civil-Military Relations in International Interventions
A New Analytical Framework
Karsten Friis

Defence Diplomacy
Strategic Engagement and Interstate Conflict
Daniel H. Katz

Management and Military Studies
Classical and Current Foundations
Joseph Soeters

Understanding Insurgent Resilience
Organizational Structures and the Implications for Counterinsurgency
Andrew D. Henshaw

For more information about this series, please visit: www.routledge.com/Cass-Military-Studies/book-series/CMS

Understanding Insurgent Resilience

Organizational Structures and the Implications for Counterinsurgency

Andrew D. Henshaw

Routledge
Taylor & Francis Group

LONDON AND NEW YORK

First published 2021
by Routledge
2 Park Square, Milton Park, Abingdon, Oxon OX14 4RN

and by Routledge
52 Vanderbilt Avenue, New York, NY 10017

Routledge is an imprint of the Taylor & Francis Group, an informa business

British Library Cataloguing-in-Publication Data
A catalogue record for this book is available from the British Library

Library of Congress Cataloging-in-Publication Data
Names: Henshaw, Andrew D, 1976– author.
Title: Understanding insurgent resilience: organizational structures and the
implications for counterinsurgency/Andrew D Henshaw.
Other titles: Organizational structures and the implications for
counterinsurgency
Description: Abingdon, Oxon; New York: Routledge, 2020. | Series: Cass
military studies | Includes bibliographical references and index.
Identifiers: LCCN 2020001460 | ISBN 9780367463168 (hardback) | ISBN
9781003028116 (ebook)
Subjects: LCSH: Counterinsurgency. | Insurgency–Case studies. |
Organizational resilience–Case studies. | Terrorism–Prevention. |
Intelligence service.
Classification: LCC U241 .H47 2020 | DDC 355.02/18–dc23
LC record available at https://lccn.loc.gov/2020001460

ISBN: 978-0-367-46316-8 (hbk)
ISBN: 978-1-003-02811-6 (ebk)

Typeset in Times New Roman
by Wearset Ltd, Boldon, Tyne and Wear

This book is dedicated to my family and my two beautiful possums who inspire my life every day. As a father the most rewarding service in life is watching you both grow, mature, and lead the most wonderful lives you can.

I also dedicate it to all those I have served with in the military and worked with in the Counterintelligence branch over the last 27 years, and to the operators around the world who do the same.

Contents

Illustrations

Figures

Tables

Abbreviations

ACCT	ASEAN Convention on Counter Terrorism
ADB	Asian Development Bank
AeH	Ahl-e-Hadith
AFP	Armed Forces of the Philippines
AHRC	Asian Human Rights Commission
AiA	al-Qaeda in Aceh
ANA	Afghan National Army
APRP	Afghan Peace and Reintegration Programme
AQ	al-Qaeda
AQI	al-Qaeda in Iraq
ARMM	Autonomous Region in Muslim Mindanao
ASEAN	Association of Southeast Asian Nations
ASG	Abu Sayyaf Group
BIFF	Bangsamoro Islamic Freedom Fighters
BIN	Badan Intelijen Negara, or State Intelligence Agency Indonesia
CCIT	Comprehensive Convention on International Terrorism
CI	Counterintelligence
CIA	Central Intelligence Agency
COIN	Counterinsurgency
CPEC	China-Pakistan Economic Corridor
CT	Counterterrorism
DET 88	Detasemen 88, or Densus 88
DI	Darul Islam
DGMI	Directorate General of Military Intelligence, Indian Army
DM	Disposition Matrix
FATA	Federally Administered Tribal Areas
FKAAI	Forum Komunikasi Alumni Afghanistan Indonesia
GCHQ	Government Communications Headquarters, UK
H-Loop	Henshaw's Loop of Manipulation
HQN	Haqqani Network
HM	Harkat-ul-Mujahedeen
HuJI	Harkat-ul-Jihadi-Islami
HuM	Hizbul Mujahedeen

HUMINT	Human Intelligence (Operations)
IED	Improvised Explosive Device
ISAF	International Security Assistance Force
ISAFP	Intelligence Service of the Armed Forces of the Philippines
ISD	Internal Security Department, Singapore
ISI	Inter-Services Intelligence, Pakistan
ISIL	Islamic State in Iraq and the Levant
Jamaat AeH	Lashkar-e-Taiba
JAT	Jamaah Ansharut Tauhid
JeM	Jaish-e-Muhammed
JI	Jemaah Islamiyah
JuD	Jama'at-ud-Da'awa
KN	Khairun Naas
LeT	Lashkar-e-Taiba
MCFF	Mujahedeen Commando Freedom Fighters
MDI	Markaz Dawa-wal-Irshad
MILF	Moro Islamic Liberation Front
MIT	Mujahideen East Timor
MMI	Majelis Mujahedeen Indonesia/Indonesia Mujahedeen Council
MNLF	Moro National Liberation Front
NCIX	U.S. National Counterintelligence Executive
NDS	|Afghanistan Riyasat-e-Amniyat-e-Milli, or National Directorate of Security
NGO	Non-Governmental Organization
NPA	New People's Communist Army
OFAC	Office of Foreign Assets Control, U.S.
POLRI	National Police, Indonesia
RAW	Research and Analysis Wing
RGA	Regional Autonomous Government
SAS	Special Air Service, UK
SCI	Strategic Counterintelligence
SDGT	Specially Designated Global Terrorist
SET	Social Exchange Theory
SIGINT	Signals Intelligence
SLSD	Sustainable Livelihoods and Social Economic Development in the Southeast Region of Afghanistan
SPCPD	Southern Philippines Council for Peace and Development
SVIED	Suicide Vest Improvised Explosive Device
SZOPAD	Special Zone of Peace and Development
TLO	The Liaison Office
TNI	Tentara Nasional Indonesia, or Indonesian Military
TSD	Technical Services Division, India
TTP	Tehrik-e-Taliban Pakistan

UJC	United Jihad Council
UN	United Nations
UNSC	United Nations Security Council
U.S.	United States
VBIED	Vehicle-Borne Improvised Explosive Device

Foreword

Combatants are the enablers of insurgency, on both sides. There cannot be an insurgency without an incumbent authority with its own forces to overthrow. Likewise, there cannot be an incumbent without a challenger. However, insurgency is not a conventional war, though it is perhaps one of the oldest forms of warfare man has fought. Therefore, this also must mean that all soldiers are not equal. What we call "regular" infantry are trained to fight conventional wars and conduct conventional operations when deployed into theatres not the norm, such as take and hold ground. But those that seek out and engage the insurgency at the primal level are different. Usually, such units occupy a military's special capabilities, and the Special Forces of air, sea, and land that operate in enemy territory under guerrilla conditions. Working in such environments gives a person unique insight into the challenges, difficulties, and the requirements needed to successfully prosecute mission objectives.

Of my 25 years in the British Army, 14 were spent actively engaged in counterinsurgency and counterterrorism operations in Borneo, Dhofar, Northern Ireland, and the UK mainland. While each is different in its own idiosyncrasies, insurgencies share some basic commonalities. In essence, they are each an armed rebellion against the legitimately elected authority competing for control of people, land, state, and law, and in some countries, insurgency has become part and parcel of everyday life. To understand counterinsurgency operations one must first understand insurgency and the dynamics of revolutionary warfare. I have learnt these first-hand in the field from 14 continuous years at war.

What is evident is that insurgent wars persist, as they have for century after century, and indeed they will probably persist for many more. If we look back at history, it is replete with examples of how insurgencies have been successfully destroyed time and again. Sadly though, history also shows that while many successes are etched into the history books, the failure to learn from them and the destiny of re-walking the same paths to failure are far more prominent. This offers a logical solution. If we do not look back into the past for the answers to defeat insurgency, we must, therefore, look forward.

Andrew poses the question of how insurgent organizations persist and remain so resilient to our efforts to counter them. To answer this, he has investigated the insurgent organizations themselves. Given the human cost of this nature of warfare it is surprising that modern military forces continue to show greater ability to repeat the failures of history rather than the successes. In his compelling book Andrew has provided not only an excellent account of where the resilience of insurgent organizations comes from, but also a means to degrade it with a new, innovative, and indeed ground-breaking intelligence doctrine to address these issues. Moreover, I know Andrew's work is largely based on experience, rather than solely on an academic or theoretical background. Andrew's military service in the Special Forces, his work in the private contracting and advisory sphere, and 16 years in counterintelligence are equally elemental foundations of the body of work presented within these pages.

This book is an essential reference for all military, intelligence, law enforcement, policy-makers, bureaucratic officers, and political leaders who have any connection to insurgency, terrorism, political violence, or communal security. Andrew provides the means to understand organizations from the inside out, and then having done so, offers the means to influence, shape, degrade, or destroy them as needed. The strategic counterintelligence doctrine Andrew presents is a complex, asymmetric, and comprehensive introduction to the craft as well as being one that can meld seamlessly with special-tasking military and law enforcement operations. This book is a paradigm shift that when applied will have significant value in addressing the enduring wars of insurgency and the human toll that comes with them.

Iain D. Townsley
Veteran – Her Majesty's 22 Special Air Service Regiment
Hereford, England

Acknowledgements

Of those I need to thank there is no fitting order, for there are many I am grateful to. Dr Adam Lockyer and Professor Grant Wardlaw, supervisors and mentors during my doctoral studies have been pinnacles of guidance, sagely advice, and sources of most-needed encouragement. My mother, next, is a bastion of stoicism, determination, and perseverance, and these traits I have inherited from her. These qualities are critical companions on this enterprise, and on my life's journey. From my father's influence I have built a life guided by the simple tenets of principle, focus, and achievement.

My wife Carmen, and my children especially, have been significant in continuing to motivate me to never give up on reaching my goal, or to undertake new adventures yet to come. Next, I am thankful to my many friends who assisted me in various ways during many years of academic study and operations, as well as the development of this book. That list is long but principal among them are Jim A, Professor Katsumata, Ghost, Lieutenant Col. F Krisamakrit, Stuart, Drew, and of course Benny. Others that need to be thanked are my very dear friends and teachers in life Rob Watt, Sensei Steven McKeown, Soke Taninobu, O-Sensei Utsuebara, and Craig Moore for the years spent in the dojo, and Reno and Grant for sharing my other passions in life. Last, I must thank my very dear friend Iain whom I have had the privilege of serving with, working with, getting out of dangerous situations with, and a man I call a true friend and mentor.

To you all I am thankful.

Part I

Introduction to insurgency and the function of organizations

1 Introduction

By July 2018, Afghanistan had already reached the highest yearly civilian death toll in over 17 years of ongoing war: 1,355 children and 544 women were among the 5,122 civilian deaths (UNAMA 2018). What is more, by September 2019 the Taliban controlled more territory in the country than it did before the U.S. and allied forces invaded. Though while Afghanistan stands out in terms of the severity and longevity of its violence, it is not the sole long-running insurgent conflict in the world. Many other countries in the Middle East (Iraq, Syria, Libya, Yemen), and states in Africa, Asia, and Southeast Asia also suffer enduring insurgencies.[1] This begs the question of how insurgent organizations persist and remain so resilient to efforts to counter them. Is it a failure of methods, doctrine, and the external pressures exerted on insurgent organizations? Alternatively, is it the resilience of the insurgents themselves and how they respond to external pressures that prolong violent political conflicts?

This book searches for answers to these questions by peering into the insurgent organizations themselves. In doing so, it contributes to our theoretical and empirical understanding of insurgent organizations so that governments can identify new ways to penetrate, counter, degrade, and destroy them. The book compares two broad types: familial versus meritocratic insurgent organizations. Familial insurgent organizations are those that draw extensively on familial connections when appointing commanders and leaders and in structuring their insurgency. Examples of familial insurgent organizations include the Islamic State-aligned Maute Group in the Southern Philippines, the Liberation Tigers of Tamil Elam (LTTE), the Revolutionary Armed Forces of Colombia – People's Army (FARC), and the Haqqani Network in Afghanistan. The Haqqani Network, in particular, exemplifies a familial organization with deep, broad-reaching, and powerfully entrenched kinship ties and clan bonds. It operates throughout Loya Paktia, the Federally Administered Tribal Areas (FATA), and Waziristan, and is responsible for some of the highest-profile attacks in the Afghan war.

Meritocratic insurgent groups, on the other hand, are those where recruitment, promotion, and senior leadership structures are based on talent and professionalism rather than any family or kin connections. A structure is how organizations build themselves and develop over time in response to internal influences and external pressures. More succinctly, structure describes the architecture of an organization. In true meritocratic organizations, everyone presumably has equal opportunities for advancement and personal gain dependent on their individual strengths and worth, regardless of their background.[2]

Examples of meritocratic insurgent organizations include Gama'a al-Islamiyya (Islamic Group), Ansar Dine, Al-Aqsa Martyrs Brigade (AAMB), al-Qaeda in Iraq (AQI), and Lashkar-e-Taiba (LeT) in Pakistan. AQI, for instance, had little in the way of an Iraqi kinship network to draw upon. As a consequence its recruitment, membership, and leadership were a varied group that included international and domestic jihadists. Indeed, the membership of AQI was an international melting pot with foreign fighters joining local Iraqis to resist the Iraqi Government and international coalition. Advancement within AQI was based on meritocracy. As a result, the top echelon were a diverse group with a range of different nationalities and backgrounds.

Ceteris paribus, which of these two types of insurgent organizations should governments expect to be the more difficult to defeat? At first glance there might be good intuitive arguments both ways. On the one hand, it might be assumed that family ties would be harder for security forces to penetrate and, if an insurgent fighter were captured, it would be more difficult for the government to convince the captive to "turn" on their family. The Mafia, for instance, might be considered the archetypal familial organization and has a worthy reputation for being difficult to infiltrate or encourage members to defect from.[3]

Alternatively, there are good intuitive arguments for why meritocratic organizations might be more resilient. First, an organization based on individual capabilities (intelligence, dedication, etc.) might be assumed to be an overall better system than one based on nepotism. Indeed, nepotism has become synonymous with ineffectiveness and graft. Second, one might speculate that the security and intelligence services would have an easier time constructing a "social network analysis" of an organization based on familial connections than on one that is not. Despite good intuitive arguments both ways, there has been little rigorous scholarly research that has compared these two types of insurgent organizations against their respective resilience. This book is an attempt to fill this gap.

The complexities of insurgency

Given the human cost of insurgent warfare it is of little surprise that these phenomena have attracted a great deal of scholarly attention. One research agenda has asked why governments find it hard to win (Mack 1975; Arreguin-Toft 2001; Sinno 2008; Meron 2012; Staniland 2014), while scholars on the other side of the coin have asked how insurgent organizations appear to be so resilient (Mockaitis 2003; Connable and Libicki, 2010). Among this second group, some scholars have made attempts at examining the specific strengths and vulnerabilities of different organizations, such as Mobley (2008) in his analysis of counterintelligence risks, and Turbiville (2009) in his research on insurgent offensive intelligence collection practices.[4] However, few have focused on the role of family and meritocracy in insurgent organizational resilience.[5]

In order to begin though we need to delineate what insurgency is. Trebbi and Weese (2015) define insurgency as armed rebellion against central authority, while Burchill (2016) describes it as actions taken to conquer existing power structures. These definitions provide a contemporary understanding. This book builds on these, and defines insurgency as an organized attempt by an armed organization to violently challenge the legitimacy of an incumbent authority and compete for control of people, land, laws, or the state itself. This expands the definition subtly to allow for the understanding of more nuanced dimensions and prismatic scope. This is achieved by viewing insurgency as actor groups in competition for authority over the whole society from which they come, rather than as actor groups in competition with others for primacy.

As Kalyvas writes on the blurred attempts of distinctions of human political violence, "Typically, they do not result from an overarching conceptual perspective; rather they are the result of practical considerations and the often-arbitrary (and solitary) development of a given subfield" (2019, 11). Therefore, the definition provided here addresses the issue of clarity by defining insurgency as a macro effort of political change, and one with a myriad of dimensions. This supports the goal of providing important understanding of how insurgency can be addressed with new ideas, approaches, and particularly a new strategic counterintelligence doctrine to exploit identified strengths and vulnerabilities.[6]

How to use this book

This book addresses a highly specialized niche within the counterinsurgency literature. Due to its design, focus on organizational resilience, and the presentation of how that can be degraded and manipulated with strategic counterintelligence, it is aimed at a multi-demographic audience. Such an audience may include operational leaders and practitioners of intelligence tradecraft and subdisciplines, scholars, academics, and researchers. Likewise, it is particularly relevant to students as a coursework book in the disciplines of security, counterinsurgency (COIN), counterterrorism (CT), conflict and military studies, law enforcement intelligence and criminal studies, and international relations social sciences.

What makes this book different?

The security studies field is highly populated and growing every day, but it is unusual that genuinely new and novel material is introduced, particularly that which can be operationalized and put into practice. Building on the comprehensive analysis of insurgent organizational resilience, the material presented in Chapter 8 does so by introducing a new strategic counterintelligence doctrine that can be deployed into COIN operations globally. Succinctly speaking, this book attempts to provide the reader with the means to understand how insurgent resilience can be weakened, as well as a tour of the toolset required to do so.

It therefore achieves two critically important goals as a learning tool, and as a framework for operationalized application. This comes with a caveat, however. Chapter 8 is an introduction to strategic counterintelligence, not the doctrine itself. Those familiar with the practice of intelligence collection and counterintelligence operations will know the methodology involved, and for them this book provides a new direction. For others who are seeking to develop such knowledge, this book is a gateway into that world. It is this dualistic approach of problem analysis and understanding, and then the bespoke solution design of strategic counterintelligence in COIN, that sets this book aside from others.

Additionally, this book is intended to be complementary to other works, methods, and doctrines of warfare. As with every endeavour, it is not possible to arrive at a point of understanding without a body of knowledge forged by others, and there are many pinnacle works in the counterinsurgency realm that have made significant contributions to COIN theory and practice. These include: David Galula's *Counterinsurgency Warfare: Theory and Practice*, Praeger, 1964; Leites and Wolf's *Rebellion and Authority: An Analytical Essay on Insurgent Conflicts*, Markham, 1970; and Fearon and Laitin's *Ethnicity, Insurgency, and Civil War*, American Political Science Review 97, 2003. Likewise, there is a healthy body of more recent texts that equally make valuable contributions, such as Shelly's *Dirty Entanglements: Corruption, Crime, and Terrorism*, Cambridge University Press, 2014; Paul Moorcraft's *The Jihadist Threat: The Re-Conquest of the West?*, Naval Institute Press, 2016; Andrew Mumford's *Counterinsurgency Wars and the Anglo-American Alliance*, Georgetown University Press, 2017; and Thomas Mockaitis's *The COIN Conundrum: The Future of U.S. Counterinsurgency and U.S. Land Power*, Department of the Army, 2017.

In the specialist academic field, works include Paul Rich and Usabelle Duyvesteyn, eds., *The Routledge Handbook of Insurgency and counterinsurgency,* Routledge, 2012; James Forest, ed., *The Making of a Terrorist: Recruitment, Training, and Root Causes* [three volumes], Praeger Security International, 2006; Walter Enders and Todd Sandler, eds. *The Political Economy of Terrorism,* Cambridge University Press, 2006; and Ekaterina Stepanova, *Terrorism in Asymmetric Conflict: Ideological and Structural Aspects*, Oxford University Press, 2008. These modern texts are some of the leading academic writings on the subjects of insurgency, counterinsurgency, and terrorism to date.

This book is a little different. Rather than assuming a phenomenological approach, it delivers nuanced understanding using detailed case studies that drill into the minutiae of insurgency, from the macro to the daily tactical levels. The analysis of familial versus meritocratic organizational structures and types enables better understanding of social capital and trust, how members rise through roles and responsibilities in different organizational types, and in turn the strengths and weaknesses of various structural systems.

Understanding this is very important because it can explain how familial and meritocratic structures affect insurgent organizational resilience in the face of an incumbent government's attempts to defeat them. Few have attempted to carefully examine the operational side of insurgent resilience and responses to external pressures, and particularly the specific relationships of organizational leadership types, insurgency systematics (i.e. the system of activities to gather inputs, process and develop them, and then produce outputs), and social capital and trust.[7] Likewise, those who have attempted to use potentially similar insights to develop new models to address insurgency are equally scarce.

At both longitudinal and chronological levels, the book makes a novel contribution to our understanding of insurgency. As insurgencies move through the three phases of inception, maturity, and cessation/current state, the differences of meritocracy and familial organizations display divergent strengths and vulnerabilities. By understanding the importance of organizational types and how they remain resilient, the book offers to the insurgency, security, and broader terrorism literature a unique framework for identifying how, and essentially when, insurgent organizations are highly potent, and how to counter them when they are most vulnerable.

Definitions and analytical overview

The book places insurgent organizations into one of two categories. These are *familial* and *meritocratic* (Figure 1.1). Familial organizations are those where the majority of the leadership (i.e. more than 50 per cent) share immediate or extended family connections. These groups also rely heavily upon family and kin networks for logistical support and recruitment. The decision-making process within familial organizations tends to be collegiate, with family members inside and outside the operational command being invited to contribute to discussions.

Meritocratic organizations are those where the leadership do not generally share familial bonds (e.g. less than 50 per cent). Promotion is thereby based on other characteristics that might include the insurgent's intelligence, leadership aptitude, military effectiveness, or ideological/religious zeal. In contrast with familial organizations, the decision-making within meritocratic organizations often is centralized more heavily on a single apex leader. Additionally, bad decisions by leaders can offer opportunities for less-senior leaders to take advantage.

In familial organizations, the leader's authority derives from the collective belief that they can be trusted to act to benefit the entire familial group over their own private gain or reward. In contrast, leaders of meritocratic organizations often possess executive power that places organizational benefit above that of members. As promotion and status within the organization is based upon performance, competition between lieutenants and junior cell-commanders is generally encouraged – as long as it remains at a level that is not harmful to the organization. At the same time though, this characteristic makes meritocratic organizations more prone to fragmenting or splitting apart.

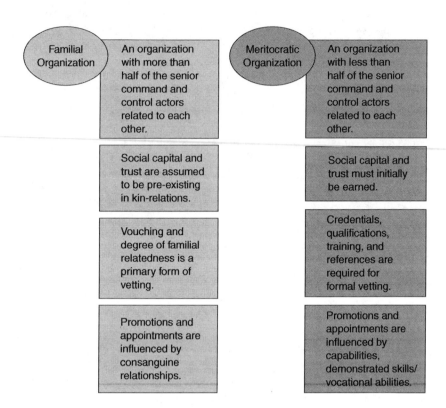

Figure 1.1 Types of insurgent organizations.

Why study insurgency at all?

Insurgencies are important for a range of reasons (Fearon and Laitin 2004; Porch 2013; Della Porta 2014).[8] The frequency and longevity of modern insurgencies and their human cost mark them out as an important phenomenon within security studies. Furthermore, insurgencies are common. Between 2003 and 2019 there were over 80 insurgencies, many of which are still raging (START 2016; ICG 2019). This compares with only six international wars over the same period, and two of those, being Afghanistan and Iraq, each went on to become insurgencies. Likewise, insurgencies are long. During the same period, the average length of an insurgency was 10 to 15 years compared to 104 weeks for conventional and international wars (Davenport 2014). Finally, insurgencies are deadly. Not including disease and famines caused by warfare, over 759,000 people have been killed in insurgencies between 2000 and 2016. Nearly 300,000 of these were in Afghanistan and Pakistan alone between 2001 and 2018 (Crawford 2018). This contrasts to 17,500 deaths that occurred as a result of terrorist attacks targeting civilians.

In addition, insurgencies are not merely localized problems. Insurgencies tend to spread to neighbouring states. They can also influence international instability between regions and between great powers, who may decide to intervene.[9] Despite this, some may still ask what possible benefit there can be in understanding the unique internal dynamics of insurgency at all. This question has largely been answered in the existing literature. For example, much work has been done to understand insurgency from policy, political, socio-economic, religious, and ideological levels; yet, insurgencies are becoming longer, not shorter (Souleimanov 2014; Anderson and McKnight 2015; Hansen-Lewis and Shapiro 2015).[10] Perhaps there are other internal facets of insurgency that have been somewhat overlooked or taken for granted. While organizations in insurgency have been closely examined (Tarrow 2007; Sinno 2008; Metelits 2010; Staniland 2014), the specific natures of familial and meritocratic structural types, and how they play a part in insurgent resilience, have received far less treatment.

One potential exception to this is the Hoffman-Sageman debate. On the one hand, Hoffman (2006) provides an authoritative understanding of the characteristics of modern terrorist organizations, including their internal organizations, autonomous control dynamics, and hierarchical structures. On the other, Sageman (2004) demonstrates a commanding knowledge of network functionality in politically violent organizations, and particularly the performance and topography of multi-layer networks. However, as intuitive as these studies are, family, meritocracy, and the different functionalities and durability of internal social capital and trust are absent, which this book argues are critical components of insurgent organizational resilience.

Social capital and trust act as a mortar that bonds groups together and allows them to achieve their goals, and in this book I argue that social capital and trust operate differently between familial and meritocratic groups. In familial ones social capital is usually facilitated organically, economically, and internally. In meritocratic ones it is generated by professionalization and utilitarianism and developed externally. In both types there are strengths and vulnerabilities. Both can be exploited with strategic counterintelligence but, as I explain, the specific methods and tradecraft must vary between organizational types. I offer to the reader that examining insurgency under these terms is an effective new method for the ongoing and future remediation of the insurgency phenomenon.

The approach

In this book I examine three central variables: (i) insurgent organizational structure (familial or meritocratic in type); (ii) social capital and trust; and (iii) external pressures. The central focus is on how the different organizational structures develop and maintain resilience. I argue that organizational structures are not what directly results in resilience. Rather, it is how different organizational structures experience, facilitate, and enable social capital and trust and their relevance to organizational efficiency that most directly affects an organization's resilience. A range of critical factors influences this as organizations pass through various stages of internal trust, and thus resilience, as represented in Figure 1.2.

This book finds that familial organizations are more resilient than meritocratic organizations in the early phases of an insurgency. Tyler (2017) references the differences between personal and institutional trust that may be a cause for this. Trust, in this context, is defined as the motivating factors that explain cooperation and collective engagement in action. This is for two reasons. First, trust is something that needs to be *earned* in meritocratic organizations but will generally be pre-existing in familial ones. Tilly (2017) puts it that trust relationships cluster and increase in strength, particularly as the duration and value of an organization's goals increase. This does not mean that meritocratic organizations have inferior internal trust throughout their lifespan, however. Trust can be earned over time and result in these organizations developing as much, if not more, internal trust than familial organizations because as Levi and Stoker remark, "trust is relational" (2000, 476). It is common to hear former soldiers and guerrillas in meritocratic organizations refer to their comrades as a "band of brothers", but fellowship is only forged over time.

Second, familial organizations often find recruiting easier in the early phases than do meritocratic organizations. They have ready-made recruitment pools that require less security vetting or political indoctrination. Conversely, the pool of potential recruits will generally be smaller for familial organizations than for meritocratic ones. These two factors could make familial organizations more resilient in the early phases of an insurgency; however, the longer an insurgency

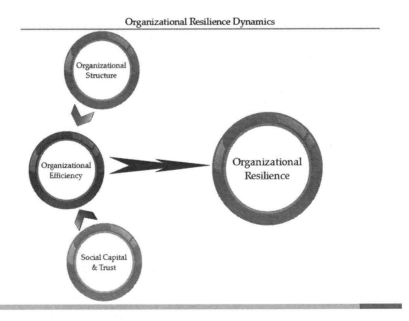

Figure 1.2 Organizational resilience dynamics.

lasts the more resilient meritocratic organizations may become. As a result it becomes evident that if a meritocratic organization can survive through its "start-up" phase, then it can generally be expected to be larger, more effective, and more resilient than its familial counterparts in the long run. I depict this situation in Table 1.1, which illustrates the general trends of organizational types for the phases of insurgency, inclusive of: (i) inception; (ii) maturity; and (iii) cessation/current state.

The data suggests that familial organizations have largely finite resources that over time are constrained by the geography of their territorial control, and by the extensions of their kinship cohorts. These can be expanded, however, as in the case of Jemaah Islamiyah (examined in Chapter 5) but must be done more rapidly than the rate at which resources are depleted. For meritocracies that can gather resources from potential global markets, this is far less of a problem.

During the early phases of conflict, meritocracies are probably more vulnerable to destruction than familial organizations due to limited resources, smaller numbers, low political and ideological acceptance, and the lack of capabilities to challenge incumbents (Mao Tse-Tung 1961; Leites and Wolf 1970; Kalyanaraman 2003). Likewise, they are possibly more susceptible to political pressures such as de-legitimization throughout their life span. Likewise, they can be undermined through initial placating political accommodations to diffuse their rebellion, because unlike familial organizations, they must grow social capital and trust as they develop popular support. If incumbents can backstop this in the early phases, meritocracies can struggle.

However, at later stages organizational change and particularly the processes of restructuring or rebuilding can require significant resources and inputs. These differ between the organizational types, especially over time as insurgent conflicts develop and as organizations are formed and build the capabilities necessary to challenge incumbents. Likewise, as conflicts progress and both sides mature through to the cessation of conflict from success, defeat, or stalemate, each will be burdened with changing resource needs. What is most apparent are the different advantages and disadvantages familial versus meritocratic organizations have over time. Familial organizations, at formation, are much more likely to have extensive resource bases to draw fighters, finances, weapons, and supporters from. The clan and supra-tribal nature of Afghanistan's society was the primary initial source of Haqqani Network resources in its formative phases for example, as it drew extensively on kinship relations. Likewise, Jemaah Islamiyah uses intermarriage to create new resource pools. Therefore, familial organizations have advantages from the start.

Conversely, meritocratic organizations do not have readily accessible resources, and they must build relationships and find socio-economic market groups to access to attract fighters and supporters. These differences do not remain the same over time, however. Rather, they exhibit a convergent/divergent relationship wherein familial insurgencies, as they grow and mature, lose resources because their bases become more and more limited. For meritocracies, their resource pools can be expanded and they can grow as they

Table 1.1 Stages of insurgent conflict

Phases of insurgent conflict					
Initial		Challenging		Conclusion	
Familial	Meritocratic	Familial	Meritocratic	Familial	Meritocratic
(i) Strong kinship resource bases. (ii) Inherent and organic social capital and trust. (iii) High initial resilience lending to efficient insurgency systematics due to cohesion across familial membership.	(i) Low resilience at inception due to small formative structures. (ii) Limited resource bases. (iii) Deficit of social capital and trust.	(i) Reaches parity with incumbents early on. (ii) Resources can become restricted as external pressure increases. (iii) Capability maturity may equal resource maturity and the point of initiation of decline.	(i) Reaches parity to challenge incumbents. (ii) Social capital and trust is stronger. (iii) Resources expanding as capabilities mature. (iv) Increasing counterintelligence vulnerabilities as recruitment is more open.	(i) Resources diminishing in returns. (ii) Familial control group shrinking due to external pressures. (iii) If not successful, resilience decline is in parallel with resource decline.	(i) Social capital and trust can be stronger. (ii) International resources can significantly increase longevity. (iii) Can exceed incumbent capabilities as resources are added.
Position: STRONG	Position: WEAK	Position: MODERATE	Position: MODERATE	Position: WEAK	Position: STRONG

Note
* (i) Inception; (ii) Maturity; (iii) Cessation/Current state

mature. This is indicative of the general trends of familial versus meritocratic insurgent organizations over time. Of course, the type and vigour of application of external pressures is a factor, as it may be the case that some organizations can sustain themselves for considerable periods, if not on an ongoing basis, with the resources they have compared to the depletion of resources by incumbent efforts.

Design and methodology

This research in this book uses a comparative case study method. Morgan *et al.* argue that case study research provides "more complete understanding of complex topics, where contextual influences are of primary concern" (2017, 1060). This is supported by Yin (2014), who posits that the case study method is an excellent way to understand how, and why, things happen when examining contemporary phenomena in real-life contexts. The comparative approach employed in this book will be both longitudinal and chronological. That is, variation in the insurgent group's resilience will be measured across time. Each group will also be compared with other insurgent groups.

The research design employs a "paired case study" approach. The literature on insurgent group longevity points to multiple factors that contribute to resilience, including international support (Fearon and Laitin 2004), geography (Galula 1964), and ideology (Williams 2011). In order to isolate the family relationship and meritocracy as the most prominent point of differences between the cases studies, it is important to "pair" them with organizations that share similarities. For example, if two insurgent groups enjoyed similar levels of international support, operated in similar terrain, and shared a similar ideology while experiencing similar amounts of counterinsurgency pressures, but one was a familial organization while the other was a meritocratic organization, then that last point of difference can be singled out to help explain any subsequent variation in resilience. Pair-matching has increasingly been used in social sciences as a way of attempting to control for factors that clearly have an influence on the dependent variable (i.e. resilience) but are not the factors of interest. By pairing the case studies in this manner we are better able to study the role of family and meritocracy in the resilience of organizations.

Measurement and observation

This book deals with three variables. The first is the organizational structure of the insurgent group. The measure of this variable will be binary: familial or meritocratic. In the simplest terms, there must be a means of distinction between types, and these are derived from the nature of their organizational structures and how they function. The use of a binary system whereby an organization is or is not familial/meritocratic strongly supports the requirements of contrast. In turn, this strengthens the validity of the research, and is a method supported by other military scholars and data scientists. For example, in their work "Taking

Time Seriously: Time-Series-Cross-Section Analysis with a Binary Dependent Variable" (1998) Beck *et al.* assert that the use of cross-sectional data of a binary dependent nature is becoming increasingly common, particularly in relation to binary analysis on military and conflict studies. Elsewhere, David Collett in his book *Modelling Binary Data* (2002) states that the use of binary analysis is highly suited to modelling data and outcomes, which is directly relevant to Chapter 8 in this book.

The second variable is social capital and trust. Trust is defined as the belief of a person's commitment and competence in the domain over which trust is being given (Levi and Stoker, 2000). It can be observed in several ways, such as: (i) the number of individuals involved in the decision-making process; (ii) the degree of authority that more junior commanders are entrusted with by the senior leadership; and (iii) the strength of a leader's command, which is observable by the loyalty of subordinates and adherence to orders. It is assumed, for example, that if a commander openly discusses strategy at a tribal gathering, the trust bonds are relatively high (i.e. no one present is expected to inform the government of the plans). Second, the more authority, independence, and capabilities that the central leadership give to different sections of the organization can act as an empirically observable measure of trust. Third, commitment to the group is observable in the dedication of members to leaders.

Strong social capital and trust probably maintain organizational cohesion and unity, whereas weak social capital and trust impact resilience over time by degrading organizational ties between commanders and fighters. Agency problems of organizational fracturing and splitting are empirically observable measures of weak or negative social capital and trust. These factors can be observed qualitatively through first-hand reports, newspaper articles, governmental reports, scholarly books written on the groups, and other observations obtained from journals and databases.

Finally, external pressures are defined in two forms: (i) hard power, and (ii) soft power. Hard-power and soft-power pressures are the means incumbents, and other actors, use to physically damage insurgents, reduce their combat capabilities, and restrict their insurgency systematics. Some of these involve the resources, recruits, mobility conditions, and partnerships organizations need, making them logical targets. Hard-power external pressures are measured empirically in the direct kinetic actions taken against insurgents, such as incumbent counterterrorism and COIN operations, large-scale attacks with conventional and special-mission forces, and targeted assassinations.[11]

Soft-power pressures are political actions taken to arrest, degrade, and delegitimize insurgency. Examples include social programmes to delegitimize insurgents and their popular support, sanctions on insurgent resources such as donors and supporters, and destroying income-producing drug-producing crops and distribution networks through arrests and the like. Because these pressures are less tangible than hard-power kinetic pressures, soft power is measurable through media releases, interviews, interrogation of government and scholastic-derived data sets, and through primary and secondary source reporting.

In order to provide a simple means of measurement of external-pressure damage to organizations, and the impact on the resilience of organizations, a coding matrix is used. Damage is coded into three types: (i) Severe – the impact on operational and political perpetuity is significant and damage may not be fully recoverable; (ii) Moderate – damage is able to be absorbed over time without enduring effects; and (iii) Low – damage is minimal and recovery is fully probable. Organizational resilience is similarly coded into three types: (i) High – the organization is likely to fully recover; (ii) Moderate – over time the organization will probably recover from damage; and (iii) Low – the organization is unlikely to recover fully.

Case selection

The case studies were selected as a cross-representational sample of insurgency. Selection was transparent to allow future replication. The factor considered was contrast in organizational structure, either familial or meritocratic. This is important to avoid bias, ensure general applicability, and maximize the extraction of theory (Eisenhardt 1989). In the selected case studies, contrast is further achieved by selecting insurgent organizations that have for the most part evolved organically, rather than being offshoots or sub-branches of other organizations. This also provides different reference points for the operationalized constructs, and once more avoids bias by using the cross-case analysis approach to allow for comparison of similarities and differences along with the variables. Next, the case studies come from different conflict theatres. Some of those theatres have overlaps, such as shared land borders or common actors (e.g. the presence of U.S., NATO, or other international forces), but are individualistic by means of geographic locations, thereby increasing validity.

The number of cases was also an important consideration. In the absence of established rules for case study thresholds in the literature, the selection was based on reference to the principles of representation and of contrast. This resulted in four units of analysis being chosen as the case studies from an initial potential field of 67. This is also consistent with other works in the field of insurgency and conflict studies that similarly employ between four and five case studies, such as: Jackson *et al.*, *Aptitude for Destruction Volume 2: Case Studies in Organizational Learning in Five Terrorist Groups*, RAND, 2005; Dolnik, *Understanding Terrorist Innovation*, Routledge, 2007; Haberfeld, "Today's Terrorism – Introduction and Analysis: The Have Nots Versus the Haves". In: *A New Understanding of Terrorism*, Haberfeld and von Hassell, eds., Springer, 2009; Klausen, *The Role of Social Networks in the Evolution of Al Qaeda-Inspired Violent Extremism in the United States, 1990–2015*, Brandeis University, MA, 2016.

The data itself was sourced from extensive interrogation and cross-referencing of multiple databases including the RAND Database of Worldwide Terrorism Incidents (RDWTI), the Global Terrorism Database (GTD-START) at the University of Maryland, the United States Bureau of Counter-Terrorism database, the TRAC terrorism database, and the International Crisis Group Global Insurgency Watch List.[12] Case studies selected for Pair One are: Haqqani Network and Lashkar-e-Taiba. For Pair Two: Jemaah Islamiyah and the Abu Sayyaf Group.

While each broadly shares a common ideological narrative, the selected case studies met other contrast requirements. As well as alternating familial/ meritocratic governance types, they are all insurgent organizations by nature. Case study organizations in each pair are in individual yet geographically similar theatres such as Afghanistan and Pakistan for Pair One, and Indonesia and the Philippines for Pair Two. This adds value to the measurement of resilience among organizations that operate in overlapping environments and that face similar external pressures. Furthermore, it provides greater empirical insight into how differently structured organizations function and address resilience issues under relatively similar circumstances. Systematic sampling was used to ensure there was no over-representation or repetitive inclusions, meaning that the case studies are fair representatives of the insurgent organization population that exhibits a natural degree of randomness along the structural metric.

The Haqqani Network

The Haqqani Network is a familial organization with strong kinship architecture in its leadership, command and control, and insurgency systematics. It has four command councils, or *Shura*, the second of which, known as the Loya Paktiya Group, consists of its most senior leadership, who are entirely related by blood. It is based in Miram Shah, North Waziristan and is currently led by Sirajuddin Haqqani. It is one of the most potent insurgent actors within Afghanistan. It demonstrates a strong emphasis on familial and kinship ties and tribal connections. The former leader and patriarch, Jalaluddin Haqqani and father of Sirajuddin, was a well-respected Mujahedeen fighter from the anti-Soviet jihad and former asset of the U.S. Central Intelligence Agency (CIA).

Rassler and Brown (2011) state that the Haqqani Network forged extensive relationships with regional jihadist organizations along tribal and clan lines as well as political and criminal ones. It also had strong ties with the U.S. CIA, Britain's MI6, and the Pakistani Inter-Services Intelligence (ISI), which continues to exercise significant influence over the Afghan-Taliban and other jihadist groups in the area to this day (Waldman 2010). The Haqqani Network is also a key ally of al-Qaeda and many other militant organizations. Its leader, Sirajuddin Haqqani (a.k.a. Siraj), has deepened organizational ties, particularly with the Pakistani security establishment, while maintaining distinct command and control across Haqqani areas and theatres of operations.

While ostensibly part of and subordinate to the Afghan Taliban, in practice the Haqqani Network maintains a great deal of autonomy to choose targets and carry out operations against the Afghan Government and coalition forces. It is distinctly structured on kinship through consanguine family and extended clan and tribal connections, which are extensive across the Zadran tribe to which it belongs. Because of its solid familial structure and strong, well-established ties through local tribes across the FATA region in Pakistan, the Haqqani Network has vast access to large populations of kin-relatives and clan members to support them and to restore destroyed human capability groups. These factors make it an ideal case study.

Lashkar-e-Taiba

The Lashkar-e-Taiba (LeT) is a meritocratic insurgent organization. Its command and control structure is an apex and consists of the founding members, between which there is no consanguine or familial relatedness. It is a potent insurgent organization, proxy force of the Pakistani ISI, and the militant wing of Jama'at-ud-Da'awa (JuD) (Siddiqa 2011). LeT is based in Muridke near Lahore, Pakistan and is led by Amir Hafiz Muhammad Saeed.[13] LeT is under considerable influence from its powerful patron the ISI, particularly with regard to its operations in Kashmir where it acts as a pseudo-independent, and thus politically deniable asset in Pakistan's enduring conflict with India. ISI backing is also a form of official endorsement and many Pakistani families have members in the Pakistani military, LeT, or both. This affords a measure of legitimacy that Fair (2011) maintains helps it sustain a huge popular support base, something other organizations around the world be envious of. This makes LeT stand out and empowers it to pursue operations against India, while furthering interests in Afghanistan with partners such as the Haqqani Network.

However, because it has sacrificed autonomy for support from the ISI, it is beholden to them for survival and caught in place as a mechanism of Pakistani foreign policy. The past violent history of LeT and its sheer size means it has been extensively studied, mapped, and documented which aids greatly in this research. LeT's professional structure, proximity to the Haqqani Network, and involvement in regional conflicts make it a strong partner case study.

Pair Two

Pair Two focuses on the Southeast Asian region, particularly Indonesia, the Philippines, Malaysia, Singapore, Sulawesi, Aceh, and Kalimantan. Pair Two organizations also share many commonalities including operational environments, external pressures, partners and affiliates, insurgency systematics, and the regional geopolitical environment. Pair Two consists of Jemaah Islamiyah and the Abu Sayyaf Group.

Jemaah Islamiyah

Jemaah Islamiyah is a Southeast Asian umbrella organization based out of Jolo and Solo on the Indonesian archipelago. The present senior leadership structures are dynamic and evolutionary, functioning largely in the absence of fixed form. A significant proportion of the senior leaders and operational commanders, over

90 per cent, are related through family or kinship (Miichi 2016). The spiritual leader is Abu Bakar Ba'asyir, though this is contested by Haron and Hussin (2015), who assert that Ba'asyir was never actually appointed Amir and never consolidated full power. Since the death of its founder Abdullah Sungkar, Jemaah Islamiyah has remained factional and conflicted.

The most likely current *primus inter pares* is Abu Rusydan (Singh 2018). The military Operations Chief is Aris Sumarson, a.k.a. Zulkarnaen, who is considered the day-to-day leader and responsible for intelligence, training, and attacks. Jemaah Islamiyah's structure evolved from a military-like hierarchy into a more flexible and integrated series of planula networks, providing it with effective rejuvenating capacity. For example, a number of hereditary autonomous cells evolved as a result of this change, largely driving the operational locomotion of the organization from the small-cell tactical level. The organization displays strong social and ideological kinship types as well as consanguine familial ties. Baker (2005) observed that an extensive network of arranged interfamily marriages between members had cemented the core organizational ideology as well as ties to other regional organizations, helping to facilitate training, intelligence sharing, fund-raising, and the movement of fighters, arms, and explosives.

Together with effective outreach and indoctrination through its madrassas, family provides added security dividends and reductions in risk adversity, such as in recruitment and communications. These have aided operationally and helped maintain security by decreasing the potential for infiltration by authorities, and by raising the risks for spies and defectors who would be betraying the organization and the family. Jemaah Islamiyah's prevalence and tempo of spectacular attacks over the years have placed it under heavy scrutiny. As a result, the organization has been well studied and its networks mapped and decoded.[14] The raft of high-quality empirical data on it is an added benefit to the study of insurgent organizational resilience.

Abu Sayyaf Group

Following the killing of former Amir Isnilon Hapilon, Abu Dar is believed to now be the supreme operational commander, with Furuji Indama leading the Basilan faction, and Radullan Sahiron the Sulu faction (Hart 2017). The factional nature of Abu Sayyaf means its leadership is distributed, with two principal leaders of the factions, and with additional dynamic leadership groups under those factions. As a meritocratic organization, interpersonal competition determines leadership positions. Kinship relations, if and where they do occasionally occur, play very little part in command and control and are more an avenue of resource collection via clan and tribal connections.

The organization grew out of the long-running Moro Islamic insurgency that has raged in the Southern Philippines since Spanish colonialism first began in the sixteenth century (Filler 2002). The insurgency continued during U.S. control of the country, beginning in 1897, and remains ongoing today under sovereign Filipino rule. Although Abu Sayyaf has experienced a brief period of oscillation between familial and professional leadership, it is firmly meritocratic with succession being based on merit. At the time of its origin it enjoyed strong ties to al-Qaeda, LeT, Jemaah Islamiyah, and other organizations. Its founder, Abubakar Janjalani, took the name Abu Sayyaf after the patron of the camp in Afghanistan where he lived, trained, and fought with Osama bin Laden and al-Qaeda.

Janjalani was deeply religious and inspired by Islamic Wahhabism. On return to the Philippines he renamed his Mujahedeen Commando Freedom Fighters (MCFF) as Abu Sayyaf, demonstrating organizational phoenixing. Originally, Abu Sayyaf sought to establish an independent Islamic State and protect the cultural and religious identities of the Filipino Muslim Moros. The MCFF was borne out of resistance to occupation by the Spanish and then the U.S., developing into an ethnic insurgency. Today its prominence in kidnapping-for-profit (K&R) and other banditry and sell-swording suggests that Abu Sayyaf's interests are far more fiscal than ideological. It quickly descended into banditry and crime-for-profit (Mendoza 2010). This was especially so after the slaying of Janjalani in 1988. Khadaffy Janjalani pushed the group back to its ideological roots, though with his death it returned permanently to more profitable endeavours.[15] Presently, Abu Sayyaf remains fragmented into several sub-groups without centralized leadership.

On 4 January 2016, former Amir Isnilon Hapilon pledged allegiance to ISIL Amir Abu Bakar al-Baghdadi (Saaduddin 2016). However, speculation remains that rather than furthering any defined ideological or political causes, the act of bay'ah, or pledge, was more to secure funding and maintain network inclusion.[16] Coupled with its close connections to regional Jihadist groups yet having divergent organizational objectives, Abu Sayyaf has suffered similar external pressures, making it a poignant case study in contrast to Jemaah Islamiyah.

The plan of the book

The remainder of the book is structured as follows. Chapter 2 presents an examination of social capital and trust in three sections. The first provides an overview, while the second reviews how social capital and trust differ between familial and meritocratic organizations. The third section compares resilience in insurgent organizations and also makes a critical analysis of dark resilience to further quantify the phenomenon and distinguish it from operational stagnation. Together they attempt to add new knowledge and understanding to the subject matter.

Chapter 3 is the first of the case studies. These begin with the Haqqani Network in Afghanistan. As the first case study and the first examination of familial insurgency, the chapter not only examines the resilience/structural phenomenon but provides the framework for the remaining case studies. Chapter 4 presents the second case study of Pair One, which is Lashkar-e-Taiba of Pakistan, a meritocratic organization. As this is the first meritocratic organization examined, it also establishes the research approach for the second pair. Lashkar-e-Taiba is highly active in Indian-controlled Jammu and Kashmir and has historical connections to the Afghan anti-Soviet jihad where it developed close relationships with many of the other case study groups presented in this book.

Chapter 5 deals with the Jemaah Islamiyah in Indonesia and the first organization of Pair Two. The case study of Jemaah Islamiyah, a familial organization, reveals that it contrasts quite significantly with the Haqqani Network in that it is a very different type of insurgency and type of organization. Additionally, in the Jemaah Islamiyah example there is significant diffusion of organizational boundaries, making it a complex example to understand. Chapter 6 follows with the case study of the Abu Sayyaf Group in the Philippines, a meritocratic organization with strong ethnic origins providing a diverse and rich historical legacy. What is interesting about Abu Sayyaf is that its ethnic roots could easily have seen it develop into a familial organization. While it has some of the necessary qualities, the leadership dynamic and the nature of its environment have shaped it into a decidedly meritocratic one instead.

Chapter 7 presents the findings of the book, reviewing the case studies against the variables and discussing the significance of the findings. It offers numerous policy prescriptions for more effectively exploiting insurgent counter-intelligence vulnerabilities, which are also applicable to terrorist groups (organizations that are unable to challenge incumbents directly), and many other organizations.[17] Chapter 8 discusses the implications for the future and, in particular, presents the strategic counterintelligence response. In that chapter I propose a new doctrine for intelligence-led influence and manipulation capabilities to mitigate insurgency and explain the significance of it for COIN, CT, and intelligence operations going forward.

This is equally important because it provides further testing and validation of the research findings. This is achieved by examining the feasibilities and practicalities of using the resilience variables, and the identified organizational weaknesses, as the means of breaking down that resilience. Incorporating these insights into extant counterinsurgency efforts offers additional inventive methods for monitoring, manipulating, and eliminating a range of organizations with hard- and soft-power external pressures and clandestine strategic counterintelligence influence operations.

Notes

1 Boko Haram in Nigeria, the Arab Spring in Libya, the Niger oil insurgency, and the Mali conflict are just some in Africa while in Asia the Nepalese insurgency, Rohingya Burmese insurgency, and insurgencies in Southern Thailand and Southern Philippines equally remain very active. SOURCES: Sunsay Aboyni and Christian Ezeh, 2017. "Terrorism/Insurgency and the Welfare of the African Child". *International Journal of Social and Management Sciences*. 1 (1): 84–90. Matt Wheeler, 2018. "Thailand's Southern Insurgency in 2017: Running in Place". *Southeast Asian Affairs* Vol. 2018 (1): 377–388.

2 Scully proposed that as a social system, meritocracy was a means of arranging people into roles and functions depending on their abilities and the assignment of appropriate rewards for their efforts. SOURCE: Maureen Scully, 2015. "Meritocracy". *Wiley Encyclopaedia of Management Volume 2.* Sydney: John Wiley & Sons, Ltd.

3 The Mafia, or "Mob", is built around both consanguine and fictive kinship that can be generated through experiential, political, or ideological sharing between individuals. Quasi kinship, or constructed, fictive, social, or defined by other terms is important because of the access it can provide to resources that are usually only accessible to blood-kin. Likewise, quasi-kinship can and does often lead to genealogical kinship through marriages. Similarly to groups comprising blood-kin family members, groups formed by choice must also have strong trust capital between interacting actors, because without trust it is likely that any positive collaboration within such institutionalized settings could fail. Moreover, for there to be genuine empathy between individuals that share similar standing across social, political, religious, or economic spheres there must be some measure of benefits. SOURCES: Helen Ebaugh and Mary Curry, 2000. "Fictive Kin as Social Capital in New Immigrant Communities". *Sociological Perspectives* 43 (2): 189–209; Ianni Francis, 1971. "The Mafia and the Web of Kinship". *The Public Interest* 22 (1): 78.

4 Operational intelligence capabilities of insurgent organizations are important because they relate to organizational security, and how they anticipate, manage, and respond to challenges across each of the variables. However, the real value of intelligence comes from the abilities of intelligent leaders and commanders to exploit it in novel ways. In and of itself, intelligence capabilities do not represent dynamics of resilience as they are a toolset rather than an endogenous organizational process. Therefore the pressures incumbents exert on insurgents are central, but it is how insurgents respond via internal processes that is important. This is because decisions are made with consideration of information from various sources that contribute to response processes.

5 Counterintelligence in the literature is sometimes used to describe what is more accurately known as counter-espionage and counterinterference. Counter-espionage and counterinterference are more accurately sub-disciplines of counterintelligence doctrine. The primary counterintelligence mission is to prevent, deter, or defend against adversaries gaining intelligence information about one's organization or nations which could be used against it. Deception and deflection operations are common in counterintelligence operations.

6 The former Director of the U.S. National Counterintelligence Executive (NCIX) Michelle Van Cleave wrote in 2007 that Strategic Counterintelligence was an operationalized form of counterintelligence, and, as such, had the potential to "advance national security policy objectives, and, at the strategic level, to go on the offense to degrade hostile external foreign intelligence services and their ability to work against us". Gaitan puts it that Strategic Counterintelligence was "aimed at exploiting the state or non-state actor's clandestine collection channel to manage the actor's objectives". In the context of insurgency, this book defines Strategic Counterintelligence as developing clandestine access to insurgent networks and organizations, and the developed or developable capabilities to extrapolate vital intelligence and to inject material of intelligence value, with the purpose being able to influence desired states and outcomes through a toolset of subtle means. SOURCES: Michelle Van Cleave, 2007. *Counterintelligence and National Strategy.* Washington, D.C.: National Defense University; John Gaitin, 2017. *Strategic Counterintelligence: An Approach to Engaging Security Threats to American Security.* Baltimore: Johns Hopkins University.

7 Social capital refers to an investment in social relationships with an expectation of productive returns. The study of social capital can be divided between sociological understanding and economics. Both actions and interactions are governed by norms

and rules, or by self-interest and utility maximization. This is consistent with many leading scholars. SOURCES: Pierre Bourdieu, 1989. "Social Space and Symbolic Power". *Sociological Theory* 7 (1): 14–25; Nan Lin *et al.*, 2008. *Social Capital: Theory and Research.* New York: Taylor & Francis.

8   While images of savage, violent militants and warlords are often conjured up in association with insurgency, there are other reasons such wars are fought. These include challenging ethnic repression, political injustice, brutal dictatorships and anti-colonialism, and securing religious and ideological freedom. SOURCES: N. Ganesan, 2015. "Ethnic Insurgency and the Nationwide Ceasefire Agreement in Myanmar". *Asian Journal of Peacebuilding* 3 (2): 273–286; Güneş Tezcur, 2015. "Violence and Nationalist Mobilization: The Onset of the Kurdish Iinsurgency in Turkey". *Nationalities Papers* 43 (2): 248–266; Michael Gross, 2017. *The Ethics of Insurgency.* New York: Cambridge University Press; Mark Juergensmeyer. 2001. *Terror in the Mind of God.* Berkeley, LA; London: University of California Press.

9   The Saudi/Iran proxy war in Yemen, the Russia/U.S. proxy war in Afghanistan, and the Pakistan/India proxy wars in Jammu and Kashmir are but a few examples. SOURCES: Simon Mabon, 2018. "Muting the Trumpets of Sabotage: Saudi Arabia, the U.S. and the Quest to Securitize Iran". British *Journal of Middle East Studies* 45 (5): 742–759; Asifa Jahangir and Umbreen Javaid, 2018. "Afghanistan Imbroglio: The Unintended Consequences of Foreign Interventions". *Journal of South Asian Studies* 33 (2): 411–433; Assad Ullah *et al.*, 2017. "Terrorism in India as a Determinant of Terrorism in Pakistan". *Asian Journal of Criminology* 1 (1): 57–77.

10   The current insurgency in Afghanistan began 18 years ago in 2001, but the country and its people had been fighting insurgent wars for many decades prior, most recently since 1979 and the Soviet invasion. In Nigeria the Boko Haram insurgency has raged since 2002, and in Southern Thailand the insurgency has been ongoing since the 1960s. SOURCES: A.Z. Hilali, 2005. *U.S.-Pakistan Relationship: Soviet Invasion of Afghanistan.* London and New York, Routledge; Samuel Oyewole, 2015. "Boko Haram: Insurgency and the War against Terrorism in the Lake Chad Region". *Strategic Analysis* 39 (4): 428–432; Duncan McCargo, 2008. *Tearing Apart the Land: Islam and Legitimacy in Southern Thailand.* Ithaca and London: Cornell University Press.

11   The use of terrorism is a deliberate strategy of most insurgencies. Usually, terrorist attacks are premeditated, politically motivated violence that are perpetrated against non-combatants, such as civilians. Most insurgent organizations utilize terrorism as a tactic in order to force incumbent responses, which in many cases can result in governmental forces committing abuses by responding with brutal crackdowns and civil oppression. This often achieves the goal of driving neutral civilians toward the insurgents and solidifying the support and loyalty of their supporters.

12   SOURCES: RAND. 2019. *Database of Worldwide Terrorist Incidents.* www.rand. org/nsrd/projects/terrorism-incidents.html. Accessed 5 March 2015; Terrorist Research and Analysis Consortium (TRAC) Database. 2019. www.tracking terrorism. org/. Accessed 12 March 2015.

13   The term "Amir" is used throughout the book in reference to a commander, and a person in high office within organizations. In contrast, "Emir" is more specifically a person of nobility, a prince, or leader of a nation.

14   A "Spectacular" attack is not a term of admiration – quite the opposite. "Spectaculars" is an increasingly common reference to large-scale, mass casualty terrorist attacks that require either complex and/or advanced planning, and/or result in significant loss of life and property destruction. Arce and Todd describe such attacks as pooling rather than being separating, and inversely related to the pressures from incumbent authorities and central government on terrorist and insurgent organizations. SOURCE: Daniel Arce and Todd Sandler, 2004. "Terrorist Spectaculars: Backlash Attacks and the Focus of Intelligence". *Journal of Conflict Resolution* 54 (2): 354–373.

15 Janjalani recruited from a diversity of young passionate Muslims throughout the Philippines who were familiar with Wahhabism and the Salafi traditions of jihad, with the focus on recruits who had studied in Saudi Arabia, Egypt, Pakistan or other countries with similar education opportunities, such as Libya. Specifically, Janjalani sought out those who had lost faith in the Moro National Liberation Front (MNLF) because of the peace agreement with the government, and so Janjalani cashed in on the anger and sentiments of betrayal many Muslims felt. SOURCES: Rommel Banlaoi, 2005. "al-Harakatul al Islamiyah: Essays on the Abu Sayyaf Group". Quezon City: Philippine Institute for Political Violence and Terrorism Research; Kenneth Bauzon, 1999. "The Philippines: The 1996 Peace Agreement for the Southern Philippines: An Assessment". *Ethnic Studies Report* 17 (2): 253–281.

16 The *bay'ah* or *'ahd* (pledge, vow) in the Arabic language means to adhere to something, in order to make it happen. SOURCE: Shafer-Ray Reed, 2015. "A Family Schism: ISIL, al-Qaeda, and the New Civil War". *Harvard International Review* 37 (1): 16–17.

17 In the wake of 9/11, the Bush Administration sought to label all foreign non-state conflict actors as "terrorists" rather than "insurgents", as Lieutenant Colonel Robert Leonhard articulates. This was an error, as the U.S. Administration's focus, for the next couple of decades, was not on the nature of the enemy, such as the insurgencies in Iraq and Afghanistan, but on their weapon of choice: terrorism. As the targets of terrorsm are usually civilians, protecting them and countering terrorism is a law-enforcement matter. Countering insurgency, on the other hand, is a military matter. The quandary arises when definitions, and in turn, roles to counter them are reversed because soliders generally make poor policemen and policemen generally make poor soldiers. SOURCES: Robert Leonhard, 2005. *The Evolution of Strategy in the Global War on Terror*. Baltimore: Johns Hopkins University; Donald Campbell and Kathleen Campbell, 2009. "Soldiers as Police Officers/Police Officers as Soldiers: Role Evolution and Revolution in the United States". *Journal of Armed Forces and Society*, 36 (2): 327–350.

References

Aboyni, Sunday and Ezeh, Christian. 2017. "Terrorism/Insurgency and the Welfare of the African Child". *International Journal of Social and Management Sciences*. 1 (1): 84–90.

Anderson, David and McKnight, Jacob. 2015. "Understanding al-Shabaab: Clan, Islam and Insurgency in Kenya". *Journal of Eastern African Studies* 9 (3): 536–557.

Arce, Daniel and Sandler, Todd. 2004. "Terrorist Spectaculars: Backlash Attacks and the Focus of Intelligence". *Journal of Conflict Resolution* 54 (2): 354–373.

Arreguin-Toft, Ivan. 2001. "How the Weak Win Wars: A Theory of Asymmetric Conflict". *International Security* 26 (1): 93–128.

Baker, John C. 2005. "Jemaah Islamiyah". In *Aptitude for Destruction, Volume 2: Case Studies of Organizational Learning in Five Terrorist Groups*, 57–92. Santa Monica, CA: RAND Corporation.

Banlaoi, Rommel. 2005. "al-Harakatul al Islamiyah: Essays on the Abu Sayyaf Group". Quezon City: Philippine Institute for Political Violence and Terrorism Research.

Bauzon, Kenneth. 1999. "The Philippines: The 1996 Peace Agreement for the Southern Philippines: An Assessment". *Ethnic Studies Report* 17 (2): 253–281.

Beck, Nathaniel, Katz, Jonathan and Tucker, Richard. 1998. "Taking Time Seriously: Time-Series-Cross-Section Analysis with a Binary Dependent Variable". *American Journal of Political Science* 42 (4): 1260–1288.

Bourdieu, Pierre. 1989. "Social Space and Symbolic Power". *Sociological Theory* 7 (1): 14–25.

Burchill, Richard. 2016. "Jihadist Insurgency and the Prospects for Peace and Security". *Small Wars & Insurgencies* 27 (5): 958–967.

Campbell, Donald and Campbell, Kathleen. 2009. "Soldiers as Police Officers/Police Officers as Soldiers: Role Evolution and Revolution in the United States". *Journal of Armed Forces and Society* 36 (2): 327–350.

Collett, David. 2002. *Modelling Binary Data.* London: CRC Press.

Connable, Ben and Libicki, Martin. 2010. *How Insurgencies End.* Santa Monica, CA: RAND.

Crawford, Neta. 2018. "Costs of War". *Brown University.* 1 November. Accessed 5 April, 2019. https://watson.brown.edu/costsofwar/files/cow/imce/papers/2018/Human%20Costs%2C%20Nov%208%202018%20CoW.pdf.

Davenport, J. 2014. *We Have Always Been At War.* 4 February. Accessed 5 May 2017. www.ifweassume.com/2014/02/we-have-always-been-at-war.html.

Della Porta, Donatella. 2014. "On Violence and Repression: A Relational Approach (The Government and Opposition/Leonard Schapiro Memorial Lecture, 2013)". *Journal of Government and Opposition* 49 (2): 159–187.

Dolnik, Adam. 2007. *Understanding Terrorist Innovation: Technology, Tactics and Global Trends.* Oxon: Routledge.

Ebaugh, Helen and Curry, Mary. 2000. "Fictive Kin as Social Capital in New Immigrant Communities". *Sociological Perspectives* 43 (2): 189–209.

Eisenhardt, Kathleen. 1989. "Building Theories from Case Study Research". *The Academy of Management Review* 14 (4): 532–550.

Enders, Walter and Sandler, Todd. 2010. *The Political Economy of Terrorism.* Cambridge: Cambridge University Press.

Fair, Christine. 2011. "Lashkar-e-Taiba beyond Bin Laden: Enduring Challenges for the Region and the International Community". Washington, D.C.: Testimony prepared for the U.S. Senate. Foreign Relations Committee Hearing on "Al Qaeda, The Taliban, and Other Extremist Groups in Afghanistan and Pakistan".

Fearon, James and Laitin, David. 2003. "Ethnicity, Insurgency, and Civil War". *The American Political Science Review* 97 (1): 75–90

Fearon, James and Laitin, David. 2004. "Neotrusteeship and the Problem of Weak States". *International Security* 28 (4): 5–43.

Filler, A. 2002. "The Abu Sayyaf Group: A Growing Menace to Civil Society". *Journal of Terrorism and Political Violence* 14 (4) (Winter): 131–162.

Forest, James, ed. 2006. *The Making of a Terrorist: Recruitment, Training, and Root Causes* [three volumes], Praeger Security International.

Francis, Ianni. 1971. "The Mafia and the Web of Kinship". *The Public Interest* 22 (1): 78.

Gaitin, John. 2017. *Strategic Counterintelligence: An Approach to Engaging Security Threats to American Security.* Baltimore: Johns Hopkins University.

Galula, David. 1964. "Revolutionary War: Nature and Characteristics". In *Counterinsurgency Warfare: Theory and Practice*, edited by David Galula, 26. Westport, Connecticut and London: Praeger Security International.

Ganesan, N. 2015. "Ethnic Insurgency and the Nationwide Ceasefire Agreement in Myanmar". *Asian Journal of Peacebuilding* 3 (2): 273–286.

Gross, Michael. 2017. *The Ethics of Insurgency.* New York: Cambridge University Press.

Haberfeld, M. 2009. "Today's Terrorism – Introduction and Analysis: The Have Nots Versus the Haves". In *A New Understanding of Terrorism*, edited by M.R. Haberfeld and A. von Hassell, 1–8. New York: Springer.

Hansen-Lewis, Jamie and Shapiro, Jacob. 2015. "Understanding the Daesh Economy", *Perspectives on Terrorism* 9 (4): 142–155.

Haron, Z. and Hussin, N. 2015. "Leadership Conflict and Identity Crisis Within Al Jama'ah Al Islamiyah: Revisited". *The Journal of Defence and Security* 6 (2): 54–73.

Hart, Michael. 2017. "Is Abu Sayyaf really Defeated?" *The Diplomat*. 23 November. Accessed 15 March 2018. https://thediplomat.com/2017/11/is-abu-sayyaf-really-defeated/.

Hilali, A.Z. 2005. *U.S.-Pakistan Relationship: Soviet Invasion of Afghanistan*. London and New York: Routledge.

Hoffman, Bruce. 2006. *Inside Terrorism*. Second edition. New York: Columbia University Press.

ICG. 2019. *International Crisis Group*. Accessed 2015–2018. www.crisisgroup.org/.

Jackson, Brian, Baker, John, Cragin, Kim, Parachini, John, Trulillo, Horacio and Chalk, Peter. 2005. *Aptitude for Destruction, Volume 2: Case Studies of Organizational Learning in Five Terrorist Groups*. Washington, D.C.: RAND.

Jahangir, Asifa and Javaid, Umbreen. 2018. "Afghanistan Imbroglio: The Unintended Consequences of Foreign Interventions". *Journal of South Asian Studies* 33 (2): 411–433.

Juergensmeyer, Mark. 2001. *Terror in the Mind of God*. Berkeley, LA; London: University of California Press.

Kalyanaraman, Sankaran. 2003. "Conceptualisations of Guerrilla Warfare". *Journal of Strategic Analysis* 27 (2): 172–185.

Kalyvas, Stathis. 2019. "The Landscape of Political Violence". In *The Oxford Handbook of Terrorism*, edited by Erica Chenoweth, Richard English, Andreas Gofas, and Stathis Kalyvis, 11–33. Oxford: Oxford University Press.

Klausen, Jytte. 2016. *The Role of Social Networks in the Evolution of Al Qaeda-Inspired Violent Extremism in the United States*. Massachusetts: Brandeis University.

Leites, Nathan and Wolf, Charles Jr. 1970. *Rebellion and Authority: An Analytical Essay on Insurgent Conflicts*. First edition. Chicago: Markham.

Leonhard, Robert. 2005. *The Evolution of Strategy in the Global War on Terror*. Baltimore: Johns Hopkins University.

Levi, Margaret and Stoker, Laura. 2000. "Political Trust and Trustworthiness". *Annual Review of Political Science* 3 (1): 475–507.

Lin, Nan, Cook, Karen, and Burt, Ronald. 2008. *Social Capital: Theory and Research*. New York: Taylor & Francis.

Mabon, Simon. 2018. "Muting the Trumpets of Sabotage: Saudi Arabia, the U.S. and the Quest to Securitize Iran". *British Journal of Middle East Studies* 45 (5): 742–759.

Mack, Andrew. 1975. "Why Big Nations Lose Small Wars: The Politics of Asymmetric Conflict". *Journal of World Politics* 27 (2): 175–200.

McCargo, Duncan. 2008. *Tearing Apart the Land: Islam and Legitimacy in Southern Thailand*. Ithaca and LondonL Cornell University Press.

Mendoza, R. 2010. "The Evolution of Terrorist Financing in the Philippines", presented at the International Conference in Countering the Financing of Terrorism at the Sulu Hotel, Philippines, 7–8 July 2008. Zamboanga City, Philippines: International Conference in Countering the Financing of Terrorism.

Meron, Gil. 2012. *How Democracies Lose Small Wars*. Cambridge: Cambridge University Press.

Metelits, Claire. 2010. *Inside Insurgency: Violence, Civilians, and Revolutionary Group Behavior*. New York and London: New York University Press.

Miichi, Ken. 2016. "Looking at Links and Nodes: How Jihadists in Indonesia Survived". *Journal of Southeast Asian Studies* 5 (1): 135–154.

Mobley, Blake. 2008. "Terrorist Group Counterintelligence – Thesis". 20 October. Accessed 15 July 2018. https://repository.library.georgetown.edu/bitstream/handle/10822/553096/mobleyBlake.pdf?sequence=1&bcsi_scan_fcaccdf017742bb0=1INgKQpKx94Vtm6dWKz J6666hSXbAAAAL1SIOA==&bcsi_scan_filename=mobleyBlake.pdf.

Mockaitis, Thomas. 2003. "Winning Hearts and Minds in the 'War on Terrorism'". *Small Wars & Insurgencies* 14 (1): 21–38.

Mockaitis, Thomas. 2017. *The COIN Conundrum: The Future of U.S. Counterinsurgency and U.S. Land Power.* Washington, D.C.: Department of the Army, Strategic Studies Institute.

Moorcraft, Paul. 2016. *The Jihadist Threat: The Re-Conquest of the West?* Annapolis: Naval Institute Press.

Morgan, Sonya, Pullon, Susan, Macdonald, Lindsay, McKinlay, Eileen and Gray, Ben. 2017. "Case Study Observational Research: A Framework for Conducting Case Study Research Where Observation Data Are the Focus". *Journal of Qualitative Health Research* 27 (7): 1060–1068.

Mumford, Andrew. 2017. *Counterinsurgency Wars and the Anglo-American Alliance: The Special Relationship on the Rocks.* Washington, D.C.: Georgetown University Press.

Oyewole, Samuel. 2015. "Boko Haram: Insurgency and the War against Terrorism in the Lake Chad Region". *Strategic Analysis* 39 (4): 428–432.

Porch, Douglas. 2013. *Counterinsurgency: Exposing the Myths of the New Way of War.* New York: Cambridge University Press.

RAND. 2019. *Database of Worldwide Terrorist Incidents.* www.rand.org/nsrd/projects/terrorism-incidents.html. Accessed 5 March 2015.

Rassler, D. and Brown, V. 2011. *The Haqqani Nexus and the Evolution of al-Qa'ida.* New York: The Combating Terrorism Centre at West Point.

Reed, Shafer-Ray. 2015. "A Family Schism: ISIL, al-Qaeda, and the New Civil War". *Harvard International Review* 37 (1): 16–17.

Rich, Paul and Duyvesteyn, Isabelle. 2012. *The Routledge Handbook of Insurgency and Counterinsurgency.* London: Routledge.

Saaduddin, M. 2016. "Abu Sayyaf rebels pledge allegience to ISIS". *The Manila Times*, 11 January: 1.

Sageman, Marc. 2004. *Understanding Terror Networks.* Philadelphia: University of Pennsylvania Press.

Scully, Maureen. 2015. "Meritocracy". *Wiley Encyclopaedia of Management Volume 2.* Sydney: John Wiley & Sons, Ltd.

Shelly, Louise. 2014. *Dirty Entanglements: Corruption, Crime, and Terrorism .* New York: Cambridge University Press.

Siddiqa, A. 2011. "Pakistan's Counterterrorism Strategy: Separating Friends from Enemies". *The Washington Quarterly* 34 (1): 149–162.

Singh, Bilveer. 2018. "Jemaah Islamiyah: Still Southeast Asia's Greatest Terrorist Threat". *The Diplomat.* 7 October. Accessed 15 December 2018. https://thediplomat.com/2018/10/jemaah-islamiyah-still-southeast-asias-greatest-terrorist-threat/.

Sinno, Abdulkader. 2008. *Organizations at War in Afghanistan and Beyond.* Ithaca: Cornell University Press.

Souleimanov, Emil. 2014. "Globalizing Jihad: North Caucasians in the Syrian Civil War". *Middle East Policy* XXI (3): 1–9.

Staniland, Paul. 2014. "Counter-insurgency and Violence Management". In *The New Counter-insurgency Era in Critical Perspective*, edited by Celeste Gventer, David Jones and M.R. Smith, 144–155. London: Palgrave Macmillan.

START. 2018. *Global Terrorism Database (GTB)*. Accessed 2015–2018. www.start. umd.edu/research-projects/global-terrorism-database-gtd.

Stepanova, Ekaterina. 2008. *Terrorism in Asymmetric Conflict: Ideological and Structural Aspects.* Oxford and New York: Oxford University Press.

Tarrow, Sidney. 2007. "Inside Insurgencies: Politics and Violence in an Age of Civil War". *Perspectives on Politics* 5 (3): 587–600.

Terrorist Research and Analysis Consortium (TRAC) Database. 2019. www.tracking terrorism.org/. Accessed 12 March 2015.

Tezcur, Güneş. 2015. "Violence and Nationalist Mobilization: The Onset of the Kurdish Insurgency in Turkey". *Nationalities Papers* 43 (2): 248–266.

Tilly, Charles. 2017. "Trust and Democratic Rule". In *Collective Violence, Contentious Politics, and Social Change: A Charles Tilly Reader*, edited by Ernesto Castaneda and Cathy Schneider, 208–240. New York and London: Routledge.

Trebbi, Francesco and Weese, Eric. 2015. *Insurgency and Small Wars: Estimation of Unobserved Coalition Structures.* Cambridge: National Bureau of Economic Research (NBER) Working Paper No. w21202.

Tse-Tung, Mao. 1961. *Mao Tse-Tung On Guerrilla Warfare.* First edition. Westport: Prager.

Turbiville, Graham Jr. 2009. *Guerrilla Counterintelligence: Insurgent Approaches to Neutralizing Intelligence Operations.* First edition. Hurlburt Field: Joint Special Operations University.

Tyler, Tom. 2017. "Procedural Justice and Policing: A Rush to Judgement". *Annual Review of Law and Social Science* 13 (1): 29–53.

Ullah, Assad, Qingxiang, Yang, Ali, Zahid, and Aness, Muhammad. 2017. "Terrorism in India as a Determinant of Terrorism in Pakistan". *Asian Journal of Criminology* 1 (1): 57–77.

UNAMA. 2018. "United Nations Assistance Mission in Afghanistan". 15 July. Accessed 19 August 2018. https://unama.unmissions.org/sites/default/files/unama_poc_midyea r_update_2018_15_july_english.pdf?bcsi_scan_fcaccdf017742bb0=QcZMOAZyobQP aYPd+xovPipK1o/bAAAArRBqOA==&bcsi_scan_filename=unama_poc_midyear_ update_2018_15_july_english.pdf.

Van Cleave, Michelle. 2007. *Counterintelligence and National Strategy.* Washington, D.C.: National Defense University.

Waldman, M. 2010. *The Sun in the Sky: The Relationship Between Pakistan's ISI and Afghan Insurgents.* Cambridge, MA: Crisis States Research Center, Harvard University.

Wheeler, Matt. 2018. "Thailand's Southern Insurgency in 2017: Running in Place". *Southeast Asian Affairs* Vol. 2018 (1): 377–388.

Williams, Kristina. 2011. "The Other side of the COIN: counterinsurgency and community policing". *Interface* 3 (1): 81–117.

Yin, Robert. 2014. *Case Study Research Design and Methods.* Fifth edition. California: Sage.

2 The foundations of resilience

It is puzzling that insurgent organizations can not only survive, but continue to evolve and develop increasingly effective attack capabilities in the face of intensive governmental attempts to defeat them. Despite valuable tactical gains made through arrests and slayings of leaders and key figures, many groups and organizations continue to show high levels of resilience that enables continuity as well as new learning and development.

Likewise, insurgent organizations are not identical. They have a myriad of organizational structures, leadership, and command and control (C2) architecture, and use information, intelligence, and resources differently. As there are no one-fits-all paradigms, perhaps there are other important aspects that drive resilience such as organizational arrangement and structural efficiency. However, as structure also differs significantly across organizations, where would such efficiency come from? This chapter reviews social capital and trust as the critical answer to that question.

To better understand this conundrum the chapter proceeds in the following manner. First, it provides a cross-section of holistic understanding of insurgent organizational strengths by presenting a focused analysis of social capital and trust in the organizational context, and particularly the roles of leaders and influence actors. The second section of the chapter specifically examines how social capital and trust differ between familial and meritocratic organizations. The third section discusses how this manifests as resilience and is facilitated differently in familial versus meritocratic organizations. The chapter then presents a review of the paradigm of dark resilience, a phenomenon specific to insurgency and many other covert organizations. Taken together, the analysis in this chapter presents a unified understanding of the efficiency of resilience in insurgent organizations, which builds our capacity to know the enemy.

Organizational structures, leadership, and efficiency

In 2003, former U.S. President George W. Bush stated in the National Strategy for Combating Terrorism that "the threat is both resilient and diffuse because of the mutually reinforcing, dynamic network structure" (2003, 8). President Bush made the connection between organizational structure (i.e. "network structure") and resilience – the argument being that because of the unique structure of insurgent organizations, they are resilient. However, not all organizations are structured similarly. Indeed, great variation exists. Some are built around family, kinship, ethnicity, clan, and tribal connections; others are structured decidedly on meritocracy and professionalized systems of function and promotion. Similarly, leaders and leadership can be differently placed with varying levels of efficiency.

What all organizations have in common, however, is social capital and trust. Putnam writes that social capital "refers to features of social organization such as networks, norms, and social trust that facilitate coordination and cooperation for mutual benefit" (1995, 2). Given the apparent differences in type and function between familial and meritocratic organizations, it is likely that socioeconomics and social capital exchange respectively involve different human and utility values. This assertion is supported by Tilly (2004), who found that the social relations in organizations affect the courses of action available and their relative costs. This also explains some differences in security efficiencies between the two types of organization.

Donckels and Frohlich (1991) report that familial organizations tend to be inward-looking with a higher likelihood of being closed systems, suggesting that their strategic behaviour is mainly conservative and centred on building lasting familial dynastic enterprises over immediate gains.[1] This is not dissimilar to the viewpoint of Arregle *et al.* (2007), who found multi-form social capital and trust to be very similar but different. They suggest that in familial organizations personal social capital and trust are used to build organizational social capital and trust. One study by McAllister (2017) describes how familial organizations are more likely to be based on associations of strong emotional connections, love, trust, and established familial bonds rather than on ideology, religion, or extremist beliefs that can attract members to meritocratic organizations.

However, this can generate agency problems. Morck and Yeung (2003) point out that familial organizations can inadvertently develop self-damaging or self-restricting issues by balancing specific needs across the whole organization to protect one area of the family system, thereby restricting capabilities or actions in other areas. According to Stewart and Kitt (2012), familial-based organizations tend to take actions that maximize benefits for family by pursuing opportunities found in informal, relationship-based operations due to efficiency dividends. Therefore, how organizational structures and their leadership operate together may be important, because leaders probably have more influence over how social capital and trust are derived and function.

Hence, it could conceivably be hypothesized that the more efficient social capital and trust are in an organization, the more resilient they may be. Levi and Stoker (2000) found that judgments of trust members make about their organizations' leaders are linked to their performance. Likewise, performance encourages responsibility diffusion that can bring added security, informal associations, and social capital and trust extensions that increase operational capabilities. This seems equally applicable to both organizational types because responsibility diffusion pushes organizational performance down to the level of individual contribution, which, in turn, may reinforce governance.

Fukuyama (1995) states that determining what constitutes good governance is a conceptual problem because there is no universal answer. For example, Katz and Kahn (1966) posit that the role of governance leaders is to clarify organizational purposes, define new objectives, dismiss old ones, manage priorities, and drive the mission. On the other hand, Lajili and Mahoney (2006) put it that governance structures are driven by demand (transaction frequency and costs), resources, and risk-reduction, which suggests that governing mechanisms do not solely rest on the recourse to the authority and sanctions of apex leadership, but rather that members have a greater investment in the organization succeeding as a whole.

This can apply to familial and meritocratic organizations, but there is a subtle variance that Dawson *et al.* (2013) describe as differences between normative commitment and continuance commitment. In familial organizations, members want the organization to succeed. In meritocratic ones, members want to be a part of the institution. It can therefore be deduced that for members in familial organizations it is about processes and belonging, whereas to members of meritocratic organizations it is about outcomes and the ownership of them. Dawson's findings support the concept of governance that includes effective leadership that builds internal organizational structures free of external impositions, which results in effective inter-organizational interactions between influencing actors and members. Perhaps these diverse views portend in the affirmative that good leadership is a mixture of such qualities, each with different yet necessary roles to play.

Sashkin (2018) argues that leaders must model the values of the organizations they lead, and explain the strategic vision to followers so that they may buy into it and do the same. Therefore, governance it is about using behaviours as tools; but whether this works equally in different types of organization is debatable. In familial organizations the family culture is the most prominently embedded behaviour, rather than "the business model". For a strategic vision to succeed it must meld well with the harmonization of familial and then professional interests, rather than be at odds with them. In meritocratic organizations leaders may "talk the talk" but often do not "walk the walk". One blatant example is how many insurgent leaders espouse violence and encourage suicide terrorism, but will not participate in it themselves.[2]

This may represent another significant difference between the two organizational types: that is, how members are viewed. Using members as tools to achieve goals is evident in both categories, but for different reasons. In meritocratic organizations people are members largely by choice, and the membership base supports the aspirations of the organization's leadership. In familial organizations the situation can be inverse wherein the leaders support the aspirations of the membership base, as it is extensive and related by kinship.[3]

Trust networks under external pressure

Different types of trust networks can be expected to react differently when they come under pressure from outside forces. More specifically, the theory on trust organizations expects that familial and meritocratic insurgent organizations will react differently when they are subjected to an incumbent government's counterinsurgency operations. Staw *et al.* (1981), for example, examined threat rigidity effects on organizational behaviour. What marks this as an important contribution is that they examined external threats and the resultant internal behavioural effects on leadership.

They claim that outside threats can be reduced by shifting them from an organizational threat as a whole and onto the leadership group, thereby attempting to manage organizational exposure to damage. This may be more effective in meritocratic organizations where blame acceptance and blame avoidance are better defined internally, or where other leaders are happy to shift blame away from themselves, rather than proactively share in others' errors.[4]

A contrary view is adopted by Worchel *et al.* (1977), who state that if there is intragroup cooperation and centralization of authority, organizations will probably be more resilient in the face of significant external threats. This not only increases leadership costs and stress but also makes sense because just as organizations look to leaders for guidance, so too do they look to them to solve the greatest problems. This can result in resilience-building processes and alignment of resources behind leadership groups to sufficiently support the required response and adaptation. Contrarily, Hamblin (1958) found that many organizations took a tack different from mustering support for leaders, and that a common practice was that organizations sought to quickly replace them when they were exposed to serious external pressures.

From this diversity of examples one may conclude that rather than being easily definable and common in design, organizational structures and the dynamics of leadership influences on the efficiency of social capital and trust functions are actually complex, opaque, and similarly evolving. The evidence presented certainly suggests that it is not a simple thing to understand, and that there is as much multiplicity of opinion as there are organizations and structural subtleties. Perhaps this is suggestive of the resilience of insurgent organizations not residing solely in the realm of structure and leadership (Table 2.1).[5]

Table 2.1 Potential responses to external pressures

	Familial insurgency	*Meritocratic insurgency*
Potential leadership responses to external pressures	Draw organizational resources together to respond holistically to treat damage effectively.	Increased pressure to find solutions and react competently to maintain control. Isolate leaders and damage from other areas of the organization.
Potential organizational responses	Consolidate behind leadership and burden-share.	Isolate leaders most responsible for damaged areas, withdraw support, and find replacements.

Internal social capital: differences in meritocracy and family

The second section of this chapter now examines differing levels of internal social capital and trust between meritocratic and familial organizations. Social capital refers to an investment in social relationships with an expectation of productive returns by investing human capital. According to Dubos (2017), the study of social capital can be divided between sociological understanding and economics. Both actions and interactions are governed by norms and rules or alternatively by self-interest and utility maximization. This reflects familial organizations and meritocracies and is evident in a significant array of social capital literature (Bourdieu 1986; Coleman 1988; Burt 1997; Tasselli *et al.* 2015; Cumberland *et al.* 2018).

Academics have developed several social capital theories to understand these concepts better. Human Capital Theory (Schultz 1974; Becker and Woessmann 2009), Cultural Capital Theory (Bourdieu 1986), and Social Cognitive Theory (Chiu *et al.* 2006) are some prominent examples. Lin *et al.* (2008) referred to these as being part of the broader neo-capital theories on social capital.[6] They argue that social relations between different classes are not fixed in social structure terms, but are layered and rely heavily on negotiation rather than obedience (Lin *et al.*, 2008).[7]

Portes (1998) takes a pragmatic approach to social capital. While acknowledging the positive consequences that participation in groups brings for individuals, organizations, and communities, he claims that conceptually, social capital ignores negative consequences. These could reside in non-monetary capital that can boost standing while power and influence can create diversity and separate the economic from the non-economic. This means that parties seeking particular outcomes will probably look for the "cheapest" option. In turn, this can lead to negative capital transactions rather than positive ones. Analysis suggests this is more prevalent in meritocracies than familial organizations. A familiar utilitarian concept is the maximum benefit for the least effort.[8] This applies to insurgency as much as it does elsewhere, such as to criminal financial gain through illicit activities. However, other variables of social capital can influence an actor's choices. Such variables include social support, group integration, cohesion, and the presence of norms and values. Conceptually these are strong in familial organizations because they establish durational dynamics that extend social capital beyond being utilitarian.

Supporting this, Adler and Kwon (2002) state that social capital is about long-term gain and investment in future returns rather than immediate ones. Interestingly, this is a concept shared by meritocracies as well as familial organizations, probably because it enables better access to socially controlled resources such as information, power, and solidarity. Furthermore, it can augment the capacity for collective action by strengthening collective identity. During the Afghan resistance to the Soviet occupation for example, the Mujahedeen successfully developed solidarity and cohesion by mobilizing the rural population and coordinating

Table 2.2 Social capital in insurgent organizations

	Familial insurgency	Meritocratic insurgency
Social capital governance	Rules and norms.	Self-interest and utility maximization.
Social capital employment	Group cohesion and long-term prosperity through belonging.	Positioning and self-gain.Benefits of leaders for organizations are based on their individual drive and achievements.

different field commanders through regional councils and clan links (Sinno 2008). This also brought resilience benefits and made it difficult for the Soviets to entice Mujahedeen to defect.

External meritocratic social relationships can be highly influential in shaping joining and signalling decisions, particularly political and ideological ones, because it is apparent that social capital has distinctly different values between the two organizational types. Putnam (2001) discusses this in terms of public and private faces of social capital. Public social capital mirrors meritocracies where external signalling is important for maintaining the requirements of insurgency, such as recruitment and retention. In familial organizations, Putnam's assertions can correspond to internal social capital values of reciprocity and kinship.

Considering these aspects, the manifestations of social capital and values across sociological, economic, moral, and self-interest based utilitarianism can differ according to the structures they are developed in. Likewise, social capital expenditure can have negative capital effects due to cheapest-option selection, as Portes (1998) describes. Furthermore, social capital has demonstrated long-term benefits such as accumulating political power and critical resources as Adler and Kwon discuss (2002). It can build solidarity through collective identity development and when used externally can maximize conflict avoidance Table 2.2).

Familial social capital and trust

We all have an idea of what family is although familial identity, kinship, and belonging can mean different things to different people. Kin-connections are utilized, leveraged, and have different values for different actors under different circumstances. What is important is not so much how people relate to others personally, but, on an organizational level, how they utilize those relationships for efficiency. Reviewing this is important to provide a clear picture of the importance of social capital and trust to family and kinship, and particularly how they function in insurgent organizations. This is accomplished by examining social capital and trust within and between family members, clans, and tribes, and externally in more extensive socio-economic activity.[9]

Relatedness and reciprocity – why do family and kin help each other?

Relatedness is a central factor in social relations. The way in which people act towards each other depends on how they feel about others, or, on following pre-established norms or rules towards those they know, even if that is very minor in extent. Siblings, parents, and uncles for example are often implicitly trusted even if personal relationships are not well established. For others, interpersonal dynamics are the determinatives of interactions, which are more likely to be found in meritocratic organizations. Therefore, why people help each other and what benefit this has for organizational efficiency is important as it may have significant relevance to resilience.

Bodenhorn and Ruebeck (2003) assert that what makes kinship real is the connection to personal identity and personal claims on others. This is a highly individualistic viewpoint however, and infers a potential for critical vulnerabilities, particularly for familial groups. If it is the individual rather than their place in a familial group that determines the relevance of kin-connections, people can presumably disassociate entirely from the natal home and family name. This would also mean that ancestry and familial hierarchy is only relevant if acknowledged and given moral authority by individuals. While this may enhance some relations because they are favoured, it risks weakening some critical ones.

Bloch and Sperber (2004) suggest that the morality of kinship is based on its irrevocability and thus leads to tolerance of unbalanced reciprocity over the short term.[10] Bloch and Sperber (1973) state that in particular cultures, such as the Merina people, it was more likely that in times of need artificial kinsmen would be called upon to render assistance rather than consanguine-kin. This has a cost however. Whereas consanguine relationships require, in theory, little renewal, fictive kinship relations would need continual reinforcement, probably through favours and the like to ensure short-term reciprocity. This seems economically more intensive than drawing on consanguine-kin who have different incentives for helping, such as group survival.

There are, however, appealing trade-offs. Providing aid to those who are bound through fictive social networks creates an obligation, which in turn creates power over the obligated to return that aid, not at a moment of their choosing but of the debt-holder. Fundamentally, morality-based kinship may balance out with long-term reciprocity, while utilitarian ones operate almost exclusively over shorter terms. Widger (2012) contends that a failure to reciprocate in the long term may not jeopardize moral relationships because they are governed by a belief in sharing and reckoning, but a lack of reciprocity in utilitarian relationships will almost certainly result in their abandonment, thereby supporting such an assertion.

From a Fortesian kinship perspective this is probably a good thing. However, Fortes (2006) may argue that reciprocal giving between kinsfolk is supposed to be done freely and not in submission to coercive sanctions or in response to contractual obligations. However, the term "freely" may have connotations of

Table 2.3 Social capital benefits in insurgent organizations

	Familial insurgencies	*Meritocratic insurgencies*
Social capital and trust costs	Continual reinforcement. Non-remunerated reciprocity.	Debts to others. Costs of incurring debts over others.
Social capital and trust benefits	Obligations of assistance in times of need. Assistance is automatic.	On-demand to assist and close debts. Assistance may be based solely on the likelihood of success.

self-benefit such as family-standing, reputation, trust capital, and perception. Although Fortes asserts exchanges between kin, consanguine or fictive, should not be based on future obligations, the very nature of aiding kin in times of need may be automatically ingrained with unspoken notions of reciprocity. Table 2.3 shows social capital costs versus benefits.

This is not dissimilar to Marxism, which views kinship functionality more negatively and ideologically. Marx (1887) emphasized the maximization of asymmetrical power relations and the claiming of rights over debt-holders, effectively using bias upon which to make property claims over individual actors. Bain (2003) maintains that exploitation of obligation is a manifestation of economic power, which suggests that obligation is a purchased commodity, not a developed one. If true, kinship could be viewed as basically another framework for social exchange but with inherent familial relatedness. Its importance would then stem from the organic connections it offers and the strengths of such ties, and perhaps more importantly, those that extend into broader communities.

Social capital and in-grouping

Building on our understanding of how social capital functions between kin, the following text examines how it operates specifically inside family groups. This is important because families are one of the most critical socio-economic institutions in society. It is within families that individuals, as children, learn about and develop social capital and trust in their nuclear group, and how they can express these externally into wider non-related social groups, which can be negative.

Strong social capital in families that depend daily on one another for survival and security can exhibit increased levels of cohesion, solidarity, and efficiency (Knack and Keefer 1997; Saegert 2001; Grootaert and Van Bastelaer 2002). This can be particularly strong in groups that have requirements for maintaining internal security, such as covert and illicit ones, similarly to insurgent organizations. Fukuyama contends "this is because solidarity in human communities is often purchased at the price of hostility towards out-group members" (2002, 2).

This suggests that the development of strong internal social capital in families fosters negative externalities. Fukuyama supports this by offering that "there appears to be a natural human proclivity for dividing the world into friends and enemies that is the basis of all politics" (1995, 4). Competitive groups and unequal groups, such as insurgent/incumbent relationships, each treat non-members similarly. Changes in attitude between those who belong and those who do not can be dramatic and strictly governed by the concept of a "radius of trust" (Realo *et al.* 2008, 447). Gambetta (1990) highlights that a critical dimension in criminal families, both consanguine and meritocratic, is that through internal group norms members are taught that only the family can be trusted.[11]

This helps to explain why people mostly stay within the familial clusters they are born into. Individuals tend not to shift between familial groups with the obvious exception of entering into new ones through marriage. Likewise, outside of civil wars, in which Kalyvas (2008) explains ethnic identities can be dynamic depending on social and political contexts, people usually do not change ethnic or cultural group heritages, whereas religious groups can be changed though sometimes with great risk. Individuals can, however, change through vocational groups. Doing so enables them to change or add allegiance connections, or switch to other better-suited organizations depending on politics and other factors at the time, yet remain in the same kinship groups. The 2012 Malian insurgency is an excellent example of this.[12]

Boundaries and family

On intimate consanguine levels of relatedness, it is not possible to physically leave a family group. However, on more macro levels of clan and tribe, it is possible to enter into new ones. This occurs temporarily or permanently. Transient kinship affiliation occurs when kin-connections are developed and drawn upon to accomplish specific purposes. Therefore, the manner in which kin interact with one another is important because even weak kinship can activate dormant relationships, or make new, temporal, and transient connections.

In contrast, enduring connections are usually forged through marriage, an essential tool in security seeking familial groups and organizations.[13] Busby (1997) determined that deliberations of marriageability rest mostly on considerations of political and collateral gain, and access to resources belonging to intended kinship parties. Moreover, gains are more relevant to fathers and patrilineal power bases than to daughters or sons, which are but commodities. Marriage is therefore an important commodity-through-process because it can bring people to insurgency who previously had little to no political or ideological affiliations.[14] Similarly, access to political and socially dominant families is beneficial. Wright (2003) states that Osama bin Laden is said to have married Amal al-Sada, who came from a powerful Yemeni tribe in Ibb, purposely to boost al-Qaeda's attractiveness to local fighters.[15]

The example of Nasir Abbas is another excellent example. Abbas bonded fighters in Jemaah Islamiyah through marriage, particularly with his daughters

(Nasir 2019). This built robust social capital systems and trust within the Jemaah Islamiyah network. It further demonstrates many reasons for parental control in creative kinship, particularly in regard to daughters, who are critically important because females invest so much into the welfare of offspring.[16] Trivers (1972) argued that access to females is more critical when scarce reproductive resources are available. Fathers particularly seek the ideal pairings for daughters that create the greatest benefit for the family in terms of material access to resources such as information, finance, and labour. This is reflected extensively in familial insurgency.

However, while there is extensive evidence that consanguine kinship increases the strengths of connections (Dyer and Handler 1994; Le Breton-Miller and Miller 2006), blood relations between people do not automatically guarantee an implicit level of trust, relatedness, or security. Both moral and utilitarian socio-economic relations can have strong trust values as well. Likewise, the "radius of trust" applies to meritocratic in-groups and vocational, political, and ideologically bonded individuals. Communal dynamics of familial and kinship connectedness represent what Tucker and Lamb call a "socially based security advantage" (2006, 2) with which insurgents can maximize cultural, social, and other heritage and legacy connections that can span centuries. However, families possess distinct intelligence disadvantages to counterinsurgent forces, largely due to the inherent strengths of connections. Collectively we can therefore conclude that claims of blood-bonds being stronger, more dependable, or more compelling than other kinds of bonds are not necessarily true. These are examined in the next section.

Social capital and trust in meritocracies

Analysis tells us that social capital values in familial groups are largely determined by the degree of connectedness. Consanguine connections are perhaps the strongest whereas distant tribal relations are probably weaker. However, each can use kinship for effective collaboration. In meritocracies, social capital connections must use a different set of value denominators. Studies largely ascribe these as the utilitarian and perfunctory nature of social capital, with less interpersonal dynamics and more socio-economic ones (Gooderham *et al.* 2011). In meritocracies, social capital can be a mercenary system in which individuals trade collateral (social capital) to get the greatest personal benefit. This makes us ask then, how could meritocratic organizations bond individuals into tightly knit groups where survival is often the daily concern?

Perhaps there is some other facet of interpersonal relations that breaches the utilitarian dimensions of social capital and melds individuals together to enable them to commit acts of political violence. This is likely to be trust. Putnam states that social capital refers to organizational features, particularly trust, that "can improve the efficiency of society by facilitating coordinated action" (1993, 167). Boon and Holmes define trust as "the positive expectation that fellow group members will act in each other's best interests in situations involving risk" (1991, 207).

One of the prime methods for studying and understanding trust is Social Exchange Theory (SET).[17] Cropanzano and Mitchell state that SET is a "conceptual paradigm" (2005, 874) for understanding behaviour. This is achieved by using SET to make conceptual distinctions of contexts and variations present in social interactions. Blau (1964) asserts explicitly that SET is a primary research tool for studying trust dynamics. Unlike with families, relationships in meritocracies take time to build, and individuals only develop trust relationships gradually to generate social capital reinforcements, such as loyalty and mutual commitment. These are exchange processes and are governed by rules and norms that have developed among participants. Once established, solidarity and cohesion take hold. Brown and Duguid (1991) report one of these as the forming of "communities of practice". Haas (1995) likewise refers to "communities of knowledge" and "epistemic communities".

Terminology aside, what SET references is the inherent human need to identify with and belong to groups. The significance of social capital and trust is highly apparent when considering the risks associated with vocational political violence. Arquilla and Ronfeldt observe that in meritocracies, a critical vulnerability is that they have "more difficulty instilling, and enforcing, a sense of personal identity with loyalty to the network" (2001, 1–19). Therefore, ideological and socio-religious norms that are developed through master narratives, as in the examples of al-Qaeda and ISIL, can be employed to counter such weaknesses and to build strength. This demonstrates a direct link between trust and actors and the correlation with group cohesion. Organizations that can effectively build close and secure relationships generally produce outcomes that are more efficient and avoid inefficient non-cooperative scenarios. Consequently, groups that can build high trust levels could have superior performance across multiple facets of the organization.

Wood (2006) links the importance of trust by illustrating the agility of diffuse, darkened networks and how their lack of clarity enables them to outmanoeuver monitoring efforts. Granovetter (1973) argues that the more diffuse a networks structure is regarding connectivity, the more conducive it is to effective action. Meritocracy therefore seems highly relevant to efficiency in security operations and practice. However, there are dangers. Analysis by Eilstrup-Sangiovanni and Jones (2008) found that a significant risk exists for organizations with diffused, decentralized nodes because there is potential for them to develop autonomy and independence from central leadership that can rupture trust bonds.[18] This could be exacerbated in meritocratic organizations with relatively few connective bonds enabling the maintenance of trust between controlling elements, particularly where leaders and commanders are geographically dispersed.

While these issues are problems for all meritocracies, there are corresponding positives. Kenney (2007) asserts that typically, meritocratic cellular organizations can have strong redundancy capacity and high security through compartmentalization, which can aid overall resilience. Williams supports compartmentalization as a resilience mechanism as well, stating that: "Compartmented networks are good at protecting not only the core membership but also information (while also having effective information flows from the periphery to core) that could compromise ... the integrity of the network" (2001, 75).

Summary of social capital and trust

Social capital and trust function differently in meritocracies and familial organizations. This is facilitated by different means and has different values. In each case there are strengths and vulnerabilities. Interestingly, offsets are present in each example that offer corresponding benefits where liabilities are present. In order for organizational efficiency to be successful, these must be balanced and managed by effective leaders to mitigate the bad and exploit the good. If this is achieved, insurgent organizations are likely to increase their resilience capabilities.

Collier (2006) contributed to initial understanding in a brief yet highly important examination of insurgent cooperation and alliancing. Collier determined that when viewed from a localized reality, an interplay of wider ally networks and partners could be established via a global-centric paradigm that correlates localized struggles back to a political and ideological wellspring. Therefore, alliances and cooperative networks may be highly relevant to the strengths and vulnerability balancing needed in insurgent organizations to ensure strong social capital and trust; and potentially a critical factor of organizational resilience, as discussed in the next section.

The resilience of insurgent organizations

So far this chapter has discussed what contributes to resilience in insurgent organizations by examining organizational arrangement, social capital and trust, structure, and efficiency. As these differ between meritocracies and familial organizations, it has examined commonalities and the facilitation of them under different circumstances. Likewise, it has established that leadership plays an important part in developing and leading the resilience of organizations. One other factor that should be considered is the state sponsorship of organizations. This is a dynamic of the Haqqani Network and Lashkar-e-Taiba, and research into this field is growing. Berkowitz (2018), for instance, examined state sponsorship through the principal-agent framework to examine the rationality of sponsorship as a tool of foreign policy.

Hastings (2003) takes a different approach and examined the relevant norms of international law to determine what tools could be employed under a legal framework to hold state sponsors accountable for the actions of organizations they support. Elsewhere, Kaunert *et al.* (2017) has examined, in-depth, the state sponsorship of insurgency because of Western democratic policy approaches to Middle-East countries, suggesting that the West plays an active part in the cycle.

However, while these approaches show the subject has already received considerable attention, and its relevance to the case studies in this book is apparent, the topic is given considerable analysis in the following case studies. As such, this section now moves back to insurgent resilience, the third section of the chapter discussing how resilience is facilitated differently in familial versus meritocratic organizations as a result.

To answer this however, we must first determine what types and levels of resilience are required for political and operational perpetuity. Is it the ability to fill leadership voids, replace the loss of fighters and supporters, the ability to run and hide, regroup and re-arm, or the ability to continue to pursue violent political agendas in the face of significant external pressures? Additionally, do needs manifest differently in meritocracies and familial organizations? To answer these questions we commence with a definition.

Defining resilience

A common description of resilience is the ability of something to bounce back to an original state after change. Organizationally, Sheffi (2015) defines resilience as a return to pre-disruption levels of performance, achieved either by redundancy or through flexibility. Folke *et al.* (2005) consider resilience as a dynamic process of ongoing adaptability to accommodate change. This is a good representation of resilience generally. However, others such as Van Der Leeuw take a contrary approach, stating that "rather than assuming stability and explaining change, as often done, one needs to assume change and explain stability" (2000, 2). This can be measured by examination of the variables and the continued demonstration of resilience over time. This suggests that resilience can be viewed as the efficiency value of any system that enables it to be restored to a similar state in the event of disruption or damage.

Adger *et al.* (2001) analysed fundamental components of resilience such as organizational growth, legacy resource investments, and the evolution and distribution of capabilities. Under such terms, resilience takes on new dynamic aspects that emphasize adaptability, transfiguration, and even metamorphosis. Resilience is not only about persistence, but also about opportunities that disruption can offer, such as the potential to evolve governance processes, change structures, and recalibrate organizational trajectories.

Organizational leadership would therefore be important to evolve practices and to learn from change to provide what we can call *strategic resilience*. This strengthens our definition of resilience by accepting continual change processes as permanent, rather than being ad hoc disruptions that occur across temporal and spatial lines. It also acknowledges findings from practice and in the literature that leadership is critical to organizational adaptation by articulating appropriate response to changing external pressures in tangible and intangible ways.[19] This provides an excellent basis to understand what resilience is, but how does it happen?

Manifesting resilience

Schoon (2006) found that resilience derives from outcomes rather than processes, stressing it is a characteristic that occurs only after exposure to disruption. In fact, what happens after an organization is subject to severe shock from external pressures seems equally, if not more, important than how it dealt with disruption before an event. This may be a critical gap. Because there are no fixed timelines, chronologies or references to determine a resilient organization accurately, nor common consensus on defining resilience, it is a fickle thing to do. Do organizations have to keep operating as they did or are there acceptable pauses and grace periods for them to recover and then re-commence? Likewise, does being resilient mean they have to continue to operate as before, or, is recovering the capability to do so in full but not exercising it the same thing? Perhaps some organizations want to lay low after being targeted by incumbent forces and re-orientate rather than getting straight back into the melee.

Khare (2015) argues that political violence in insurgency is well considered and is most often deliberate, with strategic and instrumental goals in mind supported by defined objectives and justifications. This demonstrates resilience as another strategic tool of organizations. It can be argued that like other considerations of security, secrecy, resources, and capabilities, resilience is deliberately developed and manifested in response to, and with the expectations of, probable external pressures. Similarly, the strategic nature of insurgency equally suggests that long-term considerations of survival and prosperity include an organizational understanding of internal resilience requirements.

These views are common across the literature as scholars seek to understand what makes organizations robust (Zhang *et al.* 2012; Allen and Shanock 2013; Chuang *et al.* 2016). However, there are shortcomings of validation in extant methods of understanding resilience as a strategic tool. Gall states, "The absence of effective assessment tools hampers the evaluation of adaptation actions and their effect on resilience" (2013, 25). As much focus centres on resilience in response to external pressures, the disruption of resilience is itself less apparent.

Holling (2004) addresses this by modelling resilience in the context of organizational destabilization, upon which Silverman and Hill (2018) built. They argue that when resilience is disrupted and vulnerabilities are exposed, it can be beneficial for organizational resilience because it creates favourable conditions in the adaptive cycle.[20] By modifying and visualizing Holling's model it becomes more apparent how organizations can benefit from the disruptions external pressures bring, something applicable to meritocracies and familial organizations alike (Figure 2.1).[21]

A brief comparison of two groups provides some validation of these concepts, particularly that leadership structures and organizational efficiency affect meritocracies and familial organizations in similar ways but differ significantly in terms of method and development. In criminal gangs where meritocracy is prevalent, Weisel observes that many groups demonstrate significant changes over time, "consolidating, merging, acquiring smaller gangs, reorganizing, and

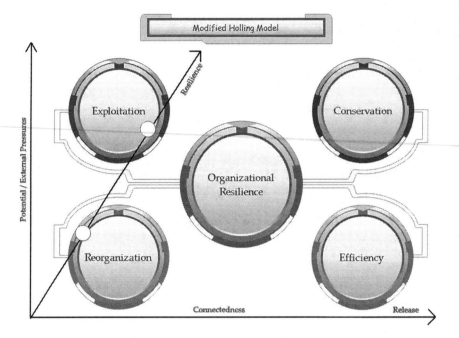

Figure 2.1 Modified Holling model.

splintering" (2002, 27). This is highly suggestive of an adaptive organic structure that actively pursues organizational efficiencies. There is further evidence of this. Morselli *et al.* (2007) determine that criminal networks consistently seek network efficiencies, balancing security with risk and reward. This indicates that adaptability in response to, and expectation of, external pressures is the critical survival tool.[22]

Work by Duijn *et al.* (2014) shows that external pressures can equally be beneficial for networked criminal gangs because it results in them "going dark" (minimizing detectability) and becoming increasingly diffused. This is reflected in the analysis of meritocracies and their decentralization in correlation with external pressures. As phenomena, this scenario is also supported by Morselli *et al.* (2007) and by Bright and Delaney (2013), who found that diffusion and decentralization occurs to meet efficiency and security requirements of networks as they are targeted.[23]

To maintain validity by comparison we next examine a criminal network with deep and extensive familial connections, culture, and organization as opposed to meritocracy. This organization is the Yakuza of Japan. The Yakuza descend from the original crime families known as Bakuto and Tekiya gangs from medieval Japan. These consisted of outcasts, jobless poor people, landless people, criminals, and petty labourers (Iwai 1986). Today's Yakuza maintain strong familial connections to them, displaying images of past godfathers and family trees linking the current groups to the past (Gragert 1997).

However, what is unusual about the familial nature of the Yakuza is that ancestral and other familial connections are not explicitly consanguine, with some obtained through adoption.[24] Family surrogacy is strictly reinforced through customs and norms by which familial social capital and trust are dictated. An Oyabun, literally meaning the "Parent", controls Yakuza gangs. All members are stringently bound by the Oyabun-Kobun relationship, meaning a father-child relationship (Gragert 1997).

Unlike in meritocracies where social capital is largely utilitarian, in the Yakuza organization it relates to belonging and reciprocity. This ingrains benefits of cohesion, organizational unity, and even what Gragert calls "fanatical devotion to the Oyabun" (1997, 22). This is part of the overall "Giri" system of obligation, i.e. loyalty, duty, gratitude, and moral debt (Roniger 1987). Giri is a social phenomenon across all levels of Japanese society but in the criminal families, it is additionally reinforced, making it particularly powerful in contributing to resilience in the Yakuza. Similar to meritocracies, external pressures also result in organizational flex and change, but rather than diffusion and darkening, it results in consolidation and reinforcement in the familial and quasi-familial organizations of the Yakuza. With regard to Holling's model, external pressures on familial criminal gangs often means activation of the Giri and Kobun social capital systems, resulting in lower-level members sacrificing themselves for the good of the family. This provides the Yakuza with what Rankin calls an "impressive record of resilience and adaptability and the safe bet that they will succeed" (Rankin 2012, 16).

Supporting a panoptic cognizance, these examples demonstrate how resilience is facilitated differently in familial versus meritocratic organizations, and what such resilience looks like in terms of ongoing political and operational perpetuity. Each has its own way of replacing leaders, filling voids in command and control, and recruiting new members, fighters, and supporters. Additionally, the extant data shows that different organizational types have different needs in terms of resilience, and particularly how they respond to external pressures and to achieve it. Some consolidate and reinforce, as in familial organizations, while others scatter, diffuse, and hide, as in meritocracies. Familial networks can be particularly dark but easily illuminated once found, whereas meritocratic networks can be easier to find but harder to map. Thus, "darkening" has reoccurred in the literature several times. The next section reviews this topic to better understand the aspects of organizational arrangement and structural efficiency that drive resilience.

Dark resilience versus stagnation

Thus far it is evident that resilience involves evolution and capacity-building. These aspects include behavioural, governance, and operational modification as well as structural strengthening. However, a critical question to ask at this point is: How do we know an organization is resilient if, in the wake of serious disruption by external pressures it does not overtly demonstrate resilience through ongoing operational and political activity? For a resilience paradigm to be true it must work over time, and not just be about immediate responses. Successfully responding to an organizational shock event does not guarantee long-term success. How long should that process be and does it have to be operationalized through attacks for organizations to be truly resilient?

This has been a novel sub-area of academic investigation that has high relevance to the examination of resilience. Organizations can fail for any number of reasons and not necessarily as a result of outside forces. Counterintuitively, organizations can "go dark" and become far less visible while retaining resilience. The asymmetrical nature of guerrilla warfare embeds covert activity into the bedrock of insurgency. Therefore understanding the dark resilience versus stagnation paradigm is critical. The answer to this means determining the difference between dark resilience and the unseen covert organizational processes that sustain, and the ineffective and failing attempts to rebuild that do not.

First, going dark should not be confused with inactivity or stagnation. They are not the same. Stagnation in common vernacular means a cessation of all activity and decay of capabilities (Cameron *et al.* 1987). Going dark means to move all activity out of the light and into the darkness where it cannot be detected without intensive effort. When going dark, most, if not all organizational capabilities, remain intact. The purpose of going dark is evasion and survival, and if organizations achieve this they can protect key capabilities, operations, members, leaders, and specialists from arrests or killings. Failures of security forces to capture or kill targets can demonstrate successful evasion and darkened insurgent organizational resilience. This is what Stern (2003) refers to as a trade-off choice organizations need to make between resilience, being the desire to live and fight another day, and capacity, referring to a desire to attack. These trade-offs need to be carefully considered.

Detecting the outcomes of these choices at first seems difficult, particularly given the very nature of darkened activity. Notwithstanding, it is likely there are a number of ways that organizations going dark could be detected. If an organization seems to have ceased activity, perhaps in response to external pressures, it may have gone dark. If organizations are damaged but not severely enough to stop all operational activity, it is likely that they are going dark. And when organizations that are intact stop communicating and overt activity ceases to be observable, they are also probably going dark.

Everton and Cunningham (2013) developed a method to detect dark network activity using the Jemaah Islamiyah, Noorudin Mohammad Top cell as a case study. Employing a modified Social Network Analysis (SNA) approach, they devised a method of monitoring dark network topography. By observing density and structural variables of centralization and fragmentation, they detected network changes and significant moves in organizational structures.[25] Elsewhere, Arquilla (2009) proposed that peripheral monitoring was the solution. By determining known actors with a high likelihood of being involved, or likely to have future involvement, it was found that it is possible that at some point they might communicate with a dark network and reveal some part of it. These approaches have made significant contributions to differentiating dark resilience from stagnation.

The Nigerian Boko Haram organization demonstrated this following the extrajudicial slaying of the group's founder, Mohammed Yusuf, by security forces in July 2009. In this example, Boko Haram reacted by retreating and going dark. This was followed by a significant display of capacity with the bombing of the police headquarters in Abuja in June 2011 (Agbiboa 2013). Periods of passivity afford organizations breathing space to avoid the brunt of security force actions. However, if external pressures remain constant and force organizations to stay low for extended periods, they can suffer from internal dissatisfaction of members. Wiegand (2010) discussed this as being a balancing act between reducing the levels of violence used to appease external conditions, but not to the extent of reducing internal supporters.

This suggests that a result of going dark may be agency issues, like splintering, desertion, or loss of external legitimacy that flows on to loss of popular support and resources. Lorenzo and Della Porta (2015) point out that, as a strategy, some incumbent state actors have deliberately seeded perceptions of growing dissatisfaction among insurgent organization members that, as in the case of the Italian Red Brigades for example, fostered collective exiting. Conversely, going on the offensive and engaging in grievance-seeking increases organizational prominence, member satisfaction, and external support, but it also increases the risk of further damage and degradation (Ballentine and Nitzschke 2003).[26] This suggests that alternating between persistence and effectiveness quickly as a strategy depends on environmental factors and the effectiveness of external pressures. For Boko Haram such a strategy worked following Yusuf's slaying.

From these examples it is apparent that periods of darkness and re-engagement in fighting have cyclical natures. Both impact the level and severity of operational activity from very low to very high and back again. Laying low enables organizations to recruit and rebuild, learn and adapt, though at the potential cost of legitimacy loss internally and externally. High operational attack tempo can raise member satisfaction and popular support but places the organization in the crosshairs. This is evident in other examples that support the resilience paradigm. Jemaah Islamiyah, for example, went through a sustained period of operational oscillation from 2000 to 2009, attacking and darkening, attacking and darkening.[27]

Dark resilience may also have structural dynamics where familial connectedness and kin relations may be important factors. Shapiro and Siegel (2007) claim that family and kinship are critical, particularly in ethnic societies where endogamy increases not only network size, but also strength and security because it reinforces, and is reinforced, by kinship-based social capital and trust. Schaffer writes that "ethnically based terrorist campaigns can be harder to end decisively than politically based ones because they often enjoy broader support among a population they seek to represent" (1999, 1). A 2006 International Crisis Group (ICG) report on the insurgency in Iraq after the U.S.-led invasion supports this empirically, stating that "the insurgency is

Table 2.4 Organizational structures – strengths and vulnerabilities

Strengths	Vulnerabilities	Strengths	Vulnerabilities
Vetting costs.	Leadership loss.	Leadership, command and control.	Internal security and counterintelligence.
Internal security and counterintelligence.	Limitations of familial recruitment.	Resource collection.	High start-up costs.
Start-up costs.	Resource limitations over time.	Open recruitment.	Vetting costs.
Strategic behaviour.	Less compartmentalization of damages.	Compartmentalization of damages.	Agency issues, splintering.

built around a loose and flexible network [and] feeds on deep-seated family, tribal and local loyalties with allegiance to a cause rather than to specific individuals" (ICG 2006, 25).

Whether to a cause or to kin, security is a significant obstacle for incumbents because identifying extraordinary communication flows between closely connected people can be very difficult. Likewise, insurgency has long-term horizons rather than a view to short-term gains, because of which, security is usually prioritized over the execution of any single attack. Therefore, operational environments with heightened risk can cause participants to focus on network security over other concerns. Erickson (1981) observed this, offering that one way network members achieved this was by relying primarily on pre-existing networks that formed the foundation upon which each covert group or network was designed, to compensate for risk.

Closed familial groups, strict centralization, and information control in meritocratic organizations are excellent examples of this. Therefore, organizational structure seems to have strong significance for organizational resilience, particularly when going dark. Similarly, organizational structures may have different resilience vulnerabilities, meaning that they are only a factor of resilience, rather than a determinant. These are shown in Table 2.4; they are explored further in Part II and in Chapter 8.

Conclusion

In this chapter I have identified several key phenomenological concepts of insurgent organizational resilience. Broadly, the data shows that resilience theorists have found social capital and trust to be able to provide efficiency, security, and legitimization, enhancing benefits in each organizational type (Putnam 1995; Levi and Stoker 2000; Fukuyama 2001; Tilly 2004; Morselli and Roy 2008; Chua *et al.* 2009). It also found that kinship can strengthen and reinforce political, ideological, and religious norms and beliefs, cement in-group cohesion, and delineate group trust (Emerson 1976; Adler and Kwon 2002; Salvatore and Le Vine 2005; Sinno 2008).

Furthermore, the literature demonstrates the diversity of approaches present in existing studies, as well as in the fields of socio-economics, exchange and communication processes, and Social Network Analysis (Blau 1964; Haas 1995; Brown and Duguid 2001; Cropanzano and Mitchell 2005; Burcher and Whelan 2018). Acknowledging the conceptual distinctions present in the plethora of socially based interchanges develops greater clarity in respect of resilience dynamics, critical to understanding how social capital and trust function in the structures of different organizations.

Examples are communities of practice and knowledge, and epistemic ones, as described by Brown and Duguid (2001). This suggests that cultural and socio-religious norms are powerful because they regulate behaviours and practices, particularly when coupled with, and occurring in, familial systems. As La Porta *et al.* (1997) and Fukuyama (2001) have asserted, these consolidate cohesion, secure relationships, and produce more efficient outcomes for organizations while reducing conflict. Emerson's (1976) work shows how exchange processes are used to describe how actors become governed by rules and norms in meritocratic organizations. This also supports cohesion and individual adaptation that shapes ethical norms and fosters cooperation (Lin *et al.* 2008). Conversely identified in the literature are some significant risks, particularly in regard to the negative implications of strong social capital and trust within organizations that can rupture and fragment overall organizational cohesion through diffusion. This is a particular concern for meritocracies.

This is exemplified in the work undertaken by Eilstrup-Sangiovanni and Jones (2008). They show that when decentralized nodes develop autonomy and independence from central leadership, trust bonds and social capital can break down into what can become almost independent entities. The validity of this is further evident in the works of Minor (2012) and Jones (2006), who reveal that diffused organizational ties could present an increased internal security risk because of disconnection between top-tier leaders and mid-level commanders and their fighters. However, decentralized groups enjoy low-cost structures, flexibility, and redundancy, which lend themselves to resilience (Govindarajan 1986).

Ultimately, the range of benefits and drawbacks identified has significant relevance to the field of counterinsurgency, to counter-terrorism studies, and to the study of political violence as a whole. This is because it opens ways to understand political violence and those who undertake it in ways far different from kinetic-, military-, and attrition-based methods used traditionally in counterinsurgency, and counterterrorism doctrines.

However, resilience takes many forms and there is no single approach that is broadly applicable. Particular characteristics of resilience can change over time to maintain sustainable future operations, just as external pressures must change in the constant pursuit of insurgent vulnerabilities to attack. This chapter is, therefore, a step towards developing a greater understanding of resilience as it pertains to insurgency, which in turn may lead to better policy and operational decision-making in countering it.

Notes

1 Ayling contends that one advantage covert organizations may have is that the need for operational secrecy necessarily militates against any kind of resilience deriving from transparent or legitimate processes that illuminated organizations must adhere to. SOURCE: Julie Ayling, 2009. "Criminal Organizations and Resilience". *International Journal of Law, Crime and Justice* 37 (4): 182–196.

2 Marazziti *et al.* (2018) claim that leaders manipulate the psychological vulnerabilities of members to create justifications and even longing for death and martyrdom. Brandebo and Alvinius (2009) put it that meritocratic organizations often use internal propaganda to do the same, and act in a narcissistic manner by placing high demands on members but offering little in return. SOURCES: Donatella Marazzitiet *et al.*, 2000. "The Mind of Suicide Terrorists". *CNS Spectrums* 23 (2): 145–150; Maria Brandebo and Aida Alvinius, 2009. *Dark Sides of Organizations and Leadership*. London: IntechOpen.

3 Forced recruitment and child soldiers are an obvious exception. Although used extensively in some African, Asian, and South American conflicts, the use of forced service is not completely meritocratic. While individuals can rise in status through meritocracy in such cases, the lack of choosing to be there initially separates those organizations from others. SOURCES: Prajakta Gupte, 2018. "Child Soldiers in Myanmar: Role of Government and Limitations of International Law". *Journal of Law and International Affairs* 6 (1): 371–397; Patricia Martuscelli and Rafael Duarte Villa, 2018. "Child Soldiers as Peace-builders in Colombian Peace Talks between the Government and the FARC–EP". *Journal of Conflict, Security and Development* 18 (5): 387–408; Oshomoh Olusesan Familusi, 2019. "Socio-Economic Implications of Boko Haram Insurgency in Northern Nigeria". *KIU Journal of Social Sciences* 4 (2): 213–223.

4 Whether this is a reflection of Jeremy Bentham's pinnacle work about the greatest good for the greatest number of people is unclear, though it does illustrate that the role of leadership is not simple. SOURCE: Jeremy Bentham, 1789. *The Principles of Morals and Legislation*. Oxford: Clarendon Press.

5 Zulaika and Douglass hold that for decades there has been much anthropological scepticism about the approaches used in studying dominant discourses of terrorism. In mainstream terrorism studies the volumes of output have exploded in the wake of 11 September 2001 and the equally expansive development of Western counterterrorism policy. Much of the academic investigation however has been sub-standard, they say, as scholars including Silke and Ranstorp have demonstrated. Conversely, others such as leftist scholars including Chomsky and Herman, Herman, Herman and O'Sullivan, and George, examined terrorism studies from politically biased perspectives, asserting that terrorism was used by the West to politically and ideologically justify the targeting of left-wing movements. SOURCES: Joseba Zulaika and William Douglass, 1996. *Terror and Taboo: The Follies, Fables, and Faces of Terrorism*. New York: Taylor & Francis; Andrew Silke, 2009. "Contemporary Terrorism Studies: Issues in Research". In *Critical Terrorism Studies: A New Research Agenda*, eds. Richard Jackson *et al.* London and New York: Routledge; Magnus Ranstorp, 2008. "Mapping Terrorism Studies After 9/11: An Academic Field of Old Problems and New Prospects". In *Critical Terrorism Studies: Framing a New Research Agenda*. London: Routledge; Edward Herman and Gerry O'Sullivan, 1982. *The "Terrorism" Industry: The Experts and Institutions that Shape Our View of Terror*. New York: Pantheon Books.

6 Lin put it that most scholars have a shared overall view of what social capital is, though there are differences of perspective about at what level it is more relevant, being profit and reciprocity at the individual level or on the group or organizational level. Addressing this, Lin *et al.*, offered that social capital works relationally at both

levels, stating that, similarly to human capital, social capital sees returns to individuals just as aggregates of individuals see returns to groups and collectives. SOURCE: Nan Lin *et al.*, 2001. *Social Capital: Theory and Research.* London and New York: Routledge.

7 Marx was responsible for much of the pioneering work on social capital. Marx put it that dominant leadership figures separated, by word or deed, those in their charge into various levels of social capital worth depending on their talents and therefore value. The work of Marx's was important because it established a foundation upon which other scholars, such as Putnam, 1993, 1995; Portes, 1998; and Cusack, 1997 have built up theories that pertain to the masses as well as individuals. SOURCE: Karl Marx, 1887. "The Capitalistic Nature of Manufacture". In *Capital: A Critique of Political Economy. Volume I, Book 1: The Process of Production of Capital*, eds. Samuel Moore and Edward Aveling. Moscow: Progress Publishers, 248–261.

8 There are several prominent efficiency-based notions that reflect this, including Productive efficiency (see Farrell), Pareto optimality (see Chinchuluun *et al.*), Kaldor-Hicks efficiency (see Stringham), and Posner's wealth maximization for example (see Posner). SOURCES: Michael Farrell, 1957. *The Measurement of Productive Efficiency.* Cambridge: Cambridge University Press; Altannar Chinchuluun *et al.*, 2008. *Pareto Optimality, Game Theory and Equilibria.* New York: Springer; Edward Stringham, 2001. "Kaldor-Hicks Efficiency and the Problem of Central Planning". *Quarterly Journal of Austrian Economics* 4 (2): 41–50; Richard Posner, 1985. "Wealth Maximization Revisited". *Journal of Law, Ethics and Public Policy* 85 (2): 85–105.

9 Nahapiet and Ghoshal developed a model to show differing dimensions of social capital and how they produce new intellectual capital from a plethora of existing research across organizational advantage and failure. Leana and Van Buren examined mechanisms by which social capital is enhanced or suppressed in organizations, while Chow and Chan showed that social trust had no effects on individual attitudes or norms of knowledge sharing. Lastly, Metnick described the origins and base theory of principal-agent exchange relationships, developing an institutional theory of agency that extends beyond economic modelling alone. SOURCES: Janine Nahapiet and Sumantra Ghoshal, 2000. "Social Capital, Intellectual Capital, and the Organizational Advantage". In *Knowledge and Social Capital: Foundations and Applications*, ed. Eric Lesser. Boston: Butterworth and Heinemann, 242–266; Carrie Leana and Harry Van Buren, 2012. "Organizational Social Capital and Employment Practices". In *Sociology of Organizations: Strucutre and Relationships*, eds. Mary Godwyn and Jody Gittel. Los Angeles, London and New Delhi: Sage Publications, 538–555; W.S Chow and L.S. Chan. 1998. "Social Network, Social Trust and Shared Goals in Organizational Knowledge Sharing". *Journal of Information and Management* 45 (7): 458–465; Barry Metnick, 1997. "Agency Theory". In *The Blackwell Encyclopaedic Dictionary of Business Ethics*, eds. Patricia Werhan and Edward Freeman. Oxford: Blackwell Publishers, 12–15.

10 Fortes defined kinship morality in terms like "prescriptive altruism", asserting that kin-based relations are characterized by a morality of "sharing" without deliberate reconciliation. Sahlins (1965) refers to the morality of kinship as "generalized reciprocity". Bloch focuses more specifically on this, claiming that inequality and absences of reciprocity are the measure of the morality of relationships. Therefore relationships in which one party does more taking is morality based, whereas ones in which immediate reciprocity is required are more utilitarian. SOURCES: Meyer Fortes, 1978. "An Anthropologist's Apprenticeship". *Annual Review of Anthropology* 7 (1): 1–30; Meyer Fortes, 1983. *Rules and the Emergence of Society.* London: Royal Anthropological Institute of Great Britain and Ireland; Meyer Fortes, 2006. *Kinship and the Social Order.* New York: Routledge; Maurice Bloch, 1974. "The Long-term

and the Short-term". In *The Character of Kinship*, ed. J. Goody. Cambridge: Cambridge University Press;. Marshall Sahlins. 1974. *On the Sociology of Primitive Exchange*. London: Tavistock Publications, 139–186.

11 The principle of trusting members of inside groups over members of outside groups was established in social psychology literature in the 1970s. SOURCES: Henri Tajfel, 1970. "Experiments in Intergroup Discrimination". *Scientific American* 223 (5): 96–102; Henri Tajfel and Michael Billig, 1973. "Social Categorization in Intergroup Behaviour". *European Journal of Social Psychology* 3 (1): 149–178; Jonathan Tan and Claudia Vogel, 2008. "Religion and Trust: an Experimental Study". *Journal of Economic Psychology* 29 (6): 832–848.

12 The social architecture of the Sahel-Sahara region is fragile at best and the interchanges between Islamist fighters, rebel insurgents, and the military are fluid. This means there are vocational inter-group shifts. This is not only true of individual fighters but of commanders and their followers as well. For instance, Walther and Christopoulos observed that individuals and groups followed opportunity more than cause. Some fighters from the Tuareg military joined with rebel forces from the MNLA to achieve local victories in the north of the country. In other instances rebels sided with Islamist forces if the tide of battle was more favourable. SOURCE: Oliver Walther and Dimitris Christopoulos, 2015. "Islamic Terrorism and the Malian Rebellion". *Journal of Terrorism and Political Violence* 27 (3): 1–23.

13 Illicit organizations can use marriage as a means to raise exits costs, meaning that, to leave, an individual must betray close relatives, which may make them choose not to. This increases security and makes networks and communication channels more secure from leaking. It can however make communication channels easier to map by authorities. Frey and Luechinger state that rather than raise exit costs, opportunity costs can be raised to encourage conformity and offer incentives to join or stay, such as access to a broader networks, resources and capabilities. SOURCE: Bruno Fery and Simon Luechinger, 2012. "How to Fight Terrorism: Alternatives to Deterrence". *Journal of Defence and Peace Economics* 14 (4): 237–249.

14 Examples of female suicide bombers is rather different situationally but similar contextually. Bloom asserts that joining a terrorist group is one of the few remaining options for women who, according to the strict honour code in some Islamic societies, must otherwise be executed by their own families if they are the victims of rape, or engage in promiscuity. SOURCE: Mia Bloom, 2005. *Dying to Kill: The Allure of Suicide Terror*. New York: Columbia University Press.

15 While bin Laden's marriage was self-arranged, in others, family members, particularly parents, have significant influence over their children regarding mate pairing. Middleton (2000) uses motherhood as an idiom of control dynamics, meaning mother exercises significant control over sons' and siblings' children, and in particular, mate selection, asserting that kinship is a creative act. SOURCE: H. Middleton, 2016. "Flourishing and Posttraumatic Growth. An Empirical Take on Ancient Wisdoms". *Health Care Annual* 24 (2): 133–147.

16 Inter-marriage is discussed at greater length in later chapters, though it is important to note here that it is an act which has reinforced the Jemaah Islamiyah organization and aided security. For instance, Mukhlas (a.k.a. Huda bin Abdul Haq and Ali Ghufron) married Nasir Abbas' sister Farida when Abbas was head of Mantiqi 3. Amrozi and al-Ghozi are his in-laws. After al-Ghozi was killed by police in 2003, his younger brother married his widow. Syawal Yassin was a midranking Jihadist from Sulawesi and married one of Abdullah Sungkar's stepdaughters, as did Ferial Muchlis bin Abdul Halim, who was head of the JI Selangor cell. SOURCE: David Jones and M.L.R. Smith, 2011. "Organization vs. Ideology: The Lessons from Southeast Asia". *Current Trends in Islamist Ideology* 12 (1): 92–123.

17 Social Exchange Theory (SET) first developed as a social studies discipline in the 1920s and was pioneered by Malinowski (1922) and Mauss (1924), and spans various other disciplines such as social psychology (Homans 1958; Thibault and Kelly 1959; Gouldner 1960; Burton and Wilson 2006), sociology (Giddens 1987; Hedstrom and Swedberg 1988; Weber 2009), and anthropology (Firth 1967; Bailey 1970; Kirsten 2005). SOURCES: Bronsilaw Malinowski, 2014. *Argonauts of the Western Pacific.* London and New York: Routledge; Marcel Mauss, 1954. *The Gift: The Form and Reason for Exchange in Archaic Societies.* New York: Cohen and West; Alvin Gouldner, 1960. *The Norm of Reciprocity.* Indianapolis: Bobbs-Merrill; George Homans, 1993. *Social Behavior as Exchange.* New York: Ardent Media Inc.; John Thibault and Harold Kelley, 1964. *The Social Psychology of Groups.* New Brunswick and London: Transaction Publishers; R.J.F. Burton and G.A. Wilson, 2006. "Injecting Social Psychology Theory into Conceptualizations of Agricultural Agency: Towards a Post-Productive Farmer Self-Identity". *Journal of Rural Studies* 22 (1): 95–115; Max Weber, 1945. *From Max Weber: Essays in Sociology.* London: Routledge; Anthony Giddens, 1987. *Social Theory and Modern Sociology.* Cambridge: Blackwell Publishing; Peter Hedstrom and Richard Swedberg, 1988. *Social Mechanisms.* Cambridge: Cambridge University Press; Raymond Firth, 1967. *Themes in Economic Anthropology.* London, Tavistock Publications; F.G. Bailey, 2001. *Stratagems and Spoils.* New York: Routledge; Kirsten Hastrup, 2005. "Social Anthropology. Towards Pragmatic Enlightenment?" *Social Anthropology* 133 (2): 133–149.

18 In networked organizations, diffuse ties may represent heightened security risks because of far lower trust and social capital levels. See: Calvert Jones, 2006. "Al-Qaeda's Innovative Improvisers: Learning in a Diffuse Transnational Network". *Cambridge Review of International Affairs* 19 (4): 555–567.

19 Tangible ways could be reflected in structural changes, and the adoption of new methods, techniques, field craft and practices, new weaponry and tactics or areas of operation (AOs). Intangible ways can be how information is controlled and shared, where decision-making lies at each level from tactical control to strategic, and the formulation and employment of goals and objectives. SOURCE: A. Carmeli and A. Tishler, 2004. "The Relationship Between Intangible Organizational Elements and Organizational Performance". *Strategic Management Journal* 25 (2004): 1257–1278.

20 Silverman and Hill propose that in ecological systems it is actually negative and attenuating influences that are stabilizing to organizations whereas positive and amplifying feedbacks are destabilizing. SOURCE: Howard Silverman and Gregory Hill, 2018. "The Dynamics of Purposeful Change: A Model". *Ecology and Society* 23 (3): 4–27. See also Stuart Chapin III et al., 2009. "A Framework for Understanding Change". New York, Springer, 3–28.

21 From a strategic counterintelligence perspective, the modified Holling's model shows opportunity at the realization/exploitation end of the resilience cycle. This potentially indicates that there could be significant weakness at the conservation-release side where the organizational focus is probably more internal than external.

22 Morselli and Roy support such a conclusion, asserting that rather than being rigid, criminal networks must be flexible and able to adapt because this determines longevity. SOURCE: Carlo Morselli and Julie Roy, 2008. "Brokerage Qualifications in Ringing Operations". *Criminology* 46 (1): 71–98.

23 Kenney's examination of the Columbian narcotics trade is an excellent example. Rather than being one large well-structured cartel, it is actually comprised of a series of smaller, dynamic networks that preserve security and coordinate activities to ensure efficiency. SOURCE: Michael Kenney, 2007. "The Architecture of Drug Trafficking: Network Forms of Organization in the Columbian Drug Trade". *Global Crime* 8 (1): 233–259.

24 This does not mean consanguine kinship is absent, quite the opposite. Many yakuza are born into the various criminal families making up a significant percentage of the membership. Paoli asserts that yakuza have a mixed nature of consanguine and non-kin, but who are considered to be as kin to one another under terms of fundamental unity. SOURCE: Letizia Paoli, 2003. *Mafia Brotherhoods: Organized Crime, Italian Style*. Oxford: Oxford University Press.

25 Contributing significantly to closing this gap, Berlusconi *et al.* developed a link prediction method to identify missing actors in criminal networks through topological analysis. Their work builds on classic Social Network Analysis (SNA) that is used extensively in CT analysis. By identifying structural dissimilarities in network nodes they were able to identify previously discarded or unknown actors. Theoretically this could be just as applicable to insurgency, including to the multi-structural types discussed. SOURCE: Giulia Berlusconi *et al.*, 2016. "Link Prediction in Criminal Networks: A Tool for Criminal Intelligence Analysis". *PLOS ONE* 11 (4): e0154244.

26 The Japanese organization Aum Shinrikyo is an example of resilience failure. After its notorious Tokyo subway sarin attack in 1995 it went dark, but it was completely dismantled within weeks as a result, and therefore had a catastrophic failure of resilience. SOURCES: K.B. Olsen, 1999. "Aum Shinrikyo: Once and Future Threat?" *Journal of Emerging Infectious Diseases* 5 (4): 513–516; Tetsu Okumura *et al.*, 2008. "The Tokyo Subway Sarin Attack: Disaster Management, Part 1: Community Emergency Response". *Academic Emergency Management* 5 (6): 613–617;

27 From the 24 December 2000 Christmas Eve bombings that killed 17 people, through further attacks in 2001, 2002, two in 2003, 2004, 2005 to the twin attacks in 2009 against the JW Marriot and Ritz-Carlton hotels, Jemaah Islamiyah had killed over 300 people and wounded some 500 more. After each attack it faced significant external pressure. During the post-attack "dark" periods Jemaah Islamiyah had a number of tasks. Not only did its members have to hide and evade authorities, but organizationally it had to maintain operational nodes, and, where they were degraded, replace and replenish them. SOURCES: Gillian Murdoch, 2009. "TIMELINE: Attacks and plots blamed on Jemaah Islamiyah in Asia". www.reuters.com/article/us-indonesia-militants-timeline-sb / timeline-attacks-and-plots-blamed-on-jemaah-islamiah-in-asia-idUSTRE58G29 X20090917. Accessed 7 March 2016; Gillian Oak, 2010. "Jemaah Islamiyah's Fifth Phase: The Many Faces of a Terrorist Group". *Studies in Conflict and Terrorism* 33 (11): 989–1018.

References

Adger, Neil, Kelly, Mick and Ninh, Nguyen Huu. 2001. *Living with Environmental Change: Social Vulnerability, Adaptation and Resilience in Vietnam*. First edition. London: Routledge.

Adler, Paul and Kwon, Seok-Woo. 2002. "Social Capital: Prospects for a New Concept". *The Academy of Management Review* 27 (1): 14–40.

Agbiboa, Daniel. 2013. "No Retreat, No Surrender: Understanding the Religious Terrorism of Boko Haram in Nigeria". *African Studies Monograph* 34 (2): 65–84.

Allen, David and Shanock, Linda Rhoades. 2013. "Perceived Organizational Support and Embeddedness as Key Mechanisms Connecting Socialization Tactics to Commitment and Turnover among New Employees". *Journal of Organizational Behaviour* 34 (3): 350–369.

Arquilla, John. 2009. *Aspects of Netwar and the Conflict with al-Qaeda*. Monterey: Naval Postgraduate School.

Arquilla, John and Ronfeldt, David. 2001. "Networks, Netwars, and the Fight for the Future". *Journal of the Internet* 6 (10): 1–19. https://firstmonday.org/ojs/index.php/fm/article/view/889/798.

Ayling, Julie. 2009. "Criminal Organizations and Resilience". *International Journal of Law, Crime and Justice* 37 (4): 182–196.

Arregle, Jean-Luc, Hitt, Michael, Sirmon, David and Very, Philippe. 2007. "The Development of Organizational Social Capital: Attributes of Family Firms". *Journal of Management Studies* 44 (1): 73–95.

Bain, William. 2003. "Trusteeship as an Institution of International Society". In *Between Anarchy and Society: Trusteeship and the Obligations of Power*, edited by William Bain, 78–107. New York: Oxford University Press.

Bailey, F.G. 2001. *Stratagems and Spoils.* New York: Routledge.

Ballentine, Karen and Nitzschke, Heiko. 2005. *The Political Economy of Civil War and Conflict Transformation.* Berlin: Berghof Research Center for Constructive Conflict Management.

Becker, Sascha and Woessmann, Ludger. 2009. "Was Weber Wrong? A Human Capital Theory of Protestant Economic History". *The Quarterly Journal of Economics* 124 (2): 531–596.

Bentham, Jeremy. 1789. *The Principles of Morals and Legislation.* Oxford: Clarendon Press.

Berkowitz, Jeremy. 2018. "Dangerous Delegation: Explaining the Rationales and Outcomes of State Sponsorship of Terrorism through the Principal-agent Framework". *Dissertation.* Binghampton: Binghampton University. https://orb.binghamton.edu/dissertation_and_theses/30.

Berlusconi, Giulia, Calderoni, Francesco, Parolini, Nicola, Verani, Marco, and Piccardi, Carlo. 2016. "Link Prediction in Criminal Networks: A Tool for Criminal Intelligence Analysis". *PLOS ONE* 11 (4): e0154244.

Blau, Peter. 1964. "Justice in Social Exchange" *Journal of Sociological Inquiry* 34 (2): 193–206.

Bloch, Maurice. 1974. "The Long-term and the Short-term". In *The Character of Kinship*, edited by Jack Goody. Cambridge: Cambridge University Press.

Bloch, Maurice and Sperber, Dan. 1973. "The Kith and the Kin". In *The Character of Kinship*, edited by Jack Goody, 75–88. London, New York and Melbourne: Cambridge University Press.

Bloch, Maurice and Sperber, Dan. 2004. "Kinship and Evolved Psychological Dispositions: The Mother's Brother Controversy Reconsidered". In *Kinship and Family: An Anthropological Reader*, edited by Robert Parkin, David Parkin, and Linda Stone, 438–455. Boston: Blackwell.

Bodenhorn, Howard and Ruebeck, Christopher. 2003. *The Economics of Identity and the Endogeneity of Race.* NBER Working Paper No. 9962. www.nber.org/papers/w9962

Boon, Susan and Holmes, John G. 1991. "The Dynamics of Interpersonal Trust: Resolving Uncertainty in the Face of Risk". In *Cooperation and Prosocial Behavior*, edited by Robert Hinde and Jo Groebel, 190–211. Cambridge: Cambridge University Press.

Bourdieu, Pierre. 1986. "The Forms of Social Capital". In *Handbook of Theory and Research for the Sociology of Education*, edited by John Richardson, 241–258. New York: Greenwood Press.

Brandebo, Maria and Alvinius, Aida. 2009. *Dark Sides of Organizations and Leadership.* London: IntechOpen.

Bright, David and Delaney, Jordan. 2013. "Evolution of a Drug Trafficking Network: Mapping Changes in Network Structure and Function across Time". *Global Crime* 14 (2–3): 238–260.

Brown, John and Duguid, Paul. 1991. "Organizational Learning and Communities-of-Practice: Toward a Unified View of Working, Learning, and Innovating". *Journal of Organization Science* 2 (1): 40–57.

Brown, John and Duguid, Paul. 2001. "Knowledge and Organization: A Social-Practice Perspective". *Organization Science* 12 (2): 198–213.

Burcher, Morgan and Whelan, Chad. 2018. "Social Network Analysis as a Tool for Criminal Intelligence: Understanding Its Potential from the Perspectives of Intelligence Analysts". *Trends in Organized Crime* 21 (3): 278–294.

Burt, Ronald. 1997. "A Note on Social Capital and Network Content". *Social Networks* 19 (4): 355–373.

Burton, R.J.F. and Wilson, G.A. 2006. "Injecting Social Psychology Theory iInto Conceptualizations of Agricultural Agency: Towards a Post-Productive Farmer Self-Identity". *Journal of Rural Studies* 22 (1): 95–115.

Busby, Cecilia. 1997. "Of Marriage and Marriageability: Gender and Dravidian Kinship". *The Journal of the Royal Anthropological Institute* 3 (1): 24–42.

Bush, George W. 2003. *National Strategy for Combating Terrorism.* First edition. Washington, D.C.: Central Intelligence Agency.

Cameron, Kim, Kim, Myung and Whetten, David. 1987. "Organizational Effects of Decline and Turbulence". *Administrative Quarterly* 32 (2): 222–240.

Carmeli, A. and Tishler, A. 2004. "The Relationship Between Intangible Organizational Elements and Organizational Performance". *Strategic Management Journal* 25 (2004): 1257–1278.

Chapin, Stuart III, Folke, Carl, and Kofinas, Gary. 2009. *A Framework for Understanding Change.* New York: Springer. 3–28.

Chinchuluun, Altannar, Pardalos, Panos, Migdalas, Athanasios, and Pitsoulis, Leonidas. 2008. *Pareto Optimality, Game Theory and Equilibria.* New York: Springer.

Chiu, Chao-Min, Hsu, Meng-Hsiang, and Wang, Eric. 2006. "Understanding Knowledge Sharing in Virtual Communities: An Integration of Social Capital And Social Cognitive Theories". *Decision Support Systems* 42 (3): 1872–1888.

Chow, W.S. and Chan, L.S. 1998. "Social Network, Social Trust and Shared Goals in Organizational Knowledge Sharing". *Journal of Information and Management* 45 (7): 458–465.

Chua, Jess, Chrisman, James, and Bergiel, Erich. 2009. "An Agency Theoretic Analysis of the Professionalized Family Firm". *The Journal of Entrepreneurship Theory and Practice* 33 (2): 355–372.

Chuang, Aichia, Shen, Chi-Tai and Judge, Timothy. 2016. "Development of a Multidimensional Instrument of a Person-Environment Fit: The Perceived Person-Environment Fit Scale (PPEFS)". *Applied Psychology* 65 (1): 66–98.

Coleman, James. 1988. "Social Capital in the Creation of Human Capital". *The American Journal of Sociology* 94 (1988): S95–S120.

Collier, Kit. 2006. "Terrorism: Evolving Regional Alliances and State Failure in Mindanao". *Journal of Southeast Asian Affairs* 29 (2): 26–38.

Cropanzano, Russell and Mitchell, Marie. 2005. "Social Exchange Theory: An Interdisciplinary Review". *Journal of Management* 31 (6): 874–900.

Cumberland, Denise, Alagaraja, Meera, Shuck, Brad and Kerrick, Sahron. 2018. "Organizational Social Capital: Ties Between HRD, Employee Voice, and CEOs". *Human Resource Development Review* 17 (2): 199–221.

Cusack, Thomas. 1997. "Partisan Politics and Public Finance: Changes in Public Spending in the Industrialized Democracies". *Journal of Public Choice* 91 (1): 375–395.

Dawson, Alexandra, Sharma, Pramodita, Irving, Gregory, Marchus, Joel and Chirico, Francesco. 2013. "Predictors of Later-Generation Family Members' Commitment to Family Enterprises". *Entrepreneurship: Theory and Practice* 39 (3): 545–569.

Donckels, Rik and Frohlich, Erwin. 1991. "Are Family Businesses Really Different? European Experiences from STRATOS". *Family Business Review* 4 (2): 149–160.

Dubos, Rene. 2017. *Social Capital: Theory and Research.* First edition. New York: Routledge.

Duijin, Peter, Kashirin, Victor, and Sloot, Peter. 2014. "The Relative Ineffectiveness of Criminal Network Disruption". *Journal of Scientific Reports* 4 (4238): 1–15.

Dyer, Gibb and Handler, Wendy. 1994. "Entrepreneurship and Family Business: Exploring the Connections". *Entrepreneurship Theory and Practice* 19 (1): 71–83.

Eilstrup-Sangiovanni, Mette and Jones, Calvert. 2008. "Assessing the Dangers of Illicit Networks: Why al-Qaida May Be Less Threatening Than Many Think". *International Security* 33 (2): 7–44.

Emerson, Richard. 1976. "Social Exchange Theory". *Annual Review of Sociology* 2 (1): 335–362.

Erickson, Bonnie. 1981. "Secret Societies and Social Structure". *Social Forces* 60 (1): 188–210.

Everton, Sean and Cunningham, Dan. 2013. "Detecting Significant Changes in Dark Networks". *Behavioural Sciences of Terrorism and Political Aggression* 5 (2): 94–114.

Familusi, Oshomoh Olusesan. 2019. "Socio-Economic Implications of Boko Haram Insurgency in Northern Nigeria". *KIU Journal of Social Sciences* 4 (2): 213–223.

Farrell, Michael. 1957. *The Measurement of Productive Efficiency.* Cambridge: Cambridge University Press.

Fery, Bruno and Luechinger, Simon. 2012. "How to Fight Terrorism: Alternatives to Deterrence". *Journal of Defence and Peace Economics* 14 (4): 237–249.

Firth, Raymond. 1967. *Themes in Economic Anthropology.* London: Tavistock Publications.

Folke, Carl, Hahn, Thomas, Olsson, Per and Norberg, Jon. 2005. "Adaptive Governance of Social-Ecological Systems". *The Annual Review of Environment and Resource* 30 (1): 1–8.

Fortes, Meyer. 2006. *Kinship and the Social Order.* New York: Routledge.

Fortes, Meyer. 1978. "An Anthropologist's Apprenticeship". *Annual Review of Anthropology* 7 (1): 1–30

Fortes, Meyer. 1983. *Rules and the Emergence of Society.* London: Royal Anthropological Institute of Great Britain and Ireland.

Fukuyama, Francis. 1995. "Social Capital and the Global Economy". *Journal of Foreign Affairs* 74 (5): 89–103.

Fukuyama, Francis. 2001. "Social Capital, Civil Society and Development". *Third World Quarterly* 22 (1): 7–20.

Fukuyama, Francis. 2002. *Social Capital and Civil Society.* IMF Working Paper No. 00/74, 1–19.

Gall, Melanie. 2013. "From Social Vulnerability to Resilience: Measuring Progress Toward Disaster Risk Reduction". *InterSecTions* 13 (1): 11–27.

Gambetta, Diego. 1990. "Trust, Making and Breaking Cooperative Relations". *Journal of Philosophy* 52 (4): 740.

Gooderham, Paul, Minbaeva, Dana and Pe dersen, Torben. 2011. "Governance Mechanisms for the Promotion of Social Capital for Knowledge Transfer in Multinational Corporations". *Journal of Management Studies* 48 (1): 123–150.

Gouldner, Alvin. 1960. *The Norm of Reciprocity*. Indianapolis: Bobbs-Merrill.

Govindarajan, Vijay. 1986. "Decentralization, Strategy, and Effectiveness of Strategic Business Units in Multibusiness Organizations". *The Academy of Management Review* 11 (4): 844–856.

Gragert, Bruce. 1997. "Yakuza: The Warlords of Japanese Organized Crime". *Annual Survey of International & Comparative Law* 4 (1): 146–204.

Granovetter, Mark. 1973. "The Strength of Weak Ties". *American Journal of Sociology* 78 (6): 1360–1380.

Grootaert, Christiaan and Bastelaer, Thierry van. 2002. *The Role of Social Capital in Development: An Empirical Assessment*. New York: Cambridge University Press.

Gupte, Prajakta. 2018. "Child Soldiers in Myanmar: Role of Government and Limitations of International Law". *Journal of Law and International Affairs* 6 (1): 371–397.

Haas, Peter. 1995. "Introduction: Epistemic Communities and International Policy Coordination". *International Organization* 46 (1): 1–35.

Hamblin, Robert. 1958. "Group Integration During a Crisis". *Journal of Human Relations* 11 (1): 67–76.

Hastings, Malzahn. 2003. "State Sponsorship and Support of International Terrorism: Customary Norms of State Responsibility". *Hastings International and Comparative Law Review* 26 (1): 83–114.

Hastrup, Kirsten. 2005. "Social Anthropology. Towards pragmatic enlightenment?" *Social Anthropology* 133 (2): 133–149.

Hedstrom, Peter and Swedberg, Richard. 1988. *Social Mechanisms*. Cambridge: Cambridge University Press.

Herman, Edward and O'Sullivan, Gerry. 1982. *The 'Terrorism' Industry: The Experts and Institutions that Shape our View of Terror*. New York: Pantheon Books.

Holling, C.S. 2004. "From complex regions to complex worlds". *Ecology and Society* 9 (1): 11–21.

Homans, George. 1993. *Social Behavior as Exchange*. New York: Ardent Media Inc.

ICG. 2006. *In Their Own Words: Reading the Iraqi Insurgency*. Amman and Brussels: International Crisis Group.

Iwai, Hiroaki. 1986. "Organized Crime in Japan". In *Organized Crime: A Global Perspective*, edited by Robert Kelly, 215. London and New Delhi: Sage.

Jones, Calvert. 2006. "Al-Qaeda's Innovative Improvisers: Learning in a Diffuse Transnational Network". *Cambridge Review of International Affairs* 19 (4): 555–567.

Jones, David and Smith, M.L.R. 2011. "Organization vs. Ideology: The Lessons from Southeast Asia". *Current Trends in Islamist Ideology* 12 (1): 92–123.

Kalyvas, Stathis. 2008. "Ethnic Defection in Civil War". *Comparative Political Studies* 41 (8): 1043–1068.

Katz, Daniel and Kahn, Robert. 1966. *The Social Psychology of Organizations*. New York: John Wiley and Sons.

Kaunert, Christian, Leonars, Sarah, Berger, Lars and Johnson, Gaynor. 2017. *Western Foreign Policy and the Middle East*. London: Routledge.

Kenney, Michael. 2007. "The Architecture of Drug Trafficking: Network Forms of Organisation in the Colombian Cocaine Trade". *Global Crime* 8 (3): 233–259.

Khare, Vijay. 2015. "Psychology of Terrorism". *International Journal of Current Research* 7 (4): 15241–15243.

Knack, Stephen and Keefer, Philip. 1997. "Does Social Capital Have an Economic Payoff? A Cross-County Investigation". *The Quarterly Journal of Economics* 112 (4): 1251–1288.

La Porta, Rafael, de Silanes, Florencio Lopez, Shleifer, Andrei and Vishny, Robert. 1997. *Trust in Large Organizations.* NBER Working Paper No. w5864. Cambridge: National Bureau of Economic Research.

Lajili, Kaouthar and Mahoney, Joseph. 2006. "Revisiting Agency and Transaction Costs Theory Predictions on Vertical Financial Ownership and Contracting: Electronic Integration as an Organizational Form Choice". *Managerial and Decision Economics* 27 (7): 573–586.

Lamb, Christopher. 2006. "Restructuring Special Operations Forces for Emerging Threats". *Strategic Forum* 1 (219): 1–6.

Le Breton-Miller, Isabelle and Miller, Danny. 2006. "Why Do Some Family Businesses Out-Compete? Governance, Long-Term Orientations, and Sustainable Capability". *Entrepreneurship Theory and Practice* 30 (6): 731–764.

Leana, Carrie and Van Buren, Harry. 2012. "Organizational Social Capital and Employment Practices". In *Sociology of Organizations: Structure and Relationships*, edited by Mary Godwyn and Jody Gittel, 538–555. Los Angeles, London and New Delhi: Sage Publications.

Levi, Margaret and Stoker, Laura. 2000. "Political Trust and Trustworthiness". *Annual Review of Political Science* 3 (1): 475–507.

Lin, Nan, Cook, Karen and Burt, Ronald. 2008. *Social Capital: Theory and Research.* First edition. New Brunswick and New Jersey: Transaction Publishers.

Lorenzo, Bosi and Della Porta, Donatella. 2015. "Processes of Disengagement From Political Violence". In *Researching Terrorism, Peace and Conflict Studies: Interaction, Synthesis and Opposition*, edited by Ioannis Tellidis and Harmoine Toros, 81–100. London and New York: Routledge.

Malinowski, Bronsilaw. 2014. *Argonauts of the western Pacific.* London and New York: Routledge.

Marazziti, Donatella, Veltri, Antonello, and Piccinni, Armando. 20009. "The Mind of Suicide Terrorists". *CNS Spectrums* 23 (2): 145–150.

Martuscelli, Patricia and Duarte Villa, Rafael. 2018. "Child Soldiers as Peace-Builders in Colombian Peace Talks Between the Government and the FARC–EP". *Journal of Conflict, Security and Development* 18 (5): 387–408.

Marx, Karl. 1887. "The Capitalistic Nature of Manufacture". In *Capital: A Critique of Political Economy. Volume I, Book 1: The Process of Production of Capital*, edited by Samuel Moore and Edward Aveling, 248–261. Moscow: Progress Publishers.

Mauss, Marcel. 1954. *The Gift: The Form and Reason for Exchange in Archaic Societies.* New York: Cohen and West.

McAllister, Daniel. 2017. "Affect- and Cognition-Based Trust as Foundations for Interpersonal Cooperation in Organizations". *Academy of Management Journal* 38 (1): 24–59.

Metnick, Barry. 1997. "Agency Theory". In *The Blackwell Encyclopaedic Dictionary of Business Ethics*, edited by Patricia Werhan and Edward Freeman, 12–15. Oxford: Blackwell Publishers.

Middleton, H. 2016. "Flourishing and Posttraumatic Growth. An Empirical Take on Ancient Wisdoms". *Health Care Annual* 24 (2): 133–147.

Minor, Tim. 2012. "Attacking the Nodes of Terrorist Networks". *Global Security* 3 (2): 1–12.

Morck, Randall and Yeung, Bernard. 2003. "Agency Problems in Large Family Business Groups". *Journal of Entrepreneurship Theory and Practice* 27 (4): 367–382.

Morselli, Carlo and Roy, Julie. 2008. "Brokerage Qualifications in Ringing Operations". *Journal of Criminology* 46 (1): 71–98.

Morselli, Carlo, Giguere, Cynthia and Petit, Katia. 2007. "The Efficiency/Security Trade-Off in Criminal Networks". *Social Networks* 29 (1): 143–153.

Murdoch, Gillian. 2009. "TIMELINE: Attacks and plots blamed on Jemaah Islamiyah in Asia". *Reuters*. Accessed 7 March 2016. www.reuters.com/article/us-indonesia-militants-timeline-sb/timeline-attacks-and-plots-blamed-on-jemaah-islamiah-in-asia-idUSTRE58G29X20090 917.

Nahapiet, Janine and Ghoshal, Sumantra. 2000. "Social Capital, Intellectual Capital, and the Organizational Advantage". In *Knowledge and Social Capital: Foundations and Applications,* edited by Eric Lesser, 242–266. Boston: Butterworth and Heinemann.

Nasir, Amalina Abdul. 2019. "Women in Terrorism: Evolution from Jemaah Islamiyah to Islamic State in Indonesia and Malaysia". *Counter Terrorist Trends and Analyses* 11 (2): 1–5.

Oak, Gillian. 2010. "Jemaah Islamiyah's Fifth Phase: The Many Faces of a Terrorist Group". *Studies in Conflict and Terrorism* 33 (11): 989–1018.

Okumura, Tetsu, Suzuki, Kouichiro, Fukuda Atsuhiro, Kohama Akitsugu, Takasu Nobukatsu, Shinichi, Ishimatsu, and Hinohara, Shigeaki. 2008. "The Tokyo Subway Sarin Attack: Disaster Management, Part 1: Community Emergency Response". *Academic Emergency Management* 5 (6): 613–617.

Olsen, K.B. 1999. "Aum Shinrikyo: Once and Future Threat?" *Journal of Emerging Infectious Diseases* 5 (4): 513–516.

Paoli, Letizia. 2003. *Mafia Brotherhoods: Organized Crime, Italian Style*. Oxford: Oxford University Press.

Posner, Richard. 1985. "Wealth Maximization Revisited". *Journal of Law, Ethics and Public Policy* 85 (2): 85–105.

Portes, Alejandro. 1998. "Social Capital: Its Origins and Applications in Modern Sociology". *Annual Review of Sociology* 24 (1): 1–24.

Putnam, Robert. 1993. "Social Capital and Institutional Success". In *Making Democracy Work: Civic Traditions in Modern Italy*, edited by Robert Putnam, 163–186. New Jersey: Princeton University Press.

Putnam, Robert. 1995. "Bowling Alone: America's Declining Social Capital". *Journal of Democracy* 6 (1): 65–78.

Putnam, Robert. 2001. "Social Capital: Measurement and Consequences". *Canadian Journal of Policy Research* 2 (1): 41–51.

Rankin, Andrew. 2012. "Recent Trends in Organized Crime in Japan: Yakuza vs the Police, & Foreign Crime Gangs". *Asia-Pacific Journal* 10 (7): 1–21.

Ranstorp, Magnus. 2008. "Mapping Terrorism Studies After 9/11: An Academic Field of Old Problems and New Prospects". In *Critical Terrorism Studies: Framing a New Research Agenda*. London: Routledge.

Realo, Anu, Allik, Juri and Greenfield, Brenna. 2008. "Radius of Trust: Social Capital in Relation to Familism and Institutional Collectivism". *Journal of Cross-Cultural Psychology* 39 (4): 447–462.

Roniger, Luis. 1987. "Coronelismo, Caciquismo, and Oyabun-Kobun Bonds: Divergent Implications of Hierarchical Trust in Brazil, Mexico and Japan". *The British Journal of Sociology* 38 (3): 310–330.

Saegert, Susan. 2001. *Social Capital and Poor Communities.* Volume 3 of Ford Foundation Series on Asset Building, edited by Susan Saegert, Phillip Thompson, and Mark Warren. New York: Russell Sage Foundation.

Sahlins, Marshall. 1974. *On the Sociology of Primitive Exchange.* London: Tavistock Publications, 139–186.

Salvatore, Armando and LeVine, Mark. 2005. "The Overlapping Dimensions of the Civic and the Public". In *Religion, Social Practice, and Contested Hegemonies: Reconstructing the Public Sphere in Muslim Majority Societies,* edited by Armando Salvatore and Mark LeVine, 29–56. New York: Palgrave Macmillan.

Sashkin, Marshall. 2018. "Leadership". In *Contemporary Issues in Leadership,* edited by William Rosenbach, 7–21. New York and London: Routledge.

Schaffer, Teresita. 1999. "Teresita Schaffer on the LTTE". *How Terrorism Ends* 5 (1): 8–11.

Schoon, Ingrid. 2006. *Risk and Resilience: Adaptations in Changing Times.* First edition. Cambridge: Cambridge University Press.

Schultz, Theodore. 1974. "Economics of the Family: Marriage, Children, and Human Capital". *National Bureau of Economic Research* 74 (1): 3–22.

Shapiro, Jacob and Siegel, David. 2007. "Underfunding in Terrorist Organizations". *International Studies Quarterly* 51 (1): 405–429.

Sheffi, Yossi. 2015. *The Power of Resilience: How the Best Companies Manage the Unexpected.* First edition. Cambridge and London: MIT Press.

Silke, Andrew. 2009. "Contemporary Terrorism Studies: Issues in Research". In *Critical Terrorism Studies: A New Research Agenda,* edited by Richard Jackson, Marie Smyth, and Jeroen Gunning. London and New York: Routledge.

Silverman, Howard and Hill, Gregory. 2018. "The Dynamics of Purposeful Change: A Model". *Ecology and Society* 23 (3): 4–27.

Sinno, Abdulkader. 2008. *Organizations at War in Afghanistan and Beyond.* Ithaca: Cornell University Press.

Staw, Barry, Sandelands, Lance and Dutton, Jane. 1981. "Threat Rigidity Effects in Organizational Behaviour: A Multilevel Analysis". *Administrative Science Quarterly* 26 (4): 501–524.

Stern, Jessica. 2003. *Terror in the Name of God: Why Religious Militants Kill.* First edition. New York: HarperCollins.

Stewart, A and Kitt, M. 2012. "Why Can't a Family Business Be More Like a Nonfamily Business? Modes of Professionalization in Family Firms". *Family Business Review* 25 (1): 58–86.

Stringham, Edward. 2001. "Kaldor-Hicks Efficiency and the Problem of Central Planning". *Quarterly Journal of Austrian Economics* 4 (2): 41–50.

Tajfel, Henri. 1970. "Experiments in Intergroup Discrimination". *Scientific American* 223 (5): 96–102.

Tajfel, Henri and Billig, Michael. 1973. "Social Categorization in Intergroup Behaviour". *European Journal of Social Psychology* 3 (1): 149–178.

Tan, Jonathan and Vogel, Claudia. 2008. "Religion and Trust: An Experimental Study". *Journal of Economic Psychology* 29 (6): 832–848.

Tasselli, Stefano, Kilduff, Martin and Menges, Jochen. 2015. "The Microfoundations of Organizational Social Networks: A Review and an Agenda for Future Research". *Journal of Management* 41 (5): 1361–1387.

Thibault, John and Kelley, Harold. 1964. *The Social Psychology of Groups* New Brunswick and London: Transaction Publishers.

Tilly, Charles. 2004. "Trust and Rule". *Journal of Theory and Society* 33 (1): 1–30.

Trivers, Robert. 1972. "Parental Investment and Sexual Selection". In *Sexual Selection and the Descent of Man, 1871–1971*, edited by Bernard Campbell, 136–179. Chicago: Aldine Publishing Co.

Tucker, David and Lamb, Christopher J. 2006. "Restructuring Special Operations Forces for Emerging Threats". *Strategic Forum* 219 (1): 1–6.

Van Der Leeuw, Sander. 2000. "Land Degradation as a Socionatural Process". In *The Way the Wind Blows: Climate, History and Human Action*, edited by Roderick McIntosh, Joseph Tainter, and Susan Keech McIntosh, 190–210. New York: Columbia University Press.

Walther, Oliver and Christopoulos, Dimitris. 2015. "Islamic Terrorism and the Malian Rebellion". *Journal of Terrorism and Political Violence* 27 (3): 1–23.

Weber, Max. .1945. *From Max Weber: Essays in Sociology.* London: Routledge.

Weisel, Deborah. 2002. "The Evolution of Street Gangs: An Examination of Form and Variation". In *Responding to Gangs: Evaluation and Research*, edited by Winifred Reed and Scott Decker, 25–67. Washington, D.C.: U.S. Department of Justice.

Widger, Tom. 2012. "Suicide and the Mortality of Kinship in Sri Lanka". *Contributions to Indian Sociology* 46 (1–2): 83–116.

Wiegand, Krista. 2010. *Bombs and Ballots: Governance by Islamic Terrorist and Guerilla Groups.* First edition. London and New York: Routledge.

Williams, Phil. 2001. "Transnational Criminal Networks". In *Networks, Netwars: The Future of Terror, Crime, and Militancy*, edited by John Arquilla and David Ronfeldt, 61–98. Santa Monica: RAND.

Wood, Jennifer. 2006. "Dark Networks, Bright Networks, and the Place of the Police". In *Fighting Crime Together: The Challenges of Policing and Security Networks*, edited by Jenny Fleming and Jennifer Wood, 246–269. Sydney: UNSW Press.

Worchel, Stephen, Andreoli, Virginia and Folger, Robert. 1977. "Intergroup Cooperation and Intergroup Attraction: The Effect of Previous Interaction and Outcome of Combined Effort". *Journal of Experimental Social Psychology* 13 (1): 131–140.

Wright, Lawrence. 2003. "The Master Plan". *The New Yorker.* 3 September. Accessed 21 May 2018. www.newyorker.com/magazine/2006/09/11/the-master-plan

Zhang, Mian, Fried, David and Griffeth, Rodger. 2012. "A Review of Job Embeddedness: Conceptual, Measurement Issues, and Directions for Future Research". *Human Resource Management Review* 22 (3): 220–231.

Zulaika, Joseba and Douglass, William. 1996. *Terror and Taboo: The Follies, Fables, and Faces of Terrorism.* New York: Taylor & Francis.

Part II
Real world analysis

3   The Haqqani Network

This chapter is an examination of the Haqqani Network. It is a structured familial organization and a highly robust and capable insurgency actor in the Afghanistan conflict. Unlike some organizations that have only familial leadership, the Haqqani Network's familial structure is fully integrated across command and control through to its tactical operations and its base-level fighters. Equally, kinship plays a key role in dictating entry, exit, and position within the organization, all of which contribute significantly to its resilience. Following a brief background introduction, this chapter is divided into three main sections.

The first section examines the morphology, structure, and leadership dynamics of the Haqqani Network to determine its core strengths. The second examines external pressures that have been exerted against it and tested its resilience. These external pressures have occurred most visibly from 2002 onwards and are manifestly observable as the external pressures from the U.S. and other international forces after the invasion of Afghanistan in late 2001. The review of external pressures includes targeted military operations, counterinsurgency activities, and secondary and soft-power projections.

The third section examines the Haqqani Network's response to those external pressures by analysing the effects that targeted operations have on it. The results show that from 2002 to the present the Haqqani Network has demonstrated robust resilience. The role of familial and kinship structural dynamics is a critical aspect, providing an expansive and critical resource base, organic organizational stability and cohesion, unity of purpose, and strong collective social capital and trust. The chapter concludes with a review of the Haqqani Network's resilience and the issues going forward.

Background

The Haqqani Network was established in 1973 by Jalaluddin Haqqani, who died in 2014 (Akbar 2015). Jalaluddin and other warlords were royalist followers of King Mohammad Zahir Shah, who was ousted in 1973 by then Prime Minister Mohammad Daud Khan (Dressler 2010). Following the coup, Haqqani family members sought military training from the Pakistani Government to fight the new Daud regime (Dressler 2010). It was then that the Haqqani's relationship with the powerful Pakistani Inter-Services Intelligence (ISI) began with the provision of training, arms, and finances. In late 1973, Jalaluddin issued the first declaration of jihad under the Haqqani Network name, marking its official creation. This was followed in 1975 by its first significant attack in the Paktika province, Afghanistan against a pro-Daud governor (Ruttig 2009b).

The Daud Government collapsed with the Soviet invasion of Afghanistan on 27 December 1979, offering the Haqqani Network a new enemy (Kakar 1995). Daud was replaced by a series of Soviet-supported puppet presidents including Babrak Karmal (1979–1986), Haji Mohammad Chamkani – interim president (November 1986 – September 1987), and then Mohammad Najibullah (1986–1992) (Smith 2014). Jalaluddin emerged as a senior anti-Soviet insurgent commander and Afghan warlord.[1] As an ethnic Pashtun from Paktia, Jalaluddin sat on the executive committee of the radical anti-Soviet Hizb-I Islam from 1976 to 1979 (Dressler 2010). In 1979 he was elected as Southeast Commander, enabling him to cement his control over the Zadran tribe and exercise power territorially beyond the Greater Loya-Paktia. This put Jalaluddin at the apex of the tribal leadership hierarchy.

The Haqqani Network survived the brutal Soviet campaign of occupation with the support of the U.S., Britain, and Pakistan. Soviet carpet-bombing of Afghanistan's second-biggest city Kandahar reduced it from a population of 200,000 to only 25,000. Coupled with a no-prisoners execution policy and extensive land-mining of the country, 1.8 million Afghans including women and children were killed (Noorzoy 2012). The Haqqani Network's focus has remained on resistance fighting and ensuring the survival of its clan, making it a keystone actor in the Afghani political security arena since 1973. Post the Soviet withdrawal the Haqqani Network became a central affiliate of the Taliban, who took power in 1996 (Hammond 2015). After the U.S. and international invasion of Afghanistan in late 2001, Graham-Harrison cites that it was "widely considered to be the most sophisticated, ruthless and well-organized of the groups that make up the Afghan insurgency" (2012, 1).

Jalaluddin became a close mentor and associate of Osama bin Laden in al-Qaeda's formative years in the 1980s, and affiliated with militant organizations in Pakistan, Uzbekistan, and Chechnya.[2] He deepened relationships with Pakistan's ISI that proved essential in later decades. These were critical in sustaining the Haqqani Network in the 1990s when Western support ended.[3] Jalaluddin also formed patronage, financial, and business connections across the Middle East and Central Asia, and he was a major proponent of protecting territorial and Islamic beliefs at all costs, particularly Pashtun culture and equality. Romaniuk and Webb state that he was known as a "devoted defender of Afghanistan against foreigners" (2015, 177). According to Nek Zaman (Coll 2006), North Waziristan congressional representative and Taliban tribal commander, Jalaluddin was and remained a hero, a Mujahid and an Islamic scholar.

This provided Jalaluddin with a significant source of social capital that added to the Haqqani Network's organizational strength. In March 1992 Taliban forces, many led by Jalaluddin, stormed Khost and Kabul and ousted President

Najibullah. Jalaluddin's notoriety as an Afghan patriot resulted in his appointment as Justice Minister in the original Mujahedeen cabinet, led by President Mojaddedi.[4] This established the Haqqani Network, and particularly Jalaluddin, as an important figure in Afghan politics. With pressure from his long-time patrons the Pakistani ISI, Jalaluddin formally affiliated with the Taliban in 1995 that took power in the country one year later. Two decades later under the Karzai Government, Jalaluddin received an invitation to become the Afghan Prime Minister, though U.S. influence stopped this from occurring. Regardless, Jalaluddin forged the essential foundations of the Haqqani Network, building a solid base and structure that has continued since the 1970s and provided the Haqqani Network with staunch resilience.

The Haqqani Network's strategic and operational control was cemented by Jalaluddin's battlefield expertise and reputation as a calculating and shrewd commander. Brown and Rassler maintained that Jalaluddin was "seen by CIA officers in Islamabad and others as perhaps the most impressive Pashtun battlefield commander in the war" (2013, 47). When leadership passed to his son Siraj Haqqani in 2005, the Haqqani Network's overall direction changed, becoming more dynamic and less focused on territorial anchors. This was primarily because Siraj was more radical than his father and foresaw an end to a continual state of war, and thus he pursued an expansion of organizational business operations beyond jihad to future-proof the Haqqani Network.[5]

Section 1: familial succession in the Haqqani Network – stability and control

Being a familial organization has had several benefits for the Haqqani Network. First, it has avoided generational transitional and political divisional issues that can disrupt meritocratic organizations due to significant shifts between leaders. Abdul Rasheed Dostam is a useful comparison. During the wars against the Taliban, Dostam possessed the largest single militia in Afghanistan. A meritocratic organization across command and leadership, his militia was a crucial element in the "Northern Alliance" with Soviet-trained and -equipped forces. Dostam built an effective administration in the territory his militia occupied in the Northern provinces around Mazare-e-Sharif with health, education, and university systems open to females.

However, his second-in-command and successor, General Malik Pahalwan, did not share Dostam's vision of governance nor his alignment with Najibullah. On 19 May 1997 Pahalwan deserted Dostam with most of his officer corps, and in a prearranged agreement with the Taliban he took control of Mazare-e-Sharif and then Dostam's hometown of Shiberghan (Matinuddin 1999).[6] It is important to note that both Dostam and Pahalwan continued to control significant fighting forces, which, although split, remained powerful, actually increasing in strength.

Afghanistan's multi-agent political power sphere is awash with examples of organizations suffering leadership splits and factionalism on the issue of secessionism while remaining potent. In 1979, for example, Malawi Khalis split from

Gulbuddin Hekmatyar's Hezb-e-Islami to form his own Hezb-e-Islami Khalis.[7] Following the death of Khalis, his son Anwar ul Haq Mujahid briefly took over before he too was succeeded by Haji Din Mohammad in a leadership battle. Mukhopadhyah (2009) observes that a significant driver of internal political turmoil in organizations was the prominence of warlordism in Afghan society that resulted in secessionist struggles being commonplace.

An additional example of this is Hezb-e Wahdat-e Islami-ye, a political party founded in 1989. It was led by Qurban Ali Erfani and was the fourth organization to phoenix from the Hezb-e Wahdat, a major unifying political party in resistance to Soviet influence (Khalilzad 1995). The split was the result of a secessionist struggle over political ideology in which senior leaders competed for the support of the organization. Another, the Hizb-i-Milli-Islami-i-Afghanistan, was also a phoenix of the Hezb-e Wahdat splitting in 1994. It was led by Ustad Mohammad Akbari, who lost a secessionist struggle for the Hezb-e Wahdat that Abdul Ali Mazari, the incumbent leader, won.

Cascading secessionist struggles are not infrequent in Afghan political organizations in which senior figures have fought for sole leadership and concentration of personal power, rather than holistic organizational unity. Afghani organizations were often amalgamations of smaller militias and warlords acting in concert, bringing together different religious, ethnic, and cultural groups. Maley puts it that many such secessionist conflicts can be attributed to animosity between factions resulting in "fierce intergroup antagonisms, with variations in doctrine and ritual" (2009, 28). This was evident when the Hizb-i-Milli-Islami-i-Afghanistan suffered a further split in 2005 when Mustafa Kazimi, a senior figure and likely successor formed his own party, the Eqtedar-e-Milli because of conflicts over political doctrine.

The Haqqani Network avoided disruption and suffered no splits because familial continuity proved to be cohesive. Exposed immediately to the harsh conflicts of the region and the strict religious authority of his father, Siraj was selected early on as the likely successor, and well ensconced in the family business he was groomed by Jalaluddin and his uncles to take over. Even on the meritocratic side, it was far more important that Siraj was the best representative and leader of the immediate Haqqani family and broader Haqqani Network. This is because Siraj was deemed most capable to take over and possessed the required attributes of leadership, rather than his brother Nasiruddin Haqqani, who was an excellent logistics manager. Therefore, one of the differences of familiarly succession over meritocratic succession is that advancement is linked to family position and to the interests of senior family leaders over the interests of individuals.

Adams (2005) makes reference to this process as the patriarchal political authority whereby family seniors regulate internal family relations, particularly the trust relationships between father and son in sucessionism. Strict rules of familial and kinship practice enforce the means of lineage and the intergenerational transitions of family power preservation. Adams (2005) also finds that patrimonial organizations have two concerns, the first being security of the organization and the support of theirs and their son's leadership, and the second, the status and power of that leadership. These are equally apparent in the Haqqani Network, making it a powerful example.

As Jalaluddin's son, Siraj was already a member of al-Qaeda's top council in 2010 and worked closely with his father for many years before the full transition of leadership. Fantz (2011) claims that since 2007, Siraj had been extending and expanding the Haqqani Network's operations, recruitment, affiliations, and partnerships as he took on more responsibility as Jalaluddin's health declined. Garamone and Mays (2007) explains that Siraj was highly successful at developing networks and capabilities outside of those inherited from his father, so much so that he became a challenger to Mullah Omar for total control of the Taliban.

The Haqqani Network therefore possessed a clear line of succession and strong support for the transition of power from Jalaluddin to Siraj, as Jalaluddin gradually stepped back and Siraj assumed more control. There was potential for sideways succession from Jalaluddin to his brother Ibrahim Omari, though this was never really a viable option for future positioning. Omari was a part of the old guard like Jalaluddin. According to Lt Col Anders of the U.S. forces, "Siraj is a part of a younger, more aggressive generation of Taliban senior leadership that is pushing aside the formerly respected elders" (Dinneen 2007, 2).

Omari continued to play a vital role acting as a liaison conduit between the Karzai Government and Siraj. He surrendered to Afghan forces in the Shahkot mountains in early 2002. This aided the patrilineal power flow by strengthening Siraj's position relative to the incumbent Karzai Government rather than hindering the Haqqani Network by moving sideways, and, probably, alienating the younger leaders. Also, Siraj did not make any significant changes to strategic goals although he did have a different management style to his father. Siraj was much more brutal and focused more on enhancing operational capability.[8] Post Jalaluddin the Haqqani Network remained the de facto authority in the federally administered tribal areas (FATA), a position it maintained with violence, secrecy, and the capacity to collect rents and enforce contracts (Paoli 2003). Siraj deepened Haqqani affiliations and alliances and expanded criminal enterprises. Mazzetti *et al.* describe the Haqqani Network as both a militia and a mini-state that "has built a sprawling enterprise on both sides of a border that barely exists" (2001, 1).

Under Siraj, the Haqqani Network retains broad support through extensive tribal and clan connections. However, some of the more noble aspects of Jalaluddin's legacy have fallen away, such as the promotion of Pashtunwali, and the development of Islamic beliefs, culture, and equality that he was known for. Conversely, Siraj instituted a sharp increase in the employment of violence as its prime governance toolset. Fantz states that Western intelligence acknowledged that Siraj turned the "Haqqani terror empire into a ruthless killing machine around 2007" (2011, 2). Despite official and often public opposition to it and pressures from international actors, this support remains evident in influential old family ties that nurture a lack of political will in Kabul, further enabling the Haqqani Network to maintain its longevity.

Structural strengths

Structurally the Haqqani Network has two essential parts. Its leadership, which is vertical, and its command and control and insurgency systematics, which are horizontal.[9] Siraj Haqqani is the Haqqani Network apex leader and second-in-command of the Afghan Taliban, giving him significant operational control and political influence. Feared and respected, Siraj directs the Haqqani Network with sole authority through his remaining siblings and closest kin associates. However, its vertical familial leadership structure has proven susceptible to degradation. In countenance, its expansive kinship group has allowed it to replace lost senior members efficiently.

Likewise, Haqqani Network horizontal resources are well established and provide it with a broad support base that has underpinned its extreme longevity. There are four Haqqani leadership councils that work side-by-side and are controlled by family members under Siraj's command. Control flows down from Siraj to his brothers and uncles, and is then diffused horizontally to areas of the organization that undertake critical processing and insurgent operations. The first Shura council is the original alumni group that served with Jalaluddin during the anti-Soviet fighting. This group included Jalaluddin, his brothers, and other tribal relations. It is probable that this council was a derivation of the Arab Mujahedeen Shura of Khost established in 1993. It has declined considerably and now is subordinate to Siraj.

Second is the leadership group comprising Siraj, his brothers, uncles, and other immediate family who do not belong to group one, as well as those who joined after 2001. This apex group has the most power and runs the strategic and daily functions. It is known as the Loya-Paktia group. The third is the North Waziristan Shura, in which members have developed extensive associations with the Haqqanis through tribal and clan networks, and probably graduated through Haqqani-run madrassas and engaged in Haqqani legal and illicit businesses. The last group are the foreign members of the Haqqani Network including Arabs, Uzbeks, and Chechens, and others. This group is almost exclusively non-Pashtun with the exception of leaders who are overlaid across all groups and have clan or tribal relations to the Haqqani (Dressler 2010). Nearly all battlefield leaders are from North Waziristan and belong to either the Zadran tribe or to the Haqqani Mezi clans (2010).

Collectively these are a complex integration of various familial, kinship, and extended clan groups, coupled with the employment of outsiders at the lowest levels for battlefield operations. Accurately distilling the intricacies of power flows within and between these four Shura has been difficult.[10] Structuring has also made it difficult to disrupt or destroy the Haqqani Network because its linkages provide diffused attribution, and comprehensive and cheap resources, contributing significantly to the Haqqani Network's resilience. Siraj chairs the Miran Shah Shura, one of three principal Taliban Shuras widely known as the "Haqqani Shura". The Haqqani Shura directs insurgent nexus operations and liaises with the Quetta Shura, the original Taliban central leadership Shura to which Siraj was appointed second-in-command in July 2015.[11] These Shura work in unison. Crews asserts that the Shuras "formed the institutional locus of Taliban policy-making under the authoritarian leadership of Mullah Omar" (Crews and Tarzi 2008, 254) with support from Siraj Haqqani.

Further, they strengthen the Haqqani Network operations by providing an additional kinship bonded resource base it can utilize. Johnson and Mason state that the Taliban nexus "has been able to build on tribal Haqqani Networks and a charismatic mullah phenomenon to mobilize a critical and dynamic rural base of support" (2007, 71). It is not only the Taliban, however. Roggio (2013) reports that Siraj is also a senior member of the Shura Majlis, the executive al-Qaeda council, which demonstrates the extent of the Haqqani Network's involvement as a central authority in the broader Afghan insurgency. This opens the way for Haqqani Network members to assume more senior roles in not just the Taliban but al-Qaeda as well, and vice versa, for the Haqqani Network to absorb members of other organizations through tribal kinship connections.

The business of family and family businesses

The Haqqani familial organizational structure is very dynamic and highly adaptive. This works well, particularly when confronted with external pressures and high risk. It has been able to strengthen its capacity as an independent organization and anticipate external pressures, demonstrating resilience in response to threats. Much of this comes from its business fronts and criminal enterprises that serve a range of functions from income generation, money laundering, criminal activities, security and support, and deniability, holistically adding to Haqqani Network resilience. Not surprisingly, these are controlled by Haqqani family members, offering several advantages over meritocratic management.

Anas Haqqani is a good example of this. Anas was at one time the Haqqani financier and propaganda master working across the region and throughout Arab countries (Roggio 2016).[12] He was taken into custody in October 2014. Replacing him was Fazl Rabbi, a member of the Taliban's Peshawar Shura of which Siraj is second-in-command. Rabbi was recruited into the highly trusted position within the intimate circle of Haqqani Network operations as the finance manager. Rabbi worked for Jalaluddin and was a trusted ally of Khalil Haqqani, Siraj's uncle, demonstrating he had deep ties with the Haqqani family that in conjunction with a supra-tribal nexus, allowed for his promotion into Anas's position. Rabbi is also a fundraiser and operational commander, and has a measure of control over business and smuggling operations as well.[13]

Khalil Haqqani is the brother of Jalaluddin and manages front businesses and Haqqani Network logistics companies.[14] Khalil Haqqani is also responsible for the detention and interrogation of captured prisoners (UNSC 2012). Another key senior Haqqani insurgent actor is Haji Khalil Zadran, related to the Haqqani through tribal connections. Haji is an Afghan businessman from Paktia, home of the Haqqani Network, who has built a construction empire that has won contracts worth more than U.S.$125 million. Khalil Zadran owns the Haji Khalil

Table 3.1 Haqqani Network businesses and fronts

Business	Address	Type	Haqqani link
Afghan-German Construction Company	Golaye Park, Shari Naw Kabul, and Dasht Qala, Takhar Province, Afghanistan	Construction	Tribal: Khalil Zadran
Palestine Liberation Front	Wazir Akbar Khan, Road Number 10, in front of the National Bank, District 10, Kabul, Afghanistan	Social Welfare	Familial: Khalil Zadran/ Siraj Haqqani
Revolutionary Front for the Liberation of Palestine	Wazir Akbar Khan, District 10, Kabul and Shahr-Now, Kabul and Paktiakoot, Jalalabad Road, District 9, Afghanistan	Social Welfare	Tribal: Khalil Zadran
Popular Front for the Liberation of Palestine	Wazir Akbar Khan, Road Number 10, in front of the National Bank, District 10, Kabul, Afghanistan	Social Welfare	Familial: Khalil Zadran/ Siraj Haqqani
Onyx Construction	Bakhtawar Palace Qasabi Street, Shahr-e-Naw, Kabul, Afghanistan	Construction	Familial: Khalil Zadran/ Ibrahim Haqqani
Zurmat Construction Company, Zurmay Group, Zurmat Foundation, Zurmat Material Testing Laboratory	H#319, St#2, Sherpor Kabul, Afghanistan	Construction/ Engineering	Familial: Yousaf Zalan/Khalil Zadran/Ibrahim Haqqani
Khalil Zadran Company	House 14, Street 13, Sector F/7/2, Islamabad, Pakistan and House 20-B, Main College Road, Sector F-7/2, Islamabad	Facilitator	Tribal: Khalil Zadran
Al Maskah Car and Spare Parts	Maliha Road, Industrial Area 6, Sharajah, U.A.E.	Vehicles	Tribal: Feroz Khan
Zurmat General Trading	Office No. 205, Platinum Business Centre, Baghdad Street, Al-Nahda 2, Al-Quasis, Dubai, U.A.E.	Construction/ Trading	Familial: Khalil Zadran/Ibrahim Haqqani

Construction Company, which is a partner company to Saadullah Khan Brothers Engineering and Construction Company (SKB), which is allegedly one of Siraj Haqqani's front companies.[15]

In Table 3.1 are listed fronts and businesses connected with, or belonging to, the Haqqani Network insurgency in Afghanistan, Pakistan, and the UAE. Importantly, unlike meritocratic organizations where the most suitable and talented members are in charge of logistics and financial operations, only close family are allowed to conduct critical business interests that support the organization.

The close familial structure of the Haqqani Network business enterprise demonstrates several advantages of its kinship organization. First, there is a significantly high degree of central control over each business and front company. Being managed and controlled by family and kin, strategic direction can be imparted on them directly from Siraj Haqqani. Second, the close proximity of these businesses to the Haqqani Network core means they are tied together, giving the advantage of burden-sharing. Third, exiting is minimized. The familial integration present between Haqqani insurgent commanders and other family members running businesses means that everyone works for the common good, and leaving the family has extreme consequences.

Fourth is commonality of purpose. All business entities work to support the Haqqani Network and are in turn supported with security and logistics by each other, strengthening the Haqqani Network holistically. Meritocratic organizations may possess highly effective and supportive front companies and businesses, but the degree of familial integration shown in the Haqqani Network makes them inseparable and bound in unity, providing significant structural and security advantages. They are also sophisticated and highly profitable. According to news reporting, the Haqqani Network via its SKB front was making U.S.$1–2 million per month (ABC 2013).[16]

The importance of family and kinship to the Haqqani Network

The Haqqani Network familial base makes it far stronger than many other organizations, giving it powerful resconstitutional capacity. This makes targeting its inputs by external pressures more challenging. As Mitsotakis (2014) reports, not only does the Haqqani Network have broad access to clan and tribal foundations from which commanders are drawn, but the nexus to organizations that traverses supra-tribal lines gives it direct and intimate access to al-Qaeda and the Taliban. Its role as a facilitator is also a powerful enabling mechanism. Dressler (2010) found that the Haqqani Network primarily gathers recruits from Paktika and Paktia, and from Khost, Logar, and Ghazni. These are essentially mercenary fighters but with some familial tribal connection to the Haqqani Network. This means it has ready access to fighting forces inside and outside of its immediate operational territories.

Conversely, the Haqqani Network has long been a recruiter, patron, and trainer of foreign fighters, but not necessarily for itself. Under Jalaluddin,

Haqqani front businesses became a primary conduit for Arabs wishing to participate in jihad, and willing to pay to do so, making it one of the first organizations in Afghanistan to welcome foreigners.[17] This not only set a precedent but it gave the Haqqani Network the most experience.[18] Acting as an incubator and supplier of foreign fighters helped cement the Haqqani Network's close ties to other militants, providing critical manpower resources to al-Qaeda and other groups like the Tehrik-e-Taliban (TTP) known as the Pakistani Taliban, and to the Afghan Taliban (Siddique 2010).[19]

This connected the Haqqani Network intimately to the Afghan jihad and the prominent actors in it by strengthening its external social capital and trust. Yobie (2009) reported that Jalaluddin commanded many Taliban forces in battle in the 1980s and 1990s. This gives the Haqqani Network the ability to very quickly gather fighters but without an ongoing requirement to maintain them, making it cost-effective and strengthening Haqqani Network offensive capabilities and resilience.[20] Equally, the provision of sanctuary in Haqqani Network territories has been critical for al-Qaeda with much of its media operations being conducted from those areas.

According to declassified U.S. documents, this provided a further source of inputs, particularly financial ones for the Haqqani Network via bin Laden and his external connections (United States Government 2008). While the Haqqani Network supports other organizations, it does so more for self-benefit because it protects familial resources by using the resources of others first. Additionally, it reinforces its social capital and trust as a patron, providing a significant modicum of influence, if not control, over affiliates.

This extends beyond Afghan actors. Dressler (2012) observed that exogenous ties between the Haqqani Network and the Pakistani army and the ISI are particularly important. This is because they are deep-running, solid reciprocal relationships that are beneficial to all parties.[21] According to Takal and Siddique (2015), the Haqqani Network's control over parts of FATA has fostered many agreements with the Pakistani military. Rohde (2009) observed first hand that this provides the Pakistani military safe passage and enables the Haqqani Network to transport illicit goods, weapons, and even kidnap victims in broad daylight throughout the area and across borders.

Stability and safe-haven in the tribal FATA region are critical for Haqqani strength and resilience because it is their familial backyard. It is also the homeland of the Pashtuns, the traditional home of the Haqqanis in a region encompassing Paktia, Paktika, and the Ghazni and Logar provinces as well as the Kurram Agency now in Pakistan.[22] The main headquarters of the Haqqani Network is in the village of Dande Darpa Khel, and it has a major operational hub in the Zambar village located in the northern Sabari district of Khost.

Additionally, Johnson (2007) identified the Taliban presence in Zabul, Paktia, and Paktika as vital to Haqqani strength because it embedded Pashtun tribalism into the Taliban senior leadership, giving the Haqqani Network deeper ties and influence due to its ancestral Pashtun connections. According to Afghan Minister Mohammad Yousafzai, "they are a fighting force that represents Pashtuns, and they are the only legitimate force fighting the foreign invasion" (Chisti 2012, 3). The Haqqani Network further propagates this through shared training bases, in particular one special group of bases that play a key role, and are known as the Haqqani "Secretariat" facilities in North Waziristan.

These are particularly important to Haqqani Network family interests and for integration with Pakistan's ISI. The roadside Dande Darpa Khel base has been home to the core Haqqani family, the wives and children of Jalaluddin and Siraj, and is only one kilometre away from a Pakistani army base. Proximity to Pakistani military facilities increases interoperability and is probably intended to deter targeting by U.S. CIA drones. This is reflected in the placement of the second and third secretariat bases. One is co-located directly in front of the Pakistani Frontier Constabulary fort in the main Miranshah bazaar, North Waziristan, and another just behind Miranshah bazaar.

These heavily fortified Secretariat bases also support operational capabilities. The first houses a computer-training institute and various compounds for different types of indoctrination. The second has several compounds and has been the probable headquarters of the Taliban, providing a secure base to move between Afghanistan and Pakistan, and to liaise and coordinate operations, according to Taj (2009).[23] Haqqani Network hosting of the Taliban demonstrates strong integration as well as Haqqani Network influence, and, particularly, social capital exchange between it, the Taliban, al-Qaeda, and the ISI, as discussed by Gabbay (2014).

However, this only exists because of the strong and central role of family and kinship. Jalaluddin, who successfully leveraged his placement in the Zadran tribe that belongs to the highland Pashtuns traversing Pakistan and Afghanistan, established the strong social capital basis of the Haqqani Network. Romaniuk and Webb (2015) posit that Islamic Deobandi principles are at the fore of tribal society. Jalaluddin Haqqani was a high-ranking Islamic scholar and religious authority, having graduated from the Dar-ul-Uloom Haqqani madrassa in Akora Khattak, as did Siraj following him.[24] Jalaluddin's religious standing was significant in further cementing social capital and, importantly, trust with other insurgent leaders.[25]

The Haqqani religious madrassa system has likewise been an important tool of kinship development by teaching and enforcing the need for tribal unity. According to Sethna (2013), many high-level al-Qaeda leaders were taught at that Haqqani Network Dar al-Ulum Haqqaniyya madrassa in Akora Khattak, including many older Taliban commanders who fought with the Haqqani Network in the anti-Soviet war. Johnston and Mason (2007) write that post 2001, the Dar al-Ulum Haqqaniyya madrassa provided tuition, food, clothing, and accommodation to students for free and gave them military and ideological training and equipment.[26]

These are just part of a system of over 80 madrassas throughout Afghanistan and Pakistan that form a critical processing capability supporting the Haqqani

Network. Sethna (2013) found that the provision of free education and training attracts recruits, lowering input-gathering costs. According to Dressler (2010), during the anti-Soviet fighting Jalaluddin personally taught many hundreds of classes, enabling him to indoctrinate countless recruits, many of whom formed the alumni that continue to fight with the Haqqani Network today, or went on to serve in government.[27]

The importance is clear. Information, intelligence, operational support, political influence, and coordination can all be potentially exploited through family and kinship.[28] Tribal and clan lines between Afghanistan, Waziristan, the FATA, and Pakistan are blurred and are not restricted by political boundaries. Pakistan has long supported organizations that are not anti-state, and in Afghanistan, supporting the Haqqani Network and others provides it with important geopolitical influence in the region. Harrison (2001) states that, during the Soviet invasion, insurgent organizations like the Haqqani Network and the Taliban were calculated strategic creations used by the ISI. Kinship ties facilitated many of these connections and the enduring relationship with the ISI provides training, resources, intelligence, and other support that has strengthened Haqqani Network resilience. According to former U.S. Commander of Eastern Afghanistan Col. Chris Toner, the "Haqqani is the most resilient enemy out there" (Partlow 2011, 3), protected from all threats in its Pakistani sanctuary of North Waziristan. Table 3.2 illustrates the beneficial effects of a familial setup on the structural dynamics of the Haqqani Network.

Table 3.2 Effects of familial setup on organization – Haqqani Network

Structural dynamics	Organizational effect
Familial organization	Cheap vetting costs and the ability to recruit through extensive kinship networks across clans.
	Increased internal security.
	Immediate access to a wide kinship resource bases.
	Stability in leadership secessionism.
Command and control	Limitations of Familial recruitment if losses occur in quick succession.
	High efficiency due to low cost socio-economics.
Resources	Extensive territorial control providing plentiful and diverse resources.
	Resource limitations will occur as growth plateaus over time.
	Extensive support from Pakistan.
Strategic behaviour	Familial unity increases whole of organization responses to external pressures.
	Less compartmentalization of damages.
	Burden-sharing.
	Daily and tactical operations support long-term prosperity.
	Beholden to Pakistani patrons as a collective proxy that imposes external goals.

Section 2: external pressures

The Haqqani Network has faced sustained external pressures on multiple fronts. After the 2001 9/11 attacks, the U.S. targeted the Afghan Taliban for hiding al-Qaeda leader Osama bin Laden, initiating the War on Terror. The Taliban was routed, sheltering with the Haqqani Network as Western forces advanced. While not targeted by the West at the beginning of the war, the Haqqani Network soon followed. Foreign external U.S. pressure was not the first challenge to the Haqqani Network however. Rather, it was an organic, tribal political power conflict for the Zadran people and its territories that occupied Jalaluddin. Padcha Khan Zadran, a few years Jalaluddin's junior and also a powerful anti-Soviet commander, sought complete tribal dominance, including over the Haqqani.

In 2002 after Western coalition forces were deployed to Afghanistan, Padcha Khan Zadran chose a side, playing a crucial role in driving the Taliban out of Paktia.[29] Probably as a political play for personal power and Western resources rather than because of any discord with the Taliban, he pursued a decidedly pro-government and pro-Western strategy. In 2002, Padcha Khan Zadran entered the Wolesi Jirga – the Afghani Upper House of Parliament and was appointed Governor of Paktia with the support of the central government. Prime Minister Karzai, who was a Northern Alliance, anti-Taliban commander when Western forces first arrived, hoped to be able to leverage greater control of the Zadran and possibly the Haqqani Network. According to Carney and Schemmer (2002) however, the leadership Shura in Gardez rejected Khan's appointment. This resulted in Khan shelling the city in retaliation, forcing Karzai to turn against Khan, damaging Khan's power base.[30]

Conversely, it offered an opportunity for Jalaluddin to strengthen his standing in the Zadran and Haqqani engagement with al-Qaeda and the Taliban. Although no longer in control in Paktia, Padcha Khan Zadran retained deep ties there and a strong militia, making him a powerful warlord in contestation with Jalaluddin. While Khan continued to seek U.S. support and maintained an anti-Taliban stance, Jalaluddin held the opposite side. Success and renown at resisting Afghan and international forces resulted in the Haqqani Network being heavily targeted by international forces.

The Haqqani Network was well known to the CIA as a formidable insurgency actor from Operation Cyclone.[31] By fighting on the other side it was marked as a substantial threat and critical target that became a priority for coalition forces. The International Security Assistance Force (ISAF) Command mobilized a significantly high level of elite forces and multiservice assets in its attempts to destroy the Haqqani Network, more than for any other target group in the theatre.

According to Ackerman, ISAF Commander General David Petraeus stated that operations against the organization were targeted, "intelligence-driven precision operations" (2010). Many have been successful; however, the Haqqani Network remains resilient and robust, and attacks and insurgent activity continue. However, it is by no means immune, and external pressures certainly damaged the Haqqani Network with many of its core familial leadership killed or dying naturally over time, though it remains defiantly resilient. The following subsection provides an examination of external pressures exerted against the Haqqani Network from 2002.

Primary pressures and targeted kinetic operations

Primary pressures are the most effective means by which incumbent forces can remove, eliminate, or isolate the command and control elements of insurgency through battlefield kinetic operations. Successfully targeting a few dozen principal actors can be far more important than killing or arresting several hundred fighters (Staniland 2014). Due to the Haqqani Network being a familial organization, it became increasingly difficult for it to replenish its commanders as there was a decreasing pool of capable kin as replacements. This makes it costly for the Haqqani Network to regenerate at leadership levels, meaning that with sufficient damage to an organization's core, insurgency-processing functions may cease because of a growing leadership deficit.

Targeting fighters has been less effective because the Haqqani Network has high reconstitutional capabilities at its broadest base levels, meaning it has been able to quickly and cheaply replace lost ranks. Likewise, the Haqqani Network not only has broad-based organic clan and tribal resources, but it has ready access to fighters from its affiliates and partners, not least of which is the Taliban with an estimated fighting force of some 25–40,000 (Victor 2019). However, it is the Haqqani familial core that manages these fighters, and as long as it remains intact it can attract partners, gather recruits, and leverage its affiliates. Therefore, killing fighters is much less effective than killing leaders.

As a result, observable damage to Haqqani Network core systems is a primary predictor of the degree of effective external pressure. Particularly in familial insurgency, the loss of core family members as critical leaders cannot be covered up for long. Overall, Afghan insurgent deaths from 2002 to 2008 are estimated at 5,000 to 15,000 (Crawford 2016). As a principal insurgent actor it is fair to surmise that Haqqani Network fighters are well represented among these. However, few senior commanders were killed during this period and even fewer familial core members. Interestingly this correlates with counterinsurgency technology, particularly armed drones. The use of unmanned aerial vehicles has been around since World War II (Bowden 2013), but it has only been since the late 2000s that they developed sufficiently to become the highly efficient tools they are today. As drones such as the Predator, the Reaper, and the Killer Bees grew in capability and in numbers, so too did their frequency of use and lethality.

Before 2008 it was very difficult to accurately target high-value Haqqani Network members. After 2008 this changed significantly as one of the greatest dangers to Haqqani leaders became drone attack. In 2008 six Hellfire missiles were fired from drones at the Haqqani madrassa in Dande Darpa Khel, aimed at killing former leader Jalaluddin Haqqani. While Jalaluddin was not there, 23 others, including Jalaluddin's sister, sister-in-law, one wife, and eight grandchildren were killed. Farmer (2010) reports that on 18 February 2010 Mohammed Haqqani, one of Jalaluddin's 12 sons and younger brother of Siraj, was killed with three other Haqqani Network members in an area of Dande Darpa Khel in North Waziristan.[32]

Siraj has been luckier, narrowing escaping the same 2010 Predator drone attack that killed his brother Mohammed. Another strike on 14 September 2010 eliminated Saifullah Haqqani, a prominent military commander. Saifullah was a cousin of Siraj and was killed with 11 additional Haqqani Network members in Dargah Mandi near Miran Shah (Mohanty 2011).[33] Targeting the Haqqani Network has had success at reducing its organizational efficiency, which has primarily been accomplished by the Disposition Matrix (DM), a targeted killing program that tracks known insurgents (Shaw 2013).

Intelligence on target locations is incorporated into the matrix and a drone is tasked for a kill mission.[34] Badruddin Haqqani was executed this way in August 2012 when a CIA multiple-missile drone strike killed him and at least 17 others. Badruddin was another of Jalaluddin's sons and the Chief of Operations for North Waziristan in charge of smuggling and logistics. According to Walsh and Schmitt (2012), Badruddin was a key commander of attacks against ISAF and allied forces as well as the commander of the August 2011 attack on the Intercontinental Hotel in Kabul.[35]

Killed in the same attack was Emeti Yakuf, a commander of the East Turkestan Islamic Movement (ETIM) comprised of Chinese Uighur Muslims from Western China, who was being sheltered by the Haqqani Network.[36] Yakut's presence reinforces the multi-ethnic transnational linkages developed by the Haqqani Network. Another counterinsurgency success was Jan Baz Zadran, a key logistician and manager for the Haqqani Network: killed by a drone strike in October 2011 (BBC 2011). However, it is not only high-value targets in the Haqqani Network familial core that are targeted. From 2004 to 2011 there were 404 drone strikes in North Waziristan and Pakistani border regions, not including strikes in Afghanistan which killed numerous fighters and affiliates. Between 2004 and 2017 there were *c.*3,120 drone strikes in North Waziristan killing nearly 8,000 Haqqani insurgents, as shown in Table 3.3, while in Pakistan (Table 3.4) there were 325 drone strikes with 2,820 Haqqani members killed as a result.[37]

The data illuminates several dimensions that are of interest. First, the new capabilities offered to counterinsurgent forces by drone technology increased at a significant pace. The significant increase in tempo from just one strike in 2004 to nearly 1,300 in 2017 showed the link between the threat and the ability to target Haqqani infrastructure, command and control, and operational capabilities remotely. The use of direct kinetic attacks afforded by drones became a core counterinsurgency methodology and a significant external pressure, and is again reflected in the results of the attacks by killing nearly 8,000 Haqqani Network members.[38]

From 2009 to 2015 there was an increased willingness to penetrate Pakistani sovereign airspace to pursue kill missions on high-value targets. Table 3.5

Table 3.3 CIA drone strikes in North Waziristan 2004–2017

Year	No. strikes	Haqqani fatalities
2004	1	5
2005	4	14
2006	2	23
2007	7	116
2008	48	455
2009	74	888
2010	205	1,799
2011	63	549
2012	53	229–425
2013	27	109–195
2014	29	128–203
2015	235–236	982–1,434
2016	1,071	1,389–1,597
2017	1,296	340–541
Totals	3,115–3,125	6,926–7,972

Table 3.4 CIA drone strikes in Pakistan 2005–2017

Year	No. strikes	Haqqani fatalities
2005	1	1
2006	0	0
2007	1	20
2008	19	156
2009	46	536
2010	90	831
2011	59	548
2012	46	344
2013	24	158
2014	19	122
2015	14	85
2016	3	7
2017	3	12
Totals	325	2,820

shows a more specific damage assessment of Haqqani Network familial core vulnerabilities to direct kinetic attacks through the Disposition Matrix program.

This data suggests that successful direct kinetic and hard-power pressures have been effective at removing Haqqani nuclear and close consanguine family members in the organizational core. In doing so, critical relationships with external patrons have been hurt. Further, processing functions have been damaged yet many have resumed under different control. As such, the

Table 3.5 Disposition Matrix damage on Haqqani familial core

Year	Date	Location	Targeted	Killed
2008	23 October	Miran Shah	Jalaluddin Haqqani – Taliban Madrassa	Jalaluddin survived
2009	15 October	Dandi/Darphakel	Haqqani fighters	4 killed
2010	18 February	Danday	Mohammad Haqqani and 4 Taliban	Mohammad Haqqani and 3 Taliban
2010	15 September	Tall/North Waziristan	Haqqani fighters	21 killed
2010	14 December	Tall/North Waziristan	Haqqani fighters	4 killed
2011	20 June	Khardand/Kurram	Haqqani fighters	12 killed
2011	10 August	Miran Shah	Haqqani fighters	25 killed
2011	16 August	Miran Shah	Haqqani fighters	4 killed
2011	13 October	Danday and Darphakel	Haqqani fighters	4 killed
2011	3 November	Darphakel Saria and Miran Shah	Haqqani fighters	3 killed
2012		NO DATA	NO DATA	
2013	5 September	Ghulam Khan	Mullah Sangeen Zadran and al-Qaeda explosives expert Zubir al Muzi	Both killed
2013	21 November	Unknown	Haqqani leader Abdullah Ahmad and 7 fighters	All killed
2014	11 June	Dargah Mandi	Haqqani fighters	6 killed
2014	29 October	Nagas/Birmal	Senior Commander Abdullah Haqqani and bodyguards	7 killed

benefits of familial processing control, such as social capital and trust, have been irrevocably damaged in some cases with the loss of Haqqani leaders, such as Badruddin Haqqani, Abu Bakar Haqqani, Mohammed Haqqani, and Haji Mali Khan. The respect and regard that died with these commanders cannot be replaced easily. Indeed, as Jordan finds on her examination of terrorist decapitation strategy, "much of the optimism surrounding the removal of terrorist leaders is grounded in theories that analyse the role of these leaders within their organizations" (2014, 7). Abu Bakar Haqqani, a key commander who was killed in a drone strike in the Hangu district of the Pakistani Khyber-Pakhtunkhwa province with two family members, is a good example of this.[39]

With the immediate familial pool of replacements shrinking, greater emphasis, responsibility, and burdens are placed on the survivors, creating more pressure on core commanders. It is not only control of insurgency operations that has been important but also the physical elements employed. Degrading primary operational activities such as mobility for fear of interception and assassination is an extreme form of external pressure that the Haqqani Network has suffered. Targeting communications, training bases, and capabilities has also damaged many of its organizational functions in numerous cases. Due to the covert nature of insurgent networks, damage to leadership can reduce strength and cohesion, making leadership succession difficult. Tactics and strategies to target and decapitate leadership figures can also have other benefits for incumbents. Freeman (2010) argues that organizations with highly active operational leaders, such as the Haqqani Network, are more susceptible.

Indeed, when mobility was restricted insurgents had to stay entrenched. However, once identified static assets became critically vulnerable. Roggio (2009) cites as examples the destruction of Haqqani Network infrastructure, including fortified bases in the mountains around Khost, and a heavily defended fort in the Wor Mamay Mountains in eastern Pakistan.[40] ISAF forces also destroyed a critical Haqqani Network facility in a remote part of Paktia province, used by the Haqqani Network to move Taliban fighters and supplies via the Khost-Gardez pass. Multiple significant caches of assorted light and heavy weapons were destroyed and numerous Haqqani Network fighters killed in the attack (Roggio 2009).

In August 2011, successful targeting of Haqqani Network infrastructure led Sartaj Aziz, advisor to former Prime Minister Dr Abdullah to state that "the infrastructure of the Haqqani Network in North Waziristan, which includes improvised explosive device factories and a number of other capacities including communications, has been disrupted" (Johnson 2015). Thus, the loss of mobility plus impaired and compromised communications, coupled with the loss of bases is significant in terms of external pressures as it reduced operational capabilities, and degraded the Haqqani Network in its static forms. In conjunction with targeting core leaders, these interventions represent the greatest external pressure it suffered.

Soft-power and secondary pressures

Unlike hard-power pressures that rely on the military capacities of incumbents and can be observed empirically and chronologically, soft-power outcomes are not as easily measured. This is particularly true in the Afghan context. Felbab-Brown writes that ongoing and endemic failures by the central government to "not only meet the expectations of the population for economic development and service delivery, but also to maintain security" (2017, 6), have contributed to significantly increased local sympathies for the Afghan insurgency. This means targeted soft-power pressures have been less emphatic. However, successfully exerting hard- and soft-power pressures is about capability as much as it is about political will. This is an internal issue for Afghanistan as much as it is an external one. This supports Malejacq's (2016) argument that external intervention frequently causes political instability rather than stability, thereby weakening instead of strengthening failing states. As a result, a mix of organic weakness and the injection of external volatility and competing priorities has resulted in a lack of strategic coherence. This has certainly been true for Afghanistan.

At tactical levels, a range of soft-power initiatives has been available to the Afghan Government and its international allies beyond kinetic military options, and these have been used with effect to reduce Haqqani Network resilience in some instances. While deficiencies exist, the interconnected Afghan insurgency nexus means that pressures on some primary actors, like the Taliban, can have ramifications for others, including the Haqqani Network. Although holistic soft-power pressures have failed in the absence of a full-spectrum approach being used, some soft-power pressures have been used to specifically target the Haqqani Network.

Those soft-power initiatives have been particularly effectively when employed in Haqqani territorial base areas.[41] Soft-power pressures projected there have been capacity-building for the government, generating economic development opportunities that have attempted to reduce underlying issues that support the insurgency, and in turn the Haqqani Network. While not as effective as envisioned, it can be argued that any positive change has an equally negative pressure effect on the enduring conflict. For example, Pate (2018) writes that while there is a strong consensus that soft-power pressures have not yielded tangible strategic gains, results are manifesting on tactical and daily levels. Similarly, since 2000, the number of Non-Governmental Organizations (NGOs) working in the Paktia, Paktika, and Logar provinces undertaking civil and socio-economic development has nearly quadrupled.[42]

Other development initiatives have also had good outcomes, particularly with regard to further enabling additional treatments of the Haqqani insurgency, including hard-power outcomes. This is made possible because soft power can assist the practice and cultivation of hard power. This relationship is evident in the massive spending in Afghanistan on building projects to develop better civic infrastructure, roads, public administration, and community health. These are equally essential for military forces operating in those areas for access and support.[43] Likewise, there has been no shortage of international aid to Afghanistan to support these initiatives.

One key, though unsuccessful, example of joint domestic and international development was the Afghan Peace and Reintegration Programme (APRP). This was aimed at building resilience to the Haqqani insurgency specifically in Paktika and Khost. The APRP was a replacement for the failed "Program Tahkim Sulh [National Program for Reconciliation or PTS]" (Derksen 2014). However, both failed to achieve much and were mainly self-undermining because they encouraged fighters to join the programme, only to arrest, punish, or execute them once they had surrendered. This did have some short-term effects of reducing fighter numbers but was detrimental to long-term success.

Another external pressure on the Haqqani Network is the Sustainable Livelihoods and Social Economic Development in the Southeast Region of Afghanistan (SLSD) programme. The SLSD is run by The Liaison Office (TLO), a non-governmental organization.[44] The TLO specifically builds infrastructure to foster socio-economic development, rural health care, and community growth. It also works in the areas of law and justice and is one of the few NGOs to make tangible gains. In 2007, the TLO established provincial- and district-level justice projects that acted as conflict-resolution commissions to mediate disputes and grievances.

Successes gave it legitimacy and recognition as an organic authority that reduced the reliance on militants, including the Haqqani Network, to resolve disputes. It achieved this by bringing together high-ranking government officials and rural elders working together through specific Shuras, many of which are in Uruzgan, Helmand, and Paktia provinces (The Liaison Office 2009). Reducing the Haqqani Network's authority and eroding its legitimacy as a provincial authority partially degraded its ability to enforce security and justice, even in its familial-dominated clan and tribal domains. The provision of education by NGOs further reduces Haqqani Network dominance of religious education, which it restricts to males only.

Of the 145 NGOs engaged in Afghanistan, more than a dozen are working directly in education programmes catering for all ages and genders (ACBAR 2020). Similarly, NGO sponsored home-based schooling has dramatically increased since 2001.[45] An increasingly educated population opens the opportunity for livelihoods beyond fighting and has had some effect at reducing insurgent recruitment. With education comes political awareness, which, when coupled with opportunity, can, and has, reduced participation in insurgency (Singh and Shemyakina 2016).

Wimpelmann concludes that power in Afghanistan was "to be found in a hierarchically structured configuration of localized authority" (2015, 181). Therefore, the organic tribal dynamics of Afghanistan have never been prone to a centralized authority, and enduring division among the various factions of tribes and clans has made political cohesion difficult, not only for incumbents but for the Haqqani Network as well.[46] Having said this, it remains the case that there are no blanket approaches and the war has been fought differently in different areas against an enduring backdrop of complex, organic power centres. This is exacerbated by soft-power pressures that erode the number of clan members associated through tribal kinship, particularly females who can begin to change the socio-cultural dynamics of the region, and wear away at the traditional family dominance of the Haqqani due to increasing education and opportunities.

Likewise, organic and regional security dynamics are relevant. The Haqqani Network is as subject to competing rivalries and internal intra-tribal pressures as any other. It too has enemies and has come into conflict with other tribal militias, including its allies on occasion. In April 2012 for instance, Haqqani Network fighters were involved in intense fighting against the TTP in the Malik Shadam Khan area of North Waziristan in which six TTP members were killed by a Haqqani attack, and two Haqqani Network fighters killed in return (ETP [The Express Tribune] 2012). While such pressures are not directly generated by incumbents, conflict zones are inherently competitive theatres with multiple actors vying for control and resources, meaning the Haqqani Network must remain vigilant on all fronts.

It is not only direct competition or direct methods that puts pressure on the Haqqani Network, however. As these examples demonstrate, skilled manipulation of intra-group dynamics can be fostered to achieve additional third-party pressures. India in particular has strong geopolitical security interests in Afghanistan, particularly in North Waziristan, which falls within its arc of instability. According to Iqbal, India seeks to "deny Pakistan strategic depth" (2015, 1). As Pakistan is India's greatest threat, this makes sense. It is therefore in India's active interests to sever Pakistan's support of the Haqqani Network and other insurgent organizations and terrorist groups.

Pakistan's control of the Lashkar-e-Taiba and the Haqqani Network has proven highly effective in undermining India in Kashmir for many years.[47] In Afghanistan, India's influence and pressures have been equally about geopolitical security as about economic self-interest. If Pakistan could cement its influence in Afghanistan via militant proxies like the Haqqani Network, India would be threatened on yet another front. Additionally, were Pakistan to gain the monopoly of power, India would lose access to Central Asian republics via Afghanistan.

Equally for Pakistan, rising Indian power and its relationship with the U.S. and Afghan Governments are troublesome. Pakistan therefore continues to maintain the Haqqani Network's resilience while India seeks to destroy it. In 2011, an Indian conglomerate won the rights to the lucrative Hajigak iron ore mines in Bamyan Province, Central Afghanistan (Nissenbaum 2011). The Hajigak mine site has the world's second-largest reserves. This example reflects and supports relations between Kabul and New Delhi, builds cooperative prosperity, creates jobs and infrastructure, and offers alternatives to conflict. It also supports India's policy goals in Afghanistan of preventing Pakistan from establishing a controlling influence and sustaining of insurgent organizations, thereby developing strategic depth that could further threaten it.

The Hajigak mine project is one example where India has developed greater influence by building economic security in Afghanistan. Kaur notes that India currently "enjoys immense goodwill among ordinary Afghans that is has earned due to its decade-long investment in Afghanistan" (2017, 1). This comes from similar initiatives from which the flow on effects provide important financial windfalls and relationship-building between Afghanistan and India. Trade increased throughout Central Asia as well as for India. D'Souza (2009) reported that economic growth had provided positive incentives in placing trade over animosities, which in turn had provided a better background in rural Afghanistan to alter the socio-economic foci.

These have been positive in placing soft-power pressures on the Haqqani Network and eroding some of its legitimacy. This is evidenced by increasing NGO activity that is representative of a much-improved security environment and of greater acceptance of charitable and development projects by the local populations. However, unlike hard power, which can be measured by tangible statistical means, soft-power outcomes are durational and are difficult to quantify in absolute terms, but there are some measurable indicators.

Significant international aid and development also offers additional exit options for fighters. Positive development in the region has increased prosperity and cheaper exit options for insurgents, undermining the lure of militancy, something very detrimental to the Haqqani Network in the longer term.[48] Likewise, development has increased access for the military, thereby developing the means to improve safety and security. Under Jalaluddin, the Haqqani Network was firmly established and Paktia was its "capital". External pressures have unfastened it to some extent and changed its nature, forcing it to become more dynamic and less fixed as its familial dominance of the area and its clan weakens.

Following an analysis of soft-power pressures it is evident they are working, to some degree, and they have been well supported internationally. Despite internal issues of corruption and misappropriation, aid does flow down to the everyday level and has made positive differences in fostering a more-secure Afghanistan. In the strategic context though, soft power must be balanced with hard power as they are mutually supportive, requiring careful balancing of national security concerns with short- and long-term solutions.

Section 3: Haqqani Network adaptation, recovery, and capabilities

This section examines the Haqqani Network's resilience and its responses to external pressures. As described in Chapter 1, insurgent organizational resilience is the efficient adaptation to endogenous and exogenous shock and the ability to respond to external pressures. This means organizations have the ability to bounce-back from shock and adapt beyond an original state after suffering damage, or change into new forms that are more efficient to reduce the likelihood of similar impacts in the future. A resilient response therefore necessitates recovering and rebuilding damaged or destroyed leadership, command and control structures, and managing external pressures in ways that avoid additional future damage that can impact political and operational perpetuity. The familial dynamics of the Haqqani Network are a critical part of this, making them the most resilient of insurgents operating in the mountains.

The Haqqani Network's ability to adapt and respond efficiently to external pressures is a significant source of its strength. It learned that just as its forces and static bases are susceptible to kinetic destruction, organic and socio-cultural pressures could be similarly damaging. Reductions to its legitimacy, social capital, and ability to exercise authority impacted its effectiveness as an insurgent actor across several operational areas. Rather than diminish though, the Haqqani Network has successfully endured. Good leadership and strong familial connectedness across clan and tribal partners have enabled the continuity of organizational functions, significantly contributing to efforts to destroy it. When Haqqani Network bases were destroyed in the north and south of Waziristan by CIA drones, it moved into areas like Baluchistan where the U.S. seemed to be unable, or unwilling, to decisively attack (Jones 2011).

Similarly, strong political lobbying by Haqqani-linked family members, like Jalaluddin's brother Ibrahim Omari, played a little-known but influential part in limiting attacks against it.[49] This has been important in alleviating some pressures, securing sanctuary, and giving operational space for the Haqqani Network to recover. This was further assisted by particularly strong relationships with the Islamic Movement of Uzbekistan (IMU), an al-Qaeda affiliate. The Haqqani Network and the IMU allow access to each other's operational areas and training camps, and share logistical support and even weapons (Jones 2011).[50] External support also enabled the Haqqani Network to effectively train foreign fighters while increasing the recruitment and training of its own fighters.

These are drawn from its extensive kinship base that enables it to replace lost fighters and commanders. Similarly, its leadership has been talented in adapting its methods of guerrilla and insurgent warfare to maintain battlefield diffusion and integration into local communities. These are legacy skills passed down the patriarchal line from Jalaluddin and his brothers to Siraj and his other sons. In fact, Jalaluddin's legacy is an important aspect of Haqqani familial resilience, not only because Jalaluddin was a strong advocate of tribal security, but also because his intricate relationships have passed to Siraj. A full transfer of social capital and trust from Jalaluddin to Siraj has only been possible in the familial context, and this has given the Haqqani Network both national and international access.

It would be imprudent to suggest that as successful as external pressures were, that the Haqqani Network was degraded or contained within the southern provinces. It has repeatedly demonstrated the ability to reach deep into the capital Kabul and strike at the heart of government. Evidence of this was identified earlier in this chapter. Strikes carried out include the 2011 Intercontinental Hotel attack, and assaults on the government Ministries of Education and Justice, the Prison Directorate, and Ministry of National Defence (Maley 2012).

Although suffering targeted attacks against its operational capabilities by the ANA/ISAF COIN campaign, Haqqani Network leadership repeatedly undertook in-kind complex and highly effective attacks. This demonstrates Haqqani Network adaptability and resilience and is further evidenced by the following examples.

In 2005 and 2008, Haqqani Network operations escalated from tactical assaults to suicide bombings in Kabul, dispatched from its base in Loya-Paktia.[51] Haqqani Network operational capacity across Afghanistan, and the ability to outmanoeuvre ISAF and ANA intelligence and security services marked it as what many call the most lethal insurgent organization in Afghanistan (Dressler 2010; Ahmad 2017).[52] Martyrdom and suicide attacks as well as other means of assassination have been prominent outputs of the Haqqani Network, used strategically to further its politico-ideological aspirations. As a result of such attacks, significant pressure is typically placed on the Haqqani Network. A primary means of Haqqani Network diffusion into the surrounding terrain is integration into localized kinship groups where Haqqani Network fighters can blend in almost seamlessly.

In 2006, a Haqqani Network suicide bomber assassinated a Governor of Paktia, Hakim Taniwal. Taniwal had served in the post since 2002 when he was appointed by the Karzai Government to replace Kamal Khan Zadran, the brother of Jalaluddin's nemesis Pacha Khan Zadran (ICG 2003). This was followed by another Haqqani Network suicide attack days later at his funeral, injuring four government ministers and killing 39 attendees (Gall 2006). As intended this altered the Zadran tribal power dynamics, making them more favourable for the Haqqani Network by removing effective leaders, discouraging capable replacements, and ensuring that the alternatives were of poor quality and easily manipulated. This showcases the Haqqani Network as a highly evolved conflict actor. These attacks also accomplished several other critical elements of insurgency such as re-shaping geopolitical conditions, furthering its cause, and weakening the incumbents. It equally demonstrates a dynamic resilience that could actively alter the power dynamics in the conflict theatre to its advantage.

Another adaptation strategy employed by the Haqqani Network was to reinforce its legitimacy through shadow governance and by enforcing law and order in Loya-Paktia, Paktika, and to some extent in the Logar and Ghazni provinces. This has been achieved by leveraging long-established familial power structures in the regional tribes and clans. The Haqqani Network eliminated virtually all non-Haqqani Network criminal enterprises and gangs from its territories and propagated the perception of itself as being the only legitimate district police service (Ruttig 2009a). However, criminal activity did not cease; rather, it was simply absorbed into the Haqqani Network's family operations. Similarly, the Network gained further authority by controlling infrastructure development. While monopolizing works within its operational areas through its front companies, it simultaneously attacked and destroyed infrastructure it was not contracted for, or that made targeting itself easier like roads, communications, and civic developments.

Dressler claims the Haqqani Network is "best known for carrying out spectacular suicide attacks in Kabul that have targeted Afghan, ISAF, and Indian infrastructure" (2011, 2). Controlling roads and movements is an essential military advantage to any conflict actor. The Haqqani Network not only targets such projects but has received protection contracts to provide security for works, from itself, providing a winning trifecta of building, protecting, or taxing and controlling infrastructure projects (Sennot 2010). What the Haqqani Network cannot tax, control, build, or be paid to protect it has attacked, often through its own dedicated network of Improvised Explosive Device (IED) cells that build, install, and detonate bombs specifically to target those projects (Maloney 2009).[53] While fatalities do occur, the IED operations in rural areas are intended more to restrict the movement of Afghan and ISAF forces. Asifkhel (2008) argues that IED attacks are meant to reduce partnership collaboration between Afghanistan and particularly India and the U.S., while conversely supporting Haqqani Network legitimizing narratives.[54] Generally, such actions work as counter-external pressure operations.

Haqqani ground forces have also supported urban area suicide IED and vehicle-borne suicide IED operations. A prime example is the May 2009 multistage assault on the provincial governor's compound in Khost, the civil administration building, and the headquarters of the Khost police (AP 2009). As Khost is home to the regional provincial operations command of the ISAF and is the provincial economic hub, the attack was highly symbolic, demonstrating the capabilities of the Haqqani Network despite being targeted continually and suffering the destruction of key infrastructure, like its fortified Khost base and heavily defended fort in the Wor Mamay Mountains.

Other complex multi-stage attacks led by the Haqqani Network hit targets including U.S. combat outposts in the Margha area's Bermal districts which border the Durand line in 2008, 2010, and 2011. During the 2011 Bermal attack, joint NATO-Afghan National Security Forces killed around 60 fighters including those of the Haqqani Network and Uzbeks, Chechens, Arabs, and Urdus (Roggio 2011). According to Mazzetti *et al.* (2011), the 2008–2011 period saw attacks grow by 20 per cent, or five fold. Urban (2012) asserts that complex assaults in the capital Kabul are the "hallmark of Haqqani Network spectacular attacks in recent years on hotels, embassies, and ministries". Likewise, Stout (2017) states the Haqqani Network "has been blamed for spectacular attacks across Afghanistan since after the U.S. invasion". These on-going multi-organizational attacks known as "spectaculars" reinforce the Haqqani Network as an insurgency leader and operational partner of choice for the Taliban, the ISI, and others.

For instance, in 2009 the Haqqani Network and Hizb-i-Islami Gulbuddin (HiG) brokered a temporary tactical alliance and undertook attacks on Afghan and ISAF troops in Loya-Paktia.[55] As Jalaluddin was a Hizb-i-Islami-Khalis leader during the anti-Soviet war this is not surprising. Other organizations like the Lashkar-e-Jhangvi (LeJ) and the Sipah-e-Sahaba also have strong ties with the Haqqani Network, having operational bases in Haqqani Network territory.[56]

The Sipah-e-Sahaba is a critical Haqqani Network partner because it controls an extensive Haqqani Network of Pakistani Sunni madrassas and is a principal supplier of suicide bombers that the Haqqani Network deploys for operations (Rashid 2008).

The Haqqani Network has maintained a high tempo of outputs driven by a highly resilient and adaptive leadership core. Attacks that achieved the dual goals of adversarial capability degradation through kinetic destruction, and reducing incumbent legitimacy and socio-political standing are another of its trademarks. The attack on Forward Operating Base Chapman on 30 December 2009 is a good example. The attack was carried out by Humam al-Balawi, a Jordanian doctor who convinced the CIA he was an al-Qaeda member with knowledge of Ayman al-Zawahiri's location. The attack was initially blamed on al-Qaeda.[57] Another was the successful attack on the American University of Afghanistan (Rasmussen 2016). In Table 3.6 are listed major Haqqani Network attacks from 2006 to 2018.[58]

Attacks like these show the Haqqani Network's ability to target and destroy hardened facilities in cities and rural areas alike, and further demonstrate that it is fully capable of meeting these goals. Regarding legitimacy-building, these attacks, particularly the spectaculars, reinforce the image of an unassailable insurgent actor. Attacking and destroying incumbent bases and personnel, and its force projection into the capital of Kabul strengthen the Haqqani Network's claim to be an official governing authority, one deeply ingrained into the Afghan tribal and clan culture, while casting the Afghan Government as merely another puppet administration, much like those of Karmal, Chamkani, and Najibullah in previous decades.

The role of family and kinship

The leadership of Jalaluddin and Siraj Haqqani differed on operational levels but remained aligned on familial, political, and ideological ones. Smooth succession eliminated disruption and maintained organizational stability as well as externally between the Haqqani Network and its affiliates, partners, and sponsors in the insurgent nexus. There have been no known internal disputes or leadership challenges nor splits or factioning, and externally it has maintained allies, affiliates, and supporters, if not increased them.

The preservation of organizational social capital and significant personal trust between Siraj and other commanders during leadership transition, as discussed, is a strong familial demonstration of Haqqani Network resilience. Ruttig (2009b) reports that for many years Jalaluddin lent his considerable authority and social capital credibility to Siraj to demonstrate familial unity, and to ensure the stability of its leadership. Siraj's appointment as the second-in-command of the Taliban after Mullah Akhtar Mansour reflects acceptance of this inside and outside of Haqqani kinship groups. Likewise, the immediate kinship circle of the senior Haqqani Network leadership has been strong, with powerful and capable men at its helm. However, as this circle shrank, predominantly due to external

Table 3.6 Haqqani Network major attacks 2006–2018

Date	Attack details
September 2006	Suicide bomb attack against Abdul Hakim Taniwal, Governor of Paktia Province and close friend to President Harmid Karzai.
September 2006	Suicide bomb attack at Taniwal's funeral. 39 killed including police and civilians, 40 wounded.
14 January 2008	Attack on the Serena Hotel, Kabul by 4 Haqqani fighters and 1 suicide bomber. 9 killed. A Norwegian delegation escaped.
3 March 2008	Suicide truck-borne vehicle attack in Sabri district headquarters of U.S. forces in Khost. 2 killed.
27 April 2008	Attempted assassination of President Harmid Karzai, who escaped unharmed. 8 others killed, 11 wounded. Haqqani Network assisted by Hizb-i-Islami and unnamed senior Afghan Defence officials.
7 July 2008	Indian Embassy in Kabul attacked using Haqqani V.B.I.E.D., killing 54. ISI believed to have provided significant support and operational direction for the attack.
18 May 2018	NATO convoy attacked killing several high-ranking Canadian officers, U.S. soldiers, and Afghan civilians. 18 dead and many wounded.
12 September 2011	Truck-borne V.B.I.E.D. in proximity of Combat Outpost Sayed Abad. 5 killed and 77 wounded.
13 September 2011	NATO headquarters in Kabul and U.S. Embassy attacked in a 19-hour siege. 5 police and 11 civilians killed. 160 wounded.
31 October 2011	V.B.I.E.D. attack in West Beirut believed to be Haqqani orchestrated. 5 killed.
22 June 2012	Kabul hotel siege by Haqqani fighters lasting 12 hours. 20 killed.
15 July 2014	Truck-borne V.B.I.E.D. in a marketplace of a remote town in eastern Afghanistan. 72 killed and many wounded.
17 July 2014	Kabul Airport attacked by suicide bomber also firing grenades. 5 killed and unknown number wounded.
22 June 2015	Haqqani attack on Afghan Parliament by V.B.I.E.D and fighters. 5 killed and 30 wounded.
25 August 2016	Haqqani fighters attack the American University in Kabul, killing 12.
27 August 2016	Haqqani and Taliban forces engage Afghan Army in Paktia in a protracted 9-day battle. Haqqani take control of the district. 27 killed include those at an Army medical post.
31 May 2017	A massive Haqqani V.B.I.E.D. attack in central Kabul near the presidential palace and embassy district. More than 80 killed and hundreds wounded.
27 January 2018	Haqqani bombing of an ambulance in Kabul kills over 100 civilians.

pressures, it forced other family members to assume higher roles as increasingly more distant kin-connections were added and promoted.

Though presenting some risks for recruitment at senior levels, on base levels extended kinship through clan and tribal ties has been highly beneficial. Keeping it in the family keeps security vetting costs down by acquiring well-known assets. Other more trusted kin can vouch for distant relations. It is also more likely that kin will be ideologically and politically aligned with shared vision, history, and culture over meritocratic selections. Ensley and Pearson argue that the unique dynamics created by the social aspects of familial organizations "will result in higher cohesion, potency, task conflict, and shared strategic consensus than those ... with less 'familiness'" (2005, 267).

This is evident in the examples of Haji Khalil and Ibrahim Haji Omari, brothers of Jalaluddin who also sat on the Miran Shar Shura, and were probably highly coordinated in the strategic vision of the organization. Similarly, Jalaluddin's other sons Badruddin, Nasiruddin, Baseeruddin, Nasir, and of course Siraj, have all been involved in the family business and know the principal goals (Dressler 2010). Before taking full leadership, Siraj and Nasiruddin were the principle liaisons with al-Qaeda, working together to coordinate between the groups and facilitate acceptance of familial power transfer.

These strengths clearly show that the benefits of kinship in insurgent organizations include security, the efficiency of recruitment, low entry costs and higher exit costs, and particularly, the use and transfer of leadership stability, social capital, and trust. The consanguine Haqqani family has provided most of the critical leaders, and the clan and tribal nature of the Haqqani Network ensconced in the Mezi and the Zadran tribes has facilitated the rest.

Conclusion

Family has been a critical aspect of resilience for the Haqqani Network. In order to continue in its present form this needs to be maintained. If, however, the familial balance changes it could become increasingly vulnerable. This is because the greater the imbalance of non-familial leaders in familial organizations becomes over time, the greater the costs for influence, incentives and the monitoring of non-familial strategic behaviour and performance. Similarly, the potential for killing or capturing Siraj and those who handle financial matters, command and control, and liaison, like Khalil al-Rahman Haqqani, could significantly degrade overall capacity and functioning.[59] The inception of drone warfare has significantly affected this however, evident in the strengths of the Haqqani Network prior to 2005, and its increasing vulnerabilities thereafter.

Such rapidly evolving and increasingly effective counterinsurgent capabilities means that Haqqani Network has little ability to evade or counter, making this perhaps the most dangerous prospect. This is because as the most important family figures are killed, new leaders are promoted, but the further from the familial core leaders are, the greater the risk of agency issues. These arise from the divergence across the phenomena of individual-level behaviours and organizational-level governance mechanisms that contribute to organizational outcomes. Similarly, exit costs are far lower for those not directly linked to the Haqqanis through intimate consanguine kinship.

White *et al.* (2017) describe such a divergence as differences between relatively short operational horizons compared to familial horizons that stretch over generations to maintain stability in organizational culture, informal networks, and operating practices. If the Haqqani Network were to see familial control reduced to a minority it could manifest as a critical risk. This could be achieved by discouraging ISAF and Afghan forces through effective military actions, undermining localized support for the central government in Kabul, and using propaganda to show the Haqqani Network as the legitimate provincial authority. However, the further loss of family members may prevent this from happening if they are necessarily replaced with members possessing different interests and malleable political visions.

It is possible friction could arise between a degraded Haqqani familial core and less-connected seniors. A change in core leadership or a draw away from family objectives could see distinct differences in orientation, or even a tangible change of politics towards a central authority. New developments in civic infrastructure and improved socioeconomic conditions may also provide new, cheap, and viable alternatives to insurgency and facilitate such moves taking place. Alternatively, it is possible that Siraj's leadership could expire, or he could be assassinated, and a new Haqqani leader may work more closely with the incumbent authority, or even embrace a legitimate provincial role. This is plausible. Siraj's uncle, Ibrahim Omari, remains close to the central government and were it not for U.S. interjections, Jalaluddin Haqqani would have been the Afghan prime minister under Karzai. Had the Americans not vetoed his appointment, the most potent insurgent organization in Afghanistan could have possibly worked intimately once more with international allies to stabilize the country.

Moving forward, it is likely that hard- and soft-power pressures will continue to be brought to bear, and that Haqqani names will be added to the covert operations kill-list Disposition-Matrix. However, even after effective targeting of its leaders, fighters, processes, and facilities with sustained pressure, the Haqqani Network has shown exceptional resilience and powerful reconstitutional capabilities. While it has not been able to counter or defeat the threat of drones, it has found a means to adapt to the damage wrought by technology by simply weathering the storm. Eventually, even the most persistent enemies have to go home.

When this may happen though remains unknown. A proposed Taliban/U.S. peace deal in September 2019 failed, and the most recent deal struck between the U.S. and the Taliban in Doha, Qatar in February 2020 is tenuous at best, but eventually, there will have to be a drawdown of forces when the few remaining international forces quit the battle theatre. At one level, this would suggest the Haqqani Network may enter a new period of growth, but on the other, this is unlikely. Any immediate absence of American troops would probably not extend to drones, many of which are stationed in adjacent territories, and they will continue to scour the skies over Afghanistan in considerable numbers, removing names from the Disposition Matrix as they can. Likewise, U.S., and indeed other regional security interests, such as those of India, Russia, and China will continue to exert soft-power pressures in their individual favours.

Therefore, reductions in U.S. forces in Afghanistan have and are providing some breathing room, but even so the Haqqani Network is not capable of any significant or continual growth. It grew quickly to convert all the available resources (land, people, and economic production) that were available within its traditional tribal lands into military power, but after it had consumed this latent power base it has not been able to expand further. Tribal and clan boundaries mean that rapid familial expansion through intermarriage is not a feasible approach to support insurgency alone. As a result, resource restrictions may be the most important point of distinction between familial insurgencies, like the Haqqani Network, and meritocratic ones.

Notes

1 Russian aspirations for Afghanistan began as early as 1734 with its Central Asian expansion, although Afghanistan specifically was not a territorial goal until the late 1830s. More recently, Snyder has put it under the pretext of propping up a communist regime, though many saw it as a blatant land grab to establish a staging area for a further push into Pakistan, India, and Iran, or to claim a seaport. Feifer suggests it had more to do with stemming American strategic influence and was a reaction to the Iran revolution. SOURCE: Bruce Amstutz, 1986. *The great game: 1837–1944*. Washington, D.C.: National Defense University.
2 It is suspected that after the routing of the Taliban in Afghanistan during Operation Dagger, that Osama bin Laden and three of his wives were given sanctuary by the Haqqani Network in Khost.
3 Developed during the 1970s, Jalaluddin built resilient connections to numerous private patrons across the Gulf lands as well as diplomatic ties enabling him to secure funding and weapons. SOURCE: Don Rassler, 2013. *Fountainhead of Jihad: The Haqqani Nexus*. London: C. Hurts and Co.
4 The Soviet withdrawal by 15 February 1989 after Gorbachev agreed to the Geneva Accords left the Najibullah Government weakened. When Kabul fell to Mujahedeen forces Najibullah and his brother took shelter in the local U.N. compound until captured, tortured, and then hanged by the Taliban in 1996. Mojaddedi had been elected President of the Afghan interim government in 1989 and arrived in Kabul as President on 28 April 1992. Under Mojaddedi the future President, Hamid Karzai, served as aide, speechwriter, adviser and foreign minister. SOURCES: Kenneth Katzman, 2013. *Afghanistan: Post-Taliban Governance, Security, and U.S. Policy*. Washington, D.C.: Library of Congress Congressional Research Service; Ahmed Rashid, 2000. "Kabul 1996: Commander of the Faithful". In *Taliban: The Power of Militant Islam in Afghanistan and Beyond*, ed. Ahmed Rashid. London and New York: I.B. Tauris and Co.; Barnett Rubin *et al.*, 2005. *Afghanistan 2005 and Beyond: Prospects for Improved Stability Reference Document*. The Hague: Netherlands Institute of International Relations 'Clingendael'.
5 "Radical" is one term. Others describe Siraj as "extreme", such as Dreazen, and "ruthless", as Kitfield does. SOURCES: Yochi Dreazan, 2015. "The Taliban's New Number 2 Is a Mix of Tony Soprano and Che Guevara". *Foreign Policy*, Accessed 15 November 2016. http://foreign policy.com/2015/07/31/afghanistan-taliban-war-terrorism-alqaeda-cia-mullahomar-haqqani/; James Kitfield, 2016. *Twilight Warriors:*

The Soldiers, Spies, and Special Agents Who Are Revolutionizing the American Way of War. New York: Basic Books.

6 Matinuddin also suggested that the actual catalyst of Pehalwan's dissatisfaction with Dostam was the suspicious death of his brother, General Rasul Pehalwan in 1996. SOURCE: Kamal Matinuddin, 1999. *The Taliban Phenomenon Afghanistan 1994–1997.* Oxford: Oxford University Press.

7 Hezb-e-Islami is an insurgent organization that was established in 1975 in Kabul to combat Soviet communism. The organization has strong Pashtun kinship roots, which it shares with the Haqqani. It is also adversarial to the Afghan Taliban and has frequently engaged them on the battlefield. Defeats by the stronger Taliban has seen Hezb-e-Islami draw closer to the incumbent government in recent years. SOURCES: Roy Oliver, 2007. *The Columbia World Dictionary of Islamism.* New York: Columbia University Press; Borhan Osman, 2013. "Adding the Ballot to the Bullet? Hezb-e Islami in Transition". *Afghanistan Analysts Network*, 6 May. www. afghanistan-analysts.org / adding-the-ballot-to-the-bullet-hezb-e-islami-in-transition.

8 Roggio, for instance, observed that under Siraj there have been "kidnappings, assassinations, beheadings of women, indiscriminate killing, and suicide bombers – Siraj is the one dictating the new parameters of brutality associated with Taliban senior leadership". While contemporary Taliban used terror and repressive methods to "win" hearts and minds, Siraj seems have little interest in the results of his fighters' crimes. SOURCE: Bill Roggio, 2007. "Targeting Taliban Commander Siraj Haqqani". *Long War Journal.* Accessed 16 July 2016. www.longwarjournal.org/archives/2007/10/targeting_taliban_co.php.

9 From inception, each insurgent organization must develop various processes, capabilities, and the raw inputs needed to make and sustain them. Likewise, when extending across new borders, organizations also need to develop newly localized systematics to challenge incumbents. This is important because as McCormak and Giordano found, in the formative stages organizations are inferior to the incumbents they are fighting across many vital levels. Primarily these are across resources, materials, weapons and equipment, political narratives, legitimacy, popular support, allies, partners, patrons, and affiliates. Insurgencies therefore need to be efficient at maximizing initial gains and exploiting opportunities. The efficiency of an organization's ability to translate resources into political advancement is, therefore, a measure of resilience. SOURCES: Gordon McCormak and Frank Giordano, 2007. "Things Come Together: Symbolic Violence and Guerrilla Mobilisation". *Third World Quarterly* 28 (2): 295–320.

10 Lanham writes that Mullah Omar, the Taliban leader, is from the Hotaki clan of the Ghilzai super-tribe, which is the largest Pashtun group in Afghanistan. The Taliban itself is an umbrella organization of smaller networks, of which the Haqqani Network is a significant force. SOURCE: Shehzad Qazi, 2011. *The Neo-Taliban, Counterinsurgency & the American Endgame in Afghanistan.* Washington, D.C.: Institute for Social Policy and Understanding.

11 The remaining two Shura are the Gerdi Jangal (Regional Military) Shura, based at and controlling Taliban operations in Helmand and Minroz provinces, and the Peshawar Shura, which broke away from the Quetta Shura in 2009 and is complemented by newer jihadists who joined the cause post-2001. The Peshawar Shura operates across central, eastern, and northern Afghanistan. The Peshawar Shura has a focus on Nuristan and the Taliban shadow government there, aligned with al-Qaeda and the Islamic Movement of Uzbekistan in northern Afghanistan. SOURCE: Bill Roggio, 2012. "ISAF captures Taliban liaison to Peshawar Shura". *Long War Journal.* Accessed 19 July 2016. www.longwarjournal.org/archives /2012/05/isaf-captures _talibal.php.

12 In October 2014 Anas Haqqani, younger brother of Siraj, was captured by U.S. Intelligence in Qatar at Bahrain airport. Anas was visiting recently released Guantanamo Bay detainees and was returning home. The U.S. handed him over to Afghan authorities, who sentenced him to death. The Taliban vowed harsh reprisals if executed, claiming that Anas was not a member of the Haqqani but rather just an ordinary student with no authority or involvement in militancy despite being a son of Jalaluddin. SOURCE: Zee News, "Afghan court sentences senior Taliban leader Anas Haqqani to death". *Zee News*. Accessed 1 April 2017. http://zeenews.india. com/news/news/asia/afghan-court-sentences-senior-taliban-leader-anas-haqqani-to-death_ 1923601.html.

13 See: United Nations. 2012. "Security Council Committee established pursuant to resolution 1988 (2011): Fazl Rabi". *United Nations*. Accessed 2 May 2017 www.un. org/sc/committees/1988/NSTI15712E.shtml.

14 Gordon states that a hallmark of the Haqqani Network's resiliency and brilliance is its financing: "Unlike the Taliban, the Haqqani Network have a lasting and significant source of income to fund the jihad and maintain its control over the area." Khalil al-Rahman Haqqani was born 1 January 1966*. Other sources place his birth year between 1958 and 1964.

  *It is common for Muslims and Arabs to have a listed DOB as 1 January as this is an indexing schema in Western Intelligence holdings when exact day and month of birth is unknown. SOURCE: Ryan Gordon, 2015. "Zarb-e-Azb: The Obama Administration's Response to the Haqqani Network and the Relationship with Pakistan". *Inquiries Journal* 7 (2): 1–3.

15 The Haji Khalil Construction Company is located in Wazir Akbar Khan, Road Number 10, in front of the National Bank, District 10, Kabul, Afghanistan. In 2011, it won a U.S.$15 million contract for the construction of a road between Khost and Gardez from the U.S. Agency for International Development, which was only partially built. Therefore, significant volumes of U.S. and international money have flowed directly back into the insurgency. SOURCE: Jessica Donati and Mirwais Harroni, 2012. "Chinese halt at flagship mine imperils Afghan future". Accessed 27 September 2012. https://uk.reuters.com/ article/uk-afghanistan-aynak/exclusive-chinese-halt-at-flagship-mine-imperils-afghan-future-idUKBRE88Q0X 20120927.

16 The Haqqani Network also has businesses in Pakistan and in the UAE. There are also connections with the Iranian Navy and Revolutionary Guards Corps that facilitate drug smuggling, safe havens, and the movement of fighters, supplies, weapons, and finances to the Taliban. SOURCE: *The Guardian*, 2010. "US embassy cables: Afghan Taliban and the Haqqani Network using United Arab Emirates as funding base". *The Guardian*. Accessed 15 January 2017. www.theguardian.com/world/us-embassy-cables-documents/242756.

17 The Palestinian scholar-activist Abdullah Azzam was perhaps the most successful and prolific international recruiter for the Afghan jihad. Volunteers were housed and trained by Abu Sayyaf and Hekmatyar. However, the quality of fighters he recruited was extremely poor. This led to a split between Azzam and bin Laden. al-Qaida then turned to the Haqqani camps in Paktia that became the staging area for the international mobilization of foreign and Arab fighters. Azzam was also responsible for the fatwa that stated supporting jihad in Afghanistan was an individual duty and that all able-bodied Muslims were duty-bound to participate. SOURCE: Rassler, *Fountainhead of Jihad: The Haqqani Nexus*.

18 UN-reported suicide bomber training is run by a mix of Arabs, Pakistanis, and even Chechens and Saudis that manipulates children, typically 13 to 15 years of age. The Pakistani ISI also plays a direct role in the training. According to the Afghan Intelligence Directorate, the ISI is known to play a central role in the provision of training and equipment to Haqqani Network suicide bombers. SOURCE: UNAMA, 2007.

Suicide Attacks in Afghanistan (2001–2007). New York: United Nations Assistance Mission to Afghanistan.

19 The Afghan Taliban differs from the Pakistani Taliban in political objectives and beliefs. Once both a part of the singular Afghan Taliban, a split emerged post-2002 when Pakistani forces under U.S. pressure entered the tribal areas to hunt for "militants". The Pakistani Taliban was originally led by Baitullah Mehsud until his death in 2009 resulting from a U.S. missile strike, and then by Hakimullah Mehsud until his death in 2013. Numbering some 35,000 members, its espoused goals are a jihad against Pakistan, strict Sharia law, and fighting and expelling NATO forces. SOURCE: Zachary Laub, 2013. "Pakistan's New Generation of Terrorists". *Council on Foreign Relations*. Accessed 5 May 2019. www.cfr.org/backgrounder/pakistans-new-generation-terrorists.

20 Rashid asserts that participating in combat operations with the Haqqani family was a significant goal of many organizations. Being invited by the Haqqani Network to fight with it would not only deepen ties as it did for al-Qaida but also meant that this form of tacit acceptance would come with a provision of sanctuary in Haqqani territory. SOURCE: Ahmed Rashid, 2008. *Descent into Chaos: How the War Against Islamic Extremism Is Being Lost in Pakistan, Afghanistan and Central Asia.* London: Allen Lane.

21 In 2008, the Pakistan Army sought out the Haqqani Network to broker a deal with its affiliate Gul Bahadar for freedom of operations in North Waziristan that brought a measure of peace to that region. SOURCE: Arif Jamal, 2010. "Floods Wash Out Counter-Terrorist Operations in North Waziristan". *Terrorism Monitor* 8 (34): 5–6.

22 The Kurram Agency like the Panjshir Valley has strategic importance to the Afghan Mujahedeen and was a primary base during the anti-Soviet war in the 1980s. Key routes from Pakistan to Kabul also pass through there. SOURCES: Lester Grau, 2002. *The Soviet-Afghan War: How a Superpower Fought and Lost.* Westbrooke: University Press of Kansas; Jeffry Dressler, 2011. "Haqqani Network Influence in Kurram and Its Implications for Afghanistan". *CTC Sentinel* 4 (3): 11–15.

23 The base commander was Maulana Bakhta Jan from Khost, a close confidant of Siraj Haqqani, who took part in the 2006 peace talks in Waziristan and that also extended Haqqani influence across Pakistan and Afghanistan. Bakhta Jan also oversaw political, ideological, and spiritual indoctrination in the Secretariat that includes significant weapons depots, guesthouses, and learning centres. SOURCE: Imtiaz Gul, 2010. *The al-Qaeda Connection.* New York: Penguin Global.

24 Siraj attended and graduated from the Dar-ul-Uloom madrassa and is considered by some to be more devout than his father. SOURCE: Anand Gopal *et al.*, 2010. "Inside the Haqqani Network". *Foreign Policy.* 3 July. Accessed 17 March 2017. http://foreignpolicy.com/2010/06/03/inside-the-haqqani-network/.

25 The Dar-ul-Uloom madrassa was a large complex near Miram Shah founded by Jalaluddin and was, until its destruction by U.S. drone strikes, the flagship madrassa in the Haqqani madrassa system teaching and indoctrinating numerous fighters and supporters. Maulana Sadiq Noor of the Daur tribe, a senior Taliban and Haqqani Network commander, was the former director of the Dar-ul-Uloom madrassa and others. When it was destroyed Sadiq and the Haqqanis lost many family members. Sadiq was the deputy to Hafiz Gul Bahadur of the Mada Khel clan of the Uthmanzai Wazir; however, his closeness to the Haqqanis meant that he came under its operational control. This bond was formed through Haqqani madrassas. SOURCES: Shadid Shamim, 2008. "U.S. Drones Bomb Madrassa in NW". *Pakistan News Daily.* Accessed 15 March 2017. www.nation.com.pk/pakistan-news-newspaper-daily-englishonline/Politics/09-Sep-2008/US-drones-bomb-madrassa-in-NW 94; Anand Gopal, 2013. "The Taliban in North Waziristan". In *Talibanistan*, eds. Peter Bergen and Katherine Tiedemann. Oxford: Oxford University Press.

26 Saudi Arabian money was a significant source of funding for many madrassas, initially in Pakistan and then Afghanistan to spread Saudi Wahhabism. Many Pakistani madrassas were run with direct oversight by the ISI, which had grown weary of the Afghan Mujahedeen leader Gulbuddin Hekmatyar and the Hizb-i-Islami (HIG, instead favouring the Taliban). SOURCE: Thomas Johnson and Chris Mason, 2007. "Understanding the Taliban in Afghanistan". *Journal of World Affairs* Winter (1): 71–89.

27 There are several other prominent Haqqani-linked madrassas, including: the Khalifa Islam Madrassa; the Abu Shoain Madrassa; the Ziul Aloom Madrassa in Datta Khel; the Dergey Manday Madrassa; the Gulsha Madrassa; the Anwarul Uloom Islamia Seminary in Mir AN; and the Darul Uloom Faredia Gulshan-Illum Madrassa destroyed in 2006. The Manba-ul-Ulum madrassa was a complex that included a Mosque and was built by Jalaluddin Haqqani in the 1980s. SOURCE: Shaiq Hussain, 2008. "U.S. Missiles Said to Kill 20 in Pakistan Near Afghan Border". Accessed 15 April 2017. www.washingtonpost.com/wp-dyn/content/article/2008/09/08/AR2008090800263html.

28 Handel argued that strategically, intelligence "in a prolonged war can considerably reduce the uncertainty of the final result". As such, intelligence has a critical, central place in insurgent organizational strength and continued resilience. SOURCE: Michael Handel, 2008. "Clausewitz in the Age of Technology". *Journal of Strategic Studies* 9 (2–3): 53–94.

29 Padcha Khan Zadran has fought on multiple fronts including against the Tani tribe, a rival tribe to the Zadran in Khost Province of which Abdel Hakim Taniwal was appointed governor by the Karzai Government in 2001. The Karzai Government hoped to undermine the Haqqani powerbase and cement their own. SOURCE: Ilene Prusher *et al.*, 2002. "Afghan Power Brokers". *Christian Science Monitor* 6 (1):1–18.

30 Far from actually being anti-al-Qaeda or anti-Taliban, Katzman references speculation that Padcha Khan helped Osama bin Laden escape Tora Bora in March 2002. SOURCE: Kenneth Katzman, 2015. *Afghanistan: Politics, Elections, and Government Performance.* Washington, D.C.: Congressional Research Service.

31 Operation Cyclone was the code name for the CIA actions to supply money, weapons and intelligence and other material support to the anti-Soviet Mujahedeen during the 1980s Cold War with Russia. At the time it was the longest covert operation the CIA had conducted. SOURCE: Andrew Hammond, 2015. "Through a Glass, Darkly: The CIA and Oral History". *The Journal of the Historical Association* 100 (340): 311–326.

32 This was the principal "secretariat" base located only 1 km from the Dande Darpa Khel Pakistani army base.

33 Kinetic external pressures require significant intelligence operations to identify and track targets as well as to filter misinformation and deception efforts. This is more so than when targeting larger fighting forces because targeting organizational cores requires time-sensitive theta-based intelligence. Haqqani Network insurgent targets were highly mobile and could blend with local populations, making them hard to track and attack. SOURCE: Andrew Henshaw, 2015. "Deploying Strategic Counterintelligence into the Counter-terrorism Space". *TRAC Intelligence Analysis* 2014 (1).

34 The Disposition Matrix is an amalgamation of several actual databases including classified U.S. military programs, CIA operational databases, and Joint Operations Centre missions. It also spans multiple countries including Afghanistan, Iraq, Iran, Syria, Yemen, Somalia, and others. The DM was created by the CIA to consolidate overlapping kill lists and streamline intelligence sharing. SOURCE: Greg Miller, 2012. "Plan for hunting terrorists signals U.S. intends to keep adding names to kill lists". *Washington Post.* 23 October. Accessed 21 May 2017. www.washington post.com /world / national-security/plan-for-hunting-terrorists-signals-us-intends-to-eep-adding-names-to-kill-lists/2012/10/23/4789b2ae-18b3-lle2-a55c-39408fbe6a4b_story.html.

35 As a senior commander and Haqqani family member, Badruddin sat on the Miran Shah Shura council as well as being an Haqqani Network media officer. SOURCE: Bill Roggio, 2013. "U.S. drones target Haqqani Network in North Waziristan strike". *Longwar Journal.* 29 September. Accessed 21 August 2017. www.longwarjournal. org/archives/2013/09/us_drones_target_haq.php.

36 Chinese authorities believe that Yakuf was hiding in the Haqqani-controlled frontier lands while planning further attacks in China. The ETIM desire an independent homeland to be called East Turkistan. SOURCE: The Bureau of Investigative Journalism, 2012. *Naming the Dead: Emeti Yakuf.* Accessed 1 May 2018. https://v1. thebureauinvestigates.com/namingthedead/people /nd513/?lang=en.

37 Data was drawn from: The Bureau of Investigative Journalism. 2018. *Drone Strikes in Afghanistan.* 5 January. Accessed 15 January 2018. www.thebureauinvestigates. com/projects/drone-war/afghanistan.

38 Data was drawn from: South Asia Terrorism Portal (SATP). 2011. "US–Pakistan: Shadow Wars in North Waziristan – Analysis". *Eurasia News.* Accessed 01 May 2017. www.eurasiareview.com/24062011-us-pakistan-shadow-wars-in-north-waziristan-analysis/.

39 One exception to the rule was Haji Mali Khan, one of the Haqqani Network's most experienced and capable battlefield commanders, and brother-in-law to Jalaluddin by his sister. He is one of the few Haqqani commanders removed from the battlefield through arrest. SOURCE: Michael Semple, 2011. "How the Haqqani Network is Expanding from Waziristan". *Foreign Affairs* 90 (5).

40 The assault occurred on May 28 and was intended to capture or kill Sangeen Zadran but he escaped. Twenty-nine Haqqani fighters were killed in the action, of which six were failed suicide bombers. SOURCE: Bill Roggio, 2009. "Afghan and U.S. forces destroy Haqqani Network training camp in Khost". *Long War Journal.* Accessed 14 July 2015. www.longwarjournal.org/archives/2009/08/afghan_and_us_forces_1.php.

41 The Haqqani Network has been fighting for its Nang Pashtun homeland since 1973, a significantly large area that encompasses Paktia, Paktika, and Khost, as well as areas of the Ghazni and Logar provinces. SOURCE: Scott Romaniuk and Stewart Webb, 2015. "The Haqqani Network Threat: Keeping Insurgency in the Family". In *Insurgency and Counterinsurgency in Modern War*, eds. Scott Romaniuk and Stewart Webb. Boca Raton, London, New York: CRC Press, 175–190.

42 In 2000, there were 158 NGOs. This rose to 701 in 2012 and slightly down to 617 in 2014. Paktia went from 14 in 2000 to 43 in 2014, Paktika from 7 in 2000 to 31 in 2014, and Logar from 17 in 2000 to 51 in 2014. SOURCE: Afghanistan Central Statistics Organization (ASCO), *Afghanistan Statistical Yearbook.* 2014–2015. Kandahar, National Statistics and Information Authority.

43 In 2001 it was estimated in that it would cost U.S.$20 billion to rebuild the country. SOURCE: Anthony Browne, 2014. "$20 Billion to start again". *The Guardian.* Accessed 22 July 2017. www.theguardian.com/world/2001/nov/18/afghanistan.

44 The TLO was established in 2003 by the Swiss-Peace pilot project with support from the Heinrich Böll Stiftung Foundation. It was set up with strong community participation from local elders who wanted to build peace and reconstruction processes. SOURCE: Swiss Peace, *Projects.* Accessed 15 April 2017. www.boell.de/en.

45 According to World Education and Reviews (WENR) there are some 350,000+ children enrolled in home-based schooling in 2016 with some 38 per cent being girls. SOURCE: WENR, 2016. "Education in Afghanistan". *World Education News and Reviews.* Accessed 9 August 2017. http://wenr.wes.org/2016/09/education-afghanistan.

46 Previous efforts in the 1990s to draw the then Taliban Government towards the West and away from supporting al-Qaeda and its founder Osama bin Laden were equally futile. SOURCE: Osama bin Laden, 2005. *Messages to the World: The Statements of Osama bin Laden.* Melbourne: Verso Publishing.

47 Paul (2005) asserts that tensions over Kashmir have contributed to the most intense and violent rivalry between India and Pakistan than nearly all others. Kashmir is equally important to both countries for strategic security and for religious and political symbolism. SOURCE: T.V. Paul, 2005. *The India-Pakistan Conflict: An Enduring Rivalry.* Cambridge: Cambridge University Press.

48 Pakistan also has made positive changes in Waziristan through Operation Zarb-i-Azb, which took a blanket targeting approach against militancy and terrorism irrespective of organization or affiliation, though what effect this had on the Haqqani Network is questionable. The operation had some success and destroyed several "militant" facilities. Civil projects included the completion of a 72 km dual carriageway highway between Miran Shah, Razmak, and Makeen and is part of the 705 km Central Trade Corridor. Also built was a 100-bed hospital with modern facilities at Sholam in South Waziristan providing aid, health care, training, and jobs to locals, but also support to insurgents, including Haqqani members. SOURCE: Mateen Haider, 2016. "Army Chief inaugurates development projects in South and North Waziristan". *Dawn News.* Accessed 5 May 2017. www.dawn.com/news/1264790.

49 It is almost ironic that the birthplace of the Taliban and the Haqqani Network is Baluchistan, they being trained, armed and supported by British Special Forces as part of a CIA programme, and it is Baluchistan now that continues to be critical in sustaining them again. SOURCE: Author interview with former British Special Air Service members who were deployed to Baluchistan as part of the anti-Soviet Mujahedeen training force. January to August 2017; May to September 2018.

50 The Haqqani Network also used covert training facilities in the Kurram and North Waziristan Agencies as well as in Quetta with accompanying madrassas for ideological indoctrination. These training bases were staffed by Haqqani and Pakistani military and ISI trainers and included a specialized and segregated suicide bomber training section. SOURCE: Anthony Lloyd, 2010. "Terror link alleged as Saudi Millions flow into Afghanistan war zone". *The Times.* Accessed 3 May 2017. www.thetimes.co.uk/ article/terror-link-alleged-as-saudi-millions-flow-into-afghanistan-war-zone-mznm5z 7tgnm.

51 There have been multiple attacks in the capital Kabul, most claimed by the Taliban but conducted with significant Haqqani Network planning and support, if not use of its suicide bombers. Some examples include the 12 March 2016 dual suicide attacks targeting former Afghan President Sibghatullah Mokaddedi; 25 April 2006 remote IED attacks on a coalition base on the Kabul-airport road; 21 May 2006 VBIED suicide attack on a U.S. military patrol in Kabul. Other high-profile attacks include the 17 January 2008 Kabul Serena Hotel attack and the 7 July 2008 attack on the Indian Embassy in Kabul by the Haqqani Network on direction from the ISI. SOURCES: Bill Roggio, 2008. "Haqqani Network behind Kabul Hotel Attack". *Long War Journal* 2008 (1); Gaurav Sawant, 2017. "Pakistan's ISI behind Kabul blast which killed 90: Afghanistan Govt. to India Today". *India Today.* Accessed 1 June 2017. www.indiatoday.in/world/story/pakistans-isi-behind-kabul-blast-which-killed-90-top-afghanistan-official-to-india-today-980407-2017-06-01.

52 More recently on 1 June 2017, it launched a devastating car bomb attack inside the fortified diplomatic area killing 90 people. SOURCE: Euan McKirdy *et al.,* 2017. "Kabul bombing: Anger as city buries dead after huge suicide blast". *CNN.* Accessed 1 June 2017. http://edition.cnn.com /2017/06/01/asia/kabul-bombing-diplomatic-quarter/index.html.

53 In urban areas the opposite holds. Maloney reported that the Haqqani Network's IED structure was comprised of individuals and small two-to-five man teams that "operated from built-up areas: towns and cities. Their sole function was to lay IEDs to target coalition vehicles and convoys". Maloney further found that urban cells in cities "employed suicide IED attacks or SVIEDs. They were also unique in that

vehicle-borne IEDs, or VBIEDs were also being manufactured somewhere in the cities". SOURCE: Sean Maloney, 2009. "Taliban Governance: Can Canada Compete"? *Policy Options* 6 (1): 63–68.

54 The Haqqani Network increased its attacks in Loya-Paktia in 2009 in line with increasing construction projects with 15 attacks against construction firms and their security. Indian firms and workers were particularly favoured as targets given Pakistan's adversarial relationship with it, reflected in the targeted selection of its proxy the Haqqani Network. The 1 June 2017 Kabul attack was a VBIED of 1,500 kilograms of explosives hidden inside a sewage tanker. SOURCES: Bashir Nadem and Sher Haider, 2008. "Over a Dozen Perish in Uruzgan & Ghazni Clashes". In *The Haqqani Network: From Pakistan to Afghanistan*, ed. Jeffry Dressler. Washington, D.C.: Institute for the Study of War; The Jerusalem Post. 2009. "10 Security Guards Killed in Afghan Bomb Blasts". *J-Post.* Accessed 19 April 2019. www.jpost.com/Breaking-News/10-security-guards-killed-in-Afghan-bomb-blasts.

55 The HiG is led by Gulbuddin Hekmatyar, who established the group in the 1980s. One of the originals, Hekmatyar was a friend and associate of Jalaluddin Haqqani and during the anti-Soviet war was supported by the CIA and the Pakistani ISI. SOURCE: Institute for the Study of War (ISW). 2017. "Hizb-i-Islami Gulbuddin (HiG)". *ISW.* Accessed 20 September 2018. www.understandingwar.org/hizb-i-islami-gulbuddin-hig.

56 The LeJ was a pinnacle driver of sectarian jihadist suicide terrorism in Pakistan. It has associations with al-Qaeda and the Afghan Taliban and has established operational capabilities there with the Haqqani. Its deep commitment to suicide terrorism resulted in LeJ being known as a primary purveyor of martyrdom operations. SOURCE: Michael McBride and Gary Richardson, 2012. "Stopping Suicide Attacks: Optimal Strategies and Unintended Consequences". *Journal of Defence and Peace Economics* 23 (5): 413–429.

57 Publicly released U.S. State Department cables indicate that the attack was actually planned and executed by the Haqqani Network on instructions, financing, and support from the Pakistani ISI. According to Fitsanakis, it was believed that the ISI and Haqqani facilitators met multiple times in the weeks leading up to the attack and that ISI officials provided U.S.$200,000 with a specific order to launch "the attack on Chapman [and] to enable a suicide mission by an unnamed Jordanian national". Others think it possible al-Qaeda had more control. SOURCE: Joseph Fitsanakis, 2016. "Were Pakistani spies behind 2009 attack that killed seven CIA employees?" *IntelNews.* Accessed 15 May 2019. https://intelnews.org/2016/04/19/01-1888/2016.

58 SOURCE: Mapping Militant Organizations. 2017. "Haqqani Network". *Center for International Security and Cooperation, Stanford University.* Accessed 12 December 2017. http://web.stanford.edU/group/mappingmilitants/cgi-bin/groups/view/363# attacks.

59 According to Zahid and Anwar, Khalil al-Rahman Haqqani is a designated terrorist and "major fundraiser for the Haqqani Network. He has reportedly engaged in weapons training and distribution by the Haqqani Network". SOURCE: Madeeha Anwar and Noor Zahid, 2017. "What is the Haqqani Network?" *Voa News: Extremist Watch.* Accessed 1 June 2017. www.voanews.com/extremism-watch/what-haqqani-network.

References

ABC. 2013. "Afghan businessman accused of channelling aid money to insurgency". *ABC News.* 22 October. Accessed 21 March 2017. www.abc.net.au/news/2013-10-22/an-afghanistan-funding-haqqa/5038854.

ACBAR [Agency Coordinating Body for Afghan Relief and Development]. 2020. "ACBAR Member List". 16 February 2020. Accessed 25 March 2020. www.acbar.org/page/8.jsp?title=ACBAR-Member-List

Ackerman, Spencer. 2010. "Drones Surge, Special Ops Strike in Petraeus Campaign Plan". *Wired.* 18 August. Accessed 7 June 2015. www.wired.com/2010/08/petraeus-campaign-plan/.

Adams, Julia. 2005. "France, England, and the Enigmatic Eighteenth Century". In *The Familial State: Ruling Familes and Merchant Capitalism in Early Modern Europe*, edited by Julia Adams, 164–196. Ithaca and London: Cornell University Press.

Afghanland. 2014. "Afghan Leaders Yearbook". 1 1. Accessed 15 November 2017. www.afghanland.com/history/leaders/leaders.html.

Afghanistan Central Statistics Organization (ASCO), *Afghanistan Statistical Yearbook 2014–2015.* Kandahar, National Statistics and Information Authority.

Ahmad, Imtiaz. 2017. "Pakistan says global terrorist tag on Syed Salahuddin 'unjustified'". 27 June. Accessed 27 June 2017. www.hindustantimes.com/world-news/pakistan-defends-syed-salahuddin-says-will-continue-to-back-kashmir-struggle/story-rSZOElJApHNQiQ1RkQnq HJ.html.

Akbar, Ali. 2015. "Jalaluddin Haqqani is dead, say Taliban sources". *DAWN.* 31 July. Accessed 16 March, 2017. www.dawn.com/news/1197598/jalaluddin-haqqani-is-dead-say-taliban-sources.

Amstutz, Bruce. 1986. *The great game: 1837–1944.* Washington, D.C.: National Defence University.

Anwar, Madeeha and Zahid, Noor. 2017. "What is the Haqqani Network?" *Voa News: Extremist Watch.* Accessed 1 June 2017. www.voanews.com/extremism-watch/what-haqqani-network.

AP. 2009. "7 Militants Killed in Taliban Attack on a Police Station in Southeast Afghanistan". *New York Times.* 25 July. Accessed 27 July 2015. www.nytimes.com/2009/07/26/world/asia/26Afghan.html?mtrref=www.google.com&gwh=5C9A0FCCE019408EF6237D5B01B91C2E&gwt=pay&assetType=REGIWALL.

Asifkhel, Syed Jamal. 2008. "Three Killed by Own Explosives". *Pajhwok Afghan News*, 2 August. 15.

BBC. 2011. "Haqqani Commander Killed in Pakistan Drone Strike". *BBC World News.* 13 October. Accessed 1 October, 2015. www.bbc.com/news/world-south-asia-15299871.

bin Laden, Osama. 2005. *Messages to the World: The Statements of Osama bin Laden.* Melbourne: Verso Publishing.

Bowden, Mark. 2013. "How the Predator drone Changed the Face of War". *Smithsonian Magazine.* 1 November. Accessed 5 January, 2016. www.smithsonianmag.com/history/how-the-predator-drone-changed-the-character-of-war-3794671/.

Brown, Vahid and Rassler, Don. 2013. "The Fountainhead: The Haqqani Network, The Taliban, and the Rise of Global Jihad". In *Fountainhead of Jihad: The Haqqani Nexus 1973–2012*, edited by Vahid Brown and Don Rassler, 47. New York: Oxford University Press.

Browne, Anthony. 2014. "$20 Billion to start again". *The Guardian.* Accessed 22 July 2017. www.theguardian.com/world/2001/nov/18/afghanistan.

Carney, John Col. and Schemmer, Benjamin. 2002. "Tungi Afghanistan". In *No Room For Error: The Covert Operations of America's Special Tactics Units from Iran to Afghanistan*, edited by John Col. Carney and Benjamin Schemmer, 1–19. New York: Random House.

Chisti, Ali. 2012. "The Afghan Taliban". *Firday Times* XXIII (50): 3–9.

Coll, Steve. 2006. "Ghost Wars". 3 October. Accessed 15 August 2017. www.pbs.org/wgbh/pages/frontline/taliban/militants/haqqani.html.

Crawford, Neta. 2016. *Update on the Human Costs of War for Afghanistan and Pakistan, 2001 to mid 2016*. Paper, Boston: Washington Institute of International & Public Affairs.

Crews, Robert and Tarzi, Amin. 2008. "Moderate Taliban?" In *The Taliban and the Crisis in Afghanistan*, edited by Robert Crews and Amin Tarzi, 238–273. Cambridge and London: Harvard University Press.

Derksen, Deedee. 2014. *Reintigrating Armed Groups in Afghanistan*. Peace Brief, Washington, D.C.: United States Institute of Peace.

Dinneen, Timothy SGT. 2007. "ANSF, Coalition forces focus on Haqqani network". 17 October. Accessed 1 September 2017. www.dvidshub.net/news/13116/ansf-coalition-forces-focus-haqqani-network.

Donati, Jessica and Harroni, Mirwais. 2012. "Chinese halt at flagship mine imperils Afghan future". *Reuters News Agency*. Accessed 27 September 2012. https://uk.reuters.com/article/uk-afghanistan-aynak/exclusive-chinese-halt-at-flagship-mine-imperils-afghan-future-idUKBRE88Q0X 20120927.

Dreazen, Yochi. 2015. "The Taliban's New Number 2 Is a 'Mix of Tony Soprano and Che Guevara'". *Foreign Policy*. 31 July. Accessed 17 September 2017. http://foreignpolicy.com/2015/07/31/afghanistan-taliban-war-terrorism-alqaeda-cia-mulla-homar-haqqani/.

Dressler, Jeffry. 2010. *Afghanistan Report No. 6 – The Haqqani Network: From Pakistan to Afghanistan*. Washington, D.C.: Institute for the Study of War.

Dressler, Jeffry. 2011. "Haqqani Network Influence in Kurram ands Its Implications for Afghanistan". *CTC Sentinel* 4 (3): 11–15.

Dressler, Jeffry. 2012. *Combating the Haqqani Terrorist Network*. Washington, D.C.: Institute for the Study of War.

D'Souza, Shanthie Mariet. 2009. "Securing India's Interests in Afghanistan". *The Hindu Times*. 22 October. Accessed 26 July 2015. www.thehindu.com/opinion/lead/Securing-Indiarsquos-interests-in-Afghanistan/article16888279.ece.

Ensley, Michael and Pearson, Allison. 2005. "An Exploratory Comparison of the Behavioral Dynamics of Top Management Teams in Family and Nonfamily New Ventures: Cohesion, Conflict, Potency, and Consensus". *Journal of Entrepreneurship Theory and Practice* 29 (3): 267–284.

ETP [The Express Tribune]. 2012. "Not allies: 8 dead as TTP, Haqqani Network clash in North Waziristan". *The Pakistan Tribune*. 19 April. Accessed 4 August 2015. https://tribune.com.pk/story/367215/not-allies-8-dead-as-ttp-haqqani-network-clash-in-north-waziristan/.

Fantz, A. 2011. "The Haqqani Network, a family and a terror group". *CNN*. 14 September. Accessed 15 November 2017. https://edition.cnn.com/2011/WORLD/asiapcf/09/14/who.is.haqqani/index.html.

Farmer, Ben. 2010. "Taliban leader's son killed by U.S. drone". *The Telegraph*. 19 February. Accessed 15 May 2015. www.telegraph.co.uk/news/worldnews/asia/afghanistan/7268756/Taliban-leaders-son-killed-by-US-drone.html.

Felbab-Brown, Vanda. 2017. *Afghanistan Affectations: How to Break Political-Criminal Alliances in Contexts of Transition*. Backgrounder, Tokyo: United Nations University Centre for Policy Research.

Fitsanakis, Joseph. 2016. "Were Pakistani spies behind 2009 attack that killed seven CIA employees?" *IntelNews*. Accessed 15 May 2019. https://intelnews.org/2016/04/19/01-1888/2016.

Freeman, Michael. 2010. Paper presented at the 51st Annual International Studies Association Convention meeting "Theory vs. Policy? Connecting Scholars and Practitioners",

New Orleans, 17 February 2010. *International Studies Association Convention.* Hilton Riverside Hotel, The Loews New Orleans Hotel: New Orleans. 1–34.

Gabbay, Shaul. 2014. "Networks, Social Capital, and Social Liability: The Case of Pakistani ISI, the Taliban, and the War Against Terror". *Social Networking* 3 (1): 220–229.

Gall, Carlotta. 2006. "Afghan Governor's Funeral Attacked". *New York Times.* 11 September. Accessed 11 July 2015. www.nytimes.com/2006/09/11/world/asia/11cnd-afghan.html?mtrref=www.google.com&gwh=59618632D3D4F887EE0D02770C6B3C DD&gwt=pay&assetType=REGIWALL.

Garamone, Jim and Mays, David. 2007. "Afghan, Coalition Forces Battle Taliban, Narcotics, Emphasize Training". *U.S. Army.* 19 October. Accessed 5 August 2018. www.army.mil/article/5663/afghan_coalition_forces_battle_taliban_narcotics_emphasize_training.

Gopal, Anand. 2013. "The Taliban in North Waziristan". In *Talibanistan*, edited by Peter Bergen and Katherine Tiedemann. Oxford, Oxford University Press.

Gopal, Anand, Mahsud, Mansur, and Fishman, Brian. 2010. "Inside the Haqqani Network". *Foreigne Policy.* 3 July. Accessed 17 March 2017. http://foreignpolicy.com/2010/06/03/inside-the-haqqani-network/.

Gordon, Ryan. 2015. "Zarb-e-Azb: The Obama Administration's Response to the Haqqani Network and the Relationship with Pakistan". *Inquiries Journal* 7 (2): 1–3.

Graham-Harrison, Emma. 2012. "Haqqani Network is considered most ruthless branch of Afghan insurgency". *The Guardian.* 7 September. Accessed 15 August 2017. www.theguardian.com/world/2012/sep/07/haqqani-network-blacklisted-terrorist-us.

Grau, Lester. 2002. *The Soviet-Afghan War: How a Superpower Fought and Lost.* Westbrooke: University Press of Kansas.

Gul, Imtiaz. 2010. *The al-Qaeda Connection.* New York: Penguin Global.

Haider, Mateen. 2016. "Army Chief inaugurates development projects in South and North Waziristan". Dawn News. Accessed 5 May 2017. www.dawn.com/news/1264790.

Hammond, Andrew. 2015. "Through a Glass, Darkly: The CIA and Oral History". *The Journal of the Historical Association* 100 (340): 311–326.

Handel, Michael. 2008. "Clausewitz in the Age of Technology". *Journal of Strategic Studies* 9 (2–3): 53–94.

Harrison, Selig. 2001. "CIA worked with Pakistan to create Taliban". 5 January. Accessed 26 June 2017. http://emperors-clothes.com/docs/pak.htm.

Henshaw, Andrew. 2015. "Deploying Strategic Counterintelligence into the Counter-terrorism Space". *TRAC Intelligence Analysis* 2014 (1).

Hussain, Shaiq. 2008. "U.S. Missiles Said to Kill 20 in Pakistan Near Afghan Border". *Washington Post.* Accessed 15 April 2017. www.washingtonpost.com/wp-dyn/content/article /2008/09/08/AR2008090800263.html.

ICG. 2003. *Disarmament and Reintegration in Afghanistan.* ICG Asia Report No. 65, Kabul/Brussels: International Crisis Group.

Iqbal, Anwar. 2015. "India wants to deny Pakistan strategic depth in Afghanistan: U.S. Report". *Dawn.* 4 November. Accessed 5 November 2015. www.dawn.com/news/1217416.

Institute for the Study of War. 2017. "Hizb-i-Islami Gulbuddin (HiG)". *ISW.* Accessed 20 September 2018. www.understandingwar.org/hizb-i-islami-gulbuddin-hig.

Jamal, Arif. 2010. "Floods Wash Out Counter-Terrorist Operations in North Waziristan". *Terrorism Monitor* 8 (34): 5–6.

Jenna, Jordan. 2014. "Attacking the Leader, Missing the Mark: Why Terrorist Groups Survive Decapitation Strikes". *International Security* 38 (4): 7–38.

Johnson, Kay. 2015. "Pakistani official says Haqqani militants weakened despite U.S. concern". *Reuters.* 31 August. Accessed 2 September 2015. www.reuters.com/article/us-pakistan-militants-idUSKCN0R018B20150831.

Johnson, Thomas. 2007. "On the Edge of the Big Muddy: The Taliban Resurgence in Afghanistan". *China and Eurasia Forum Quarterly* 5 (2): 93–129.

Johnson, Thomas and Mason, Chris. 2007. "Understanding the Taliban and Insurgency in Afghanistan". *Journal of World Affairs* Winter (1): 71–89.

Jones, Sidney. 2011. "Why the Haqqani Network is the Wrong Target: To Save Afghanistan, Deal With the Taliban". *Journal of Foreign Affairs* Winter (1): 1–10. www.foreignaffairs.com/articles/afghanistan/2011-11-06/why-haqqani-network-wrong-target.

Kakar, Mohammad. 1995. "The Soviet Invasion". In *Afghanistan: The Soviet Invasion and the Afghan Response, 1979–1982*, edited by Mohammad Kakar, 21–31. Berkeley CA: University of California Press.

Katzman, Kenneth. 2013. *Afghanistan: Post-Taliban Governance, Security, and U.S. Policy.* Washington, D.C.: Library of Congress Congressional Research Service.

Katzman, Kenneth. 2015. *Afghanistan: Politics, Elections, and Government Performance.* Washington, D.C.: Congressional Research Service.

Kaur, Jasmeet. 2017. "Working of Jemaah Islamiya: A Radical Trajectory from 2000–2009". *Journal of Arts, Humanities and Social Sciences* 5 (9B): 1210–1219.

Khalilzad, Zalamy. 1995. "Afghanistan in 1995: Civil war and a Mini-Great Game". *Asian Survey* 36 (2): 190–195.

Kitfield, James. 2016. *Twilight Warriors: The Soldiers, Spies, and Special Agents Who Are Revolutionizing the American Way of War.* New York: Basic Books.

Laub, Zachary. 2013. "Pakistan's New Generation of Terrorists". *Council on Foreign Relations.* Accessed 5 May 2019. www.cfr.org/backgrounder/pakistans-new-generation-terrorists.

Lloyd, Anthony. 2010. "Terror link alleged as Saudi Millions flow into Afghanistan war zone". *The Times.* Accessed 3 May 2017. www.thetimes.co.uk/article/terror-link-alleged-as-saudi-millions-flow-into-afghanistan-war-zone-mznm5z7tgnm.

Malejacq. 2016. "Warlords, Intervention, and State Consolidation: A Typology of Political Orders in Weak and Failed States". *Journal of Security Studies* 25 (1): 85–110.

Maley, William. 2012. "Afghanistan in 2011: Positioning for an Uncertain Future". *Asian Survey* 55 (1): 88–89.

Maley, William. 2009. "The Road to War". In *The Afghanistan Wars: Second Edition*, edited by William Maley, 1–31. New York: Palgrave Macmillan.

Maloney, Sean. 2009. "Taliban Governance: Can Canada Compete?" *Policy Options* 6: 1–11.

Mapping Militant Organizations. 2017. "Haqqani Network". Stanford University, Centre for International Security and Cooperation. Accessed 12 December 2017. http://web.stanford.edU/group/mappingmilitants/cgi-bin/groups/view/363# attacks.

Matinuddin, Kamal. 1999. *The Taliban Phenomenon Afghanistan 1994–1997.* Oxford: Oxford University Press.

Mazzetti, Mark, Shane, Scott, and Rubin, Alissa. 2001. "A brutal Afghan clan bedevils the U.S.". 25 September. Accessed 19 April 2017. www.bendbulletin.com/news/1607215-151/a-brutal-afghan-clan-bedevils-the-us.

Mazzetti, Mark, Shane, Scott, and Rubin, Alissa. 2011. "Brutal Haqqani Crime Clan Bedevils U.S. in Afghanistan". *New York Times.* 24 September. Accessed 30 June 2015. www.nytimes.com/2011/09/25/world/asia/brutal-haqqani-clan-bedevils-united-states-in-afghanistan.html?mtrref=www.google.com&gwh=428E985FD6FC43A5D83 7DCC907CB3439&gwt=pay&assetType=REGIWALL.

McBride, Michael and Richardson, Gary. 2012. "Stopping Suicide Attacks: Optimal Strategies and Unintended Consequences". *Journal of Defence and Peace Economics* 23 (5): 413–429.

McCormak, Gordon and Giordano, Frank. 2007. "Things Come Together: Symbolic Violence and Guerrilla Mobilisation". *Third World Quarterly* 28 (2): 295–320.

McKirdy, Euan, Popalzai, Ehsan, Van Heerden, Dominique, and Lila, Muhammad. 2017. "Kabul bombing: Anger as city buries dead after huge suicide blast". *CNN.* 1 June 2017. http://edition.cnn.com/2017/06/01/asia/kabul-bombing-diplomatic-uarter/index.html.

Miller, Greg. 2012. "Plan for hunting terrorists signals U.S. intends to keep adding names to kill lists". *Washington Post.* 23 October. Accessed 21 May 2017. www.washington post.com/world/national-security/plan-for-hunting-terrorists-signals-us-intends-to-keep-adding-names-to-kill-lists/2012/10/23/4789b2ae-18b3-11e2-a55c-39408fbe6a4b_story. html.

Mitsotakis, Spyridon. 2014. "Understanding the Haqqani-Taliban-Al Qaeda Relationship–in the Haqqanis' Own Words". *Breitbart.* 12 June. Accessed 18 September 2017. www.breitbart.com/national-security/2014/06/12/understanding-the-haqqani-taliban-al-qaeda-relationship-in-the-haqqanis-own-words/.

Mohanty, Tushar. 2011. "North Waziristan: Shadow Wars". *South Asia Intelligence Review.* 20 June. Accessed 15 April 2015. www.satp.org/satporgtp/sair/Archives/sair9/9_50.htm.

Mukhopadhyay, Dipali. 2009. *Warlords as Bureaucrats: The Afghan Experience.* Washington, D.C.: Carnegie Endowment for International Peace.

Nadem, Bashir and Haider, Sher. 2008. "Over a Dozen Perish in Uruzgan & Ghazni Clashes". In *The Haqqani Network: From Pakistan to Afghanistan*, edited by Jeffry Dressler. Washington, D.C.: Institute for the Study of War.

Nissenbaum, Dion. 2011. "India Wins Bid for 'Jewel' of Afghan Ore Deposits". *Wall Street Journal.* 30 November. Accessed 15 July 2015. www.wsj.com/articles/SB10001 424052970203802204577067303633783544.

Noorzoy, Siddieq. 2012. "Afghanistan's Children: The Tragic Victims of 30 Years of War". *The Middle East Institute.* 20 April. Accessed 15 August 2015. www.mei.edu/publications/afghanistans-children-tragic-victims-30-years-war.

Oliver, Roy. 2007. *The Columbia World Dictionary of Islamism.* New York: Columbia University Press.

Osman, Borhan. 2013. "Adding the Ballot to the Bullet? Hezb-e Islami in Transition". *Afghanistan Analyst Network.* 6 May. www.afghanistan-analysts.org/adding-the-ballot-to-the-bullet-hezb-e-islami-in-transition

Paoli, Letizia. 2003. "Mafia, State and Society". In *Mafia Brotherhoods*, edited by Letizia Paoli, 178–179. Oxford: Oxford University Press.

Partlow, Joshua. 2011. "Haqqani insurgent group proves resilient foe in Afghan war". *The Washington Post*, 29 May. www.washingtonpost.com/world/asia-pacific/haqqani-insurgent-group-proves-resilient-foe-in-afghan-war/2011/05/27/AG0wfKEH_story. html.

Pate, Tanvi. 2018. "Soft Power, Strategic Narratives, and State Identity: Re-Assessing India-Afghanistan Relations Post-2011". *India Review* 17 (3): 320–351.

Paul, T.V. 2005. *The India-Pakistan Conflict: An Enduring Rivalry.* Cambridge: Cambridge University Press.

Prusher, Ilene, Baldauf, Scott, and Girardet, Edward. 2002. "Afghan Power Brokers". *Christian Science Monitor* 6 (1):1–18.

Qazi, Shehzad. 2011. *The Neo-Taliban, Counterinsurgency & the American Endgame in Afghanistan.* Washington, D.C.: Institute for Social Policy and Understanding.

Rashid, Ahmed. 2000. "Kabul 1996: Commander of the Faithful". In *Taliban: The Power of Militant Islam in Afghanistan and Beyond,* edited by Ahmed Rashid. London and New York: I.B. Tauris and Co.

Rashid, Ahmed. 2008. *Descent into Chaos: How the War Against Islamic Extremism Is Being Lost in Pakistan, Afghanistan and Central Asia.* London: Allen Lane.

Rasmussen, Sune Enhel. 2016. "American University attack: at least 12 dead and 44 injured in Afghanistan". *The Guardian.* 24 August. Accessed 3 January 2017. www.theguardian.com/world/2016/aug/24/american-university-afghanistan-attacked-kabul.

Rassler, Don. 2013. *Fountainhead of Jihad: The Haqqani Nexus.* London: C. Hurts and Co.

Roggio, Bill. 2008. "Haqqani Network behind Kabul Hotel Attack". *Long War Journal* 2008 (1).

Roggio, Bill. 2009. "Afghan and U.S. forces destroy Haqqani Network training camp in Khost". *Long War Journal.* 6 August. Accessed 14 July 2015. www.longwarjournal.org/archives/2009/08/afghan_and_us_forces_1.php.

Roggio, Bill. 2011. "ISAF Beats Back Assault on Eastern Afghan Base". *Long War Journal.* 11 November. Accessed 22 July 2015. www.fdd.org/analysis/2011/11/09/isaf-beats-back-assault-on-eastern-afghan-base/.

Roggio, Bill. 2013. "U.S. drones target Haqqani Network in North Waziristan strike". *Long War Journal.* 29 September. Accessed 21 August 2017. www.longwarjournal.org/archives/2013/09/us_drones_target_haq.php.

Roggio, Bill. 2016. "Targeting Taliban Commander Siraj Haqqani". *Long War Journal.* 16 July. Accessed 5 September 2016. www.longwarjournal.org/archives/2007/10/targeting_taliban_co.php.

Rohde, David. 2009. "You Have Atomic Bombs, but We Have Suicide Bombers". *Post-Gazette.* 21 October. Accessed 2 March 2017. www.post-gazette.com/news/world/2009/10/20/You-Have-Atomic-Bombs-but-We-Have-Suicide-Bombers/stories/200910200192.

Romaniuk, Scott and Webb, Stewart. 2015. "The Haqqani Network Threat: Keeping Insurgency in the Family". In *Insurgency and Counterinsurgency in Modern War,* edited by Scott Romaniuk and Stewart Webb, 175–190. Boca Raton, London, New York: CRC Press.

Rubin, Barnett, Hamidzada, Humayun, and Stoddard, Abby. 2005. *Afghanistan 2005 and Beyond: Prospects for Improved Stability Reference Document.* The Hague: Netherlands Institute of International Relations 'Clingendael'.

Ruttig, Thomas. 2009a. "Loya Paktia's Insurgency". In *Decoding the Neo-Taliban,* edited by Thomas Ruttig, 64–65. New York: Columbia University Press.

Ruttig, Thomas. 2009b. "Loya Paktia's Insurgency: The Haqqani Network as an Autonomous Entity". In *Decoding the New Taliban. Insights from the Afghan Field,* edited by Antonio Giustozzi, 57. New York: Columbia University Press.

Sawant, Gaurav. 2017. "Pakistan's ISI behind Kabul blast which killed 90: Afghanistan Govt. to India Today". *India Today.* Accessed 1 June 2017. www.indiatoday.in/world/story/pakistans-isi-behind-kabul-blast-which-killed-90-top-afghanistan-official-to-india-today-980407-2017-06-01.

106 *Real world analysis*

Semple, Michael. 2011. "How the Haqqani Network is Expanding from Waziristan".
Foreign Affairs 90 (5).
Shamim, Shadid. 2008. "U.S. Drones Bomb Madrassa in NW". *Pakistan News Daily*.
Accessed 15 March 2017. www.nation.com.pk/pakistan-news-newspaper-daily-
englishonline/Politics/09-Sep-2008/US-drones-bomb-madrassa-in-NW 94.
Sennot, C.M. 2010. "Taxpayer money funneled to Taliban". *Global Post*. 30 September.
Accessed 23 July 2015. www.rawa.org/temp/runews/2010/09/30/taxpayer-money-
funneled-to-taliban.html.
Sethna, Razeshta. 2013. "The Haqqani network: talent for survival". *Dawn*. 2 December.
Accessed 17 April 2017. www.dawn.com/news/1059995.
Shaw, Ian. 2013. "Geopolitics". In *Predator Empire: The Geopolitics of U.S. Drone
Warfare*, edited by Ian Shaw, 536–559. Glasgow: Taylor & Francis Group.
Siddique, Abubakar. 2010. "U.S. Push To Blacklist Taliban Networks Could Reap Little
Reward". *Eurasianet*. 18 July. Accessed 26 October 2015. https://eurasianet.org/us-
push-to-blacklist-taliban-networks-could-reap-little-reward.
Singh, Prakarsh and Shemyakina, Olga. 2016. "Gender-Differential Effects of Terrorism
on Education: The Case of the 1981–1993 Punjab Insurgency". *Economics of Educa-
tion Review* 54 (C): 185–210.
Smith, Shane. 2014. "Afghanistan after the Occupation: Examining the Post-Soviet
Withdrawal and the Najibullah Regime It Left Behind, 1989–1992". *The Historian* 76
(2): 308–343.
South Asia Terrorism Portal (SATP). 2011. "U.S.–Pakistan: Shadow Wars in North
Waziristan – Analysis". *Eurasia News*. Accessed 01 May 2017. www.eurasiareview.
com/24062011-us-pakistan-shadow-wars-in-north-waziristan-analysis/.
Staniland, Paul. 2014. *Networks of Rebellion*. Ithaca: Cornell University Press.
Stout, David. 2017. "Meet the Haqqanis, former CIA assets". *Agence France Presse*. 18
October. Accessed 1 November 2018. http://62.75.195.47/News/World/2017/Oct-
18/423051-meet-the-haqqanis-former-cia-assets.ashx.
Swiss Peace. *Projects*. www.boell.de/en. Accessed 15 April 2017.
Taj, Farhat. 2009. "Target: terror secretariat". 4 April. Accessed 13 March 2017. https://
defence.pk/pdf/threads/target-terror-secretariat.24466/.
Takal, Ahmad and Siddique, Abubakar. 2015. "Dangerous Afghan Taliban Network Pre-
pares Return To Pakistani Sanctuary". *Gandhara*. 31 March. Accessed 28 August
2017. https://gandhara.rferl.org/a/pakistan-waziristan-haqqani-network/26930083.html.
The Bureau of Investigative Journalism. 2012. *Naming the Dead: Emeti Yakuf*. 24
August. Accessed 1 May 2018. https://v1.thebureauinvestigates.com/namingthedead/
people/nd513/?lang=en.
The Bureau of Investigative Journalism. 2018. *Drone Strikes in Afghanistan*. 5 January.
Accessed 15 January 2018. www.thebureauinvestigates.com/projects/drone-war/
afghanistan.
The Guardian. 2010. "US embassy cables: Afghan Taliban and the Haqqani Network
using United Arab Emirates as funding base". *The Guardian*. Accessed 15 January
2017. www.theguardian.com/world/us-embassy-cables-documents/242756.
The Jerusalem Post. 2009. "10 Security Guards Killed in Afghan Bomb Blasts". *Jerusa-
lem Post*. Accessed 19 April 2019. www.jpost.com/Breaking-News/10-security-
guards-killed-in-Afghan-bomb-blasts.
The Liaison Office. 2009. *Tribal Jurisdiction and Agreements: The Key to Sub-National
Governance in South-Eastern Afghanistan*. Policy Brief, Berlin: The Green Political
Foundation.

U.N. 2012. "Security Council Committee established pursuant to resolution 1988 (2011): Fazl Rabi". 6 January 2012. Accessed 2 May 2017 www.un.org/sc/committees/1988/NSTI15712E.shtml.

UNAMA. 2007. *Suicide Attacks in Afghanistan (2001–2007)*. New York: United Nations Assistance Mission to Afghanistan.

United States Government. 2008. "PTQ4530 Document 3". 12 June. Accessed 16 September 2017. https://nsarchive.gwu.edu/search/node/ptq4530.

UNSC. 2012. "Nasiruddin Haqqani". *United Nations Security Council*. 1 January. Accessed 16 August 2017. www.un.org/sc/suborg/en/sanctions/1988/materials/summaries/individual/nasiruddin-haqqani.

Urban, Mark. 2012. "Afghan spectacular bears hallmarks of Haqqani Network". *BBC*. 16 April. Accessed 15 July 2015. www.bbc.com/news/world-17731774.

Victor, Daniel. 2019. "Need a Refresher on the War in Afghanistan? Here are the Basics". *New York Times*. 28 January. Accessed 15 August 2019. www.nytimes.com/2018/12/21/world/asia/afghanistan-war-explainer.html.

Walsh, Declan and Scgmitt, Eric. 2012. "Militant Leader Believed Dead in Pakistan Drone Strike". *The New York Times*. 24 August. Accessed 5 October 2015. www.nytimes.com/2012/08/25/world/asia/us-drone-strikes-kill-18-in-pakistan.html?mtrref=www.google.com&gwh=459324F61AFE69D6AA9C8DE990E34706&gwt=pay&assetType=REGIWALL.

WENR. 2016. "Education in Afghanistan". *World Education News and Reviews*. Accessed 9 August 2017. http://wenr.wes.org/2016/09/education-afghanistan.

White, Bowen, Albers-Schoenberg, Alexandra, and Zeisberger, Claudia. 2017. "The Institutionalization of Family Firms". Wendel International Centre for Family Enterprise. Paris.

Wimpelmann, Torunn. 2015. "Nexuses of Knowledge and Power in Afghanistan: The Rise and Fall of the Informal Justice Assemblage". In *The Afghan Conundrum: Intervention, Statebuilding and Resistance*, edited by Jonathan Goodhand and Mark Sedra, 168–184. New York and London: Routledge.

Yobie, Benjamin. 2009. "The top 15 terrorist groups in Afghanistan & Pakistan". 1 October. Accessed 5 October 2017. http://blog.sfgate.com/ybenjamin/2009/10/01/the-top-15-terrorist-groups-in-afghanistan-pakistan/

Zee News, "Afghan court sentences senior Taliban leader Anas Haqqani to death". *Zee News*. Accessed 1 April 2017. http://zeenews.india.com/news/asia/afghan-court-sentences-senior-taliban-leader-anas-haqqani-to-death_1923601.html.

Zeisberger, Claudia and Schoenberg, Alexandra. 2017. *The Institutionalization of Family Firms – From Asia-Pacific to the Middle East*. Report, Fontainebleau: INSEAD.

4 Lashkar-e-Taiba

Lashkar-e-Taiba (LeT) rose to international infamy following the 2008 Mumbai attacks that killed 166 people. However, this was not its birth. LeT's history of major attacks against India can be traced back to the 5 January 1996 massacre of 16 Hindus at Barshalla, Doda (Baweja 2013). This chapter examines LeT as a meritocratic organization. As outlined in Chapter 1, this means it is an organization in which the leadership is unrelated by kinship, and the majority of appointments across the organization, including joining, are based on individual capability, accomplishment, and organizational "fit".[1] What makes LeT an informative case of a meritocratic organization is not its potency, which is significant, but how it has survived the unique yet significant external pressures used against it.

LeT is a constituent part of the Haqqani Network pair that was examined in the previous chapter, with which it shares many characteristics. Both are powerful insurgent actors; each operates from bases in Afghanistan and Pakistan, both trace their origins back to the Afghanistan anti-Soviet jihad, and both have strong legacy connections to Osama bin Laden, al-Qaeda, and the Afghan Taliban. Comparing LeT and the Haqqani Network allows for many important variables to be held relatively constant while singling out the relationship between kinship, meritocracy, and external pressures. Equally as important, LeT and the Haqqani Network have confronted similar external pressures in the forms of national and international counterinsurgency and counter-terrorism operations over the past 35 years. Consequently, LeT's meritocracy and the Haqqani Network's familial structure are two of the main differences between the two organizations, making them well suited for a comparison of the role of organizational structures and their resilience.

This chapter is divided into three main sections. The first section examines the LeT organizational structure. It discusses meritocratic foundations, leadership, command and control, organizational morphology, and the importance of LeT nexus affiliates. The second section examines the external pressures exerted against LeT and the Indian intelligence failures to realize the threat, or to take any pre-emptive actions to develop intelligence coverage to penetrate Pakistani-based insurgents leading up to, and in the wake of the 2008 Mumbai attacks. It begins with an examination of LeT strengths to gauge the effects of external pressures. This includes how it has been targeted and by whom, and how effective this has been. The third section reviews the data and discusses if LeT has successfully adapted to endogenous and exogenous shocks in response to external pressures. In particular, it looks at how the LeT meritocratic organizational structure has been a vehicle of adaptation, and how this may have influenced resilience by comparing it to LeT's latent resilience to pressure and damage sustained. Finally, the chapter concludes with a discussion of the results, which are somewhat mixed. For instance, LeT shows a strong organic resilience and its meritocratic organizational structure plays a part in that, but, its unequal relationship with the Pakistani State and Inter-Services Intelligence Directorate (ISI) is highly controlling. The ISI provides significant protection and support, but it comes at the cost of indebtedness to a powerful institution, meaning that LeT is not holistically self-resilient. Meritocracy, and in turn self-interest, are central to this.

Meritocratic foundations

Similarly to other organizations that grew out of the anti-Soviet war in Afghanistan, LeT initially enjoyed substantial support from the U.S., U.K. and Pakistan. In 1990, the U.S. ended its support, forcing LeT to develop a greater reliance upon Saudi donors and on Pakistan. In particular, Pakistani patronage gave LeT exogenously derived strength that was important to overall resilience, but it became a lynchpin and a critical point of failure. Over its history LeT has experimented with a number of organizational structures, but while it continues to change and evolve, some things remain constant. These include the organization's core political ideology and its meritocratic leadership, which was established at its inception.[2]

Lashkar-e-Taiba's origins are similar to those of other Afghan insurgent organizations like the Haqqani Network and the Taliban groups. After the 1989 Soviet withdrawal from Afghanistan, Pakistan guided LeT to seek a new enemy in India, and since then it has been an anti-Indian, pro-Kashmiri insurgent organization. Graff argues this is largely because "partition of the subcontinent was to prove a disaster in many ways, especially for the large Muslim population who could not or would not migrate eastwards or westwards to a nascent Pakistan" (2006, 9). The bulk of LeT insurgency operations take place in Jammu and Kashmir, but its most prominent attacks have been in the Indian heartlands including Mumbai, Hyderabad, New Delhi, Varanasi, Gujarat, and Kolkata (Fair 2009).

Lashkar-e-Taiba rose to international infamy in 2001 after the suicide attack on the Indian Parliament. This was followed by several more major attacks such as the October 2005 three-stage Delhi bombings, the July 2006 Mumbai commuter-train attacks that killed over 180, and the March 2007 Varanasi attack killing 21. However, the highly evolved Mumbai attacks in 2008 were the deadliest in Indian history, and the largest undertaken by LeT. Any of these operations should have resulted in significantly increased external pressures being exerted upon LeT, but they never materialized as hard-power responses. There are several reason for this including a lack of tangible political will in New Delhi, operational obstacles due to the U.S. presence in Pakistan, and notably, a catastrophic failure by India's principal intelligence service, the Research and Analysis Wing (RAW). These are discussed in the following sections.

The genesis of LeT meritocracy

Lashkar-e-Taiba's origins can be traced back to 1986 and an earlier organization named the Markaz Dawa-wal-Irshad (also referred to as MDI). Four men, all un-related by kinship, founded the MDI. Three were university professors from Pakistan: Hafiz Saeed, Abdul Rehman Makki, and Zafar Iqbal. The fourth was Sheikh Abdullah Azzam, a Palestinian who was a mentor to Osama bin Laden and had ties to the Muslim Brotherhood, recruited Arabs for training with the Haqqani Network, and was active in Maktab ul-Khidmat (MaK – Bureau of Services for Arab Jihadist).[3] Sheikh Abdullah Azzam was also the spiritual founder of the Palestinian resistance group Hamas. In its early days, MDI was primarily a charitable organization working in Afghanistan to help relieve the impact of the war on civilians.

Sheikh Azzam was a central figure in MDI and was a conduit of significant nexus connections to insurgent organizations in Afghanistan, meaning he was a bridge between multiple groups.[4] This provided MDI with an expanded network of resources. Markaz Dawa-wal-Irshad remained extremely active in Afghanistan until the 1989 Soviet withdrawal. With the Russians gone it searched for a new ideological enemy. Fair (2017) contends that due to ISI influence, LeT focused on India and its perceived oppression of Muslims in Jammu and Kashmir, which aligns with Graff's (2006) earlier assertions. The first LeT operations began in Kashmir in 1990 as the organization set about building an insurgent infrastructure in Pakistan.

These coincided with expanding Ahl-e-Hadith religious activities to cement connections between Afghanistan and Pakistan, providing powerful religious and ideological means of bonding people together. In 1993 the functions of militancy, proselytization, and education were divided between LeT and MDI.[5] The move to Lahore, Pakistan, provided important defence-in-depth, insulating LeT inside Pakistani sovereign territory against pressures from India and the U.S. that had no will at the time to operate covertly inside Pakistan. However, LeT remained susceptible to hard-power kinetic pressures outside of Pakistan in Afghanistan, and especially in Indian-controlled Jammu and Kashmir.

That susceptibility grew as it developed an increasing presence and, in turn, organic anchoring in those areas by deriving more of its inputs and processing locally. India began targeting LeT's local leadership with direct kinetic actions shortly thereafter. In January 2002 MDI was re-named Jamaat-ud-Dawa and continued the MDI mission. Jamaat-ud-Dawa became known widely by the moniker JuD. As of 2020, the LeT/JuD organization remains active in Pakistan, Jammu and Kashmir, India, Afghanistan and its tribal regions, Syria, Bangladesh, and Southeast Asia.

Meritocracy in LeT: leadership, command and control,
and positioning

LeT organizational bonds do not rely on kinship in the same way as with the Haqqani network, but rather on the pursuit of politico-ideological goals, which are discussed in this section. LeT recruitment is vocational and meritocratic rather than based on family, enabling LeT to recruit from all walks of Pakistan society. LeT apex leadership is comprised of the founders and longest-serving members. Under Amir Saeed, there are several top-tier commanders with subordinates under them in an apex structure. These men manage the most critical portfolios and functions of the organization. As of 2020, all are Specially Designated Global Terrorists by the U.S. State Department.[6]

Zafar Iqbal is a LeT co-founder and the deputy Amir, while Abdul Rehman Makki is Chief of the External Affairs Department, the most potent arm of LeT. Zaki-ur Lakhvi is a critical founder and the Supreme Commander Jammu and Kashmir. He was the first to lead Ahl-e-Hadith jihadists into Afghanistan to fight the Soviets years before Saeed and Iqbal even went there. Lakhvi's local knowledge and experience made him an ideal, merit-based leader in LeT. When Saeed and Iqbal arrived, they recruited Lakhvi and fused as the genesis of MDI/LeT.

This model of leadership with the core alumni leaders has worked well for the past 30 years and continues to do so. Publicly, however, the division of leadership and responsibility in LeT has not always been a clean one. Wilson (2008) reports that Zafar Iqbal, co-founder of the MDI and professor at the University of Engineering and Technology, came into conflict with Saeed. According to Sareen (2005), Saeed appointed Hafiz Abdul Rehman Makki, his brother-in-law, and MDI co-founder, to the position of head of the Department of External Affairs, held at the time by Iqbal.

This was a unique situation. While Hafiz Abdul Rehman Makki has standing as a co-founder, appointments in LeT are meritocratic, and because of LeT's merit-based structure any promotions based on kinship are strictly taboo. Hafiz Abdul Rehman Makki has a strong familial relationship with Saeed, being the son of Saeed's maternal uncle Maulana Hafiz Abdullah. Saeed also married Makki's sister, and Makki married the younger sister of one of Saeed's wives. His appointment to a role held at the time by Iqbal caused significant internal conflict because it was seen as a clear case of nepotism and Iqbal levelled this accusation at Saeed. So serious was the matter that he challenged for the leadership. For Saeed, making a familial appointment without making consultations seemed to be a clear case of building familial dominance over the command and control structure. Internal negotiations managed to calm the incident but saw Makki ultimately take the post.

Between senior leaders in the remaining functions of LeT there is little to no familial connection, reinforcing LeT's meritocratic basis. LeT senior leadership positions and responsibilities, shown in Figure 4.1, span intelligence, finance, divisional and regional commands, media and spokespeople, international operations, training, and social services.

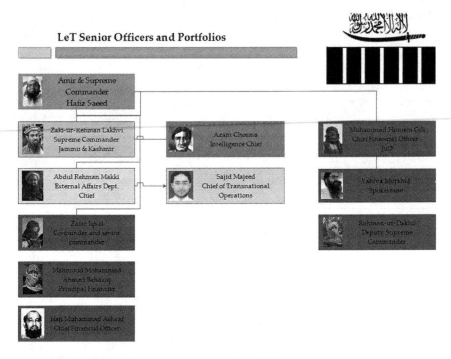

Figure 4.1 Lashkar-e-Taiba senior officers and portfolios.

Further demonstrating LeT meritocracy, Jamal (2002) reports that students who excelled at LeT-run Ad-Da'Wah schools were expected to be the new leaders, holding important positions in LeT and replacing the JuD leadership in the future. As students came from all castes and were promoted on merit alone, nepotism before the Makki incident was unheard of.[7]

Of the senior officers, Mahmoud Mohammad Ahmed Bahaziq was an early inclusion in MDI who was promoted into the LeT senior officer corps. Jaffrelot (2017) maintains Bahaziq was already a well-connected jihadist financier in the early 1980s with strong connections to Saudi Arabia and the Gulf States. Although MDI received considerable funding from the CIA during Operation Cyclone, as discussed in the previous chapter, new Saudi money was an essential source of support for LeT and many others like al-Qaeda and the Haqqani network. For LeT, Bahaziq was the conduit. Jaffrelot and Louer (2017, 238) suggest he was appointed leader of LeT in Saudi Arabia and coordinator of LeT fund-raising activities with Saudi NGOs and businessmen as a result of his effectiveness.

Meritocracy repeats

Muhammad Hussein Gill was an LeT alumnus from the 1990s and a senior LeT accountant. Due to his financial acumen, in 2014 he was appointed as JuD's Chief

Financial Officer (Roul 2015).[8] This mirrors the promotion of another vital financier, that of Haji Muhammad Ashraf. Subrahmanian *et al.* (2008) claim that Ashraf was the LeT chief financier from at least 2003, with suggestions that he had an association with LeT for some time before this. The UN Security Council listed Ashraf on 9 March 2009 as a Specially Designated Global Terrorist.[9] Besides financing, two further positions of Spokesman and Intelligence Chief have critical roles in LeT. LeT media releases are not coordinated through a single point but through various people. Amir Saeed for instance has made numerous public announcements. Officially though, Abdullah Muntazir (a.k.a. Abdullah Khan) is the appointed "Spokesman for International Media" and JuD website editor.[10] Other LeT spokesmen include Abdul Wahid, a senior commander, and Yahya Mujahid.

Abdul Wahid was a LeT commander in Kashmir and the head of the Majlis-e-Shura, the LeT command council. Wahid's title of Maulana marks him as a scholar and religious authority, which is probably the reason for his appointment, coupled with his leadership experience in Jammu and Kashmir. Zahab (2007) contends that the Majlis-e-Shura was formed in December 2001 under the JuD banner to divert resources away from LeT in expectation of external pressures from India after the 2001 attack on the Indian Parliament.

Maulana Abdul Wahid's appointment as LeT Commander in Jammu and Kashmir was also a meritocratic promotion. According to Bukhari, this was intended to give LeT legitimacy as an anti-Indian insurgent actor and to add a "pure Kashmir color" (2017, 1). Wahid is a Kashmiri by birth and was a respected Islamic scholar. This combination made him an ideal candidate and in December 2001 he was promoted to Amir of Jammu and Kashmir insurgency operations. Wahid had no kinship relations to Saeed or Zaki-ur-Rehman Lakhvi; rather, it was his credentials that reinforced the Kashmiri connection. He was replaced in 2017 by Zeenat-ul-Islam to run Kashmir military operations (Chaubey 2017).[11]

Yahya Mujahid is another critical and meritocratically appointed leader. He heads the media department of JuD and has been a LeT spokesman for many years. His business card lists his position as "Secretary of Information" (Balasubramaniyan and Raghavan 2017). Yahiya is well known for his statements following the December 2001 LeT attack on the Indian Parliament, and the 2008 Mumbai attacks in which he praised the fighters as holy warriors. Collectively this group represents the Tier 1 leadership of LeT. The remaining senior officers are regional and area commanders, who all attained their positions through meritocratic appointment and promotion, having come through the ranks to seniority. Tier 2 senior officers are deputy and divisional commanders and others with senior leadership roles (Figure 4.2). The meritocracy apparent in each tier of the senior officer corps continues to replicate at lower levels, supporting meritocracy right across the LeT organization.

Meritocracy and organizational culture

In meritocracies, organizational culture is akin to that of family identity in familial organizations as it too sets the course and purpose. Driving the organizational culture

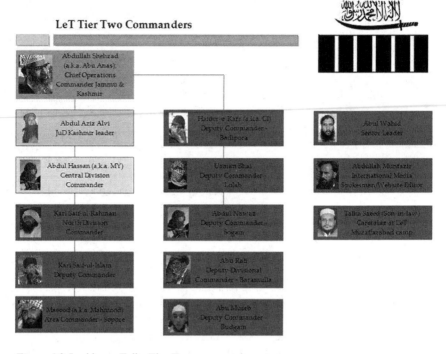

Figure 4.2 Lashkar-e-Taiba Tier-Two commanders.

and modelling individual leadership on it are essential traits for leaders in merito-cratic organizations, particularly in the profession of arms. Senior officers are responsible for implementing and pursuing executive goals. In LeT, Ali and Shehzad report these to be the defence of Islam from foreign influences and a "desire for political power – with the use of Islamic slogans and narratives – that lies at the heart of their strategic objectives" (2009, 3). This is most visibly reflected in "Hum Kyun Jihad Kar Rahe Hain" (Why We Are Waging Jihad), the manifesto that was authored by Amir Saeed in 1998.[12] The manifesto sets out LeT's ideological course through its organizational culture, which directly influences its insurgent operations employed to pursue its strategic goals. The continuous leadership of Saeed has posi-tively affected LeT's organizational culture and delivered stability. This is important because, as Wilson argues, when an organization's culture is strong "people did not always have to be told what to do; they knew what to do, and what is more important, wanted to do it well" (2016, 18).

Bourdieu (1989) likewise maintains that formal organizational culture is a fundamental element of social and socio-economic capital. Saeed drew exten-sively from LeT's long-standing involvement in Afghanistan and the anti-Soviet jihad when drafting Hum Kyun Jihad Kar Rahe Hain. The manifesto represents a written narrative of policy alignment with the Pakistani State and also melds

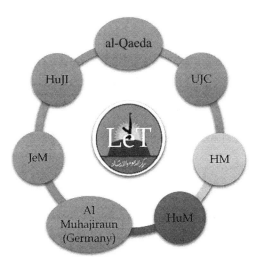

Figure 4.3 Lashkar-e-Taiba affiliate nexus.

LeT to the nexus of al-Qaeda, the Haqqani Network, and the Afghan Taliban. It is evident in the manifesto that meritocracy is central to the organizational structure of LeT, and while family and a sense of community is important, they are a secondary concern. According to Brown and Rassler (2012), LeT is careful not to recruit from the Ahl-e-Hadith Islamic tradition from which is descends, even though many of its members retain family adherents thereto.

Fair (2014) considers that this is because LeT has drifted from its theological roots, and therefore is cautious not to involve family members that may unduly influence it. Additionally, the Ahl-e-Hadith community is only around 180 million in size, less than a tenth of the Pakistani population. LeT therefore finds greater diversity in the Barelvis and Deobandi communities, and particularly those individuals who are attracted to insurgency, violence, and the extensive militant and cultural indoctrination so provided. This also creates organizational overlap through which LeT shares some operational support and training, as well as joint combat operations with the Haqqani Network, al-Qaeda, and Afghan Taliban. This nexus also includes Jaish-e-Muhammed (JeM), Hizbul Mujahedeen (HuM), the United Jihad Council (UJC), Harkat-ul-Jihadi-Islami (HuJI) and Harkat-ul-Mujahedeen (HM) (Figure 4.3). D'Souza and Routray (2016) state such affiliations were facilitated by LeT senior leaders and as a result of meritocratic connections.[13]

At LeT's core, the recruitment of middle management and base-level fighters is a little different. According to Khan (2010), LeT has little issue with recruiting members from across Pakistan, and many are drawn from the North West Frontier and Punjab. These are also the Pakistan Army's primary recruiting areas (Rotella 2013).[14] These regions offer a broad multi-demographic pool to recruit from. Joshua (2016) cites that almost 90 per cent of LeT recruits come from Punjab, also where the army has its highest recruitment levels, as well as from the border provinces with India. Rassler *et al.* argue that "there is considerable overlap among the districts that produce LeT militants and those that produce Pakistan army officers, a dynamic that raises a number of questions about potentially overlapping social networks between the army and LeT" (2013, 11).

Charles Faddis, a veteran CIA counterterrorism officer, has stated that LeT "had the ability to make connections with military officers, well-educated people abroad, and scientists" (Rotella 2013). LeT is known as both an active recruiter and as a sought-after employer. This dual approach is achieved by actively screening potential recruits via its madrassas, schools, and religious institutions, and secondly by attracting recruits to it through is social work, media, and propaganda units. Those recruits that align with LeT meritocratic organizational culture make up the bulk of its command and fighting corps. Likewise, LeT's meritocracy is not nationalist but extends to other nationalities as it accepts external recruitment from Arabs, Persians, Uzbeks, and other Muslim denominations across Iraq, Afghanistan, Europe, Central Asia, Africa, Turkey, Libya, Bahrain, and the Sudan. LeT also has a long history of recruiting Westerners from the U.S., the U.K., and Australia. Figure 4.4 shows LeT fighter recruitment by province in Pakistan.

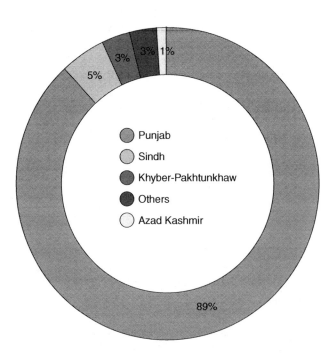

Figure 4.4 Lashkar-e-Taiba recruitment by province.

Equally, LeT enjoys the benefits of being able to recruit through organizations it has spawned. The Khairun Naas, or People's Welfare organization, led by Zaki-ur-Rehman Lakhvi, is a good example. Khairun Naas was more of a "pop-up" organization as there is little evidence of any ongoing activity specifically under this guise. It was therefore never really a new organization but rather a LeT front developed as a stratagem for a specific purpose, with many top commanders, trainers, and operatives temporarily serving in it. This allowed LeT to shift important assets to Khairun Naas in order to protect them from potential punitive actions against it. This demonstrates the importance of maintaining ongoing operational capabilities as a key to organizational resilience, of which the 2008 Mumbai attacks are a significant example.

With no familial connections between the two organizations there was little to connect them, providing Saeed the opportunity to obfuscate LeT. Similarly, as Lakhvi was a principal planner of the operation, Saeed claimed that it was Khairun Naas that carried out the Mumbai operation, not LeT (Reuters 2017). While this is not the case, there has been very little political will in Pakistan to link the two. Clarke (2012) disputes that Khairun Naas was even an organization in any tangible form. Similarly, Raman reports that, according to LeT members, "Khairun and Lashkar-e-Taiba are basically the same, but the LeT is banned in Pakistan, so we adopted the name Khairun Naan" (2004, 2) and undertook the Mumbai operations.[15]

The use of obfuscating stratagems by LeT to avoid external pressures are clear evidence of its core cultural ideology of protecting the Paksistan State, and striking at the enemies of Islam as it sees them, according to its manifesto. Laskar (2014) observes that the return from Khairun Naan of its Amir, Zaki-ur-Rehman Lakhvi, to his previous position in LeT directly after the attacks cements thinking that the split really was a deception.

The influence of meritocracy on organizational structure

LeT commanders are chosen through merit, and those who are most capable are appointed to senior roles. As meritocracy involves social capital exchange, those with much to offer are likely to prosper. Zaki-ur Lakhvi for example, a LeT founder and Operations Chief, has had a long career in LeT. It was Lakhvi that first developed geographic anchors to Afghanistan by establishing important training camps through which LeT could recruit additional members. Foremost was Camp Muaskar-e-Taiba at Jali in Paktia Province, and the second, Camp Muaskar-e-Aqsa in the Kunar Province. The third, Camp Tango, was a Haqqani Network stronghold also in the Kunar Province (Laskar 2014). These bases provided critical insurgency resources and served as operational bases from which to launch attacks. Zaki-ur Lakhvi was the central architect and played a further important role by connecting LeT to AeH Jihadists in Afghanistan.[16] Unlike Pakistan's AeH community, the Afghan AeH were happy to embrace insurgency as a way of life.[17]

LeT's later focus in Indian controlled Jammu and Kashmir brought it and the Pakistani ISI into a closer relationship that provided it with additional support and funding. Tellis claims the relationship is underpinned by Saeed's unwavering dedication and "uncompromising commitment to jihad that could be manipulated to advance Pakistan's own strategic goals" (2009, 2). With ISI support and an extensive recruitment base, including army officers to meet its need for professional and experienced combat commanders, LeT was well prepared. Meritocracy was additionally important for LeT to strengthen its infrastructure, external relationships, corporate experience base, and capabilities, with each of these enhancements adding to its organic resilience. However, it was ISI patronage that would prove most critical, and this came directly from Saeed's relationship with the Pakistani State. As Galula (1964) spoke of, state-actor patronage is very important to the successful insurgency, an example LeT and the ISI strongly reflect. Indeed, throughout the world, LeT enjoys a level of support practically unparalleled elsewhere.

Shah (2012) maintains this arose from Saeed's position on, and involvement in, the Council on Islamic Ideology, a body that gave Islamic rulings and advice to the government and lawmakers. According to Shafqat (2004), Saeed was appointed in the late 1970s by then Pakistani leader General Zia ul-Haque.[18] The Council had a strong adversarial focus on India that especially influenced Saeed. It was also a gateway for membership on the United Jihad Council (commonly known as UJC) since 1993. The UJC bound LeT and other organizations under a common anti-Indian cause. According to Shahid, the UJC is a "conglomerate of 13 jihadist groups" (2017, 1) not least of which are LeT, Jaish-e-Muhammed (JeM), and Hizbul Mujahedeen.[19] This also provided deep-running connections al-Qaeda's senior leadership an opportunity to develop transnational partners, affiliates, patrons, and donors.[20]

The distinct organizational structure of LeT and relationships with its key stakeholders and allies makes such integration and cooperation possible. Figure 4.5 shows the style and structure of corporate LeT divisions. The departments of External Affairs; Social Welfare; Education; and the Department of Dawah (spreading the faith) are the primary mechanisms of LeT insurgent operations. The Department of External Affairs is the liaison partner to other insurgent organizations, both internally and externally of Pakistan. It is headed by Abdul Rehman Makki.

The Department of Social Welfare plays a critical role and is the largest. It is probably Commanded by Saifullah Khalid, a senior JuD official and head of the Milli Muslim League (MM) political party. Khalid's experience in dawah and community development make him an ideal leader, and he is another critical ideological actor that binds LeT to the Pakistani State. The provision of education through 137 schools and mosques, and 40 madrassas is used as the base-rung of LeT's meritocratic ladder. Through these, LeT indoctrinates and anchors cadres to it, many of whom go on to serve in the military or other arms of government and return to LeT later on (Rotella 2013).

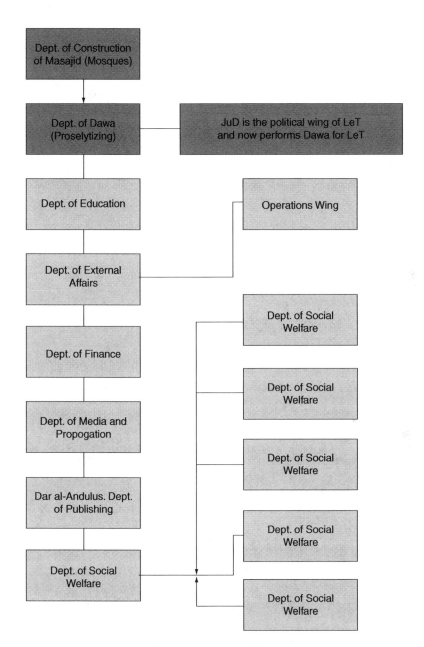

Figure 4.5 Lashkar-e-Taiba structural architecture.

Table 4.1 Effects of meritocratic setup on organization – Lashkar-e-Taiba

Structural dynamics	Organizational effect
Meritocratic organization	Open recruitment across class, ethnicity and citizenship. Attractive employer. Internal security vulnerabilities and high vetting costs. Recruitment from military and police families provides access to extensive resources. Leaders are promoted on basis of skills, capabilities, and what they offer to the organization.
Command and control	Formalized and hierarchical but is dynamic. In-fighting and internal politics can disrupt organizational cohesion and stability. Agency issue can arise as control is pushed down.
Resources	Extensive but conditional patronage from Pakistan that provides diverse resources. Is well supported by the public and able to operate freely in Pakistan. Has extensive regional and international resource networks.
Strategic behaviour	Organizational goals must be balanced with the needs of Pakistan. High compartmentalization of damages. Extensive support from Pakistan comes with the cost of obedience. Operations support tactical gains and short-term political goals. Beholden to Pakistani patrons as a collective proxy that imposes external goals.

When interrogated, its American operative David Headley stated that LeT was "filled with former Pakistani army officers" and that "every major official with the group had a handler from the spy agency [ISI]" (AP 2010). Each promising new recruit is also assigned an ISI handler to ensure their service in LeT reflects the state's needs (2010). Overseeing this is Saifullah Khalid, the administrator of LeT's extensive education and recruitment system, including the Markaz Taiba madrassa in Muridke at the headquarters of LeT. This is the central and primary vetting and recruitment centre. LeT co-founder Professor Zafar Iqbal is the madrassa Director of Education. According to Huggler, "local people refer to the students as Mujahedeen. The school is openly run by an organization (LeT) that everybody in Pakistan knows is linked to militants fighting in Kashmir" (2005, 2).

Likewise, the open nature of recruitment in Pakistan from all levels of society demonstrate that LeT is afforded significant freedoms from Islamabad. According to Zahab and Roy, "the center of Muridke served as an autonomous zone outside the jurisdiction of the State" (2004, 42). This provides LeT with freedom of coordination with its partners, evident in its open hosting of al-Qaeda planners Aimal Kansi and Ramzi Yusuf, who were given shelter from U.S. efforts to hunt them down, probably with the acquiescence of the ISI.[21] Table 4.1 shows the organizational effects of LeT structural dynamics.

External pressures

Given its significant focus and operational presence in Jammu and Kashmir, hard-power pressures on LeT in those areas have been consistent, with frequent escalations in counterinsurgent activity from Indian forces. Shah (2018) observes that it is almost self-perpetuating as the common reaction to counterinsurgent activities is more violence, with cycles of gunfights, attacks, bombings, and civilian fatalities that continually result in the further recruitment of local youths into the ranks of insurgents. Conversely, soft-power pressures on LeT in Pakistan and elsewhere have been relatively weak because of its defence-in-depth.[22] From the 1990s to the present, the main direct kinetic losses have been suffered in Jammu, Kashmir, and the Ladakh area because these are the main battlegrounds, and these have come from clashes with Indian security forces. Fareed (2017) states that India maintains a fighting force of nearly half a million that has been effective at suppressing anti-Indian insurgents. These are vastly superior to LeT's forces.

According to the Indian Ministry of External Affairs (2002), some 2,358 foreign fighters were killed in Jammu and Kashmir between 1990 and 2001, the vast majority of those being LeT insurgents. Between 2002 and 2013 there were 7,499 insurgents killed, which represented a four-to-one ratio of 1,984 security force personnel killed (SATP 2018). Sandhu (2017) reports that from 2014 onwards, Indian security force claimed to be killing LeT insurgents faster than they could infiltrate, at a rate of about 200 a year. According to Naseem (2017), in 2013, 2014, 2015, and 2016 there were 97, 65, 33, and 112 LeT infiltrations respectively and more than 75 in 2017, totalling 382, with 555 insurgents killed overall. In 2018 and 2019, there were over 100 infiltrations each year as well (Gurung 2019).

In addition to pressures on LeT operational capabilities there was localized damage against LeT command and control. In October 2015, Abu Qasim, a high-ranking LeT commander, was killed by Indian police in Srinagar in the Kashmir Valley (Kumar 2017). In July 2017 Salim Mukim Khan, a LeT leader with strong ties to the ISI, was arrested in Mumbai, India. This followed the arrest in May 2017 of an ISI intelligence officer, who was Khan's handler, by the Indian Uttar Pradesh Anti-terrorism Squad (Bidwal 2008). The Anti-terrorism Squad also arrested ISI agents Govardhan Singh in 2015 and Jamaluddin in 2016, who were supplying information on Indian military activity to insurgents (Lucknow 2016). These arrests and killings further impacted LeT operations in Jammu and Kashmir. However, the same cannot be said for LeT in Pakistan where it has been challenging the exertion of hard-power pressures directly against it.

As a result, India sought to target LeT using its own proxies. Despite substantial political resistance in India to undertaking covert operations in Pakistan, India's external intelligence service, the Research and Analysis Wing (RAW), took action. Azizi (2014) reports that India commenced joint operations in conjunction with the Afghanistan Riyasat-e-Amniyat-e-Milli, or National Directorate of Security (NDS), to target LeT. Hassan (2017) refers to the example of Indian and Afghan intelligence services jointly providing support, financing, and targeting information to the Tehrik-e-Taliban Pakistan (TTP) to hurt Pakistani interests and proxies.[23]

Swami (2016) highlights that the NDS has intelligence assets within various jihadist groups that have fallen out with Pakistan, including the TTP. Through these, the NDS and RAW have supported counterattacks against Pakistan in retaliation for ISI support of LeT and the Haqqani network (Swami 2016). In direct kinetic terms this has become India's most effective means of exerting external pressure on LeT outside of Jammu and Kashmir, something that was a long time in coming.[24]

Many observers thought that after the 2008 Mumbai attacks India would retaliate militarily (Menon 2016; Vij 2019). The reason why India did not respond was simple: RAW had no reliable intelligence on LeT training bases or the locations of key leaders, and it had not developed any intelligence coverage or penetration of LeT, or affiliated organizations, even though LeT was an ongoing and significant national security threat.[25] Starr (2008) highlights that Pakistan was on high alert in the expectation of attacks, but the failures of Indian intelligence coupled with the need for India to have fly-through designated U.S. air corridors made any counterstrikes untenable.

This forced India to consider other methods. After Mumbai, retired Indian Army Chief General VK Singh was tasked with creating the Technical Services Division (TSD).[26] The TSD was explicitly formed to conduct covert operations on foreign soil, particularly Pakistan, to counter the ISI and LeT through infiltration and intelligence operations. Baweja (2013) cites that former members claim the unit conducted at least eight such operations though to date official actions remain unknown, as do what, if any, real pressures were placed on LeT organizationally.[27]

On 20 March 2009, LeT re-engaged Indian forces in a protracted battle with the 1st Para and 6th Battalion Rashtriya Rifles in Kashmir near the Line of Control.[28] Indian forces took losses that it ascribes to the direct operational support provided to LeT fighters by the ISI, evidenced by the use of military technology, GPS, army maps, rations, and secure communications and satellite phones (Roul 2003). The minimal damage to LeT by Indian and Afghan intelligence operations, and the TSD, show that hard-power, kinetically based pressures have mostly been ineffective at an organizational level.

Soft-power pressures

International actors like the U.S., Israel, and China have used soft-power pressures against LeT as they share concerns that it could be a serious threat to their security and economic interests. Former U.S. Director of Intelligence Dennis Blair remarked in February 2010 that LeT was "placing Western targets in Europe in its sights" (2010, 11) raising fears of possible transnational attacks. In 2016, the U.S. Office of Foreign Assets Control (OFAC) tried to stymie LeT financial networks by targeting LeT financial masters Muhammad Sarwar and Shahid Mahmood, though this had little effect outside of U.S. jurisdictions (United States Government 2016). Saudi Arabia and the U.S. have also imposed sanctions on joint LeT/al-Qaeda front organizations: the Pakistani Al-Rahmah Welfare Organization, Jamia Asariya Madrassa, and the Al-Furqan Foundation Welfare and Trust. Paul and Torbati (2016) report that Abdul Aziz Nuristani, Saudi-based Muhammad Ijaz Safarash, and Naveed Qamar, all LeT facilitators, were also sanctioned, but again it is not known if the actions taken were detrimental in any substantial ways.

Israeli concerns come from LeT's strong anti-semitic stance and political rhetoric. Berman states that LeT has "described Hindus and Jews as the main enemies of Islam and India and Israel are the main enemies of Pakistan" (2010, 2). Politically this places Israel on a par with India as a target. Haider highlights that in response, Israel stated that the Jewish nation "completely supports New Delhi in its fight against terrorism emanating from Pakistan and within the country" (2017, 1). Israel also maintains concerns about its diaspora in India, particularly in the Kullu district in Himachal Pradesh, known as "the mini-Israel of India" and a known target of LeT (Sharma 2017).

LeT provocations against Jews has inadvertently strengthened the Indo-Israeli relationship. Since 2016 this has been built around a central pillar of defense cooperation spanning counter-terrorism, intelligence sharing and weapons sales (Kaura 2017). SIPRI data indicates that Indian arms purchases from Israel increased over 120 per cent from 2015 to 2017 with India being the primary customer, responsible for 41 per cent of Israeli arms sales. Indeed, trade between the countries in 2016 and 2017 amounted to U.S.$767 and $715 million per year (Pant and Sahu 2019).

However, while this indicates a healthy relationship, weapons sales and intelligence sharing that together may increase hard-power capabilities do not translate directly into usability which reflects the situation on the ground.[29] United efforts by Israel and India to pressure Islamabad politically have been correspondingly ineffective because Pakistan largely ignores its detractors. Pakistan can afford to do so because it is often rewarded for staying its course. Ramarao identified for example that the U.S. Government "removed a provision from the National Defence Authorization Act 2018 that would have required the U.S. Secretary of Defense to certify that Pakistan has taken steps to 'significantly disrupt' the activities of both the Lashkar-e-Taiba (LeT) and the Haqqani Network" (2017, 1). This is a strong signal from the U.S. that it is unconcerned about the ISI's proxy and does not have the inclination to follow through on any of its threats concerning LeT, or its most lethal protagonist in Afghanistan, the Haqqani Network.

Conversely, there are two other actors Pakistan does need to be responsive to. China and Russia are key influencers, critical allies, and share an agenda of Pakistan clamping down on its support to militants. China is a long-time advocate against UN sanctions on Pakistan over terror support, though for the first time at the 2017 BRICS Summit it condemned Pakistan-based groups including

LeT, while stopping short of condemning Islamabad itself according to Kumar (2017). To Pakistan, China is a critical protector and patron. According to Blank (2015), Chinese veto power on the UN Security Council protects Pakistan, and without Chinese assistance the Pakistani nuclear programme would not have succeeded.[30]

Additionally, China and India have an adversarial relationship with a long-running conflict since the 1962 territorial war over Bhutan (Garver 2004). With long-standing animosities present, Beijing seems happy to antagonize India while supporting Pakistan. Likewise, China has had its own problems with the East Turkestan Islamic Movement (ETIM), an organization Reed *et al.* call a "true terrorist force, with an ideology that is both separatist and fundamentalist" (2011, 2).[31] However, Riedel (2015) says that even with China's strong counter-terrorism stance it understands the importance of the ISI/LeT relationship, which is a critical caveat in the Sino-Paki relationship.

Panda (2015) remarks that as a favour to Pakistan, China exercised its little-used veto power on the UN Security Council several times to block JuD's listing as a proscribed organization. This was a strategic move. China's U.S.$46 billion Economic Corridor (CPEC) development connecting Kashgar in Xinjiang to the Arabian Sea port of Gwadar runs through Baluchistan. Katoch argues that in return for China's continued support, Pakistan "is responsible for the security of the CPEC with all costs to be borne by Islamabad" (2016, 1) to guarantee the security of the project. The cooperation of various militant groups is key to this and something only Pakistan and its ISI can do.

This is important because up until this point the ISI conducted its affairs, and its use of proxies, largely as it saw fit. With more now at stake, maintaining favoured treatment from China places serious constraints on the ISI and on Pakistan's strategic ambitions. China wants stability and peace in the region for its economic success while Pakistan wants its proxy war with India. The ISI must exercise a controlling influence on LeT to ensure interests are met without deviation, constraining it and LeT to China's ambitions. Undoubtedly it is Pakistan that needs China more. While China has buffered Pakistan in the past, tensions are present in the relationship. Should ISI pressure or oversight ease on LeT, the Paki-China relationship could suffer. China does not want the CPEC disrupted, which could happen if LeT leverages some form of autonomy from the ISI and exacerbates tensions with India.

Likewise, Russia has similarly stepped up political pressure on Islamabad to take action. Russia does not accept the militant proxy organizations of the ISI. Menon asserts this is because it is "alarming for Russia, which is wary of Islamists in Central Asian States" (2016, 2). As with its relationship with China, Pakistan also needs a good relationship with Russia to enable it to pursue its power projections into Afghanistan. The Russia-Pakistan relationship was normalized in 2007 and in 2011 was significantly bolstered as both countries shared deteriorating relations with the United States. According to Ramani, this caused strong anti-American sentiments in both nations and "caused Russian and Pakistani policymakers to view the United States as the leading force for instability in South Asia" (2018, 1). This accelerated bilateral cooperation and efforts to degrade U.S. strategic influence there.

Additionally, Russia and Pakistan align on supporting insurgent organizations in Afghanistan like the Haqqani Network and the Taliban. According to Ramani "Russia has countered U.S. efforts to contain Pakistan's influence in Afghanistan" (2017, 1). In turn, Pakistan's influence over the Taliban and the Haqqani Network is important to Russia because it cooperates with the Taliban in attempts to stop the Islamic State from establishing a permanent presence in Afghanistan. It also wants to "deter the United States from maintaining a long-term military presence in the country" (Ramani 2017, 1). However, any organization not similarly aligned could be viewed as a threat to Russia, and Lashkar-e-Taiba is one such. Therefore, just like China, Pakistan also needs to adhere to Moscow's wishes when employing its proxies.

This is not a situation LeT wants either. Chalk (2010) reports that among other capital cities, LeT has vowed to plant the Islamic flag in Moscow. Russian backing of the Comprehensive Convention on International Terrorism (CCIT), which is highly supportive of India, and heavily biased towards Pakistan and LeT, has put President Putin and Amir Saeed at odds with little prospect of change (Sasikumar 2010).[32] Therefore, geo-political and political-economic considerations over what is best for Pakistan may divide the ISI, or pressure it to choose control in Afghanistan over deniability in Indian Kashmir. If the former is the case the ISI buffer between LeT and the rest of the world could shrink. As Kumar observes, "China's increasing economic stakes and evolving security concerns in the region seem to be forcing Beijing to re-orientate its internal calculus and tighten its grip over security in Pakistan" (2017, 2). Pakistan and notably the ISI could then tighten its grip on LeT, especially if Russia makes LeT a key issue.

As soft-power pressures, the needs and wants of China and Russia are tangible and are being felt on the ground by LeT, which has little love for either, particularly Russia. The ISI is being pressured to not only rein in LeT and its actions against India, but to police LeT's conformity to new rules. Pakistan, and by default its proxy organizations, need to guarantee security and stability in the region for China and be part of the process to further Russian power projection into Afghanistan and the region. Not only is this a restrictive pressure on LeT, but it is an aggravating one that could see friction ignite into conflict with its masters by limiting its own political and operational activities that are critical to its resilience.

Summary of external pressures

LeT has been fighting India for three decades and has had some extraordinary successes. These should be met with, at the least, an equal level of countermeasures by India. While India possesses the intent to destroy LeT, it never translated into actions due to significant intelligence and political failures. This was not because India lacked the required capabilities, but because it feared the political ramifications of attacking LeT in Pakistan and igniting a conventional conflict. In Jammu and Kashmir India did have many successes, but inside Pakistan LeT remained secure, lending significantly to its resilience. The examination of external pressures in this chapter has identified multiple reasons why.

First, LeT has enjoyed enormous insulation and buffering from hard- and soft-power pressures thanks to Pakistan, specifically the ISI, Army, and key government figures. Second, the pressures exerted on LeT have principally been political, not kinetic as in the Haqqani Network example with the exception of operations in Jammu and Kashmir. Even there, LeT has quickly and efficiently replaced damaged capabilities because of its resilient meritocratic organization. After the 2008 Mumbai attacks, LeT activities and attack planning paused for a short period in expectations of reprisals, but they never came. It resumed insurgent operations in Jammu and Kashmir shortly afterwards in 2009. Third, while India has been effective kinetically in Jammu and Kashmir, killing LeT fighters and commanders by the score, it has failed to target LeT leadership and core commanders inside Pakistan in any tangible ways. Cooperation with Afghanistan demonstrates that an Indian operational capability to exert direct kinetic pressure on LeT exists, but it is limited because of LeT's security-in-depth inside Pakistan, and the weak political appetite in New Delhi. Similarly, India's relationship with Israel is strong, and cooperation is deeply integrated on some crucial fronts. However, even with significant Israeli arms and intelligence support, India's hard-power projection outside of Jammu and Kashmir has not been increased to any significant degree, or resulted in any new capabilities.

Lastly, a unified international effort is absent, despite many nations making public statements about the violent nature of LeT. The U.S. is chief among these. Perhaps the most significant international hope for action has failed to take a leadership role and worse, has backflipped and seems uninterested. In Afghanistan, LeT fighters have suffered casualties from engagements with Western troops, but outside of that theatre the U.S. has clearly signalled its non-involvement, including in Pakistani internal politics and support for LeT.

Conversely, soft-power pressures have been demonstrated in other ways beyond punitive ones. China and Russia are the most capable actors of incentive-based diplomatic, political, and economic options to influence Pakistan. Collectively they could encourage Islamabad to reduce its reliance on LeT. ISI patronage is a cornerstone of LeT resilience, as highlighted, and is the primary buffer against external international pressures. As Pakistan seeks greater influence in Afghanistan, and China and Russia seek deeper integration and control in Central Asia, soft-power pressures from them will continue.

Islamabad is not insensitive to the regional opinions of China and Russia, and if Pakistan comes to believe it is better served strategically by its economic and transnational security partnerships, LeT will find itself in a disadvantageous position with respect to its patron. In the aftermath of Mumbai in 2008, Pakistan closed several LeT camps in Pakistan-occupied Kashmir, forcing it to move to transient camps set up in vulnerable forested areas to avoid detection (Ul-Hassan 2010). This reminded LeT it is susceptible and in an unequal relationship with

Pakistan. Should LeT become a political burden its value as a proxy to the ISI could come into question.

LeT resilience and responses to external pressures

This section examines the impact of external pressure on Lashkar-e-Taiba's resilience, its responses, and the efficiency of its adaptations. It reveals how LeT's meritocratic leadership enables organizational recovery from impacts on its governance structures and operations, thereby ensuring political and operational perpetuity.

Adaptation and recovery – correlating meritocracy and resilience

LeT adaptation and recovery is multifaceted. The meritocratic structure of LeT contributes significantly to its resilience by drawing on vast and highly efficient regeneration systems. Beyond Pakistan, LeT maintains recruitment offices in Nepal, Bangladesh, the Maldives, and the Gulf region (MMP 2017), demonstrating its broad recruitment focus irrespective of kinship, geography, class, or socio-economics. Likewise, enduring stability across its strategic apex leadership group has remained consistent and enabled Amir Saeed, Rehman Maki, and Zafar Iqbal to considerably influence LeT structure, processes, and operations in which meritocracy is promoted.

Slawinski finds that this enables commanders to "make voluntary decisions that contribute to short-term stability and long-term viability of the organization" (2015, 299). The development of a strong organizational culture is one of the most apparent manifestations thereof, and has been particularly influential on LeT as a meritocratic organization by institutionalizing its merit-based enlistment and promotion practices. According to Tellis, this makes LeT highly attractive and has "proven to be an invaluable recruiting tool" (2012, 13).

A result of the above has been the melding of organizational culture to efficiency and efficiency to resilience by reinforcing social capital and trust; particularly LeT's transnational ambitions that necessitate the meritocratic recruitment of professional appointments across boundaries and borders. Recruits are extensively vetted and their credentials checked, common in merit-based organizations where new entrants lack pre-existing social capital ties, such as family (Hedberg 2016). Recruits must also pass selection and specialist training to progress in the organization, which also instils in-group belonging and a professional standardized cadre across the organization.[33]

One of the strongest indicators of LeT resilience is its operational continuance. Several factors identified in previous sections support this. For example, there has been ongoing expansion of organizational infrastructure in Pakistan, and theatres of operations in Jammu and Kashmir supported by strong organic capability development. Additionally, its strong Salafi-Wahhabi ideological narratives have contributed to the success of its advocacy of the plight of indigenous Kashmiris at social and political levels (Mahapatra 2018). Likewise, kinetic effectiveness, LeT attacks, bombings, and general violence show continued success at engaging a target-rich environment that consists of Indian military personnel, government members, and civilians in Jammu and Kashmir and in India's biggest cities.

Despite these strengths however, LeT has suffered significant losses. The massive presence of Indian security forces means that LeT is likewise sought out and attacked. The Indian Ministry of External Affairs reports there were almost 57,000 terrorist incidents in Jammu and Kashmir from 1990 to 2001 (2002), resulting in nearly 52,000 deaths. While not all casualties were LeT fighters, India ascribes many of them directly to it or to organizations it says belong to LeT (see Table 4.2).[34]

From 2002 to 2018 there was a sharp reduction to 22,223 terrorist incidents, with 18,701 deaths, due in large part to direct kinetic pressures on LeT and in turn, the nexus it controls (see Table 4.3).[35]

Some key conclusions can be drawn from the data. First, the number of insurgents killed is considerable during both time frames. The number of attacks and the ratio of attacks to insurgents killed also remained relatively constant. This shows that the operational capacity and efficiency to continue to launch attacks remained steady, despite fluctuations in numbers and damage to LeT operations.[36]

Second, according to Rassler *et al.* (2013), the average life expectancy of an LeT fighter is 5.14 years. In 2018, Mishra (2018) put this figure for LeT fighters in Jammu and Kashmir at just six months. Compared to Indian soldiers, who are overwhelmingly expected to survive their tours and live to an age of between 58 and 78 (Dikshit 2005), this is extremely low. However, even with significant losses LeT's tempo of attacks remained high.

Table 4.2 Insurgency-related deaths Jammu and Kashmir 1990–2001

Year	Attacks	Civilian deaths	Security force deaths	Insurgent deaths
1990	4,158	461	155	564
1991	3,765	382	173	856
1992	4,817	634	189	833
1993	5,247	747	198	1,329
1994	5,829	820	200	1,614
1995	5,938	1,031	237	1,407
1996	5,014	1,336	184	1,348
1997	3,420	948	139	1,272
1998	2,932	857	236	1,318
1999	3,071	821	355	1,387
2000	3,074	762	400	1,956
2001	4,522	919	536	2,642
Total	51,787	9,718	3,002	16,526

Table 4.3 Insurgency-related deaths Jammu and Kashmir 2002–2018

Year	Attacks	Civilian deaths	Security force deaths	Insurgent deaths
2002	4,038	1,008	453	1,707
2003	3,401	795	314	1,494
2004	2,565	707	281	976
2005	1,990	557	189	917
2006	1,667	389	151	591
2007	1,092	158	110	472
2008	708	91	75	339
2009	499	71	78	239
2010	488	47	69	232
2011	340	31	33	100
2012	220	11	38	50
2013	170	15	53	67
2014	222	28	47	110
2015	208	17	39	108
2016	322	15	82	150
2017	342	40	80	213
2018	429	129	77	223
Total	18,701	4,109	2,169	17,925

Director-General of the Jammu and Kashmir police, SP Vaid said, "we will get nothing simply out of killing militants. We have killed 200 of them [in 2017]. They will recruit 200 fresh [in 2018]. How long can we kill militants?" (Raina, 2018, 1). This is evidence that direct kinetic pressures exert little tangible long-term pressures on LeT.

Third, between 2015 and 2018 there was a rise in both civilian and insurgent fatalities, but these were disproportionate with overall civilian deaths rising by 164 per cent, while insurgent deaths rose only 18 per cent. Civilian casualties are not merely collateral damage but are deliberate, with Hindus being the overwhelming victims. Fair writes that a review "of LeT literature demonstrates a commitment to targeting Indian Hindus" (2009, 7). This aligns with the LeT political ideology of attacking non-Muslims and demonstrates its ongoing political perpetuity, another measurement of resilience.

LeT's continued success in Jammu and Kashmir is interesting because of the substantial damage it has suffered. However, this can be explained by observing Indian external pressures. Although direct kinetic pressures in Jammu and Kashmir resulted in the killing of literally thousands of LeT insurgents, it remains resilient. Why? Most likely it is because Indian security force efforts have been aimed principally at killing fighters, rather than attacking LeT capabilities, therefore leaving its organizational efficiency intact. If this form of hard power is to be effective at reducing the LeT insurgency, it needs to be recalibrated to target the mechanisms of LeT efficiency, such as infrastructure in Pakistan and Afghanistan, as well as commanders and senior operational planners. A failure to do so has meant India has had little success in stopping LeT's infiltration into the region and its ability to replenish its lost forces.

To offset the absence of hard-power pressures on LeT beyond Jammu and Kashmir, India and other actors in the international community have sought to target LeT with soft-power pressures via financial restrictions and sanctions. LeT uses several means of financing including State sponsorship via the ISI, charities, NGOs, legitimate front businesses, and the drug trade. Actions taken against LeT moneymen target its finance network in Pakistan and around the world. In 2016 for example, the U.S. placed sanctions on Abdul Aziz Nuristani and Muhammad Ijaz Safarash, Saudi-based businessmen connected to the LeT Jamia Asariya Madrassa, and the Al-Rahmah Welfare Organization (Reuters 2016).

However, these had minimal impact. This is because external pressures targeting LeT financing ultimately lead back to Pakistan, where the government does not take any action against the organization or its financial networks. This is not surprising. Trehan (2002) claims that the ISI is directly involved in LeT narcotics operations, processing Afghan opium in LeT facilities and using ISI transport networks to move it across borders, raking in billions of dollars per year. Because it is so profitable, ISI cooperation with LeT is unlikely to stop.

LeT political perpetuity: diffusion, adaptation, and resilience

Despite strong international rhetoric, soft-power pressures against Pakistan and LeT specifically have been difficult to apply effectively, particularly in areas where LeT has state supporters. LeT has adapted by misdirecting external pressures and creating new mechanisms that serve out its insurgency functions and agenda. Its patrons Pakistan and particularly the ISI, have been responsible for providing advanced warning and assistance in these processes. *Ceteris paribus*, the necessity of self-preservation has seen Pakistan take some actions against LeT.

These have been token efforts however, sufficient only to maintain a guise of being tough on terrorism. For example, LeT has a myriad of fronts and sub-organizations. It has phoenixed into new groups such as Tehreek-e-Tahafuz Qibla Awal and Tehreek Azadi Jammu Kashmir. LeT's principal input apparatus, JuD, is a further example. Advanced warning from the ISI of impending political actions against LeT helped it adapt, and through its non-proscribed fronts it effectively skirts sanctions placed upon it. After the proscription of LeT, its JuD offshoot ran various social and development programmes across Pakistan that provided mass public support and fresh resources (Bashir and Khalid 2019). JuD was eventually banned in January 2018 under the Pakistani Anti-Terrorism Act of 1997, and by the UNSC Act of 1948 (PTI 2018b). Just before this however, LeT's Amir Saeed phoenixed JuD into Milli Muslim League Pakistan (MMLP) in August 2017 (Dutta 2017).

As new front organizations have evolved, LeT has had fewer external pressures exerted against it, and working inside the friendly environment of Pakistan allows the transfer of resources and recruits to be immediately utilized for insurgency operations. LeT also achieves this through its affiliate network through which it can take actions that are deniable. Membership in the UJC, as discussed in the first section of this chapter, adds a level of public endorsement to LeT, supports its political, social, and religious legitimacy and mainstream acceptance, and importantly provides proxy capabilities.[37]

For these reasons LeT is difficult to target. Aside from the ISI and UJC, LeT has developed other vital relationships. Along the tribal belt region of Pakistan's northwestern frontier, LeT works closely with al-Qaeda, the Afghan Taliban, and Tehrik-i-Taliban Punjab or Punjabi Taliban (Nomani 2011). Other key connections include Paasban-i-Ahle-Hadith, Al Mansoorian, the Army of Madinah, the Falah-i-Insaniat Foundation, and several more, shown in Figure 4.6. This network shares recruitment, financing, operational planning, and training. Equally, transferring and gathering inputs, process-sharing, and joint outputting through the UJC nexus are strong diffusion mechanisms that reduce direct external pressures against any single point in the network.

The development of organic Jammu and Kashmir ties has also been a factor in LeT resilience. Rather than a foreign organization based in Pakistan, LeT has developed a string of local indigenous leaders to anchor and reinforce its social capital externally. As an illustration, in 2015 Abu Dujana replaced Abu Qasim as LeT Commander in Kashmir (ITVND 2015), and in 2016 Wani (2016) reported that Junaid Matto replaced Majid Zargar as LeT South Kashmir Commander, who was killed by Indian forces. In September 2017, Zeentat-ul-Islam,

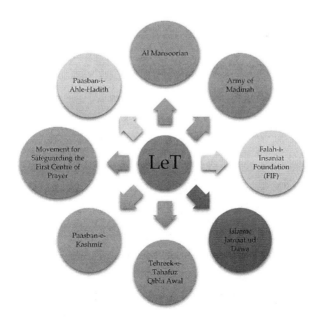

Figure 4.6 Lashkar-e-Taiba United Jihad Council (UJC) nexus.

a Kashmiri and an experienced jihadist and IED expert, was then promoted to lead LeT Jammu and Kashmir operations. The ongoing drive to localize LeT as an indigenous actor in Jammu and Kashmir has paid off in social capital terms, but has been somewhat costly in processing terms.

Bengali (2017) cites that in many areas of Jammu and Kashmir, anti-Indian protests have grown in size and intensity. He states: "Tensions are rising and show a clear turn toward further support for the insurgency, resulting in month-long crackdowns by Indian forces" (Bengali 2017). Such actions historically serve to foster increasing anti-Indian sentiments. It is only recently that some benefits have manifested. On 18 November 2017, Indian forces reported that they had killed several high-ranking leaders. Srivastava (2017) reports that one of these was Osama Jungvi, the nephew of Zaki-ur-Rehman Lakhvi. LeT commanders Mushtaq Zargar and Mehmood Bhai have also been killed in the area.[38]

In 2017 four more local LeT Kashmiri commanders were killed. These were Gulzar Ahmad Mir, Waseem Shah, Nasir Ahmad Khan, and Abu Ismail (PTI 2018a). The slayings put strong external pressure on LeT that affected command and control of localized operations, but demonstrate output vulnerabilities rather than core command and leadership weaknesses. The continuous appointment and promotion of new commanders, increasingly Kashmiri in origin, demonstrate this, thereby reducing any long-term impact on LeT.

Succinctly, despite a range of external pressures on LeT it has, organizationally, adapted and been resilient. LeT suffered severe short-term damage to its operations through direct kinetic actions in Jammu and Kashmir, and some temporary disruption to its command and control in that region, but holistically these were ineffective. Pressures targeting LeT financial systems have failed because they are either too specific or not supported by Pakistan, which ignores and nullifies UN and international actions against it. Similarly, LeT has expanded its capabilities across multiple organizations, networks, and affiliates, increasingly anchoring it to the Pakistani social fabric from which it gathers key inputs, providing redundancy.

Conclusion

This chapter has examined Lashkar-e-Taiba's meritocratic structure, the external pressures it has faced, and its organizational resilience. LeT organizational morphology has also been discussed, highlighting deep integration with the Pakistani State and ISI, and the benefits of diffusion and political misdirection that come with it. Its meritocratic organization has shown it is functionally robust and has resilient mechanisms of insurgency that have forged strong, enduring ties to the military, and to intrastate insurgent networks. Likewise, LeT insurgency systematics have been shown to be particularly strong with organic, patronage, and external organic development occurring in Jammu and Kashmir, representing a multifaceted system of leadership, command, recruitment, and operations.

LeT has successfully pursued an ongoing expansion of organizational infrastructure in Pakistan, and in theatres of operations in Jammu and Kashmir that are supported by strong organic capability development. This is a critical point of distinction between LeT and the Haqqani Network. In its tribal homelands in Afghanistan, the Haqqani Network has achieved a state of near critical mass. It has developed its resource bases and plateaued. In contrast, LeT's membership base is truly international and it has an evolving nexus of international partners and patrons that add new resource inputs.

LeT's nexus relationships to the Pan-Asian jihadist network dating back decades to the 1980s have also played an important role in resilience and organizational capabilities, creating enduring relationships with al-Qaeda, the UJC, various Taliban groups, and more widely in South Asia, Saudi Arabia, and the Gulf States. Additionally, the resilience of individual leadership figures including Hafiz Saeed, Zafar Iqbal, and Rehman Makki has been critical in driving its organizational culture and maintaining a dominant and durable command and control hierarchy, as articulated by Everly (2011).

The review of soft-power political pressure shows that there are international actors practising it that, in the longer term, may manifest results, but which represents little real concern for the present. However, holistically LeT is not impervious. ISI support of LeT, like the Haqqani Network, is detrimental to the security interests of Afghanistan and India, and is of concern to China and Russia. This has resulted in an alignment of goals and a unification of efforts to destroy both organizations. Conversely, international political pressures including multilateral and United Nations undertakings require cooperation, information sharing, and real political will to effect change. As Ramarao (2017) reports, U.S. back-flipping on LeT, despite tough rhetoric to the contrary, has signalled to Pakistan that LeT is not a U.S. problem outside of Afghanistan.

This has helped LeT entrench its social legitimacy in Pakistan and Jammu and Kashmir, and develop strong social capital and trust relationships in Afghanistan and throughout Central Asia. Resilient insurgent organizations like LeT do this in environments of ongoing and expected volatility in which unpredictability becomes a norm. As Kapisthalam (2009) demonstrates, this has allowed LeT to adapt and respond efficiently to sanctions, crackdowns, proscription, and direct pressures. Furthermore, LeT resilience has been about developing the right balance of efficiency, capability, and recovery. The intelligence advantage it gains from its ties to the ISI is a cornerstone of this. LeT has a binary resilience of endogenously self-developed resilient capabilities and exogenous support from Pakistan and other patrons. These make LeT an extraordinarily potent and resilient organization, demonstrated on many occasions by its continual attacks, such as Mumbai 2008.

Combined, these have a saturation effect across multiple forums of the Pakistani socio-cultural and economic spectrum. When these are built around a strong organizational culture supported by strong leadership, robust resilience is a likely outcome. LeT accesses recruits from all strata of the socio-economic scale, and demographics show that most have a higher-than-average education and come from the middle and lower-middle classes, with some from privileged castes also seeking to join (Shelley 2015). As Rotella (2013) reports, it is important also to note that inside of Pakistan there are no restrictions on joining LeT.

Shafiq (2007) argues that LeT ties to the ISI enable the secondment of current and former intelligence and military officers as training staff, and as operational advisers that help it develop new leaders. This is reinforced by the effectiveness of its social service activities that continually develop and reinforce social capital and trust, making LeT recruitment and training cheaper and more efficient. It is necessary to reiterate the absolute importance of the ISI relationship through which many major operations have made LeT far more dangerous than it would otherwise have been. Many Western nations have challenged Pakistan about its support of LeT, but responses from Islamabad have always been lacking. Dill argues this is because the Pakistan Government "contends LeT is too dangerous and capable and a crackdown would result in LeT turning on the government" (2012, 8). There is no doubt that LeT is powerful and a conflict with it would be violent and bloody. However, four considerations render the Pakistani response flawed.

First, although legally banned it must be remembered that for Pakistan, LeT is first and foremost an auxiliary force in case of war with India, and a militant proxy arm of the government in Jammu and Kashmir. It is widely known Pakistan uses LeT as a tool of foreign policy it will not give up so long as it perceives India as a threat to Islamabad. Second, LeT's strength and resilience come mainly from what the government, and the ISI in particular, have given it, principally sanctuary and resources. These can be withdrawn at any time. Third, LeT is encircled inside of Pakistan. Should it choose to do so, Pakistan could dismantle the majority of LeT infrastructure, leadership, recruitment, financial networks, and insurgent activities in short order.

Therefore, any argument that LeT is not able to be brought to heel is a political shake-off. Although LeT should not be underestimated it exists only because it is allowed to by the state. Fourth, as a meritocratic organization LeT is vulnerable in other ways. The durable nature of its apex control structure has strong redundancy, but ISI support is not contingent on Saeed remaining as Amir because he is only an office-holder rather than a patriarch, making him replaceable. This is inverse to the ISI's support of the Haqqani Network because organizational control is intrinsically linked with family and kinship. Should leadership change be desired in LeT there are many ways it could be quickly achieved.

For example, the ISI could foster change by manipulating socio-cultural pressures to reduce Saeed's legitimacy and ability to exercise authority. Likewise, there are historical social capital and trust issues present in LeT which Saeed is at the centre of, as identified by Sareen (2005). These could form a basis for change, with either Iqbal or Makki taking over with little disruption and minimal loss of face.

Lastly, it is evident that LeT is a highly resilient insurgent organization in its own right when viewed as an independent entity. This comes from its grass-roots support, social capital and trust gained through its extensive social services and organic anchoring to the Pakistani and Jammu and Kashmiri peoples, based mainly on anti-Indian narratives and Islamic ideologies. The patronage relationship with the ISI and Pakistani State make it more resilient than nearly any of its contemporaries. This makes LeT largely impervious to external pressures, political or kinetic, hard or soft. However, meritocratic resilience is double-edged and represents LeT's most significant vulnerability.

Notes

1 Dineen *et al.* put it that organizational "fit" is the balance of demands and abilities of individuals and organizations and how well these align, creating good, or bad, fits. SOURCE: Brian Dineen *et al.*, 2017. "Who cares about demands-abilities fit?" *Personal Psychology* 71 (4): 122–152.

2 Jamaat ud-Dawa (JuD), an alias of LeT, is considered to be LeT and is referenced as such.

3 The Maktab al-Khidmat was a non-governmental organization created in the 1980s that assisted the Afghani people during the anti-Soviet fighting. It became entrenched in al-Qaeda as a linear descendant known as the Centre of Mujahedeen Services that formed to provide similar assistance to the Iraqi jihadists. SOURCES: Daveed Gartenstein-Ross and Kyle Dabruzzi, 2008. "Is Al-Qaeda's Central Leadership Still Relevant?" *Middle East Quarterly* 15 (2): 27–36; Michael Scheuer, 2007. "Chasing bin Laden's Money". In *Through Our Enemies' Eyes: Osama bin Laden, Radical Islam, and the Future of America*, ed. Michael Scheuer. Nebraska: Potomac Books Inc., 31–44.

4 Sheikh Abdullah Azzam was assassinated on 23 November 1989 by a roadside IED in Peshawar Pakistan as he and his two sons were being driven to local prayers. Speculation continues about which party was responsible including the U.S., Israel, and Jordan, but heavy suspicion also falls on Ayman al-Zawahiri. SOURCE: Ayrn Baker, 2009. "Who Killed Abdullah Azzam?" *Time*. Accessed 6 February 2016. http://content.time.com/time/specials/packages/article/0,28804,1902809_1902 810_1905173–1,00.html.

5 The assassination of Jamil al-Rahman of JDSQ, MDI's affiliate in Afghanistan and the slaying of Allama Ehsan Elahi Zaheer, the leader of Jamaat AeH in Lahore in 1987, played a critical role in enabling LeT to develop and phoenix out of MDI. The Jamaat al-Dawa al-Quran Wal-Sunnah was a hard-line Salafist group that was led by Jamil al-Rahman, who provided strong support to Saeed and the MDI until his slaying in 1987. SOURCES: Razia Musarrat *et al.* 2012. "The Predicament of Ethnicity in Divided Society of Pakistan". *International Journal of Human Resource Studies* 2 (1): 199–209; John Solomon, 2011. "9/11 Legacy: More Resilient Skyscrapers". *CBRNE Terrorism Newsletter* 39 (2011): 192–197.

6 Zaki ur-Rehman Lakhvi, LeT Operations Chief, was listed on the 27 May 2008 along with Haji Muhammad Ashraf and Sajid/Saeed Majeed. Yahya Mujahid was designated in 2009 and Sajid Mujahid in 2012. Azam Cheema was designated in November 2010. SOURCES: United States Government. 2008. "Specially Designated Nationals and Blocked Persons". *U.S. Department of the Treasury*. Accessed 5 December 2018. www.treasury.gov/resource-center/sanctions/sdn-list/pages/default.aspx 2008; United States Government. 2012. "Treasury Designates Lashkar-e-Tayyiba Leadership". *U.S. Department of the Treasury*. Accessed 26 November 2018. www.treasury.gov/press-center/press-releases/Pages/tg1694.aspx.

7 SOURCES: Countering Extremism Project. 2017. "Lashkar-e-Taiba". Accessed 15 November 2017. www.counterextremism.com/threat/lashkar-e-taiba; Stanford University, "Mapping Militant Organizations". Accessed 28 October 2018. http://web.stanford.edu/group/mappingmilitants/cgi-bin/groups/view/79; SATP. 2016b. "Terrorist Outfits: Lashkar-e-Taiba". *South Asia Terrorism Portal.* Accessed 5 March 2016. www.satp.org/satporgtp/countries/india/states/jandk/terrorist_outfits/Lashkar_etoiba.htm.

8 According to a U.S. Treasury Department report, Gill "has been an accountant for Lashkar for more than ten years and more specifically, has served as Lashkar's chief financial officer and headed Lashkar's accounts department for several years. He also has served in Lashkar's revenue wing and has maintained Lashkar's expense records". SOURCE: Muzamil Jaleel, 2014. "U.S. identifies JuD as Lashkar alias, names two new global terrorists". *The Indian Express.* Accessed 5 June 2016. https://indianexpress.com/article/world/americas/us-identifies-jud-as-lashkar-alias-names-two-new-global-terrorists/.

9 The UN QDi.265 stated: "Ashraf assisted Saudi Arabia-based LeT leaders to expand its organization and increase its fundraising activities. He maintains and manages funding networks in Saudi Arabia." SOURCE: United Nations Security Council, 2014 "QDi.265 Haji Muhammad Ashraf". *Al-Qaida Sanctions Committee.* Accessed 2 March 2016. www.un.org/sc/suborg/en/sanctions/1267/aq_sanctions_list/summaries/individual/haj i-muhammad-ashraf.

10 Muntazir is also known as Abdullah Muntazer and was born in Abbottabad, Pakistan on 17 January 1974. His Pakistani National Identity Number is: 3520203526763. The official JuD website is available at: https://judofficial. wordpress.com/. SOURCE: United States Government, 2016. "Treasury Sanctions Lashkar-e-Tayyiba Financial and Leadership Officials". *U.S. Department of the Treasury.* Accessed 26 November 2017. www.treasury.gov/press-center/press-releases/Pages/jl0691.aspx.

11 Zeenat-ul-Ilsma took over when Abu Ismail was killed in 2017. Ismail took over from Abdul Rehma, who in turn took over from Gazi Shahab-ud-din. SOURCES: Bashaarat Masood, 2011. "Lashkar face in south Kashmir killed". *The Indian Express.* Accessed 6 March 2016. http://archive.indianexpress.com/news/lashkar-face-in-south-kashmir-killed/855448/; Praveen Swami, 2017. "Lashkar commander killed". *The Indian Express.* Accessed 6 March 2017. http://indianexpress.com/article/india/lashkar-commander-killed-in-rise-and-fall-of-abu-dujana-a-tale-of-falsehood-and-ambition-4778106/.

12 Heneghan referenced eight primary goals: (i) to eliminate evil and facilitate conversion to and practice Islam; (ii) to ensure the ascendancy of Islam; (iii) to force non-Muslims to pay jizya (poll tax, paid by non-Muslims for protection from a Muslim ruler; (iv) to assist the weak and powerless; (v) to avenge the blood of Muslims killed by unbelievers; (vi) to punish enemies for breaking promises and treaties; (vii) to defend a Muslim state; (viii) to liberate Muslim territories under non-Muslim occupation. SOURCE: Tom Heneghan, 2008. "Lashkar-e-Taiba's goals". *Reuters.* Accessed 16 September 2017. http://blogs. reuters.com/faithworld/2008/12/03/lashkar-e-taibas-goals/.

13 JeM, Hum, UJC, HuJI, and HM are monikers in common use and how those organizations are often referred to.

14 The exact numbers of the LeT are unknown though it is believed to be several thousand strong with nearly a thousand fighting in Jammu and Kashmir at any one time. SOURCE: American Foreign Policy Council, 2014. "Lashkar-e-Taiba". *AFPC.* Accessed 3 June 2017. http://almanac.afpc.org/sites/almanac.afpc.org/files/Lashkar-epercent20Taiba_0.pdf.

15 There was strong speculation that Khairun Naas was an orchestrated move by the ISI to shelter LeT from the Mumbai attacks in anticipation of increasing U.S. pressures to

ban it. After the attacks the ISI continued to support Saeed and LeT, as well as other essential LeT officers such as Yahya Mujahid the LeT spokesman, JuD Amir Abdul Rehman Makki, and Saifullah Qasoori, a former LeT commander and Chairman of Daawat-o-Islah. Walsh reported that one of the most public, yet passive, demonstrations of state support is the presence of armed police as bodyguards to Saeed. Walsh states "police officers screened visitors at checkpoints near his house, while other officers patrolled an adjoining park, watching by floodlight for intruders". SOURCES: Ryan Clarke, 2010. *Lashkar-i-Taiba: The Fallacy of Subservient Proxies and the Future of Islamist Terrorism in India.* Strategic Studies Institute, U.S. Army War College. Accessed 22 May 2018. www.jstor.org/stable/resrep11768; Myra Mac-Donald, 2011. "Blacklisted group says Pakistan needs peace, prosperity". *Reuters.* 12 July. Accessed 5 August 2016. www.reuters.com/article/us-pakistan-jud/blacklisted-group-says-pakistan-needs-peace-prosperity-idUSTRE76B05M20110712.

16 JuD stalled after its creation due to competition from Jamaat AeH that was also built on an extremist interpretation of the Ahl-e-Hadith, the South Asian version of Arab Salafist-Wahhabism according to Rad. Jamaat AeH was led by Zakiur-Rehman Lakhvi, who went on to mastermind the 2008 Mumbai attacks. Rather than competing, Saeed and Lakhvi amalgamated Jamaat AeH into MDI in 1986, also known as the "Centre for Call and Guidance" located near Lahore, Pakistan. SOURCES: Ghorbanali Soltani and Omid Sepehri Rad, 2015. "Theoretical Investigation of Salafi Thought by Emphasizing Akhbarygary". *Ijtihad Network.* Accessed 24 July 2018. http://ijtihadnet.com/article-theoretical-investigation-salafi-thought-emphasizing-akhbarygary/.

17 According to Noonan and Stuart it was in 1990 in Kunar province that MDI changed its name to Lashkar-e-Taiba, reflecting the importance of Lakhvi's contributions, though Tellis puts it some years earlier in 1987. SOURCES: Sean Noonan and Stuart Levey, 2011. "The Evolution of a Pakistani Militant Network". *CBRNE Terrorism News Letter* 39 (2011): 193–197; Ashley Tellis, 2012. "The Menace That is Lashkar-e-Taiba". *Carnegie Endowment For International Peace.* Accessed 15 November 2017. http://carnegieendowment.org/files/LeT_menace.pdf.

18 General ul-Haque's Council on Islamic Ideology was formed to cement his dictatorial rulership, which was based on appeasing the religious and military elites. It was also critical to promoting Afghanistan as a place for jihad for Pakistani extremists, and by doing so enabled ul-Haque to fight a proxy war with the Soviets without direct Pakistani engagement. SOURCES: Jamal Shah, 2012. "Zia Ul-Haque and the Proliferation of Religion in Pakistan". *International Journal of Business and Social Science* 3 (21): 310–323; Tahir Amin, 1982. *Afghanistan Crisis: Implications and Options for Muslim World, Iran, and Pakistan.* Institute of Policy Studies, Pakistan.

19 The HJI is a Deobandi group originally established as the Jamiat Ansarul Afghaneen (JAA) to fight the Soviets in Afghanistan. Once the Soviets withdrew, its founder Qari Saifullah renamed it the HuJI to take up the fight in Kashmir. The Harkat-ul-Mujahedeen changed its name from the Harakat-ul-Ansar due to listing by the U.S. as a terrorist organization. Its founder Fazlur Rehman Khalil was a signatory to the al-Qaeda/bin Laden fatwa declaring war on the United States. The Jaish-e-Muhammed is known to have additional links to the Iraqi Ansar al-Islam and the Lashkar-e-Jhangvi and has cooperated in tactical and strategic operations together. SOURCES: Ramachandran Sudha, 2007. "PART2: Behind the Harkat-ul-Jihad Al-Islami". *Asia Times Online.* Accessed 7 July 2016. www.atimes.com/atimes/South_Asia/FL10Df06.html; SATP, 2017. "Harkat-ul-jihad-al-Islami (JuJI) (Movement of Islamic Holy War)". *South Asian Terrorism Portal.* Accessed 12 August 2016. www.satp.org /satporgtp/countries/india/states/jandk/terrorist outfits/HuJI.htm.

20 According to Yasir, the "United Jihad Council or Mujahedeen Jihad Council – head-quartered in Muzaffarabad, Pakistan controlled Kashmir – came into being in 1990 to

centralise command among dozens of militant groups, and to create a unified command among Pakistan-based groups and Kashmir-based militant outfits." SOURCE: Sameer Yasir, 2016. "United Jihad Council claims Pathankot attack". *First Post.* Accessed 5 April 2016. www.firstpost.com/politics/united-jihad-council-claims-pathankot-attack-heres-why-this-admission-is-an-exercise-in-subterfuge-2571098.html.

21 Aimal Kansi murdered two CIA officers in the U.S. state of Virginia, at 07:50 am on the morning of 25 January 1993. Kansi opened fire, killing Lansing Bennett, a CIA medical doctor and Frank Darling, a communications expert, as they waited in their cars to enter the CIA Langley headquarters. Three other CIA officers were wounded in the AK-47 attack by Kansi, who then flew to Quetta, Pakistan and was then smuggled into Afghanistan. Three years later after his return to Pakistan a CIA black team captured Kansi in a sting operation. He was rendered and executed. SOURCES: CIA, 2013. "A Look Back ... Murder at CIA's Front Gate". *Central Intelligence Agency.* Accessed 10 July 2017. www.cia.gov/news-information/featured-story-archive/murder-at-cia.html; Mariam Abou Zahab and Oliver Roy, 2004. "Pakistan: From Religious Conservatism to Political Radicalism – Salafism and Jihadism". In *Islamist Networks: The Afghan-Pakistan Connection,* eds. Mariam Abou Zahab and Oliver Roy. London: C. Hurst and Co. Publishers, 32–47.

22 LeT suffered losses during its anti-Soviet campaigning and well into the post 2001 fighting in Afghanistan, and to a smaller extent in Iraq where it sent thousands of fighters to attack Western forces. SOURCE: Praveen Swami and Mohammed Shehzad, 2004. "Lashkar raising Islamist Brigades for Iraq". Accessed 10 July 2016. www.thehindu.com/2004/06/13/stories/2004061306050100.htm. Accessed 10 July 2016.

23 On 26 July 2017 an off-shoot of the TTP, the Taliban Special Group (TSG), launched a deadly commando-style suicide attack in Lahore, Pakistan. Twenty-six were killed and 54 injured, including police. It is Pakistan's assertion that such attacks are supported by Indian RAW and NDS with finance and training. SOURCE: Asif Chaudhry, 2017. "New TTP wing of trained suicide commandos behind Lahore attack". *Dawn.* Accessed 18 May 2016. www.dawn.com/news/1347712.

24 While this in itself doesn't run counter to U.S. ambitions, the use of the TTP as a proxy of Pakistan and India does. In 2013 U.S. forces took senior PTT Commander Latif Mehsud from the custody and protection of the Afghan Government. Mehsud was working with them and Indian operatives to target the LeT, though the U.S. Government sought him for operations against coalition forces. SOURCE: Kashmira Gander, 2013. "Latif, Mehsud, senior commander of Pakistan Taliban, captured by US forces". *The Independent.* Accessed 17 June 2016. www.abc.net.au/news/2013-10-12/us-captures-senior-commander-of-pakistani-taliban/5018260.

25 Not only was the British Intelligence eaves-dropping service GCHQ tracking Zarrar Shah's online activities as he set up his phase of the Mumbai operation, but the U.S. CIA passed on signal intercepts of LeT about the attack plan several times to RAW in the months before the attack. SOURCE: James Glanz *et al.*, 2014. "In 2008 Mumbai Attacks, Piles of Spy Data, but an Uncompleted Puzzle". *The New York Times.* Accessed 22 June 2016. www.nytimes.com/2014/12/22/world/asia/in-2008-mumbai-attacks-piles-of-spy-data-but-an-uncompleted-puzzle.html.

26 The TSD was controlled through the Army's Directorate General of Military Intelligence (DGMI). Operations were run by Colonel Munishwar Bakshi of the Army Intelligence corps with a complement of 32 men. Its mandate was to "enable the Military Intelligence Directorate to provide a quick response to any act of state-sponsoring terrorism with a high degree of deniability". However, the classified nature of these efforts make any estimation of effect difficult irrespective of the strong potential for black operations to target critical core members. SOURCE: Sushant Singh, 2015. "Simply Put: The working and controversies of TSD, the Army's shadowy MI unit". *The Indian*

Express. Accessed 23 June 2016. http://indianexpress.com/article/explained/simply-put-the-working-and-controversies-of-tsd-the-armys-hadowy-mi-unit/.

27 The TSD unit was apparently disbanded by the government in 2012 after allegations it was used to spy on Indian officials in Kashmir. SOURCE: Harinder Baweja, 2013. "Army spook unit carried out covert ops in Pakistan". *Hindustan Times*. 21 September. Accessed 24 June 2016. www.hindustantimes.com/delhi-news/army-spook-unit-carried-out-covert-ops-in-pakistan/story-4j1WTC.xyj8ObRmktfl3zWN. html?isab=true&meta-geo.

28 The battle took place in the Shamasbari forest range in the Kupwara District in proximity to the Line of Control, also referred to as the "LoC". The LoC is a pseudo border separating Indian control and Pakistani control between Kashmir and Pakistani Gilgit. SOURCE: Animesh Roul, 2003. "Lashkar-e-Taiba Resumes Operations against Indian Forces in Jammu and Kashmir". *Terrorism Monitor* 7 (1): 4–6.

29 For example, Ambassador Syed Akbaruddin, the Indian Permanent Representative to the UN speaking of the new UN Office of Counter-Terrorism said that "India believes that the creation of the office of Counter-Terrorism Coordinator is a much awaited first step in our efforts to enhance coordination of the UN's CT (counter-terrorism) efforts." SOURCE: Yoshita Singh, 2017. "India welcomes creation of new UN Office of Counter Terrorism". *Outlook India*. Accessed 13 July 2016. www.outlookindia.com/newsscroll/india-welcomes-creation-of-new-un-office-of-counter-terrorism/1076928.

30 China has previously acted on Pakistan's behalf in blocking a UN Security Council vote to proscribe the Jaish-e-Mohammed (JeM) as a terrorist entity due to the close relationship the ISI has with JeM leader Masood Azhar. In regard to Chinese assistance to Pakistan's nuclear programme, Abdul Qadeer Khan, Pakistan's father of the Atomic bomb, disclosed that in 1982 China gave 50 kilograms of bomb-grade uranium to Pakistan and set up a special centrifuge plant in Hanzhong China which produced 15 tons of hexafluoride (UF6) for Pakistan's own centrifuges. China also provided ongoing technical expertise. SOURCES: James Dorsey, 2017. "Protecting Militants: China Blocks UN Listing of Pakistani as Globally Designated Terrorist". *Eurasia Review*. Accessed 13 July 2017. www.eurasiareview.com/09022017-protecting-militants-china-blocks-un-listing-of-pakistani-as-globally-designated-terrorist-analysis/; Financial Express, 2017. "When China 'gifted' 50 kilograms of Uranium to help Pakistan make nuclear bombs against India". *FE Online*. Accessed 13 August 2017. www.financialexpress.com/india-news/china-gifted-50-kilogram-of-uranium-to-help-pakistan-make-nuclear-bomb-against-india-know-about-the-dreaded-chapter-of-history/800966/.

31 Contrarily, this suggests that the ETIM is more an insurgent organization than a terrorist group because of its ability to wage sustained guerrilla war for independence.

32 The CCIT was originally drafted in 1996 with the core aims of, first, developing a universally accepted definition of terrorism that all 193 member nations could adopt into law, and, secondly, to make cross-border terrorism an extraditable offence globally. To date the United States has been the strongest obstacle to the CCIT due to fears that its own military forces could be defined as terrorists when intervening and operating on foreign soil under what many consider to be questionable international legal authority. SOURCE: Suhasini Haider, 2016. "Delhi hopes UN will push global terror convention". *The Hindu*. Accessed 3 July 2016. www.thehindu.com/news/national/Delhi-hopes-UN-will-push-global-terror-convention/article14467324.ece.

33 Tankel describes several stages of training for LeT recruits at various camps and facilities in Pakistan and Afghanistan that recruits must either pass or be forced out of. See: Stephen Tankel, 2011. *"Storming the World Stage: The Story of Lashkar-e-Taiba"*. London: C. Hurst & Co.

34 SOURCE: Indian Government, 2002. "Fact Sheet on Jammu and Kashmir". *Ministry of External Affairs*. 20 May. Accessed 15 March 2018. http://mea.gov.in/in-focus-article.

htm?18987/Fact+Sheet+on+Jammu+amp+Kashmir&bcsi_scan_d2f7438883b2c67d=m
++Fnbhp7XSQDdV0oMvfsWA/5TrBAAAAF0kxzg==&bcsi_scan_filename=in-focus-article.htm.

35 SOURCE: SATPb, "Data Sheets: Trends of Violence". *South Asian Terrorism Portal.* Accessed 3 March 2016. www.satp.org/satporgtp/countries/india/states/jandk/datasheets/trendsofviolence.htm.

36 In 2016, over half of all terrorist attacks in India occurred in Jammu and Kashmir across four states. These are Jammu and Kashmir (19 per cent), Chhattisgarh (18 per cent), Manipur (12 per cent), and Jharkhand (10 per cent). Attacks in Jammu and Kashmir represent a 93 per cent increase from 2015. SOURCE: U.S. Department of State. 2018. *National Consortium for the Study of Terrorism and Responses to Terrorism: Annex of Statistical Information.* Department of State. Bethesda: Bureau of Counterterrorism and Countering Violent Extremism.

37 United Jihad Council leader and close associate of Hafiz Saeed, Syed Salahuddin is another extremely important enabler of Pakistani foreign policy in Jammu and Kashmir. Ahmad reports that Pakistan considers any reference to Salahuddin and the UJC as terrorist is "completely unjustified" and that Pakistan will always continue to completely support the Kashmiri struggle. SOURCE: Imtiaz Ahmad, 2017. "Pakistan says global terrorist tag on Syed Salahuddin 'unjustified'". *Hindustan Times.* Accessed 5 September 2017. www.hindustantimes.com/world-news/pakistan-defends-syed-salahuddin-says-will-continue-to-back-kashmir-struggle/story-rSZOElJApHNQiQ1RkQnqHJ.html.

38 Mushtaq Zargar is known as a long-time and ruthless Kashmiri terrorist. Mehmood Bhai is a Jaish-e-Mohammed commander who has cooperated with LeT operations. SOURCES: Ankit Panda, 2015. "Why China Snubbed India on a Pakistan-Based Terrorist at the UN". *The Diplomat.* Accessed 16 February 2016. https://thediplomat.com/2015/06/why-china-snubbed-india-on-a-pakistan-based-terrorist-at-the-un/; PTI, 2018c. "Around 170 militants including top commanders killed in Kashmir in 2017". Economic Times. Accessed 23 August 2018. https://economictimes.Indiatimes.com/news/defence/around-170-militants-including-top-commanders-killed-in-kashmir-in-2017/articleshow/6156 3545.cms.

References

Ahmad, Imtiaz. 2017. "Pakistan says global terrorist tag on Syed Salahuddin unjustified". *Hindustan Times.* Accessed 5 September 2017. www.hindustantimes.com/world-news/pakistan-defends-syed-salahuddin-says-will-continue-to-back-kashmir-struggle/story-rSZOElJApHNQiQ1RkQnqHJ.html.

Ali, F and Shehzad, M. 2009. "Lashkar-i-Tayyiba Remains Committed to Jihad". *CTC Sentinel* 2 (3): 13–15.

American Foreign Policy Council. 2014. "Lashkar-e-Taiba" *AFPC.* Accessed 3 June 2017. http://almanac.afpc.org/sites/almanac.afpc.org/files/Lashkar-epercent20Taiba_0.pdf.

Amin, Tahir. 1982. *Afghanistan Crisis: Implications and Options for Muslim World, Iran, and Pakistan.* Institute for Policy Studies, Pakistan.

AP. 2010. "Indian report: Pakistan spies tied to Mumbai siege". 19 October. Accessed 15 September 2017. www.ctvnews.ca/indian-report-pakistan-spies-tied-to-mumbai-siege-1.564652.

Azizi, Parviz. 2014. "Pakistan, India, and the Secret War for Afghanistan". *Geopolitical Monitor.* 3 December. Accessed 11 November 2017. www.geopoliticalmonitor.com/pakistan-india-secret-war-afghanistan/.

Baker, Aryn. 2009. "Who Killed Abdullah Azzam?" *Time.* Accessed 6 February 2016. http://content.time.com/time/specials/packages/article/0,28804,1902809_1902 810_1905173-1,00.html.

Balasubramaniyan, V. and Raghavan, S.V. 2017. *Terror Funds in India: Money Behind Mayhem*. Lancer Publishers Atlanta 2017

Bashir, Usman and Khalid, Iram. 2019. "Religion and Electoral Politics in Punjab: A Case Study of 2018 General Elections". *Journal of South Asian Studies* 34 (1): 7–24.

Baweja, Harinder. 2013. "Army spook unit carried out covert ops in Pakistan". *Hindustan Times*. 21 September. Accessed 24 June 2017. www.hindustantimes.com/delhi-news/army-spook-unit-carried-out-covert-ops-in-pakistan/story-4j1WTCxyj8ObRmktfl3zWN.html?isab=true&meta-geo.

Bengali, Shashank. 2017. "Anti-Indian protests in Kashmir have grown in size and intensity in the year". *LA Times*. 17 May. Accessed 18 November 2017. www.latimes.com/world/la-fg-india-kashmir-20170527-story.html.

Berman, Eran. 2010. "Lashkar-e-Toiba's Jewish Problem". 16 April. Accessed 26 October 2017. www.ict.org.il/Article.aspx?ID=1072#gsc.tab=0.

Bidwal, Praful. 2008. "Confronting the Reality of Hindutva Terrorism". *Economic and Political Weekly* 43 (47): 10–13.

Blair, Dennis. 2010. *Annual Threat Assessment of the U.S. Intelligence Community for the House Permanent Select Committee on Intelligence*. Threat Assessment, Washington, D.C.: Office of the Director of National Intelligence.

Blank, Jonah. 2015. "Pakistan and China's Almost Alliance". *RAND*. 15 October. Accessed 29 October 2017. www.rand.org/blog/2015/10/pakistan-and-chinas-almost-alliance.html.

Bourdieu, Pierre. 1989. "Social Space and Symbolic Power". *Sociological Theory* 7 (1): 14–25.

Brown, Vahid and Rassler, Don. 2012. *Fountainhead of Jihad: The Haqqani Nexus 1973–2012*. New York: Columbia University Press.

Bukhari, S. 2017. "Lashkar Moves to Give Struggle a 'Pure Kashmir Colour'". *The Hindu*. 26 December. Accessed 26 September 2017. www.thehindu.com/2001/12/26/stories/2001122601431200.htm.

Chalk, Peter. 2010. "Lashkar-e-Taiba's Growing International Focus and Its Links with al-Qaeda". *Jamestown Terrorism Monitor* 8 (30): 6–9. Accessed 9 November 2017. https://jamestown.org/program/lashkar-e-taibas-growing-international-focus-and-its-links-with-al-qaeda/.

Chaubey, S. 2017. "New Lashkar commander in Kashmir: who is Zeenat-ul-Islam?" *India Today*. 16 September. Accessed 4 October 2017. http://indiatoday.intoday.in/story/lashkar-commander-kashmir-zeenat-ul-islam/1/1049118.html.

Chaudhry, Asif. 2017. "New TTP wing of trained suicide commandos behind Lahore attack". *Dawn*. Accessed 18 May 2016. www.dawn.com/news/1347712.

CIA 2013. "A Look Back … Murder at CIA's Front Gate". *Central Intelligence Agency*. Accessed 10 July 2017. www.cia.gov/news-information/featured-story-archive/murder-at-cia.html;

Clarke, Ryan. 2012. *Lashkar-i-Taiba: The Fallacy of Subservient Proxies and the Future of Islamist Terrorism in India*. Washington, D.C.: Strategic Studies Institute, US Army War College. Accessed 22 May 2018. www.jstor.org/stable/resrep11768.

Countering Extremism Project. 2017. "Lashkar-e-Taiba". Accessed 15 November 2017. www.counterextremism.com/threat/lashkar-e-taiba.

Dikshit, Sandeep. 2005. "Life expectancy of soldiers low: study". *The Hindu*. 29 December. Accessed 15 May 2018. www.thehindu.com/2005/12/29/stories/2005122904610900.htm.

Dill, Eric (Maj.) 2012. *Lashkar-e-Taiba: A Global Threat Today, A Threat to Pakistan Tomorrow*. Quantico, VA: USMC Command and Staff College Marine Corps University.

Dineen, Brian, Vandewalle, Don, Noe, Raymond, and Wu, Lusi. 2017. "Who cares about demands-abilities fit?" *Personal Psychology* 71 (4): 122–152.

Dorsey, James. 2017. "Protecting Militants: China Blocks UN Listing of Pakistani as Globally Designated Terrorist". *Eurasia Review*. Accessed 13 July 2017. www.eurasiareview.com/09022017-protecting-militants-china-blocks-un-listing-of-pakistani-as-globally-designated-terrorist-analysis/.

D'Souza, Shanthie Mariet and Routray, Bibhu Prasad. 2016 "Jihad in Jammu and Kashmir: Actors, Agendas and Expanding Benchmarks". *Small Wars & Insurgencies* 27 (4): 557–577.

Dutta, Prabhash. 2017. "Hafiz Saeed to register Jamaat-ul-Dawa as political party, renames it as Milli Muslim League Pakistan". *India Today*. 3 August. Accessed 27 November 2017. http://indiatoday.intoday.in/story/hafiz-saeed-political-party-jamaat-ud-dawah-milli-muslim-league-pakistan/1/1018115.html.

Everly, Jr, George. 2011. "Building a Resilient Organizational Culture". *Harvard Business Review*. 24 June. Accessed 16 November 2017. www.gystconsulting.com.au/userfiles/files/building_a_resilient_organizat.pdf.

Fair, Christine. 2009. *Antecedents and Implications of the November 2008 Lashkar-e-Taiba (LeT) Attack Upon Several Targets in the Indian Mega-City of Mumbai*. Washington, D.C.: RAND.

Fair, Christine. 2014. "Insights from a Database of Lashkar-e-Taiba and Hizb-ul-Mujahideen Militants". *Journal of Strategic Studies* 37 (2): 259–290.

Fair, Christine. 2017. "The 2008 Mumbai Attack". In *The Evolution of the Global Terrorists Threat: From 9/11 to Osama bin Laden's Death*, edited by B. Hoffman and F. Reinares, 571–599. New York: Columbia University Press.

Fareed, Ritaf. 2017. "Two Lashkar-e-Taiba fighters killed in Kashmir raid". *Aljazeera*. 17 October. Accessed 6 November 2017. www.aljazeera.com/news/2017/10/lashkar-taiba-fighters-killed-kashmir-raid-171014113822031.html.

Financial Express. 2017. "When China 'gifted' 50 kilograms of Uranium to help Pakistan make nuclear bombs against India". *FE Online*. Accessed 13 August 2017. www.financialexpress.com/india-news/china-gifted-50-kilogram-of-uranium-to-help-pakistan-make-nuclear-bomb-against-india-know-about-the-dreaded-chapter-of-history/800966/.

Forbes. 2009. "An Alphabet Soup of Terror". *Forbes*. Accessed 21 November 2017. www.forbes.com/2009/05/29/taliban-isi-let-jem-lashkar-jaish-pashtun-afghanistan-opinions-contributors-pakistan.html#174e2c3c4d16.

Galula, D. 1964. "The Prerequisites for a Successful Insurgency". In *Counterinsurgency Warfare: Theory and Practice*, edited by F. Praeger, 13–31. New York: Praeger.

Gander, Kashmira. 2013. "Latif, Mehsud, senior commander of Pakistan Taliban, captured by US forces". *The Independent*. Accessed 17 June 2016. www.abc.net.au/news/2013-10-12/us-captures-senior-commander-of-pakistan-taliban/5018260.

Gartenstein-Ross, Daveed and Dabruzzi, Kyle. 2008. "Is Al-Qaeda's Central Leadership Still Relevant?" *Middle East Quarterly* 15 (2): 27–36.

Garver, J. 2004. "India, China, the United States, Tibet, and the Origins of the 1962 War". *India Review* 3 (2): 171–182.

Glanz, James, Rotella, Sebastian, and Sanger, David. 2014. "In 2008 Mumbai Attacks, Piles of Spy Data, but an Uncompleted Puzzle". *The New York Times*. Accessed 22

June 2016. www.nytimes.com/2014/12/22/world/asia/in-2008-mumbai-attacks-piles-of-spy-data-but-an-uncompleted-puzzle.html.

Graff, Violette. 2006. *Hindu-Muslim Communal Riots in India (1947–1986)*. Michigan: Inter-University Consortium For Political and Social Research.

Gurung, Shaurya. 2019. "Over 100 terrorists ready at launch pads to enter India via Pakistan occupied Kashmir: Intelligence ". *Economic Times.* 23 August. Accessed 5 September 2019. https://economictimes.indiatimes.com/news/defence/over-100-terrorists-ready-at-launchpad-in-pok-intelligence/articleshow/70797354.cms?from=mdr.

Haider, Suhasini. 2016. "Delhi hopes UN will push global terror convention". *The Hindu.* Accessed 3 July 2016. www.thehindu.com/news/national/Delhi-hopes-UN-will-push-global-terror-convention /article14467324.ece.

Haider, Suhasini. 2017. "Israel backs India's fight on terror". *The Hindu.* 4 July. Accessed 2 November 2017. www.thehindu.com/todays-paper/israel-backs-indias-defence-against-terror/article19207057.ece.

Hassan, Syed Raza. 2017. "India, Afghanistan gave help to Pakistan Taliban, says group's ex-spokesman". *Reuters News.* 26 April. Accessed 28 October 2017. www.reuters.com/article/us-pakistan-militants/india-afghanistan-gave-help-to-pakistani-taliban-says-groups-ex-spokesman-idUSKBN17S1VN.

Hedberg, Masha. 2016. "Top-Down Self-Organization: State Logics, Substitutional Delegation, and Private Governance in Russia". *Governance* 29 (1): 67–83.

Heneghan, Tom. 2008. "Lashkar-e-Taiba's goals". *Reuters.* Accessed 16 September 2017. http://blogs.reuters.com/faithworld/2008/12/03/lashkar-e-taibas-goals/.

Huggler, J. 2005. "Inside the Pakistani school accused of teaching terrorism". *The Independent.* 15 July. Accessed 27 October 2017. www.independent.co.uk/news/world/asia/inside-the-pakistani-school-accused-of-teaching-terrorism-299440.html.

Indian Government. 2002. "Fact Sheet on Jammu and Kashmir". *Ministry of External Affairs.* 20 May. Accessed 15 March 2018. http://mea.gov.in/in-focus-article.htm?18987/Fact+Sheet+on+Jammu+amp+Kashmir&bcsi_scan_d2f7438883b2c67d=m++Fnbhp7XSQDdV0oMvfsWA/5TrBAAAAF0kxzg==&bcsi_scan_filename=in-focus-article.htm.

ITVND. 2015. "Abu Dujana likely to be new commander of Lashkar-e-Taiba in Kashmir". *India TV News Desk.* 31 October. Accessed 28 November 2017. www.indiatvnews.com/news/india/abu-dujana-likely-to-be-new-commander-of-lashkaretaiba-kashmir-55655.html.

Jaffrelot, Christophe. 2017. "The Saudi Connection". *Indian Express.* 5 July. Accessed 19 September 2017. http://indianexpress.com/article/opinion/columns/the-saudi-connection-4735754/.

Jaffrelot, Christophe and Louer, Laurence. 2017. "Conclusions". In *Pan-Islamic Connections: Transnational Networks Between South Asia and the Gulf*, edited by Christophe Jaffrelot and Laurence Louer, 233–244. New York and London: Oxford University Press.

Jaleel, Muzamil. 20014. "U.S. identifies JuD as Lashkar alias, names two new global terrorists". *The Indian Express.* Accessed 5 June 2016. https://indianexpress.com/article/world/americas/us-identifies-jud-as-lashkar-alias-names-two-new-global-terrorists/.

Jamal, Arif. 2002. "From Madrasa to School". *The News*, 15 December: 50.

Joshua, Anita. 2016. "Young, educated and dangerous". *The Hindu.* 18 October. Accessed 26 November 2017. www.thehindu.com/opinion/op-ed/Young-educated-and-dangerous/article12191626.ece.

144   *Real world analysis*

Kapisthalam, K. 2009. "Banned Pakistani Terror Group Re-Emerges Under New Name". *The Long War Journal.* 15 January. Accessed 11 May 2017. www.longwarjournal.org/archives/2008/12/un_declares_jamaatud.php.

Katoch, P. 2016. "China-Pakistan Economic Corridor: 'Highway of Terror' turns operational at last". *First Post India.* 16 November. Accessed 24 October 2017. www.firstpost.com/india/china-pakistan-economic-corridor-highway-of-terror-turns-operational-at-last-3107800.html.

Kaura, Vinay, 2017. *Indo-Israeli Security Cooperation: Onward and Upward.* Ramat Gan, Israel: BESA Centre Perspectives Paper No. 522.

Khan, R. 2010. "Untangling the Punjab Taliban Network". *CTC Sentinel* 3 (3): 7–9.

Kumar, Arushi. 2017. "China Pressuring Pakistan on Terrorism?" *The Diplomat.* 17 September. Accessed 5 November 2017. https://thediplomat.com/2017/09/china-pressuring-pakistan-on-terrorism/.

Laskar, R. 2014. "Revealed: How Mumbai attacks mastermind runs LeT from Pakistan jail". *Daily Mail.* 29 August. Accessed 1 November 2017. www.dailymail.co.uk/india-home/indianews/article-2737132/Revealed-How-Mumbai-attacks-mastermind-runs-LeT-Pakistan-jail.html.

Lucknow. 2016. "Inter-Services Intelligence Agent Arrested in Lucknow". *Indo-Asian News Service.* 24 August. Accessed 17 November 2017. www.ndtv.com/lucknow-news/inter-services-intelligence-agent-arrested-in-lucknow-1449387.

MacDonald, Myra. 2011. "Blacklisted group says Pakistan needs peace, prosperity". *Reuters.* 12 July. Accessed 5 August 2016. www.reuters.com/article/us-pakistan-jud/blacklisted-group-says-pakistan-needs-peace-prosperity-idUSTRE76B05M20110712.

Mahapatra, Debidatta. 2018. "Gandhi, International Relations, and War". In *Gandhi and the World,* edited by Debidatta Mahapatra and Yashwant Pathak, 13–37. Lanham, Boulder, New York, and London: Lexington Books.

Masood, Bashaarat. 2011. "Lashkar face in south Kashmir killed". *The Indian Express.* Accessed 6 March 2016. http://archive.indianexpress.com/news/lashkar-face-in-south-kashmir-killed/855448/.

Menon, Shivshankar. 2016. *Choices: Inside the Making of India's Foreign Policy.* Washington, D.C.: Brookings Institution Press.

Mishra, Kashmir Mohan. 2018. "Average age of a terrorist in Jammu and Kashmir is six months". *Zeenews.* 26 October. Accessed 5 January 2019. http://zeenews.india.com/india/average-age-of-a-terrorist-in-jammu-and-kashmir-is-six-months-2151149.html.

MMP. 2017. *Mapping Militants Project – Lashkar-e-Taiba.* Stanford: Stanford University. http://web.stanford.edu/group/mappingmilitants/cgi-bin/groups/view/79.

Musarrat, Razia, Ali, Ghulam, and Azhar, Salman. 2012. "The Predicament of Ethnicity in Divided Society of Pakistan". *International Journal of Human Resource Studies* 2 (1): 199–209.

Naseem, Ishfaq. 2017. "Despite Bandipora encounter, Lashkar-e-Taiba remains deadliest militant outfit in Kashmir". *First Post.* 19 November. Accessed 25 March 2018. www.firstpost.com/india/despite-bandipora-encounter-lashkar-e-taiba-remains-deadliest-militant-outfit-in-kashmir-4217983.html.

Nomani, Asra. 2011. "Salmaan Taseer and the Punjabi Taliban". *Foreign Policy.* 5 January. Accessed 18 November 2017. http://foreignpolicy.com/2011/01/05/salmaan-taseer-and-the-punjabi-taliban/.

Noonan, Sean and Levey, Stuart. 2011. "The Evolution of a Pakistani Militant Network". *CBRNE Terrorism News Letter* 39 (2011): 193–197.

Panda, A. 2015. "Why China Snubbed India on a Pakistan-based Terrorist at the UN". *The Diplomat.* 25 June. Accessed 21 May 2017. http://thediplomat.com/2015/06/why-china-snubbed-india-on-a-pakistan-based-terrorist-at-the-un/.

Pant, Harsh and Sahu, Ambuj. 2019. *Israel's arms sales to India: Bedrock of a strategic partnership.* Special Report, New Delhi: Observer Research Foundation.

Paul, Katie and Torbati, Yeganeh. 2016. "U.S. and Saudi Arabia sanction alleged Lashkar-e-Taiba supporters". *Reuters.* 1 April. Accessed 27 November 2017. www. reuters.com/article/us-usa-saudi-sanctions/u-s-and-saudi-arabia-sanction-alleged-lashkar-e-taiba-supporters-idUSKCN0WX2JM.

PTI. 2018a. "5 LeT, HM militants killed in J&K encounter; civilian killed in protests". *moneycontrol.* 15 September. Accessed 4 October 2018. www.moneycontrol. com/news/world/5-let-hm-militants-killed-in-j-civilian-killed-in-protests-2953871. html.

PTI. 2018b. "Pakistan bans 72 groups including Hafiz Saeed's JuD, LeT; says those funding them will face up to 10 years in jail". *First Post.* 7 January. Accessed January 16, 2018. www.firstpost.com/world/pakistan-bans-72-groups-including-hafiz-saeeds-jud-let-says-those-funding-them-will-face-up-to-10-years-jail-4291011.html.

PTI. 2018c. "Around 170 militants including top commanders killed in Kashmir in 2017". *Economic Times.* Accessed 23 August 2018. https://economictimes.Indiatimes. com/news/defence/around-170-militants-including-top-commanders-killed-in-kashmir-in-2017/articleshow/6156 3545.cms.

Raina, Anil. 2018. "Operation All Out: Killing Militants Not Going To Solve Any Problems". *Mumbai Mirror.* 14 January. Accessed 25 March 2018. https://Mumbaimirror. indiatimes.com/news/india/operation-all-out-killing-not-going-to-solve-any-problems. articleshow/62495001.cms.

Raman, B. 2004. *Split in Let: A Charade.* Paper No. 1059, New Delhi: South Asia Analysis Group. Paper 1054. Accessed 2 November 2017. www.southasiaanalysis.org/ paper1059.

Ramani, Samuel. 2017. "What's Driving Russia-Pakistan Cooperation on Afghanistan?" *The Diplomat.* 9 May. Accessed 3 November 2017. https://thediplomat.com/2017/05/ whats-driving-russia-pakistan-cooperation-on-afghanistan/.

Ramani, Samuel. 2018. "Russia and Pakistan: A Durable Anti-American Alliance in South Asia". *The Diplomat.* 21 April. Accessed 5 May 2018. https://thediplomat. com/2018/04/russia-and-pakistan-a-durable-anti-american-alliance-in-south-asia/.

Ramarao, Malladi. 2017. "U.S. Congress against including action against LeT as a condition for funds to Pakistan?" *Policy Research Group.* 14 November. Accessed 14 November 2017. www.policyresearchgroup.com/us-congress-against-including-action-against-let-as-condition-for-funds-to-pakistan/.

Rassler, D., Fair, C., Chosh, A., Jamal, A., and Shoeb, N. 2013. *The Fighters of Lashkar-e-Taiba: Recruitment, Training, Development and Death.* West Point: CTC – Combating Terrorism Center.

Rath, Sarok. 2014. "LeT: From Regional to Global". In *Fragile Frontiers: The Secret History of Mumbai Terror Attacks,* edited by S. Rath, 63–92. New York: Routledge.

Reed, Todd, Raschke, Diana, and Bovington, Gardner. 2011. "The ETIM: China's Islamic Militants and the Global Terrorist Threat: The Uyghurs: Strangers in Their Own Land". *Foreign Affairs.* 1 February. Accessed 2 November 2017. www. foreignaffairs.com/reviews/capsule-review/2011-01-01/etim-chinas-islamic-militants-and-global-terrorist-threat-uyghurs.

Reuters. 2016. "U.S. and Saudi Arabia sanction alleged Lashkar-e-Taiba supporters". *Reuters.* 1 April. Accessed 27 March 2018. www.reuters.com/article/us-usa-saudi-sanctions/u-s-and-saudi-arabia-sanction-alleged-lashkar-e-taiba-supporters-idUSKCN0WX2JM.

Reuters. 2017. "Cleric accused of masterminding 2008 Mumbai attacks under house arrest". 31 January. Accessed 5 June 2017. www.theguardian.com/world/2017/jan/30/cleric-2008-mumbai-attacks-house-arrest-hafiz-saeed-us-pakistan-india.

Riedel, B. 2015. "The China-Pakistan axis and Lashkar-e-Taiba". *Brookings Institute.* 26 June. Accessed 3 November 2017, www.brookings.edu/opinions/the-china-pakistan-axis-and-lashkar-e-taiba/.

Rotella, Sebastian. 2013. "A Terror Group That Recruits From Pakistan's 'Best and Brightest' ". *The Atlantic.* 4 April. Accessed 26 November 2017. www.theatlantic.com/international/archive/2013/04/a-terror-group-that-recruits-from-pakistans-best-and-brightest/274682/.

Roul, Animesh. 2003. "Lashkar-e-Taiba Resumes Operations Against Indian Forces in Jammu and Kashmir". *Terrorism Monitor* 7 (1): 4–6.

Roul, Animesh. 2015. "Jamaat-ud Daawa: Into the mainstream". *ETH Zurich – Center for Security Studies.* 19 May. Accessed 6 June 2015. https://css.ethz.ch/en/services/digital-library/articles/article.html/190666/pdf.

Sandhu, Kamaljit. 2017. "Indian Army's 'Operation All Out' in Kashmir killed 190 terrorists, but there is reason to worry". *Daily O.* 27 November. Accessed 27 March 2018. www.dailyo.in/politics/kashmir-militancy-hizbul-mujahideen-indian-army/story/1/20687.html.

Sareen, S. 2005. "Dividing Jihad to Control It". In *The Jihad Factory: Pakistan's Islamic Revolution in the Making*, edited by S. Sareen, 134–181. New Delhi: Har-Anand Publications.

Sasikumar, Karthika. 2010. "State Agency in the Time of the Global War on Terror: India and the Counter-Terrorism Regime". *Review of International Studies* 36 (3): 615–638.

SATP. 2016a. "Terrorist Outfits: Lashkar-e-Taiba". *South Asia Terrorism Portal.* Accessed 5 March 2016. www.satp.org/satporgtp/countries/india/states/jandk/terrorist_outfits/Lashkar_etoiba.htm.

SATP. 2016b. "Data Sheets: Trends of Violence". *South Asian Terrorism Portal,* Accessed 3 March 2016. www.satp.org/satporgtp/countries/india/states/jandk/datasheets/trendsofviolence. htm.

SATP. 2017. "Harkat-ul-jihad-al-Islami (JuJI) (Movement of Islamic Holy War)". *South Asian Terrorism Portal.* Accessed 12 August 2018. www.satp.org/satporgtp/countries/india/states/jandk/terrorist outfits/HuJI.htm.

SATP. 2018. "Fatalities in Terrorist Violence 1988–2018". *South Asia Terrorism Portal.* 15 March. Accessed 28 March 2018. www.satp.org/satporgtp/countries/india/states/jandk/data_sheets/annual_casualties.htm?bcsi_scan_d2f7438883b2c67d=0&bcsi_scan_filename=annual_casualties.htm.

Scheuer, Michael. 2007. "Chasing bin Laden's Money". In *Through Our Enemies' Eyes: Osama bin Laden, Radical Islam, and the Future of America,* edited by Michael Scheuer, 31–44. Nebraska: Potomac Books, Inc.

Shafiq, A. 2007. "The Jihad Within". *Herald (Karachi, Pakistan),* 1 April: 92–93.

Shafqat, S. 2004. "From Official Islam to Islamism: The Rise of Dawat-ul-Irshad and Lashkar-e-Taiba". In *Pakistan: Nationalism Without a Nation,* edited by C. Jaffrelot, 131–148. London, New York, and New Delhi: ZED Books.

Shah, J. 2012. "Zia Ul-Haque and the Proliferation of Religion in Pakistan". *International Journal of Business and Social Science* 3 (21): 310–323.

Shah, Khalid. 2018. "Why Kashmir needs a new counterinsurgency strategy". *Observer Research Foundation.* 18 May. Accessed 13 June 2018. www.orfonline.org/expert-speak/kashmir-needs-new-counterinsurgency-strategy/.

Shahid, K. 2017. "What Syed Salahuddin's 'Global Terrorist' Designation Means for Pakistan". *The Diplomat.* 29 June. Accessed 2 November 2017. https://thediplomat.com/2017/06/what-syed-salahuddins-global-terrorist-designation-means-for-pakistan/.

Shams, Shamil. 2017. "China's 'betrayal' – BRICS leaders slam Pakistan-based jihadi groups". Accessed 15 September 2017. www.dw.com/en/chinas-betrayal-brics-leaders-slam-pakistan-based-jihadi-groups/a-40365244.

Sharma, Tishta. 2017. "Israelis in Himachal Pradesh At Risk As Lashkar-e-Taiba Conducts Secretive Research". *India-Aware.* 8 December. Accessed 9 December 2017. www.india-aware.com/latest/israelis-himachal-pradesh-risk-lashkar-e-taiba-conducts-secretive-research/.

Shelley, L. 2015. "Corruption and Youth's Recruitment into Violent Extremism". In *Countering Radiaciztion and Violent Extremism Among Youth to Prevent Terrorism,* edited by E. Lombardi, E. Ragab, and V. Chin, 37–47. Amsterdam, Berlin, Tokyo, Washington, D.C.: IOS Press.

Singh, Sushant. 2015. "Simply Put: The working and controversies of TSD, the Army's shadowy MI unit". *The Indian Express.* Accessed 23 June 2016. http://indianexpress.com/article/explained/simply-put-the-working-and-controversies-of-tsd-the-armys-hadowy-mi-unit/.

Singh, Yoshita. 2017. "India welcomes creation of new UN Office of Counter-Terrorism". *Outlook India.* Accessed 13 July 2016. www.outlookindia.com/newsscroll/india-welcomes-creation-of-new-un-office-of-counter-terrorism/107 6928.

Slawinski, Natalie. 2015. "Strategic Leadership". In *Cases in Leadership,* edited by Glenn Rowe and Laura Guerrero, 297–334. New York: SAGE Publications.

Solomon, John. 2011. "9/11 Legacy: More Resilient Skyscrapers". *CBRNE Terrorism Newsletter* 39 (2011): 192–197.

Soltani, Ghorbanali and Rad, Omid Sepehri. 2015. "Theoretical Investigation of Salafi Thought by Emphasizing Akhbarygary". *Ijtihad Network.* Accessed 24 July 2018. http://ijtihadnet.com/article-theoretical-investigation-salafi-thought-emphasizing-akhbarygary/.

Srivastava, Samarth. 2017. "LeT top leadership in Kashmir Valley wiped out: Indian Army". *News Track.* 19 November. Accessed 28 November 2017. https://newstrack.com/india-news/let-top-leadership-kashmir-valley-wiped-indian-army/.

Stanford University "Mapping Militant Organizations". Accessed 28 October 2018. http://web.stanford.edu/group/mappingmilitants/cgi-bin/groups/view/79.

Starr, B. 2008. "U.S.: India's air force 'on alert' after Mumbai attacks". *CNN.* 15 December. Accessed 15 September 2017. http://edition.cnn.com/2008/WORLD/asiapcf/12/15/india.pakistan.tension/.

Subrahmanian, V.S., Mannes, Aaron, Silva, Amy, Shakarian, Jana and Dickerson, John. 2008. "A Brief History of LeT: LeT's Top Leaders". In *Computational Analysis of Terrorist Groups: Lasker-e-Taiba,* edited by V.S. Subrahmanian, Aaron Mannes, Amy Silva, Jana Shakarian, and John Dickerson, 23–68. New York: Springer.

Sudha, Ramachandran. 2007. "PART2: Behind the Harkat-ul-Jihad Al-Islami". *Asia Times Online.* Accessed 7 July 2016. www.atimes.com/atimes/South_Asia/FL10Df06.html.

Swami, P. 2016. "India's new langauge of killing". *The Hindu.* 23 May. Accessed 11 August 2017. www.thehindu.com/opinion/lead/indias-new-language-of-killing/article5963505.ece.

Swami, Praveen. 2017. "Lashkar commander killed". *The Indian Express.* Accessed 6 March 2017. http://indianexpress.com/article/india/lashkar-commander-killed-in-rise-and-fall-of-abu-dujana-a-tale-of-falsehood-and-ambition-4778106/.

Swami, Praveen and Shehzad, Mohammed. 2004. "Lashkar raising Islamist Brigades for Iraq". *The Hindu.* Accessed 10 July 2016. www.thehindu.com/2004/06/13/stories/2004061306050100.htm.

Tankel, Stephen. 2011. *Storming the World Stage: The Story of Lashkar-e-Taiba.* London: Hurst & Co. Ltd.

Tellis, Ashley. 2009. "Lessons From Mumbai". Washington, D.C., Moscow, Beirut, Bejing, and Brussels: Carnegie Endowment for International Peace.

Tellis, Ashley. 2012. "The Menace That is Lashkar-e-Taiba". *Carnegie Endowment For International Peace.* 1 March. Accessed 15 November 2017. http://carnegieendowment.org/files/LeT_menace.pdf.

Trehan, Jyoti. 2002. "Terrorism and the Funding of Terrorism in Kashmir". *Journal of Financial Crime* 9 (3): 201–211.

Ul-Hassan, Ishfaq. 2010. "Arrested Lashkar-e-Taiba militant spills the beans to Jammu and Kashmir Police, lays bare neighbour's nefarous designs". 27 November. Accessed 5 October 2017. www.dnaindia.com/india/report-pakistan-cocks-a-snook-revives-terror-centres-closed-after-2611-1472732.

United Nations Security Council. 2014. "QDi.265 Haji Muhammad Ashraf". *Al-Qaida Sanctions Committee.* Accessed 2 March 2016. www.un.org/sc/suborg/en/sanctions/1267/aq_sanctions_list/sum maries/individual/haj i-muhammad-ashraf.

United States Government. 2008. "Specially Designated Nationals and Blocked Persons". *U.S. Department of the Treasury.* Accessed 5 December 2018. www.treasury.gov/resource-center/sanctions/sdn-list/pages/default.aspx.

United States Government. 2016. "Treasury Sanctions Lashkar-e-Tayyiba Financial and Leadership Officials". *U.S. Department of Treasury.* 28 December. Accessed 26 November 2017. www.treasury.gov/press-center/press-releases/Pages/jl0691.aspx.

United States Government. 2018. *National Consortium for the Study of Terrorism and Responses to Terrorism: Annex of Statistical Information.* Department of State. Bethesda, Bureau of Counterterrorism and Countering Violent Extremism.

Vij, Shivam. 2019. "Why Indians and Pakistanis Want a War". *Foreign Policy.* 19 September. Accessed 15 October 2019. https://foreignpolicy.com/2019/09/19/why-indians-and-pakistanis-want-a-war/.

Wani, Ashraf. 2016. "Exclusive: Meet the new face of Lashkar-e-Taiba in Kashmir". *India Today.* 15 December. Accessed 24 November 2017. http://indiatoday.intoday.in/story/lashkar-e-taiba-in-kashmir-new-face-jammu-and-kashmir/1/835223.html.

Wani, Fayaz. 2017. "Zeenat-ul-Islam likely to be first Kashmiri militant to head Lashkar-e-Taiba in Valley". *New Indian Express.* 17 September. Accessed 16 November 2017. www.newindianexpress.com/nation/2017/sep/17/zeenat-ul-islam-likely-to-be-first-kashmiri-militant-to-head-lashkar-e-taiba-in-valley-1658681.html.

Wilson, J. 2008. "Resurgent Radicalism in Pakistan: A Case Study of Jamaat-ud-Dawa". *CLAWS* (Winter) (1): 60–73.

Wilson, James in Long, Austin. 2016. "Culture, Doctrine, and Military Professionalization". In *The Soul of Armies: Counterinsurgency Doctrine and Military Culture in the*

US and UK, edited by Austin Long, 13–34. Ithaca and London: Cornell University Press.

Yasir, Sameer. 2016. "United Jihad Council claims Pathankot attack". *First Post*. Accessed 5 April 2016. www.firstpost.com/politics/united-jihad-council-claims-pathankot-attack-heres-why-this-admission-is-an-exercise-in-subterfuge-2571098. html.

Zahab, Mariam Abou. 2007. "I Shall be Waiting for You at the Door of Paradise: The Pakistani Martyrs of the Lashkar-e-Taiba (Army of the Pure)". In *The Practice of War: Production, Reproduction and Communication of Armed Violence*, edited by Aparna Rao, Michael Bollig, and Monika Bock, 133–160. New York and Oxford: Berghahn Books.

Zahab, Mariam Abou, and Roy, Oliver. 2004. "Pakistan: From Religious Conservatism to Political Radicalism – Salafism and Jihadism". In *Islamist Networks: The Afghan-Pakistan Connection*, edited by Mariam Abou Zahab and Oliver Roy, 32–47. London: C. Hurst & Co. Publishers.

5   Jemaah Islamiyah

This chapter examines Jemaah Islamiyah, an organization of deep familial networks and strong kinship bonds. However, it differs importantly from other familial organizations, notably the Haqqani Network examined in Chapter 3. In Jemaah Islamiyah, familial and kinship bonds exist vertically through median levels, and also horizontally across base levels, whereas in the Haqqani Network consanguine kinship often constricts at the tactical command level. In Jemaah Islamiyah, family is a mechanism of resilience and structural strength across both vertical and horizontal axes, and family and kinship dynamics strongly influence its command and control, daily operations, and strategic direction. These have manifested holacratically as a result of external pressures and have actively contributed to its efficiency and resilience.

Jemaah Islamiyah is paired with the meritocratic organization the Abu Sayyaf Group examined in the next chapter. Each shares many characteristics including proximity, significant international attention and external pressures, particularly from Australia, Singapore, the United States, Malaysia, and Singapore, and strong external pressures at home. Additionally, Jemaah Islamiyah and the Abu Sayyaf Group often work collaboratively and have many levels of connection to each other, al-Qaeda, Afghanistan and the Haqqani Network, and the Islamic State group.

However, Jemaah Islamiyah is a familial organization while Abu Sayyaf is clearly a meritocracy. A comparison between the two organizations shows that in the Abu Sayyaf Group, social capital and trust have different socio-economic values of utilitarianism, professionalism, and resource provision. This allows the Abu Sayyaf Group to recruit the most proficient, ruthless, and proven fighters, and for lower-level commanders to rise up the ladder by proving themselves as they gain supporters and experience. In Jemaah Islamiyah, social capital and trust are facilitated across family, largely by marriage and consanguine kinship. This provides strengths and efficiencies in information, recruitment, vetting, and operational security, and also gives it significant counterintelligence advantages. These features also enable Jemaah Islamiyah to be highly adaptable.

Fealy and Borgu report that Jemaah Islamiyah has maintained "considerable resilience and capacity for change" (2005, 4). Despite having come close to being destroyed a number of times over its 25-year history, it has come back after each disruption demonstrating an impressive ability to adapt, recover, and reconstitute its political and operational capacities. This turbulence extends to governance where it has experienced a number of apex leadership transitions and splinters such as the Noorudin Top cell, al-Qaeda in Aceh (AiA), and the Dulmatin cells, and Jamaah Ansharut Tauhid (JAT).[1] Despite these dynamic changes, core operational capabilities have remained efficient and therefore resilient. This is an interesting phenomenon as the instability of strategic leadership in Jemaah Islamiyah inversely fosters greater tactical endurance.

This derives from Jemaah Islamiyah's familial command and control as leaders emerge as adaptive agents when overall strategic direction has been missing. Between 2002 and 2015, there were over half a dozen leaders in the Jemaah Islamiyah Amir-ship while operations continued, driven largely by individual commanders. As leaders rose they cemented correlational bonds, mostly from inside Jemaah Islamiyah's densely populated familial groups, resulting in aggregated tactical leadership across the organization as strategic direction oscillated. That same support base of family and kinship is important for another reason. Unlike its affiliates in the Southeast Asian jihadi nexus, Jemaah Islamiyah has no judicial patronage or powerful state actors supporting it.[2] For example, the Abu Sayyaf Group has enjoyed strong support from Libya (CFR 2005), and the Haqqani network and Lashkar-e-Taiba are supported by Pakistan (Krasner 2012). As a consequence, Jemaah Islamiyah's familial nature supports its resilience in organic ways.

The examination of this is presented in four sections. The first section provides the foundational analysis of Jemaah Islamiyah operations and organization, and how family and kinship are a critical part of its success. It develops our understanding of family and kinship in Jemaah Islamiyah's structure by specifically looking at its organizational morphology and its strong insurgency efficiencies. The second section presents the examination of external pressures exerted against Jemaah Islamiyah, particularly after the December 2000 Christmas Eve bombings and the Singapore plots, and in the wake of successive attacks beginning with Bali 2002.[3]

Where and by whom Jemaah Islamiyah has been targeted, and the effectiveness thereof are also discussed. The third section analyses Jemaah Islamiyah's resilience, its adaptation to endogenous and exogenous shock from external pressures, and its efficiency in doing so. The concluding analysis is presented in the fourth section, finding that family and kinship have been central to Jemaah Islamiyah's resilience, and while it suffered considerable hard-power external pressures that came close to destroying it, family and social capital and trust were central to its ability to efficiently reconstitute and bounce back.

Background: the importance of family in Jemaah Islamiyah operations

Jemaah Islamiyah is a well-established, mature, and highly experienced insurgent organization with extensive involvement in domestic and international conflicts.[4]

Due to this, it has been drawn on by Afghan organizations to supply Asian fighters, as well as members from Filipino insurgent organizations to facilitate fighting in Afghanistan. As a result, Jemaah Islamiyah later formed joint training camps with the Moro Islamic Liberation Front (MILF), Moro National Liberation Front (MNLF), and Abu Sayyaf Group in the Southern Philippines. Family, kinship, and social capital have critical roles in the development of these relationships, with many leading to deeper inter-organizational consanguine ties. Helfstein and Wright (2011) observe that the geographic origins of Jemaah Islamiyah members, and the familial and social capital ties with other insurgent groups, are critical facets of its extensive operational network.

This network was built upon a territorially based administrative structure with an Amir at the top who was the spiritual and operational leader. Under the Amir, then Abu Bakar Ba'asyir, Jemaah Islamiyah had a central command governance council that set strategic direction and operational goals. The organization was further divided into four territorial Mantiqi groups that had operational control over their respective districts across the Asia Pacific region.[5] Prior to his arrest in 2003, Jemaah Islamiyah Operations Chief Hambali, an Afghan war veteran, was a critical part of the Jemaah Islamiyah central core, the overall head of the Mantiqi network, and commander of Mantiqi I.[6]

Hambali was also a close friend of Mohammed Jamal Khalifa, the brother-in-law of Osama bin Laden (Berger 2007). Khalifa was the al-Qaeda financing conduit to Jemaah Islamiyah and the Abu Sayyaf Group. When living in the Philippines he had regular contact with Hambali, helping him establish a front business, the Konsojaya Trading Company in 1994 with his wife, Noralwizah lee Abdullah, who was the sister-in-law of Jemaah Islamiyah commander Abu Yusuf.[7] The Konsojaya Trading Company was a major source of covert al-Qaeda funding to Jemaah Islamiyah in the 1990s (Comras 2005).

As well as being the overall Mantiqi leader, Hambali was the key operational command and control actor in Jemaah Islamiyah. Mantiqi I focused on recruiting new members from existing conflict areas, forging new familial connections, and re-activating experienced field commanders. These provided an efficiency dividend to Jemaah Islamiyah because it reduced vetting, training, and indoctrination costs substantially. Indoctrination molds recruits into the required format, but for those not already connected through kinship it is what happens after joining that truly bonds members to it. Jemaah Islamiyah is an intricate network of arranged marriages between subordinates and leaders, creating a "giant extended family that keeps the organization secure" (ICG 2003, i).

The emphasis on kinship is reflected in its social capital investments and encouragement of recruits to intermarry. While recruitment generally occurs through family, in cases where recruits have no existing ties, marrying into Jemaah Islamiyah is typically required. Ressa reports, "Marriages have long cemented alliances among jihadi networks, and women played key roles in Jemaah Islamiyah's plots, from translators to accomplices" (2015, 1). Ressa (2015) goes on to argue that with increases in technology, recruits often do not meet in person before marrying, only communicating via Facebook and online before a ceremony by video conference. Jones' assertions support this, stating that "Jemaah Islamiyah men married the sisters or daughters of other Jemaah Islamiyah members, or chose wives from Jemaah Islamiyah schools where the girls had been carefully inculcated with the organization's values" (2015, 1). Therefore, marrying into Jemaah Islamiyah is the norm.

Family and marriage is not simply symbolic, but confers real social support. Partners of Jemaah Islamiyah fighters not only accompany men into combat areas like Syria, often with children in tow, but increasingly the wives of fighters have engaged directly in operations.[8] This strong kinship focus is a distinguishing feature of the organization, as is the importance the organization places on supporting members and their immediate families in the event of death, serious injury, or simply through illness or old age. Hastings (2010) notes explicitly the importance of providing social services and making regular payments to slain members' families for instance. Conversely, Osman (2010) reports that Indonesian authorities also recognized the importance of family and kinship to Jemaah Islamiyah, and that they have programmes in place to support families in the event that a bread-winning fighter is killed or captured.[9]

This continually reinforces a sense of community and works as a trust vehicle to new members and new generations. It likewise provides access to membership, cements Jemaah Islamiyah as a familial patron, and builds popular political support outside of Jemaah Islamiyah networks. These vehicles of trust also support community integration. Long before the wars in Iraq and Syria, Jemaah Islamiyah aimed to establish its own Islamic State. It used its Mantiqi structure, consisting of several divisions with regional responsibilities, as its means to do so, as depicted in Figure 5.1. Within the Mantiqi were wakalah – geographically based military brigades (Hastings 2010). Mantiqi I was led by Hambali, Mantiqi II by Abu Rusdan, and Mantiqi III by Nasir Abbas. These covered Singapore and Malaysia, mainland Indonesia, and Sulawesi, and the Philippines and Eastern Malaysia. Mantiqi IV was led by Abdul Rahim Ayub in Australia, but it achieved little except for a failed plot involving British-born convert Jack Roache (Jeffry 2004).

Into the late 1990s Mantiqi I was the central insurgency group, establishing the infrastructure for the transfer of al-Qaeda funds and materials and coordinating training for hundreds of Jemaah Islamiyah members in Afghanistan (Abuza 2011). Mantiqi II became the principal operational and attack division and was directly responsible for significantly dialing up the operational tempo on Amir Ba'asyir's direction. This was observable in the violence leading up to, and including, the 2000 Christmas Eve church bombings and the Bali 2002 attacks. Mantiqi II also provided the bulk of some 2,000 members as well as being a major source of financing via front companies and charities, as Stillwell (2015) notes. This supported Jemaah Islamiyah's core insurgency strategy and other functions, such as those conducted by Mantiqi III, which was responsible for training and weapons procurement, as well as working directly with regional partners. Kippe (2010) observes it was Mantiqi III that developed and maintained Jemaah

Islamiyah's strong operational cooperation with the Philippines-based MILF and Abu Sayyaf Group, enabling cross-training, support, and logistics.[10]

Following Bali 2002, the Mantiqi structure fell apart because of external pressures. Many of Jemaah Islamiyah's senior commanders were hunted down, and the Muslim fatalities from the attack caused some rifts in the organization that led to a breakdown of formal cohesion. Scholars like Acharya (2006) claim that this made Jemaah Islamiyah less resilient. Others such as Stillwell assert that it "severely hurt Jemaah Islamiyah's operational capabilities" (2015, 1), and would seriously restrict any further attacks. However, the 2003 Superferry 14 and Jakarta JW Marriot bombings, and the 2004 Australian Embassy and Davao airport attacks demonstrate this simply was not the case. In other words, the structure changed but not the capabilities.[11] The reason for this was family.

Significant and multi-agent connections between senior operational leaders has created a system of extreme efficiency, one in which operations work principally on the basis of informal relations outside of structural hierarchies, or strict lines of management and control. Rather, familial connectedness provides the networks for commanders and fighters to engage in secure and often highly cellular attack planning and operational activities with restricted oversight from others. The high saturation of family and the connectedness of the central senior echelon commanders is shown in Figure 5.2. The interconnections represent direct consanguine relations and close kinship through intermarriage between member families that form strong nuclear family links. These links collectively form an extremely strong and efficient organizational operational network.

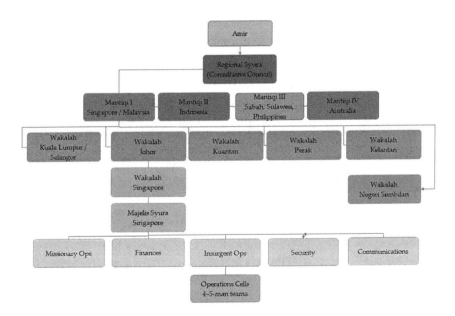

Figure 5.1 Mantiqi structure.

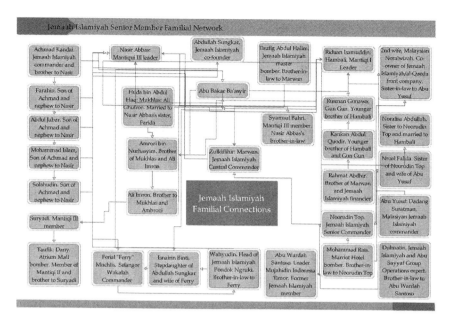

Figure 5.2 Jemaah Islamiyah senior member familial network.

A number of critical features are clearly evident. First, intermarriage is frequent, particularly between senior members. Second, directly or indirectly, practically all of Jemaah Islamiyah's senior officer corps are connected by kinship. It is possible this contributes to increased organizational efficiency, security, and the facilitation of social capital and trust that is so vitally important to it. Von Lampe and Johansen (2003) assert that kinship and ethnicity provide a powerful basis for trust. Similarly, Ayling finds that strong trust between kin-connected members in organizations speeds information flows, thereby "making possible lightning adjustments" (2009, 190) to plans, and enhancing longer-term strategic operations. Jemaah Islamiyah's operational capabilities post the collapse of the Mantiqi structure appear to reflect this.

The third critical feature the figure reveals is how Jemaah Islamiyah's diffused operational methodology developed. For example, sibling groups often work together on operations without the oversight of the Amir or other commanders, using only their closest family to assist. An example of this can be seen in the actions of Mantiqi III leader Nassir Abbas's brother Achmad Kandai, and sons Mukhlas, Ambrozi, and Ali Imron. This may suggest that the resilience of Jemaah Islamiyah to withstand significant structural turbulence and change could stem, at least partially, from the efficiency of its adaptability, commensurate with the saturation of familial connection within it. Eti-Tofinga *et al.* (2017), for instance, have linked individual and family welfare to the welfare performance of organizations, as have Cantanese *et al.* (2016) and Walsh (2015).

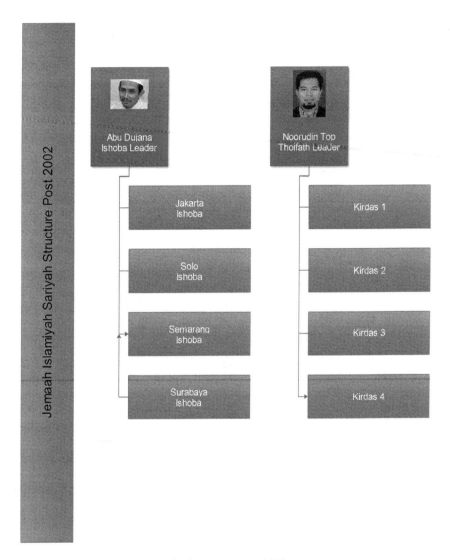

Figure 5.3 Jemaah Islamiyah Sariyah structure post 2002.

   Jemaah Islamiyah efficiency seeking structural changes reflect this. After the complete collapse of the Mantiqi system in October 2002, a new structure was formed based on a *sariyah* (or leadership system) with four smaller units under the sariyah leader Abu Dujana (Figure 5.3). The smaller units, known as *ishoba*, spanned Jakarta, Solo, Semarang, and Surabaya. While Abu Dujani controlled Jakarta, Dani, Gulam (a.k.a. Maulana Tanmin), and Sarwo Edi led the remaining units respectively (ICG 2003). Meanwhile, Noorudin Top's Jemaah Islamiyah sub-group adopted a smaller *thoifath* structure of highly clandestine squads.[12]

Noorudin Top commanded the intelligence and planning cell under which were four *kirdas*, or platoons, in which were four smaller combat sections. These represent largely autonomous but highly operational sub-units connected through the sariyah structure. That Jemaah Islamiyah was able to reorientate itself so quickly and so effectively in such little time is a testament to the resilience of its familial nature.

Kinship and effective capabilities

Building on the understanding of familial saturation in Jemaah Islamiyah, this section examines how kinship has developed the organization's effective capabilities beyond its core structures, and secondly, the role it has internally. Jemaah Islamiyah has a powerful morphological nexus to key partners that increases its insurgent capabilities. A primary means of achieving this is through kinship. Many members of the Jemaah Islamiyah who are staying in the Philippines are known to marry Filipino women. One of the prime fugitives from the Jemaah Islamiyah 2002 Bali bombings, Zulkifli bin Hir (a.k.a. Marwan) was known to have married the widow of slain Abu Sayyaf Group leader Khadaffy Janjalani. This is a very good example of Jemaah Islamiyah using external anchoring to partners and building geo-strategic capabilities, something that was more common than not.

According to Ressa (2015), Marwan had two further Filipino wives besides Janjalani's widow, including a 17-year-old bride in Jolo through whom Marwan became brother-in-law to Abu Sayyaf Group fighter Aljebir Adzhar a.k.a. Embel.[13] Marwan's first brother-in-law was Abu Sayyaf Group member Ren-Ren, whose sister was the wife of the slain Janjalani. Ren-Ren took command of the Abu Sayyaf Group after Abdurajak Janjalani, brother to Khadaffy Janjalani, was killed (AP 2007). There are others also. Joko Pitoyo (a.k.a. Dulmatin), the infamous 2002 Bali nightclub bomber, had an Indonesian wife and two Filipino Tausug wives (KBK/RSJ 2010). Dulmatin's Indonesian wife was the sister of his long-time bodyguard Niko (a.k.a. Jundi or Ridwan) (ICG 2010).

She was arrested in October of 2009 in the Philippines with their two children in Patikul, a town on the Southern Jolo Island (Collins 2009). Ridwan likewise married into the leadership family of the Ring Baten organization that had fought with Jemaah Islamiyah in Poso, and cooperated with it on the 2002 Bali bombings, and Australian Embassy attack in 2004 (ICG 2010). In Indonesia, Jemaah Islamiyah had similar connections to the Mujahedeen KOMPAK, Majelis Mujahedeen Indonesia/Indonesia Mujahedeen Council (MMI), and JAT through family.[14] There were also strong familial connections with Filipino counterparts in the MNLF and MILF dating back to the 1980s.

Abu Bakar's sons play important roles as well. Rohim Ba'asyir lived in Pakistan and Afghanistan with Khalid Shaikh Mohammad, the al-Qaeda 9/11 mastermind. Rohim was the Jemaah Islamiyah-appointed al-Qaeda propaganda chief for several years according to Fitzpatrick (2010). The younger Ba'asyir son, Rahim, was also in Afghanistan during the anti-Soviet jihad fighting alongside Zulkarnaen.[15] According to Atran, Abu Bakar enrolled Rahim "in an Islamic high school in Faisalabad, Pakistan. Seeking a stricter Salafist education for his son, Ba'asyir directed Rahim in the mid-nineties to Sana'a, Yemen, to study under Abdul Madjid al- Zindari" (2005, 2). Both Rahim and Rohim Ba'asyir played critical roles by connecting Jemaah Islamiyah to al-Qaeda in Afghanistan, Pakistan, and Yemen in significant ways.[16]

Abu Bakar Ba'asyir is of Yemeni heritage from his mother's line, the Ba'Ashar, in the Yemen Hadramout region. This family connection has facilitated a significant transfer of Salafist ideology to Indonesia and the Philippines via Jemaah Islamiyah. Eliason finds that in Yemen in 2010, there were "more than 2000 Indonesians studying Islam with some students from the Philippines reportedly receiving Jemaah Islamiyah scholarships" (2010, 1). By 2015, this was estimated to be several thousand. Siblings are, therefore, very important to Jemaah Islamiyah and not just the Bakars.

When recruiting, Jemaah Islamiyah uses paired and multi-sibling recruitment as a strategy because it has several benefits. For instance, when brothers are recruited into Jemaah Islamiyah they provide familial anchoring and personal support during ideological training and operational development. Ismail (2006) writes about the Achmad Kandai family as a good example. Kandai was a Darul Islam member and the brother of Mantiqi III Commander Nasir Abbas. Like him, Kandai was also a compatriot of Abdullah Sungkar and Abu Bakar Ba'asyir and went to Afghanistan with their assistance in 1985 to fight the Soviets (Hastings 2010).[17]

Kandai had four sons who were active in insurgency. These were Solahudin, Mohammed Islam, Abdul Jabar, and Farihin bin Ahmad. Solahudin was involved in several attacks including the 2001 Atrium shopping mall bombing and was later arrested in Wonosobo. Solahudin was part of the Jemaah Islamiyah Malaysia cell, of which Dedi Setiono a.k.a. Abas was also a member (Utusan 2001). Abas had planted bombs near the Jakarta Roman Catholic Cathedral in the December 2000 Christmas Eve attacks. Both Solahudin and Abas had bomb-making and combat experience from Maluku. However, according to Kunkler and Stepan (2013), authorities had not connected the Christmas Eve bombings to an active cell in Maluku, and it was only after a Malaysian bomber in the Atrium attack blew his foot off that they discovered the Jemaah Islamiyah link.

Mohammed Islam was a third-generation insurgent. Osman writes that Mohammed and his brother Farihin "travelled to Poso to join in the violent clashes against the Christians there at the height of communal violence in Central Sulawesi" (2010, 9). Farihin bin Ahmad also joined Jemaah Islamiyah and had spent time in Afghanistan fighting the Soviets with al-Qaeda, and on his return to Indonesia participated in the anti-Christian fighting in Indonesia with his brothers. Following his involvement in the Philippines Consulate bombing in Jakarta in 2000 he was arrested.[18]

The other brother, Abdul Jabar, was also highly active. He too had been involved in the bombing of the Philippines Embassy as revenge for the Philippine

Army's attacks on the joint Jemaah Islamiyah/MILF camps Abu Bakar and camp Hudaibiyah, according to Magouirk and Atran (2008). The Philippines Embassy operation demonstrates the depth of familial importance and the role of kinship in Jemaah Islamiyah. Also involved were Ali Imron, Amrozi, and Mukhlas, the three brothers from the Bali bombing, as well as al-Ghozi, Amrozi's cousin. Likewise, Abdul Jabar and his brother Farihin were the critical actors in supplying the materials and the bomb-making groups respectively.

Further examples included Al-Ghozi, who was a second-generation jihadist and son of a Darul Islam member. His younger brother Ahmad Rofiq Ridho sheltered Noorudin Top for a period, and then married the widow of his brother after his death (Ismail 2008). Similarly, Ali Ghufron married the younger sister of Nasir bin Abas, the Mantiqi III commander and brother-in-law to Jemaah Islamiyah fighter Syamsul Bahri. A further example is the injured Jemaah Islamiyah operative who blew his foot off in the Atrium mall attack, Taufiq Abdul Halim. He is the brother-in-law of Zulkifli Hir, who took part in the assassination of Dr Joe Fernandez, a former Perak State Assembly member (Chun Wai and Zolkepli 2014).

This intricate web of intermarriages is not accidental. Senior Jemaah Islamiyah figures play matchmaker to members to forge permanent intra-organizational kinship bonds. This acts as a means of internal security by maintaining confidentiality, raising exit costs, and making organizational processing more efficient. An example of this is the radical Darul Islam leader Haris Fadillah who married his daughter, Mira Augustina, off to Omar al-Faruq.[19] This union in particular demonstrates the utility and benefit of new familial couplings. Al-Faruq was a senior al-Qaeda leader in Southeast Asia and an Afghan veteran who lived in the Philippines from 1995 training MILF and Jemaah Islamiyah fighters. Abuza claims that from early 1999 "he was dispatched to Indonesia, where he relied heavily on the Jemaah Islamiyah network. Faruq relied not just on Jemaah Islamiyah personnel for his operations, but he indicated that he even worked through Ba'asyir to plan all operations" (2003a, 144). This was an additional link to al-Qaeda that was essential in supporting Jemaah Islamiyah operations.

Succinctly, these examples demonstrate that family and kinship is important for network efficiency and security, as well as for expansion, affiliation, recruitment and logistics, operational planning, and of course attacks. Likewise, the scope and scale of Jemaah Islamiyah's familial dynamics make it more of a supra-organization that spans several others, and weaves bonds throughout the regional and indeed global jihadist nexus. This highlights the importance of extensive kinship relationships and the complexity of the systematics they can build, support, and sustain that lend heavily to organizational resilience.

A long and powerful legacy of family and insurgency

The analysis so far demonstrates that family has always been central to Jemaah Islamiyah. Where this comes from and how Jemaah Islamiyah has developed around the centrality of kinship is examined in this section. It identifies that family is not just about the present for Jemaah Islamiyah, but very much about the past as well. Therefore, understanding the relevance of family in this context goes some way to understanding the efficiencies it brings to the present. In doing so we commence with Jemaah Islamiyah's ideological birth. The organization grew out of the Darul Islam movement in Indonesia as the result of a splintering of the Darul Islam leadership. The Darul Islam movement came from Darul-Islamism, which undertook armed revolt from 1948 to 1965 against the secular Indonesian Government.[20] Around 25,000 people died in the fighting but the deep familial and communal roots of Darul Islam were never defeated.[21]

Familial insurgent networks across Indonesia absorbed fighters not killed or captured and enabled them to go underground, resurfacing after the fall of the Suharto regime in 1985. This was not just a nationalistic ideology that lent to their survival, however. Buehler concludes, "Family relations among many of the Islamist leaders provide additional glue to this network" (2016, 140). Darul Islam idealism lived on through multiple generations with allegiance passed down through families, providing a deep socio-ideological river for Jemaah Islamiyah that essentially became the new manifestation of the Darul Islam vision. This is unsurprising. Riviere maintains that "the co-founders of Jemaah Islamiyah, Sheik Abdullah Sungkar, and Abu Bakar Ba'asyir, had been close associates of the Darul Islam leader, Kartosuwirjo, and for over 30 years they remained fervently dedicated to establishing Indonesia as an Islamic State" (2016, 6).

Eliraz (2004) similarly contends that Islam in Indonesia provides some historical references and ideological underpinnings of contemporary radicalism, which is characterized by the close relationship between family, religion, and political activism. From the mid-1940s Darul Islam fought the anti-Dutch colonial insurgency as a representative of the *Jemaah*, or community, which incorporated the familial and kinship connections of society to the organization and the struggle. This is important, because, as former Darul Islam members, Ba'asyir and Sungkar melded these with their own *Jemaah* community's blueprint in Pondok Ngruki, known as the Al-Mukmin Islamic boarding school in Solo, Indonesia.[22] It remains an important tool to carry the kinship and familial connection forward, as Jemaah Islamiyah weaves a strong and resilient organizational fabric.

Spanning multiple generations, the Darul Islam legacy is one of the central facets of Jemaah Islamiyah's resilience. This assertion is indirectly supported by the findings of several scholars. Daskon, for example, argues that socio-cultural resilience increases survival through "customs, values, and experiences shared through a common culture, and their moral and spiritual systems" (2010, 1081). This equally applies to familial groups, communities, and organizations. Kalathil *et al.* spoke of socio-cultural resilience as pertaining to "collective resilience" (2011, 5) regarding shared experiences across communities surviving collective pressures like colonialism, neo-colonialism, and oppression.

This mirrors the Jemaah Islamiyah and Darul Islam experiences. What is more, those social conditions and particularly the emphasis on family and kinship automatically included, and compounded, the value of social capital and trust. These are valuable dynamics of resilience and are particularly evident in Jemaah Islamiyah that has capitalized on its long, and enduring Darul Islam roots of communal sentiment. These beliefs and social conditions have persisted throughout Indonesia since the anti-colonial, anti-Dutch movement, and are now a cornerstone of Jemaah Islamiyah's master narratives.[23]

However, after several decades there has been a danger of new generations becoming disenagaged from the sentiments of Darul Islam's golden years. Jemaah Islamiyah has overcome this by remaining connected socially, politically, and ideologically to the *Jemaah* by reframing new conflicts like Iraq, Afghanistan, and Syria with the al-Qaeda master narrative of a shared sense of grievance, as Ramakrishna (2017) carefully articulated. These social connections provide new capabilities beyond its organizational boundaries and reinforce the importance of family in the struggle of the people.

Amir Ba'asyir in particular was a powerful figure in re-framing insurgent struggles, tying the familial legacies of previous generations to the far enemy and the West.[24] From the 1990s to 2014, al-Qaeda's macro master narratives of fighting the far enemy because the West was at war with Islam, and freeing Islamic lands from Takfir governments who did not impose sharia law, offered Jemaah Islamiyah new framing opportunities (Schmid 2014). Understanding what drives the reframing of historical violence through transnational macro narrative descendancy is highly relevant to understand legacy resilience supports, such as those Jemaah Islamiyah was drawing from (Henshaw 2015). Particularly after the September 2001 attacks in America, al-Qaeda's prominence meant its narratives were highly influential in Southeast Asian insurgencies.

What al-Qaeda framed as a war on Islam was a second and much-needed catalyst for Jemaah Islamiyah that Bonura remarked was "durable" (2010, 49). Bartolucci and Corman state that al-Qaeda's "message of anti-Muslim oppression, a Western-led war on Islam and call to jihad for all Muslims appeals to those (especially young) people who seek revenge as a way of overcoming frustration, to those seeking identity through group membership, and those seeking adventure" (2014, 15). Jemaah Islamiyah offered all of this within the secure folds of family. The bridging and narrative descendancy from al-Qaeda by Jemaah Islamiyah was therefore extremely effective.

In particular, Jemaah Islamiyah was highly successful at narrative vertical integration.[25] Bartolucci and Corman describe this as using cultural master narratives "as analogies for local narratives about the here-and-now, and encourage their audience to align their personal narratives with the local ones" (2014, 7). This seems to have been extremely persuasive and has resulted in binding legacies with familial kinship connections over multiple generations, increasing social capital and trust within its networks (see Table 5.1). This also has internal efficiency benefits. Griswold puts it that inside Jemaah Islamiyah, groups are "interwoven through training camps, intermarriage, and violent common purpose" (2010, 217). It is common for new recruits to marry the daughters and sisters of other members. Ismail writes: "this was a unique tool utilized for

Table 5.1 Effects of familial setup on organization – Jemaah Islamiyah

Structural dynamics	Organizational effect
Familial organization	Extensive recruitment through trans-generational kinship networks.
	Increased internal security through intermarriage.
	Immediate access to a wide kinship resource bases.
	Operational efficiency maintained through familial connections in the absence of formalized structures and leadership.
Command and control	Diffused and holacratic with little strategic oversight.
	High efficiency due to intimate family networks and low-cost socio-economics.
Resources	Local resource collection is limited to family members and petty crime.
	International support from al-Qaeda has been minimalized.
	International partnerships with Filipino organizations are strong.
Strategic behaviour	Some strategic coordination at inter-organizational levels.
	Cellular structure increases compartmentalization of damages.
	Familial core networks follow a collective ideology outside of Abu Bakar Ba'asyir.
	Tactical actions rather than strategic insurgency.

recruitment and further engagement in the Jemaah Islamiyah cause, thus limiting disengagement options for Jemaah Islamiyah members and blocking effective counter-terrorism tactics" (2006, 2).

External pressures

In this section external pressures are analysed. The Bali 2002 bombings were a catalyst for international pressure on Jemaah Islamiyah after Singapore's highly successful counterterrorist operation in 2001, which is discussed later. Some, such as Abuza (2007), Hoare (2005), and Gacad (2010), had thought the Bali 2002 attacks to be the beginning of the end for Jemaah Islamiyah.[26] However, while external pressures after Bali 2002 caused the Mantiqi structure to collapse fully, Jemaah Islamiyah endured and undertook many more significant actions. Likewise, Bali 2002 was not the start of the destruction of the Mantiqi system. It was being successfully dismantled before then. Additionally, no end ever came.

Subsequent attacks resulted in more deaths and more operations that caused new and additional pressures against Jemaah Islamiyah, but the death knell was never rung. Therefore, the purpose of this section is to identify how Jemaah Islamiyah was targeted, with what types of pressures, where, and by whom, and to determine what effects external pressures had, if any, in damaging the organization. The types of pressures considered are those defined in Chapter 1, i.e. hard-power, direct kinetic pressures, including arrests and slayings, and soft-power political-, social-, economic-, and policy-based efforts.

Hard-power pressures

Prior to the 2002 Bali bombings, Jemaah Islamiyah suffered very little, if any attention from the Indonesian Government. For example, in the wake of President Suharto's fall in 1998, Jemaah Islamiyah openly participated in the fighting in Maluku and Poso, experiencing little to no resistance. A 2005 International Crisis Group report states the violence there provided "legitimate theatres for armed jihad, and holy war, by violent jihadists across Indonesia" (2005, 1). The fighting in these two areas raged until 2001, and was a sectarian conflict between Muslims and Christians. Freedom to engage in the conflict strengthened many jihadist organizations as it was an important opportunity for building capabilities.

The lacklustre responses to Jemaah Islamiyah's 2 May 2000 Medan church bombing, the August 2000 Philippine Embassy attack in Jakarta by VBIED (Conboy 2004), and the December 2000 Christmas Eve bombings each separately signalled that the Indonesian Government was reluctant to take action. Sim writes that "until the Bali bombings of October 2002, the Indonesian Government denied the existence of such a movement, playing to public opinion of a western conspiracy to undermine Muslims" (2013, 11). Similarly, Bonner and Perlez write that "for nearly a year, Indonesia has dismissed claims that the organization was a threat, or that it even existed" (2002, 1). This noticeably demonstrates the Indonesian Government's ambivalence towards the existence and very nature of Jemaah Islamiyah, something that has been present in Indonesian politics for many years.

This approach likewise extends beyond a single administration. President Yudhoyono's administration claimed Jemaah Islamiyah was a phantom, as did his predecessor and mentor Megawati Sukarnoputri (Pavlova 2007). Had Sukarnoputri acted it is possible Jemaah Islamiyah may not have become what it is today, but not only did her administration ignore its insurgent nature, it was fearful of the political backlash that might have resulted from going against the nationalist Darul Islam sentiments Jemaah Islamiyah propagated. Conversely, before Bali 2002 regional authorities in the Association of Southeast Nations (ASEAN) were actively dismantling Mantiqi I in Singapore and Malaysia, at a time Indonesia was uninterested in considering, or even recognizing Jemaah Islamiyah as a threat of any kind.

These external pressures on Jemaah Islamiyah outside of Indonesia are very important because they effectively ended attack capabilities in other countries. Additionally, it signalled to Indonesia that Jemaah Islamiyah was considered to be a very real threat that was being addressed by the international community. When combined, the Singapore operational gains and political gravitas on Indonesia constituted effective external pressures that in no small part instigated a possibly reluctant, yet necessary, Indonesian response.

Singapore's counter operations

From September 2001, Singaporean intelligence, the Internal Security Department (ISD), became aware of an ambitious Jemaah Islamiyah plot to detonate six massive truck bombs. With three tonnes of ammonium nitrate in each, the trucks were to be deployed to various diplomatic missions and soft targets around the city-state. According to Nirmala (2013), had this succeeded it would probably have killed more than a thousand civilians. A principal actor in the operation was al-Qaeda member Mohammad Aslam bin Yar Ali Khan (a.k.a. Aslma). Aslma was a Singaporean citizen but left Singapore in October 2001 and was arrested in Afghanistan in November of that year. During his interrogation he provided details of the Jemaah Islamiyah plot that al-Qaeda was involved in, and which had been under operational planning since 1997 (Yew 2002).

Aslma had fought with Jemaah Islamiyah in Afghanistan and was involved in attack planning for many years. His arrest was a significant blow to the organization. When the ISD became aware of his capture it moved swiftly, and within two weeks arrested 13 tier-1 Jemaah Islamiyah Mantiqi I cell members, including the leader Ibrahim Maidin and his deputy commanders Faiz bin Abu Bakar Bafana, Mohamed Khalim bin Jaffar, and Singapore Wakalah leader Mas Selamat (Rekhi 2013).[27] Interrogations informed the ISD that the planning was in the advanced stages and that cell members had safe houses and bomb-making materials, and had conducted extensive reconnaissance of targets (Mydans 2002).

In order to fund these operations, Jemaah Islamiyah deputy commander Abu Bakar Bafana contacted his old friend Mohammed Atef a.k.a. Abu Hafs, a central figure in the al-Qaeda 9/11 plot in the United States. Atef agreed to send money and suicide bombers to Jemaah Islamiyah for the attacks once Jemaah Islamiyah had sent videotapes of the reconnaissance and proposed targets.[28] By September 2002, the ISD had progressed its investigation and 18 more Jemaah Islamiyah members had been arrested. About half of those were Singapore citizens and full-time National Service members who were on reserve duties at the time (U.S. State Department 2002).[29]

The crippling of the planned Singapore attacks coupled with ongoing Internal Security Department vigilance put so much pressure on Jemaah Islamiyah that it was unable to recover. What marks this as a significant external pressure event is that it destroyed one of Jemaah Islamiyah's most important Mantiqis, and represents a loss that was never recovered fully. In Singapore, this demonstrates a significant failure of Jemaah Islamiyah's organizational resilience. However, while its Singapore branch was destroyed it concurrently conducted the joint Jemaah Islamiyah-MILF Rizal Day Manila bombings in the Philippines, and then the Bali 2002 bombings, discussed next.[30]

Bali 2002, the Densus 88 and other actors

The 11 October 2002 Bali bombings announced to the wider international community that Jemaah Islamiyah was a serious insurgent actor and capable international threat. Absent from Singapore, Jemaah Islamiyah maintained significant operational bases in Indonesia and the Philippines, with smaller cells in Malaysian Sabah, Borneo, and Australia at that time (Kaur 2017). The attacks on the Sari Club, Paddy's Bar, and the U.S. Consulate came at a time when the so-called War on Terror had just begun. The reaction from the international community was one of condemnation.

The massive loss of life, particularly foreign tourists, saw Australia, the U.S., and other international actors become more involved. The threat from Jemaah Islamiyah and militant Islam in Southeast Asia was such that Bond called it the "second front in the War on Terrorism" (2005, 1). Two weeks after the bombings, the United Nations Security Council added Jemaah Islamiyah to its list of proscribed terror organizations.[31] This was a significant development because it gave Indonesia's security actors like *Polri* (National Police), the *Tentara Nasional Indonesia*, or TNI (Military), and the *Badan Intelijen Negara*, or State Intelligence Agency (BIN) a stage to compete on and vie for additional funding and powers to confront Jemaah Islamiyah.

Per contra, due to the poor human rights records of those organizations, perceived endemic corruption and suspected involvement in criminal enterprises, Australia and the U.S. wanted a new organization created that they were directly involved in (Butt 2009). Doing so required them effectively to influence Indonesian politics to develop a new legislative framework. This was step one. Indonesia had been drafting its 2002 Anti-Terrorism Law since September 2001, and this became the means of access. Whitaker writes that the "Bush administration's twin foreign policy goals of strengthening international security and promoting democracy" (2007, 1017) played a part in its amendment and accelerated its passage after 11 October 2002. On 18 October 2002, it was signed into law by President Sukarnoputri and adopted on 4 April 2003.

This was the essential second step that empowered Indonesia to develop the toolbox of resources that would enable it to exert direct kinetic, hard-power pressures on Jemaah Islamiyah. Most importantly, it provided the means to establish a new counterterrorism unit called Densus 88, known as Detachment 88, or simply Det 88. A tactical and intelligence gathering organization, it was inaugurated on 30 June 2003 with equipment, funding, and training from Australia and the U.S.[32] The "88" has several meanings ranging from community and continuity, to law enforcement, and even a representation of Australia's involvement in setting up the unit as a tribute to the 88 Australians killed in Bali 2002.[33] However, it took time to establish, and for the next few years Jemaah Islamiyah continued its attacks while authorities, particularly Det 88, employed their new capabilities to counter Jemaah Islamiyah, which by late 2005 was making serious progress.

Kinetic pressure

After Singapore, Jemaah Islamiyah began to suffer increasingly effective hard-power and specific direct kinetic pressures that resulted in critical losses and organizational damage. One of the first significant occurrences was the killing of Dr Azahari Husin, a key logistician and planner of Bali 2002, as well as the mastermind behind the 2004 JW Marriot and Australian Embassy bombings and the second 2005

Bali bombings. The increased intelligence and tactical capabilities of Indonesian security forces, thanks largely to training by Australia and the U.S., led directly to Dr Husin being shot dead during a raid on his villa in Batu, East Java on 11 November 2005 by a Det 88 sniper (Forbes 2005). A fellow Jemaah Islamiyah member hiding with Dr Azahari Husin killed himself with an explosives belt, wounding police officers, in preference to being taken alive.

The killing of Dr Husin was the first of many. Following the East Java operation several more of Jemaah Islamiyah's senior and most wanted operatives were captured or killed in quick succession. In June 2007 Abu Dujana was arrested in Central Java. It was Australian intelligence agencies that allegedly provided telephone intercepts and geo-data; Signals Intelligence (SIGINT)-derived location information led Det 88 to him, landing a crippling blow to the Jemaah Islamiyah Java cell, as well as to the wider organization (Murdoch 2007).[34] Following that success, in August 2009 police and Det 88 raided the hideout of Noorudin Top in the village of Temanggung in Central Java. After surrounding him, Det 88 sent a surveillance robot in to the house, at which point Noorudin Top fled to a bathroom and detonated a bomb, killing himself and his wife and children (Blomfield 2009).

As the lead commander of several of Jemaah Islamiyah's most successful attacks, and with more planned, including the assassination of President Susilo Bambang Yudhoyono, Noorudin Top's death was another noteworthy blow. Shortly after this was yet another momentous loss, that of Dulmatin who was also killed by Det 88 at an internet café in Jakarta on 9 March 2010. Dulmatin's killing came ahead of a visit by former U.S. President Barack Obama on 20 March. Killed in the same raid were Ridwan, Dulmatin's brother-in-law, bodyguard, and Ring Baten senior commander, and Hasan Noor (a.k.a. Blackberry), an Abu Sayyaf sub-commander from the Philippines (Mcguirk 2010).[35]

With these deaths, Jemaah Islamiyah activity dropped off to the point that no major attacks followed the 2009 JW Marriot and Ritz-Carlton hotel attacks until the Jakarta attack in January 2016.[36] Meanwhile, external pressures continued. In May of 2011, Amir Abu Bakar Ba'asyir was sentenced to 15 years in jail for his involvement in the Aceh training camp that was disrupted by Det 88 in 2010. On 9 June 2011, Det 88 and Polri arrested Jemaah Islamiyah member Sudirman (a.k.a. Yasir), in the village of Pemalang, Central Java. The 42-year-old was the apprentice of Dulmatin and served for many years as his right-hand man and master trainer to other Jemaah Islamiyah fighters and affiliates (Syafputri 2011).

Analysis of this damage to Jemaah Islamiyah reveals a pattern. They were not singularly brought about by good work or good luck on the part of Det 88 and the security services. Chapter 1 examined how familial networks and organizations suffer a counterintelligence deficit because once discovered they are more easily mapped and addressed with increasingly effective counterintelligence treatments. This is a symptom of resilience weakness and vulnerability present in Jemaah Islamiyah. On the same day as Yasir was captured, Dulmatin's brother-in-law Heri Kuncoro and 15 Jemaah Islamiyah fighters were arrested in Central Java. The interrogations of Heri and Yasir led police to two further suspects in Palu, Sulawesi, home of the Mujahideen East Timor (MIT), that were wanted for police shootings (Priyambodo 2011).

Two days later Jemaah Islamiyah fighter Muhammad Sibghotulloh was arrested by Polri in East Kalimantan. Sibghotulloh (a.k.a. Faisal, Mus'af, Hani, or Yuardi) was wanted for the attempted shooting of Polri officers and his involvement in the Cirebon Mosque bombing.[37] Faisal was also a Jemaah Islamiyah trainer, sheltered Dulmatin's bodyguard Niko (a.k.a. Jundi or Ridwan), and was a key arms smuggler for Jemaah Islamiyah from the Philippines (Zahara 2011). These points are important because analysis suggests that even though familial security may have remained high across these Jemaah Islamiyah operatives, the kinship bonds between them significantly increased the correlational intelligence value of the data, meaning that under interrogation kinship became a security liability.

This was proven by intelligence-led follow-up action that once more yielded additional gains. In rapid succession Det 88 arrested several more Jemaah Islamiyah militants in Central Java and in Yogyakarta who were linked with Upik Lawanga, a master bomb maker trained by Dr Azahari Husin. Lawanga assembled the bombs that were used in the JW Marriot attack and is known to have been a close friend of Abu Wardah Santoso, leader of the Mujahedeen Indonesia Timor who remained at large at the time (Suriyanto 2016).[38]

Another success for the Indonesian authorities was the imprisonment of Jemaah Islamiyah leader and master operational planner Umar Patek. In July 2012, an Indonesian court found him guilty of direct involvement in the 2000 Christmas Eve bombings and the 2002 Bali attacks, sentencing him to 20 years in jail. Patek was arrested the year before on 25 January 2011 in Abbottabad, Pakistan in the same town and area where Osama bin Laden was killed just a few months later (Marks 2018). According to Indonesian Defence Minister Purnomo Yusgiantoro, Patek and his Filipino wife, travelling under the aliases Anis Alawi Jaafar and Fatima Zahra, had been instructed to meet bin Laden there to discuss joint Jemaah Islamiyah/al-Qaeda operations (Karmini 2011). Fatima Az Zahara was not idle company but an active Jemaah Islamiyah member. She had assisted in establishing Mantiqi I and had written a book about the role of wives in Jihad.[39] She was therefore very much an operational asset of Jemaah Islamiyah, as many wives are.

The example of Patek shows the relationship between family, kinship, Jemaah Islamiyah, and al-Qaeda as organizations, especially between the most senior leaders. The social capital bonds between senior al-Qaeda and Jemaah Islamiyah figures are similar to those it shares with the Abu Sayyaf Group. While the benefits of close kinship integration have been presented extensively, it is undeniable that many forms of the kinetic damage Jemaah Islamiyah suffered are due to those same kinship ties that enabled authorities and intelligence services to map Jemaah Islamiyah's networks. The results of which have been the removal of key members and principal nodes and actors in Indonesia and Singapore, and internationally. These are shown in Table 5.2.

Table 5.2 Key Jemaah Islamiyah commanders removed 2005–2019

Name	Rank/Position	Status	Date
Azahari Husin	Senior operational planner and explosives expert	Killed	11 November 2005
Abu Dujan	Amir	Arrested	13 June 2007
Noorudin Mohammed Top	Sub-group commander and explosives expert	Killed with wife and children (suicide)	17 September 2009
Dulmatin	AiA sub-group commander	Killed	9 March 2010
Ridwan	Dulmatin's bodyguard and Ring Baten commander	Killed	9 March 2010
Hasan Noor	Abu Sayyaf commander and Jemaah Islamiyah affiliate	Killed	9 March 2010
Abu Bakar Ba'asyir	Jemaah Islamiyah and MMI Amir	Imprisoned	16 June 2011
Sudirman a.k.a. Yasir	Bomb-maker apprentice to Dulmatin	Imprisoned	9 June 2011
Heri Kuncoro and 15 Jemaah Islamiyah fighters	Dulmatin's brother-in-law and senior commander	Arrested	9 June 20111
Muhammad Sibghotulloh	Senior members and weapons smuggler	Arrested	11 June 2011
Umar Patek	Operational planner and al-Qaeda liaison officer	Imprisoned	21 June 2012
Ustadz Sanusi	Amir – Jemaah Islamiyah Philippines and trainer of the Maute Brothers	Killed	22 November 2012
Zulkifli Bin Hir a.k.a. Marwan	Sneior commander and bomb master. Liaison to Abu Sayyaf, MIT, and MNLF	Killed	25 January 2015
Joko Supriyono	Training coordinator – Central Java	Arrested	15 May 2019
Agus Suparnoto	Foreign fighter logistics manager	Arrested	15 May 2019
Taufik Teguh Prasety	Jemaah Islamiyah Syria commander	Arrested	15 May 2019
Para Wijayanto	Senior Bomb-maker	Arrested	29 June 2019

It is important to note that those killed largely represent Jemaah Islamiyah's old guard. There are many younger and perhaps more militant junior leaders gaining prominence, including Ba'asyir's sons. The familial nature and the strong focus on bringing new members into the Jemaah Islamiyah family means that new generations are replenishing the ranks, and fighting prospects in Syria, Iraq, and Afghanistan continue to offer members extensive development opportunities.

Soft-power pressures

Pressure is not merely one-way. Whenever a force is exerted on something there is resistance. The opposite of this is an absence of pressure, which is a vacuum, and in a vacuum what was resistance turns into growth. It is more difficult to discuss soft-power pressures because there are noticeable weaknesses in them. While some soft-power pressures did eventually manifest in later years, they were largely not organic to Indonesia, being imposed or influenced by external international actors. In Indonesia, soft-power pressures were lower than those in other countries. Singapore, for example, has very robust legislation and low tolerances to terrorism while possessing a stable, politically powerful anti-corruption system (Gregory 2015). These were highly effective in destroying Mantiqi I, but overall represent a duality where a languor of organic soft-power pressures, hesitancy in cooperation, and a system at times supportive of Jemaah Islamiyah in Indonesia inversely affect its resilience in positive ways.

Analysis thus far has shown that successive Indonesian Governments were reluctant to take any action against Jemaah Islamiyah until they could no longer ignore the threat it posed, especially in the wake of the Bali 2002 attacks. Following that, Indonesian authorities in concert with, and as a result of pressures from, international actors Australia and the U.S., undertook a range of changes and new initiatives in response. However, as the following examination shows, these were not necessarily the result of an all-inclusive political commitment to counterinsurgency, or to countering the ideology of militant Islam. Rather, it demonstrates mostly political decisions to act on terrorism as a phenomenological symptom of insurgency while ignoring the sources of it.

This is evident in the initial political reactions to the Bali 2002 attacks, which were to speed up and broaden the legal framework for addressing acts of terrorism. As successive Indonesian Governments have decidedly shown, few if any believed there was a problem with political militant Islam, or terrorism and the insurgent organizations using it. The Sukarnoputri and Yudhoyono Governments are the prime cases. Their actions suggest it was easier and more politically manageable for them to deal with the attacks as crimes of terror, rather than as an integral part of Jemaah Islamiyah's insurgency.

The short-term focus on direct-kinetic pressures is a good reflection of this. In the years following 2002, Det 88 killed many high-profile Jemaah Islamiyah leaders and arrested many more. On the surface this would seem to constitute significant gains, but the failure of soft-power pressures to support hard-power initiatives means that, overall, soft-power pressures were weak and ineffective, and the examples are numerous. In the three years following 2002, Indonesian authorities arrested 700 accused insurgents but over half were released. Toohey (2014) reports that all those convicted of terrorist offences and sentenced to anything less than a life term, which is just five years, have all been freed. At the start of 2013 there were more than 300 insurgents behind bars, but 80 of those were released in late 2014, and 90 more in 2015 (Williams 2015). Coupled with outdated legislation that remained unrevised until late 2016, weaknesses in political and judicial systems facilitated the mass release of insurgents.

Singh states that "despite six major attacks and more than 20 minor ones, Indonesia's anti-terrorism framework remains relatively weak" (2016, 1). Not only was the judicial system flawed, but the underpinning political leadership was equally lacking. In the days immediately following Bali 2002, polls showed that right across the country people had an unprecedented 80 per cent dissatisfaction rating with the Megawati Government when it came to law and order, security, corruption, and government performance (Nakashima 2002). When Susilo Bambang Yudhoyono became President in 2004, many feared his tendency for caution and excessive indecision would see him being similarly inattentive at addressing security issues. This was proven when he failed to directly address collusion and corruption in his government, evidenced by the arrest and imprisonment of several of his senior ministers. During his second presidential term an additional 300 government office-holders came under investigation for corruption and nepotism (Wardhana and Wira Usaha 2016). Despite promising to stamp out such activity, it continued under Yudhoyono's leadership. Similar weakness of leadership extended into the security arena.

A prominent example of this occurred in February 2011 when Yudhoyono refused to condemn the killings of Ahmadiyya sect members, a religious minority group, by an Islamist mob in the Banten province until a gruesome video of the murders was published online (BBC 2011). Even then, the government refused to revoke a 2008 anti-Ahmadiyya decree.[40] A report by the Asian Human Rights Commission (AHRC) (2018) stated that this is most apparent in the gap between local and central authorities, where many local governments have banned minorities with decrees like the Ahmadiyya, but the central government is loath to interfere. Although this is an example of a localized event, whereas Jemaah Islamiyah represented a much broader nationalist one, the hesitancy and reluctance of Jakarta to impose political, security, or religious authority outside of the capital is reflective of a pervasive weakness.

Endemic political issues

The fear of being perceived as interfering at grassroots levels kept the Megawati and Yudhoyono Governments from effectively tackling militant Islam, and in turn Jemaah Islamiyah's insurgency in Indonesia. This harks back to the Indonesian Pancasila political Islamic system of state ideology. Pancasila has been in Indonesia for a long time, several decades in fact, since 1945 when the

First Principle was established in Article 29, Section 1 of the Constitution, stating, "The state shall be based on belief in the One and Only God" (Purdy 1982/1983).

In the 1980s then-President Suharto started investing heavily in Islamic institutions and promoting Muslim involvement in the daily political life of the country. When this occurred, Pancasila became problematic to political leaders. As an all-encompassing doctrine, Pancasila was difficult to reconcile with the wide range of Islamic ideologies. Weatherbee (1985) puts it that non-establishment groups became convinced that government institutions were hostile, and had become enemies to the people, forcing them to find solutions outside of legal processes, such as by armed jihad.[41]

The U.S. International Business Association reports that in an attempt to appease jihadist elements in opposition to his government, "Suharto himself went to great lengths to demonstrate that he was a good Muslim, including making the Hajj to Mecca in May 1991" (IBA 2008, 103). According to Nash, Salafi-Wahhabi teaching "not only survived but thrived under the oppression of Suharto's New Order regime from 1966 to 1998" (2018, 1). As a result, Saudi Arabia has spread Salafi-Wahhabism to Indonesia with over 85 per cent of Indonesia's Muslims following Wahhabi Islamic teachings. Varagur states that Saudi alumni are now deeply integrated into "Indonesian public life, holding a position in Muhammadiyah, the Prosperous Justice Party, and the Cabinet" (2017, 2).[42]

This was to be mirrored by Yudhoyono who, like Suharto, also sought to demonstrate his strong religious credentials by developing a solid relationship with Saudi Salafi-Wahhabi ideology. This resulted in Saudi-financed Islamic education thriving under Yudhoyono as it did under Suharto, even though his was a repressive regime. It has therefore been unpalatable politically for Megawati, Yudhoyono, or any future president to take any actions against the ideology that Jemaah Islamiyah, Darul Islam before them, and modern fellow-travellers like JAT and MMI continue to promulgate. Not only is Salafi-Wahhabism ingrained into many facets of the political reality in Indonesia, but it is effectively a tangible form of soft-power pressure on moderate Indonesian politics to refrain from taking action. This was discussed after Suharto's fall when Jemaah Islamiyah took strong advantage and openly joined the fighting in Poso and Maluku. It equally makes the Indonesian political landscape difficult for leaders to challenge the ingrained acceptance of Salafi-Wahhabism that Jemaah Islamiyah draws from; meaning soft-power pressures are often feeble.

The ephemerial effectiveness of external pressures

In the immediate aftermath of the 2002 bombings, pressures on Jemaah Islamiyah and Mantiqi III resulted in change through direct kinetic redress, but it came with resistance from Indonesia's elites. Some members of the incumbent political authority blocked efforts to target Jemaah Islamiyah. Former Indonesian Vice President Hamzah Haz said that there might be others behind the attack, mainly the United States, avowing, "the Bali bomb blast I'm sure was not an act of Muslims ..." (Moore 2003a, 1). Amien Rais, the Speaker of Parliament, also claimed it was not possible to blame Jemaah Islamiyah or al-Qaeda for the attacks (Synovitz 2002). It is unclear if these statements are more an anti-Western stance, or alternatively an alignment with Jemaah Islamiyah's broader political ideology. Nevertheless, it is clear from previous analysis that the deep integration of Salafi ideology in Indonesia politics probably played a significant part in the formation of such perspectives.[43]

This is also apparent in the immediate response. While even the naysayers could not ignore the significance of Jemaah Islamiyah's Bali attacks, the localized police and security response took weeks to gain traction, demonstrating either reluctance or weaknesses of indigenous external pressures. This is in stark contrast to the international response, which was immediate. As an al-Qaeda affiliate, Jemaah Islamiyah was placed quickly under international crosshairs. Before establishing Det 88, Australia and the U.S. rallied international partners and took immediate action in the UN. Realuo and Stapleton write, "52 countries united on October 23, 2002, to request and/or to support the United Nations terrorist designation of Jemaah Islamiyah. More than 150 jurisdictions have agreed to freeze the assets of Jemaah Islamiyah-related individuals" (2004, 15). This impacted not only international sentiments but pressured domestic Indonesian ones as well, the results of which were to force President Megawati off the fence.

However, this was not simple. Chiefly, the ramifications of moving against powerful political actors such as parliamentary speaker and leader of the New Order Golkar Party, Akbar Tanjung, were not favourable, and probably contributed directly to the lack of tangible pressures on Jemaah Islamiyah. As a powerful political party, the New Order Golkar Party had deep ties to industry, the security establishment, and criminal networks as well (Ulla 2016). Equally, endemic corruption in government and support for Jemaah Islamiyah became even more evident. Sherlock reports that Indonesia's "legal system was regularly thwarted by delaying tactics, quite often with the complicity of judges and law enforcement officials themselves" (2002, 8). When Megawati urged authorities to arrest Abu Bakar Ba'asyir, he was suddenly admitted to hospital and police leadership refused to intervene (Siddiq 2018).

The trial of Abu Bakar Ba'asyir did go ahead but he was quickly acquitted of the most severe charge of treason, and of any connection to Bali. Instead, he was jailed only for minor immigration offences. A charge of subversion was upheld but it was thrown out a few months later at appeal. These were not isolated cases. In July 2004, Indonesia's Constitutional Court ruled that the Anti-Terrorism legislation used to jail the bombers Imam Samudra and his brothers was unconstitutional, and could no longer be used for the prosecution of cases related to the attacks (Larue 2017). This further weakened Indonesia's toolset of external pressures. In time Ba'asyir did face justice. After a short prison term he was immediately re-arrested on release and charged with a string of serious offences, including planning acts of terrorism, conspiring to commit terrorist acts, and having knowledge of terrorist acts (Djuhari 2004).

These pertained to the JW Marriot bombings, the Mindanao training camp in the Philippines, and weapons and equipment caches. However, the changes to the Anti-Terrorism legislation meant that he could not retrospectively be charged with Bali 2002, though prosecutors did have a charge upheld for his involvement in the attacks under Indonesian's criminal code. This was an important win for Indonesia regarding external pressure capabilities because it shows that there are mechanisms that can be applied to achieve results. Ba'asyir received a 15-year jail sentence, which at 72 years of age should have effectively been a life sentence (Ward 2011). Yet again though, the Yudhoyono Government showed its capacity for political survival over its commitment to anti-terrorism and to combating insurgency by seeking to free Abu Bakar Ba'asyir, only nine years into his sentence and just three months short of the Presidential election.[44]

Although the judicial system is capricious, imprisoning one of the most prominent jihadist leaders in the country was supposed to send a strong message. Further arrests and prosecutions led to more jailings, like those of Abu Dujana, the Jemaah Islamiyah mastermind, and Zarkashi, the Jemaah Islamiyah Amir who replaced Adung in 2004, though both were released on good behaviour after serving only half terms. Again, this appears to show thinly veiled if not tacit support for Jemaah Islamiyah with any message of being tough on militancy essentially nullified.

Pressures from outside and conflicts within

Just as there were missed opportunities from the incumbent Indonesian Government, international pressures also suffered from effectiveness issues. International asset freezes had been in place for years, but they were ineffective as many Jemaah Islamiyah members had little to no assets, particularly outside of Indonesia. As Jemaah Islamiyah were the end-users of assets and financing rather than the wealthy patrons, it is difficult to see the point of such sanctions beyond political signalling. Elsewhere, it was not the apparatus of pressure itself but the lack of political will to use it properly that led to weaknesses. ASEAN is an excellent demonstration of this. It introduced a new legal instrument in 2007 called the ASEAN Convention on Counter Terrorism (ACCT). The ACCT's purpose was to enable member states to coordinate CT activities through a common framework (Ahmad 2013).

As an instrument the ACCT was not without overall merit, but its strengths lay in multi-lateral engagement by member nations, which was lacking. Chau (2008) observes that as it was, the ACCT was soft, very slow to be adopted regionally, and not fully ratified for several years until 2011. Similarly, Tan and Hitoshi state ASEAN members did not draw on ACCT because of "the perception that the sources of militancy and terrorism stem from neighboring territories – hence potentially complicating, if not compromising, ASEAN-based efforts" (2016, 1220). This meant that nations would not compromise the sovereignty of others, thereby limiting inter-member joint operations. For Jemaah Islamiyah that operated in Indonesia, Philippines and Malaysia, it always had somewhere to hide, plan, and operate out of.

Global conflicts likewise impacted Indonesian soft-power initiatives in different ways. When ISIL rose to prominence between 2011 and 2013, conflicts in Iraq, Libya, Syria, and Afghanistan saw an outflow of fighters leaving to join, but also a return home of additionally skilled and ideologically potent adherents shortly afterwards, many of whom were looking to continue to support insurgency. Ba'asyir aligned with ISIL in July 2014 in a move that caused stresses and divisions in Jemaah Islamiyah, as well as for authorities who uncovered Jemaah Islamiyah's fund-raising for the Islamic State group.[45] This is because the ideology of ISIL, so different from the far enemy doctrine of al-Qaeda, was as attractive to insurgents in Indonesia as much as it was to Africans, European Muslims, and insurgents in the Middle East (Winter 2015). As a consequence, ISIL quickly gained many transnational adherents.

Beyond jihadists and insurgents, local reactions to ISIL were mixed. The majority of everyday Muslims did not explicitly endorse ISIL and were generally against the extreme violence it espoused, while a minority supported it strongly. A 2015 Pew study (Poushter 2017) found that 4 per cent, or about 9 million Indonesian Muslims, nearly 40 per cent of the population of Australia in equivalence, did support ISIL.[46] A survey in December 2016 by the Institute for the Study of Islam and Society reported "78 per cent of 505 religious teachers in public schools supported implementing sharia law in Indonesia. The survey also found that 77 per cent backed Islamist groups advocating this goal" (Thompson 2017).

This indicates that ISIL ideology has been appealing to a small percentage of people overall, yet a numerically significant number, correlating to sentiments about the role of Islam and the state. However, Indonesia already had a nationalist political ideology, the Pancasila, which conflicts with ISIL narratives.[47] Pancasila was constitutionally endorsed in 1945 and has five principles focused on belief, humanity, national unity, democracy, and social justice (Morfit 1981). These conflict strongly with IS narratives, particularly on democracy.

Notwithstanding, Pancasila has been successfully leveraged under the auspices of national unity to beef up Indonesian national security legislation, and to increase the powers of police and security services. President Yudhoyono tried to use Pancasila holistically to address poverty, inequality, and religious teachings that are harmful to political stability. In 2017, he established the Presidential Working Unit for Fostering of the State Ideology of Pancasila (UKP-PIP) as a tool to influence Indonesians at a grass-roots level (Shamasundari 2017). Equally, this approach has been sold to the West as being a significant soft-power means of dealing with insurgency and Islamic militancy. How effective this has been is controversial because Pancasila is both a prop for supporters of the Darul Islam vision and a tool to be used against actors like Jemaah Islamiyah.

Therefore, the constitutional value of Pancasila is questionable. It has led to new counterterrorism methodologies, particularly police de-radicalization programmes and community policing, as the analysis of Noorhaidi *et al.* (2012) asserts, but it has also fostered corruption and the abuse of power. For Indonesia's political elites, Pancasila is a powerful mechanism of control, and as such will not be given up easily, even by those who do not conform to it, such as Akbar Tanjung. The most significant problems with employing and promoting Pancasila are that the initiatives undertaken do not address causes and endemic socio-political sentiments, or religious-based indoctrination throughout Indonesia that supports insurgency through the propagation of Saudi-funded Salafi-Wahhabism.

In summary, Indonesia's soft-power approach to combating Jemaah Islamiyah and Islamic insurgency more broadly has been lacking. Jemaah Islamiyah has successfully adapted to pressures that have impacted it and taken advantage of the flaws and weaknesses in the judicial system and in law-enforcement reforms. In turn, the myriad of opposing agendas and a plethora of ulterior motives and processes, flawed by endemic corruption and competing personalized power politics, have made it difficult for leaders to sufficiently support hard-power initiatives. To an extent, this is understandable in the multi-polar Indonesian political theatre with power actors spanning the TNI, Polri, BIN, and religious and social authorities, each circumventing, collaborating, or outmaneuvering each other as self-interests dictate.

Externally, international efforts of policy and security frameworks to support Indonesia have been best applied to the hard-power kinetic approaches rather than to soft-power ones. As a result, there are no simple answers to how best to apply soft-power pressures on Jemaah Islamiyah that will impact its insurgency systematics to any tangible degree. External actors like Saudi Arabia have the will, money, and influence to shape the socio-political landscape into one that is unlikely to accept ideological change to Salafi-Wahhabi beliefs, which are the foundations of al-Qaeda, Jemaah Islamiyah, and the Islamic State. This leaves others like Australia and the U.S., who can only support a flawed multi-agent system, to push for the outcomes they want.

Resilience and the familial organization of Jemaah Islamiyah

Following the examination of external pressures in the previous section, we now examine Jemaah Islamiyah's resilience and the role of family and kinship as an inherent part of that. Overall, Jemaah Islamiyah has demonstrated strong organizational efficiency and remarkable adaptability through holistic structural change, rather than by redundancy. Family and kinship are central aspects of this, more so than regeneration values or conflict economics (Warneryd 2014). As discussed, Jemaah Islamiyah's formal command and control system and Mantiqi structure started to weaken after December 2000, but it was in Singapore in 2001, and Indonesia following Bali 2002, that complete collapse was seen to be inevitable. In response to these pressures, Jemaah Islamiyah remodelled itself into an organization with separated and flatter holacratic structures, while retaining strategic and tactical governance through its familial linkages.

This is highly important because the flexibility that allowed this to happen came from family, and from the existing familial hierarchy and the efficiency of inter-family adaptation. This is supported by Zahra (2005), who finds that familial organizations are more likely to be efficient at accepting sudden and significant changes. In Jemaah Islamiyah this manifested as a powerful capability for rapid change, in which command and control became less centralized. Rather than degrade operational capabilities as Abuza (2005), Stillwell (2015), and Acharya (2006) contend, it enabled active familial cells to operate with heightened autonomy.[48] The holacratic change further enabled distributed decision-making by pushing it down to tactical levels. It also enhanced security and efficiency by restricting information flows outside of family groups. According to Galamas (2015), these changes resulted in Jemaah Islamiyah re-emerging as two broad divisions, one covering logistics, Dakwah, and education as primary activities and the other, insurgency.

This was also the catalyst that instigated the shift of power dynamics into Jemaah Islamiyah's horizontal familial membership and away from the apex leadership, meaning that changes followed familial groupings rather than structural ones. This had external impacts because inter-organizational cooperation was no longer driven by vertical leadership figures like the Amir, resulting in a significant change to Jemaah Islamiyah's strategic governance by reducing Apex power. In turn, this allowed powerful familial leadership actors such as Mukhlas, Dulmatin, and Patek to exert significant tactical control in divergence from the strategic direction of the Amir. There is evidence this began prior to the collapse of the Mantiqi structure. In August 2000, Amir Ba'asyir created a new political organization known as the Majelis Mujahedeen Indonesia, or MMI. As apex power waned in Jemaah Islamiyah and the Amir was essentially relegated to the position of spiritual adviser with little to no tactical control, the MMI gave Abu Bakar Ba'asyir full control of a new organization.[49]

Despite the separation of power, the MMI remained politically and ideologically entwined with Jemaah Islamiyah. It was formed as an umbrella organization to bring together smaller jihadist groups, political associations, and NGOs to work towards creating an Islamic State. It was also a new political front for Ba'asyir to secure funding via Saudi financiers (BIN 2002).[50] Abuza called it "Ba'asyir's overt political organization" (2004, 334). Tan states MMI "engaged in Proselytizing, the spread of radical ideology and the promotion of an Islamic State, though it publicly stressed it was committed to doing so through peaceful means" (2013, 240). While technically separate from Jemaah Islamiyah, the MMI was but another layer, though one with little to no strategic or operational control.

New leadership

The changes in Jemaah Islamiyah between 2000 and 2007 were very important for the organization for three key reasons. First, it was at the peak of its operational activities. Second, it suffered its greatest external pressures during this phase. Third, this was the greatest period of change. The cessation of control by Abu Bakar Ba'asyir was important because his focus on the MMI was welcomed by other Jemaah Islamiyah commanders, rather than shunned, as it provided opportunities for new leadership.[51] Abu Rushdan, a moderate, was the first to take over as Amir in 2002, but before he could mend the fences he was arrested in 2003. This was at the same time Abu Bakar Ba'asyir was tried and imprisoned for his involvement in the bombing of 38 churches on Christmas Eve 2000. After this there was a rapid change of senior operational leadership. Each new Amir was increasingly militant and tried to re-centralize Jemaah Islamiyah command and control and the operational functions of the organization.

Kamarulnizam reports that when Abu Rushdan was jailed, the "Amir Position was taken over by a little-known personality named Abu Dujana, and later by Nuaim, alias Abu Irsyad" (2011, 37). Although unknown in Western media, Abu Dujana was a jihadist veteran with strong credibility. According to Abuza, he was born in West Java around 1968 and had "close family connections to the Darul Islam movement, and in turn many of Jemaah Islamiyah's old guard. He was educated by Dadang Hafidz, a militant Islamist with deep ties to the Darul Islam organization" (2006, 1). Abu Dujan trained and fought in Afghanistan with the Haqqani Network and other Mujahedeen and was an experienced fighter. He met Jemaah Islamiyah members Hambali, Nasir bin Abbas, who is brother-in-law to his mentor Dadang, and Zulkarnaen in a training camp in Pakistan in 1986 (Hariyadi 2007). It was there that the more militant core of Jemaah Islamiyah that would go on to have operational control probably formed.

Abu Dujana was himself quickly replaced as overall leader. According to Ridley (2012), another Jemaah Islamiyah veteran, Sunarto bin Kartodiharjo (a.k.a. Adung), took the leadership while Abu Dujana returned to military operations until his arrest in 2007 in Solo by Detachment 88.[52] Shortly afterwards, Adung was quickly replaced by Zarkashi in 2004.[53] Although leaders frequently changed due to external pressures, the ability to replace them with highly capable new ones exemplifies Jemaah Islamiyah's re-generational resilience quantum.

Zarkashi was the fifth Amir in as many years. This tells us several salient facts about Jemaah Islamiyah's resilience. First, it demonstrates the high degree of flexibility and adaptability present in the organization. Second, it shows that social capital and trust economics in the organization remained high. As each new leader came into the Amir position they were readily accepted, due very much so the extant familial nexus. Third, the constant turnover of leaders shows resilience, not weaknesses, as the organization was clearly able to immediately recover from leadership losses.

Likewise, Jemaah Islamiyah sub-groups managed to undertake several complex and large-scale attacks. The turbulent flux of apex leadership and the Indonesian Government's focus on pursuing the Amir provided the very operational freedom militant Jemaah Islamiyah commanders including Hambali, Noorudin Top, Umar Patek, and Qotada needed to successfully undertake their various operations.

These include the Davao Super ferry bombing in March 2003, the Jakarta JW Marriot hotel bombing on 5 August 2003 by Azahiri bin Husin, the 9 September Australian Embassy bombing in Jakarta by Noorudin Top, and the second Bali bombing on 12 October 2005. These operations were extensively undertaken by family groups operating covertly and with significant autonomy.[54]

Jemaah Islamiyah's operational resilience

This section examines Jemaah Islamiyah's operational resilience and how the organization maintains its attack capabilities. Jemaah Islamiyah has demonstrated several important factors of change management, each contributing to its success. First, the quick transition from the Mantiqi to the Sariyah and Thoifath structures, and the effectiveness of its familial networks in adapting to it were central to the transformation process. Consequently, it has been difficult for authorities to disrupt Jemaah Islamiyah attack planning because of the security efficiencies that family and the new cellular arrangement afford it. Third, smaller control loops, restricted communications, and the increased autonomy in the conduct of operations each contribute to a heightened counterintelligence awareness.[55] Subsequently, the diffusion of operational control in Jemaah Islamiyah down to lower levels, and the strengths and benefits of its familial sub-groups have proven particularly resilient when used in concert.

Calderoni *et al*. (2017) state that sub-groups commonly occur in larger organizations, but in Jemaah Islamiyah this seemed to be more of a natural evolution as family and kinship became further embedded as mechanisms of operations, which morphed into a flatter holacratic method of governance. Conversely, Crossley *et al*. (2012) find that sub-grouping can frequently mean an operational efficiency/security trade-off where one is favoured to the detriment of the other. In Jemaah Islamiyah it seems this is less the case, with efficiency and security conjointly increasing equally. However, these strengths derive from Jemaah Islamiyah's covert nature. While this proves to be robust there are inherent dangers. Familial groups can be darker in networks but once discovered they can be more easily mapped and dismantled, quickly shifting efficiencies to counterintelligence vulnerabilities.

Without knowing with confidence that every sub-group has been identified, it is difficult to understand with precision the specifics of Jemaah Islamiyah's strengths at any given time. Adding to this is a lack of clarity around exact numbers from familial linkages, and the fact that Jemaah Islamiyah has many affiliations and partnerships that lend transient and non-permanent dynamics to it. Equally, these factors also make it difficult to determine exact levels of Jemaah Islamiyah's internal attack planning compared to nexus attacks in mixed-organization operations. Family and kinship contribute to the porous nature of operational boundaries, and because operations are often not coordinated through a central strategic command, correctly attributing attacks has been challenging at times. Smith for example writes that "no accusations were directed at Jemaah Islamiyah until years later when the investigation into the

Bali bombings of 2002 revealed a common cast of actors that all belonged to Jemaah Islamiyah" (2011, 22).

Substantial fluctuations in membership levels have likewise added to the opaqueness of Jemaah Islamiyah. According to the Australian Government (2017), there have not been any officially established numbers for Jemaah Islamiyah, though it is thought to have gone from a core of nearly 1,000 with several thousand second-tier and supportive members prior to 2002, to only a few hundred dedicated members following the series of attacks in 2002, 2004, and 2005. From 2007 it is believed that the membership numbers of Jemaah Islamiyah recovered to earlier levels and that in 2016 was at, or very near to, its peak levels before 2000, if not exceeding them.

During these fluctuations Jemaah Islamiyah has adapted in synchronicity. In contrast, other organizations like Lashkar-e-Taiba and the Haqqani Network have needed to maintain their size and stability in line with organizational capabilities. In Jemaah Islamiyah however, size and stability was definitively secondary to efficiency. There are multiple examples in this chapter of concurrent operations undertaken by small familial cells that have been extremely efficient, secure, and effective despite major organizational external pressures. Each major attack post-2002 is strong evidence of this.[56]

Additionally, the robust familial nature of Jemaah Islamiyah's new cellular-familial structures in the Sariyah and Thoifath architecture inoculate it against infiltration, further strengthening its operational security. Everton and Cunningham's assertion support this. They argue, "Resilient dark networks will fall more toward the decentralized end of the continuum than a hierarchical one" (2013, 96). Jemaah Islamiyah's successful attack regime, as shown in Table 5.3, suggests the new decentralized structure better supports operational resilience compared to the rigid Mantiqi structure of the past, particularly in the three years immediately after the Bali bombings in 2002.[57] This can be attributed to the efficiency of the new architecture and to the efficiency of how family-derived social capital and trust enable it. Consolidating operational planning, direction, and execution into the Sariyah and Thoifath, the scope of transactions and approvals is minimized, logistics probably streamlined, and overall operational security increased to protect Jemaah Islamiyah from operational disruption.[58]

Several of these attacks were orchestrated with other insurgent organizations external to Indonesia. All attacks on Indonesian soil were undertaken by Jemaah Islamiyah, but the operational coordination of simultaneous attacks in neighbouring countries required complex inter-organizational planning. The multiple bombings across Jakarta on Christmas Eve of December 2000 were coordinated with several attacks in the capital of the Philippines, Manila.[59] There, they were carried out by Jemaah Islamiyah's operational partners the MILF, with the operational direction and funding coming from Jemaah Islamiyah's senior command.[60]

The next major attack was the first of two Bali bombings on 12 October 2002 that killed 202 civilians. Bali 2002 was another cooperative mass-casualty event. In conjunction with al-Qaeda, three of Jemaah Islamiyah's sibling commanders

Table 5.3 Jemaah Islamiyah operations and fatalities, 2000–2016

Date	Operations and fatalities
24 December 2000	Christmas Eve blasts targeting churches in Jakarta, Indonesia. 17 killed and 100 wounded.
30 December 2000	With funding from Jemaah Islamiyah, the MNLF sets 5 bombs in Manila, Philippines. 22 killed.
December 2001	Plans to assault U.S., British, and Israeli Embassies in Singapore disrupted.
12 October 2002	Bali bombings kill 222, 88 of which are Australians.
5 March 2003	Jemaah Islamiyah and MNLF kill 38 in Superferry 14 bombing.
5 August 2003	Jemaah Islamiyah bombs the Jakarta JW Marriot Hotel. 12 killed and 100+ wounded.
9 September 2004	The Australian Embassy in Jakarta is attacked with a bomb that kills 10 locals and wounds over 100.
11 October 2004	Jemaah Islamiyah and MNLF bomb Davao airport killing 18.
2 October 2005	Second Bali bombing kills 23 and wounds more than 100 with the bombing of 3 resorts.
24 October 2005	3 Christian schoolgirls beheaded in Poso, Sulawesi. One other escapes with injuries.
17 July 2009	Jemaah Islamiyah bomb the JW Marriot and Ritz-Carlton in Jakarta for a second time.
14 January 2016	Jakarta Capital attacks. 7 dead and 20 injured.

planned and executed the complex operation. Brothers Mukhlas, Amrozi, and Imam Samudra were the key actors. The security and efficiency advantages provided by kinship is evident in the success of the attacks that went completely undetected from the initial planning and reconnaissance stages, through to completion.[61]

This is also seen in follow-up attacks including the JW Marriot Hotel Jakarta attack on 5 August 2003, and the Australian Embassy Jakarta attack on 9 September 2004. The bomb-maker for both attacks was Gempur Angkoro (a.k.a. Jabir) (Ismail 2006). Jabir is closely linked to Noorudin Top by his cousin Faturrahman al-Ghozi, who was a Jemaah Islamiyah bomb-master. Al-Ghozi was also well known for being the operational mastermind and bomb-maker that was used in the Rizal Day Manila attacks in 2008, in which Jemaah Islamiyah member Mukhlas from Bali 2002, and possibly one of his brothers, was also involved (GMA 2009).

In the Philippines, Jemaah Islamiyah continued to work with other affiliates besides al-Qaeda, such as the Abu Sayyaf Group, MNLF, and MILF, as well as training external insurgents in advanced bomb-making, drawing heavily on its extensive familial expertise. The 2003 Superferry 14 and 2004 Davao airport bombings were both carried out by means of the close cooperation of Jemaah Islamiyah, Abu Sayyaf, and MILF members, who grouped together through personal and familial connections to undertake the operations (Abuza 2003a). These are just a few examples that show the familial dynamics and how they

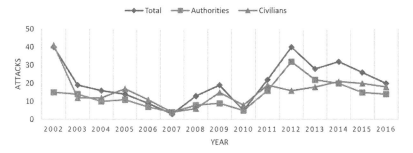

Figure 5.4 Jemaah Islamiyah attack victim groups, 2002–2006.

develop, forge, and exploit kinship connections to positively affect organizational capabilities and resilience.

This is reflected in Figure 5.4, which shows Jemaah Islamiyah operations in Indonesia from 2002 to 2016, including total casualties, and the division of the targets of the attacks being either civilian and incumbent security forces.[62] Of particular interest is the significant increase in operations from 2007 onwards when Jemaah Islamiyah gained increasing attention from authorities. That it was able to continue attacks largely unhindered indicates that the attention focused on it was not being translated into effective external pressures. As a result of the significance that family and kinship have in Jemaah Islamiyah, it can be inferred that this was the most significant obstacle to authorities in developing critical intelligence coverage because it was so difficult to penetrate.[63] In this particular instance, this was less a failure of authorities and more so a strength of Jemaah Islamiyah.

Conclusion

The data and analysis presented in this chapter shows that finding tangible, persistent, and effective ways to deal with Jemaah Islamiyah has been difficult. This is for many reasons. First, family and kinship have made security and operational economics cheap and efficient. Jemaah Islamiyah can replace fighters and leaders easily. Second, Jemaah Islamiyah has very strong internal security and counterintelligence awareness, due largely to its exclusive familial membership in sensitive operational and attack-planning activities.

This means Jemaah Islamiyah is very hard to penetrate, and the closeness of familial groups ensures information is not inadvertently seeded out. From an intelligence perspective, network analysis and surveillance of Jemaah Islamiyah's senior leaders and command and control actors no longer provides ideal coverage of attack planning and other covert activities. For hard-power, direct kinetic pressures to be effective, increasingly complex intelligence operations must work down to the cellular level, where they are often hard to find and tougher to penetrate.

Third, family provides Jemaah Islamiyah with improved logistics networks drawn from members and their families, which is substantially broad and diverse. Fourth, Jemaah Islamiyah has developed very close links with many keystone actors in regional and global insurgencies, making resource acquisitions of financing, weapons, arms, training, and expertise readily available. Fifth, family and kinship connections ensure recruitment is more comfortable and quicker than vetting unknown, un-associated new members, and when new members are introduced they are usually married into the family to sisters or cousins. These resilience strengths are certainly robust and enduring, but they are by no means imperishable.

Jemaah Islamiyah has been susceptible to hard-power, direct kinetic pressures and lost many fighters, leaders, organizational divisions, and significant expertise and capabilities. However, the outcomes have been transient. Leaders and fighters have been replaced from its base to the most senior levels, and the role of Amir has changed hands multiple times, though in some cases this has taken considerable time to do so. The data in this chapter shows clearly that the greatest resilience dynamic of Jemaah Islamiyah has been its familial and kinship architecture, because it is within this that the organizational culture and ideology lives on.

Externally, Jemaah Islamiyah members have married into al-Qaeda, Ring Baten, Darul Islam, JAT, the MILF, MNLF, Abu Sayyaf Group, and others, increasing resources, capabilities, and access. It has therefore achieved the dual measurements of political and operational perpetuity. Although there were chronological failings of successive Amirs in establishing unity and a clear strategic purpose, the aims of Jemaah Islamiyah persisted cohesively across senior commanders such as Hambali, Dulmatin, Noorudin Top, Dujana, and familial middle members such as Mohammad Rais, Rahmat Abdhi, Kankan Abdul Quodir, Dadang, and many others.

Holistically the data in this chapter also tells us some additional important findings about Jemaah Islamiyah's resilience. For example, it has been able to move operational and planning centres from one province to another, and from one country to another, facilitated via kinship networks. This has resulted in a geographically dispersed insurgency and load-sharing across partner organizations; creating what Carter *et al.* (2017) refer to as "fusion groups", many of which share kinship.

Figure 5.5 shows the rise in insurgent-based political violence between 1990 and 2015, going from a dip to just 1,000 incidents in 2004 to 17,000 in 2015.[64] Thirty-five per cent of that rise has occurred in Southeast Asia. As a result, Jemaah Islamiyah enjoyed a growing theatre of potential partners that increased the proliferation of skills, expertise, operational and intelligence sharing, and joint attack planning.

Additionally, the continuance of influence actors like Saudi Arabia to fund and propagate Salafi-Wahhabism in Indonesia and surrounding countries, and the maturation of global Islamic State and al-Qaeda transnational narratives,

INSURGENT POLITICAL VIOLENCE 1990-2015

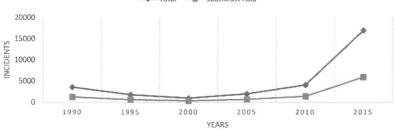

Figure 5.5 All-group insurgent violence, 1990–2015.

means that others are already propagating the ideologies necessary for Jemaah Islamiyah's insurgency to succeed. Building popular political support is now largely an off-the-shelf product, provided through technology and by international mainstream and social media. All Jemaah Islamiyah has to do is bridge local issues and bond them to communal sentiment by creating narrative-bridges, and then offer itself as the most suitable vehicle for change.

In regard to soft-power pressures, the data shows it has been more a case of taking the opportunity of the lack of extant ones, and leveraging the absence of effective ones. The international tools are there, such as the United Nations resolutions and ASEAN frameworks that are well supported by Australia and the U.S., but a notable lack of organic political will means they are not used as they could be. Similarly, the competing priorities and power contests of Polri, BIN, TNI, political actors, and the corrupt and weak judicial and legislative systems work at odds with each other and provide Jemaah Islamiyah room to operate.

So long as it can mature new familial connections faster that they are degraded, Jemaah Islamiyah will retain ongoing access to strong regenerative capacities, recruiting former Darul Islam members as fighters and leaders, as well as new members through its extensive radical madrassa network.[65] Indeed, political inaction to dismantle Jemaah Islamiyah's schools like the Al-Mukmin Islamic boarding school in Solo and its affiliates supports such a finding. These schools are just a part of a structure that provides Jemaah Islamiyah with redundancy through multiple sources of resource acquisition, indoctrination of recruits, and access to multi-generational social, cultural, and familial networks sympathetic and aligned to Jemaah Islamiyah narratives.[66]

Notes

1 For more on JAT see Chris Rottenberg, 2012. *Jamaah Ansharut Tauhid (JAT): The Perpetual Threat.* Washington, D.C.: The Osgood Centre for International Studies. Other groups include Dulmatin's Al-Qaeda of the Veranda of Mecca Group and Jemaah Ansharut Tauhid (JAT) created by Abu Bakar Ba'asyir as a phoenix

organization. SOURCE: Aubrey Belford, 2010. "Rise and Fall of a Terror Cell". *The Diplomat*. Accessed 26 October 2018. https://thediplomat.com/2010/04/rise-and-fall-of-a-terror-cell/.

2 Lacking state patronage, Jemaah Islamiyah has received significant support from al-Qaeda, which is often referred to as Jemaah Islamiyah's "Parent organization". SOURCE: Zachary Abuza, 2003b. "Militant Islam in Southeast Asia". *Survival* 46 (3): 153–184.

3 The first Bali 2002 bombings killed 202 people and many Australians. Authorities reacted swiftly with a joint Indonesian/Australian federal police task force investigation called "Operation Alliance". On 4 March 2003 Jemaah Islamiyah was linked as a prime operational partner in the bombing of a ferry terminal in Davao City, Philippines that killed 23 people and injured more than 150. Again Jemaah Islamiyah partnered with its MILF affiliates and provided operational training, direction, and funds for the attack. The attacks in 2005 became known as the "Second Jemaah Islamiyah Bali Bombings" and targeted Jimbaran Bay and the Kuta shopping and tourists district. The bombs detonated at 8 pm local time on Saturday the 1st of October and killed 26 with over 100 wounded including many international visitors. SOURCES: David Royds *et al.*, 2005. "A Case Study in Forensic Chemistry: The Bali Bombings". *Talanata* 67 (2): 262–268; Seth Mydans, 2003. "16 Die in Bombing in Southern Philippines: Rebels Deny Link". *New York Times*. Accessed 17 May 2019. www.nytimes.com/2003/04/03/world/16-die-in-bombing-in-southern-philippines-rebels-deny-link.html; Elaine Quijano *et al.*, 2002. "Bali terrorist blast kills at least 26". *CNN*. Accessed 26 September 2018. https://edition.cnn.com/2005/WORLD/asiapcf/10/01/bali.blasts/.

4 Locally Jemaah Islamiyah was involved in fighting in Poso, Maluku, and Central Sulawesi, and abroad in Afghanistan since 1985, the Philippines since 1989, Iraq from 2003 after the U.S.-led invasion, and Syria since at least 2013. SOURCES: Mohamed Salleh, and Muhammad Hassan, 2009. "The Disconnection of Indonesia's Jemaah Islamiyah and al-Qaeda from the Afghan Jihad Experience". *Terrorism Monitor 7* (39): 5–8; Tricia Bacon, 2017. "Why al-Qaida is still strong 16 years after 9/11". *The Conversation*. Accessed 28 September 2017. https://theconversation.com/why-al-qaida-is-still-strong-16-years-after-9-11-83403; Muh Taufiqurrohman, 2015. "The Road to ISIS: How Indonesian Jihadists Travel to Iraq and Syria". *Counter Terrorist Trends and Analyses* 7 (4): 17–25.

5 Hwang puts these as being Mantiqi I: Malaysia and Singapore where much fundraising was done; Mantiqi II: Sumatra and Java where recruit inputs were primarily collected; Mantiqi III: Eastern Malaysia, the Philippines, and Indonesian Sulawesi used largely for covert training bases; Mantiqi IV: Papua New Guinea and Australia though these largely failed to become established. SOURCE: Julie Hwang, 2009. "Conclusion: Patterns of Mobilization". In *Peaceful Islamist Mobilization in the Muslim World*, ed. Julie Chernov Hwang. New York: Palgrave Macmillan, 161–174.

6 The ties Hambali forged in Afghanistan exhibit strong social capital and trust that continued to serve the Jemaah Islamiyah/al-Qaeda relationship for many years to come. Three years before his arrest in the temple town of Ayutthaya, Thailand by Thai authorities, Hambali was filmed in a January 2000 meeting with Nawaf Alhazmi and Khalid Almihdhar, who were two of the 9/11 hijackers. SOURCE: Maria Ressa *et al.*, 2003. "Asia's most wanted in U.S. hands". *CNN*. Accessed 21 June 2018. http://edition.cnn.com/2003/WORLD/asiapcf/southeast/08/15/hambali.capture.

7 Abu Yusuf is the alias of Dadang Suratman, a Jemaah Islamiyah senior operational planner and close associate of the organization's founder Abdullah Sungkar. Abu Yusuf married the sister of one Jemaah Islamiyah's most wanted leaders, Hambali. SOURCE: ICG, 2003. *Jemaah Islamiyah In Southeast Asia: Damaged But Still Dangerous. ICG Asia Report No. 63*. Jakarta/Brussels: International Crisis Group.

Accessed 1 January 2018. www.crisisgroup.org/asia/south-east-asia/indonesia/
jemaah-islamiyah-south-east-asia-damaged-still-dangerous.

8 Nisa and Saenong report that while this is relative new, it is not an uncommon phenomenon. In fact, they state that female martyrdom, or "amaliyah", is increasing.
Additionally, the May 2018 East Java attacks involving an entire family, including
children, demonstrates this is not only not an increasing trend but an expanding one.
SOURCES: Eva Nisa, 2018. "Female suicide bombers: how terrorist propaganda radicalises Indonesia women". Australian National University; Hannah Ellis-Petersen
and Kate Lamb, 2018. "Surabaya blast: family of five carried out bomb attack on
Indonesian police station". *The Guardian.* Accessed 16 May 2018. www.theguardian.
com/world/2018/may/14/indonesia-car-bomb-surabaya-police-station-attacked.

9 Authorities use this tactic as a means to entice families out of Jemaah Islamiyah once
the primary connection is broken, such as the arrest of a father and husband.
However, this reinforces Jemaah Islamiyah's focus on family as well and is therefore
a rather questionable method as little data exists to show its effectiveness. SOURCE:
Sulastri Osman, 2010. "Jemaah Islamiyah: Of Kin and Kind". *Journal of Current
Southeast Asian Affairs* 29 (2): 157–175.

10 According to a 2003 ICG report, the MILF and Jemaah Islamiyah supported each
other by Jemaah Islamiyah facilitating MILF operatives to train with al-Qaeda in
Afghanistan. In turn, MILF gave Jemaah Islamiyah significant amounts of explosives
and other weapons. The Jemaah Islamiyah/MILF relationship is still active in Southeast Asia to the present time. SOURCE: ICG, 2003. Report No. 63: Sri Yunanto and
Angel Damayanti, 2017. "The Root Causes and Nexus of Militant Islamic Movements in Indonesia: Case Studies of Darul Islam and Jemaah Islamiyah". *Journal of
Asia Pacific Studies* 1 (2017): 1–39.

11 Data was drawn from Ken Micchi, 2016. "Looking at Links and Nodes: How Jihadists in Indonesia Survived". *Journal of Asian Ethnology* 75 (1): 1535–1543.

12 A similar structure is in use in Palestine where the al-Quds brigades, al-Qaeda, and
Saraya Ansar al-Taweed brigades have similar systems. SOURCE: Author observation.
pdf?bcsi_scan_fcaccdf017742bb0=0&bcsi_scan_filename=b063_indonesia_jemaah_
islamiyah_s_current_status.pdf. Accessed 6 July 2017.

13 Embel was the right-hand man of Abu Sayyaf leader Gumbahala Jumdail a.k.a. Doc
Abu, whose group was responsible for the kidnapping of ABS-CBN journalists in
cooperation with two other Abu Sayyaf Group factions, led by Radullan Sahiron
and Albader Parad respectively. SOURCE: Maria Ressa, 2013. "From Bin Laden to
Facebook: 10 Days of Abduction, 10 Years of Terrorism". London: Imperial
College Press.

14 Majelis Mujahedeen Indonesia/Indonesia Mujahedeen Council (MMI), and Jamaah
Ansharut Tauhid (JAT) were each founded by Abu Bakar Ba'asyir in 2000 and
2008 respectively. The Mujahedeen KOMPAK is a part of the Lashkar
Mujahedeen, a network comprised of Jemaah Islamiyah, al-Qaeda, Darul Islam, and
other members from the MILF and MNLF. SOURCE: Francisco Galamas, 2015.
*The Militant Groups of Radical Ideology and Violent Nature Series Area: Indian
Subcontinent and Southeast Asia.* Ceseden, Spain: Del Instituto Espanol de
Estudios Estrategicos (IEEE).

15 Zulkarnaen was the head of military and intelligence operations of Jemaah Islami-
yah's Central Command, and a very powerful actor in the organization. SOURCE:
Dolores Yuvienco, 2005. "Circular Letter-Jemaah Islamiyah". Bangko Sentral Ng
Pilipinas. Available at: www.bsp.gov.ph/regulations/regulations.asp?id=1829.

16 Conboy asserts that allegedly an al-Qaeda Yemeni national with a U.S. Passport
travelled to Indonesia and "provided key technical assistance and had been in Bali
during the days immediately before the bombing [2002]". SOURCE: Kenneth
Conboy, 2004. "The Provocateurs". In *The Second Front: Inside Asia's Most*

Dangerous Terrorist Network, ed. Kenneth Conboy. Jakarta, Singapore: Equinox Publishing, 109–111.

17 Hwang reports that Kandai Ahmad was a central figure in the 1957 assassination plot to kill President Sukarno. SOURCE: Julie Hwang, 2012. "Terrorism in Perspective: An Assessment of 'Jihad Project' Trends in Indonesia". *Asia Pacific Issues* 104 (1): 1–12.

18 After his release, Farihin worked for the Forum Komunikasi Alumni Afghanistan Indonesia (FKAAI), an organization that aimed to stem radicalization of youths. However, his work was not benevolent but rather remained firmly entrenched in insurgent jihadism. Rather than deter extremism he sought to only deter aspiring fighters from joining IS in favour of local Indonesian organizations. Chopra states that Farinha believed the 2002 Bali bombings were the right thing to do, quoting him as saying that "it was necessary to cleanse the place of immoral, lewd foreigners bringing their sins to our country. They spread Aids in our country." SOURCE: Anuj Chopra, 2010. "Indonesia tries rehabilitation to wipe out extremism". *The National.* Accessed 11 September 2018. www.thenational.ae/world/asia/indonesia-tries-rehabilitation-to-wipe-out-extremism-1.590716.

19 Two of Abdullah Sungkar's daughters were married off by their father to Jemaah Islamiyah fighters and Sungkar also arranged the marriage of Hambali to a half-Chinese Indonesian Muslim convert. SOURCE: ICG, 2003. Report No. 63.

20 Ramakrishna is an excellent source on the early days of Darul Islam in Indonesia. See: Kumar Ramakrishna, 2009. *Radical Pathways: Understanding Muslim Radicalization in Indonesia.* Santa Barbara: Praeger Security International.

21 In 1942 the Japanese invaded and fought the Dutch over control during a brutal conflict lasting until 1945. According to Reid, the Japanese triumph over the Dutch initially was seen by many Indonesians as meaning that colonial powers could be defeated. However, when the allies defeated the Japanese, the Dutch regained power and Indonesia entered a new period of insurgency and the rise of Darul Islam. SOURCES: Rachel Leow, 2016. *Taming Babel: Language and the Making of Malaysia.* Cambridge: Cambridge University Press; Anthony Reid, 1974. *The Indonesian National Revolution 1945–1950.* Harlow, UK: Longman Publishing.

22 Pondok Ngruki is an Islamic boarding school (pesantren) founded by Abu Bakar Ba'asyir and Abdullah Sungkar. It is a training and indoctrination centre for Jemaah Islamiyah Alumni and used the work of Al-Banna and that of Abd al-Qadir, *Baraja's Jihad and Hiraj*, as standard texts. An ICG report states it was an ideological hybrid with a mixture of Egyptian Islamic radicalism, jihad, and secrecy with a strong Darul Islam current and anti-Christian sentiments. There are over fifty Islamic schools associated with Jemaah Islamiyah that work to indoctrinate future generations into the familial organization. SOURCE: ICG, 2002. *Indonesia Backgrounder: How The Jemaah Islamiyah Terrorist Network Operates.* International Crisis Group. Report No. 43.

23 The Dutch East Indies, as Indonesia was known prior to WWII, was a colony restructured to support the Dutch economy. SOURCE: Dien Madjid and Johan Wahyudi, 2018. "Local Resistance in Kerinci in the 20th Century". *Tawarihk – Journal of Historical Studies* 9 (2): 137–150.

24 The far enemy, also *al-Adou al-Baeed*, is a term used by jihadists to refer to the United States and its Western allies. SOURCE: Fawaz Gerges, 2005. *The Rise of Trans-nationalist Jihadi's and the Far Enemy.* Cambridge, Cambridge University Press.

25 Jeffry Halverson *et al.*, 2011. *Master Narratives of Islamist Extremism.* New York, Palgrave Macmillan.

26 Former Australian Foreign Minister Gareth Evans said in 2005 that "the threat posed by the South East Asian terrorist group, Jemaah Islamiyah, has effectively been

thwarted." Romeo Gacad of Stratfor assessed that after Indonesian authorities' raided an AiA camp in Aceh it seemed that former Jemaah Islamiyah members had been trying to re-establish the organization, suggesting that it was no longer a viable entity. Gacad went on to suggest that in Indonesia, "jihadist groups have never gained a significant following", and security forces consistently captured and killed militants. Given that successive governments were extremely hesitant to even recognize insurgent jihadists, or take action against them because of the perceived social and political backlashes, this seems a very odd assessment indeed. SOURCES: Daniel Hoare, 2005. "Gareth Evans downplays terrorist risk in Australia". *ABC News*. Accessed 18 April 2018. www.abc.net.au/worldtoday/content/2005/s1469369.htm; Romeo Gacad, 2010. "JI Assessments". *Stratfor.* Accessed 19 April 2018. https://worldview.stratfor. com/article/indonesia-dismantling-another-militant-cell.

27 Faiz bin Abu Bakar Bafana was the Mantiqi I treasurer. During the trial of Jemaah Islamiyah Amir Ba'asyir he supplied key evidence against the accused. He maintains Ba'asyir had personally approved both Bali bombing attacks and an operation to assassinate then Prime Minister Megawati Soekarnoputri. SOURCE: Matthew Moore, 2003b. "Insider says Jemaah Islamiyah in Australia". *The Age*. Accessed 21 April 2016. www.theage.com.a /articles/2003/06/26/1056449367273.html.

28 The tapes were later recovered by U.S. forces in Afghanistan in 2001 but they did not share the intelligence with Singapore for another month, by which stage the IDS had already commenced arresting Jemaah Islamiyah members. SOURCE: SOURCE: Seth Mydans, 2002. "Singapore Details Terrorist Plot to Bomb U.S. Ships and Soldiers". *The New York Times.* Accessed 15 March 2018. www.nytimes.com/2002/01/11/ international/singapore-details-terrorist-plot-to-bomb-us-ships-and-soldiers.html.

29 This second round of arrests ended Jemaah Islamiyah operations in Singapore including a planned sea-borne attack against U.S. interests such as naval vessels, the Paya Lebar Air Force Base, Singaporean Changi Airport, and Biggin Hill radar station. SOURCE: Muhammad Hassan and Tuty Mostarom, 2011. *A Decade of Combating Radical Ideology: Learning From the Singapore Experience (2001–2011)*. RSIS Monograph No. 20. Singapore: S. Rajaratnam School of International Studies.

30 The Rizal Day metro Manila bombings were developed by Mukhlas and MILF member Hadji Onos. Mukhlas had been sent to the Philippines in 1996 by the Singapore Manti commander Faiz bin Abu Bakar Bafana to develop closer ties with the MILF. SOURCE: GMA, 2009. "Rizal Day Bombing Chronology". *GMA News*. Accessed 16 April 2018. www.gmanetwork.com/news/news/content/145645/rizal-day-bombing-chronology/story.

31 SOURCE: UN, 2015. *Security Council Committee Persuant to Resolutions 1267 (1989) (1999) (2011) and 2253 (2015) Concerning ISIL (Da'esh) al-Qaeda and Associated Individual Groups Undertaking Entities. QDe.092 Jemaah Islamiyah.* United Nations Security Council. Accessed 22 April 2017. www.un.org/sc/suborg/en/ sanctions /1267/aq_sanctions_list/summaries/entity/jemaah-islamiyah.

32 The U.S., under its Anti-Terror Assistance Program, gave Indonesia U.S.$130 million to start Det 88, and ongoing funding from U.S.$1.3 in 2003 rising to U.S.$40+ million in 2006. Australia annually provides over A$16 million and in 2004 gave A$35 million to build a joint law enforcement training centre in Jakarta. SOURCE: UNODC, 2017–2020. *Country Programme 2017–2020: Making Indonesia safer from crime, drugs and terrorism.* New York: United Nations Office on Drugs and Crime.

33 Davies and Rondonuwu reported that according to Jakarta-based security analyst Ken Conboy, the name actually came about because a senior police official who was present at discussions about starting the new unit, misheard Anti-Terrorism Assistance [programme] "A-T-A", as "eighty-eight", and as a lucky number in Asian culture, believed it to be an auspicious sign. SOURCES: Ed. Davies, and Olivier Rondonuwu, 2010. "U.S.-funded Detachment 88, elite of Indonesia security". *Reuters.* Accessed

14 April 2016. www.reuters.com/article/us-indonesia-usa-security/u-s-funded-detachment-88-elite-of-indonesia-security-idUSTRE62H13F20100318; BRIMOB, "Indonesian Police's Detachment 88". Accessed 14 April 2016. http://indonesiaelite forces.tripod.com/id37.html.

34 SOURCE: Jonathan Lord, 2015. "Undercover Under Threat: Cover Identity, Clandestine Activity, and Covert Action in the Digital Age". *International Journal of Intelligence and Counterintelligence* 28 (4): 666–691.

35 The presence of these other senior commanders from the Ring Baten and Abu Sayyaf Groups further illustrates the deep inter-organizational nexus Jemaah Islamiyah is part of.

36 The unexpected attacks by Jemaah Islamiyah in the capital on 14 January in a series of bombings and gunfire by insurgents, resulted in seven being killed and more than 20 wounded. SOURCE: Prashanth Parameswaran, 2016. "Islamic State Attack in Indonesia?" *The Diplomat.* Accessed 25 March 2017. https://thediplomat.com/tag/ indonesia-and-the-islamic-state/.

37 The nature of aliases can be confusing, particularly so in Asia where militants often have several aliases of aliases. Jacob Zenn mistakenly reported this incident as involving two Jemaah Islamiyah fighters, Sibghotulloh and Yuardi, when in fact they are the same person. SOURCE: Jacob Zenn, 2011. "Indonesia's 'Ghost Birds' Tackle Islamist Terrorists: A Profile of Densus 88". *Terrorism Monitor* 9 (32). https:// jamestown.org / program / indonesias -ghost -birds -tackle -islamist -terrorists-a-profile-of-densus-88/. Accessed 25 April 2016.

38 Abu Wardah Santoso was also the brother-in-law to Jemaah Islamiyah's Operations mastermind Dulmatin.

39 The book is titled *Perjalanan Cinta Istri Seorang Mujahid* (Love Journey of a Mujahid's wife). Jemaah Islamiyah's media arm Arrahmak Media published the book in 2009. SOURCE: Ahmad Saiful *et al.*, 2016. "Women's Proactive Roles in Jihadism in Southeast Asia". *Counter Terrorist Trends and Analysis* 8 (5): 9–15.

40 SOURCE: ICG, 2008. *Indonesia: Implications of the Ahmadiyya Decree. Report No. 78.* International Crisis Group. Briefing 78 (Asia). Jakarta/Brussels: International Crisis Group.

41 As an established political doctrine, later leaders including Megawati could not ignore Islamic nationalist sentiments, and had little choice but to embrace Pancasila as a moral counter-balance to secular political-economic development. SOURCE: Gregory Coles, 2018. "What Do I Lack as a Woman? The Rhetoric of Megawati Sukarnoputri". *A Journal of History of Rhetoric* 36 (1): 58–91.

42 In 1980, Saudi Arabia built the Institute for the Study of Islam and Arabic (LIPIA) in Jakarta in a modern, state-of-the-art centre. Initially it produced 3,500 graduates annually which rose to over 10,000 a year by 2016, and campuses were added in Medan, Makassar, and Surabaya. SOURCE: Margaret Scott, 2016. "Indonesia: the Saudis are coming". *Financial Review.* Accessed 5 March 2016. www.afr.com/news/ world/asia/indonesia-the-saudis-are-coming-20161017-gs3u7j.

43 Atran points out that the Indonesian Parliamentary Speaker even visited Ba'asyir when he was in jail in 2003 for his role in the December 2000 Christmas Eve bombings, to show solidarity with him as a victim of international pressures. SOURCE: Scott Atran, 2009. "To Jihad and Back". *Foreign Policy.* Accessed 1 November 2005. https://jeannicod.ccsd.cnrs.fr/ijn_00000648.

44 Despite significant protests from Australia and international allies, in January 2019 President Widodo said Ba'yasir, 81, would be unconditionally freed on humanitarian grounds, citing his age and poor health. However, this was later reviewed. SOURCES: Anne Barker, 2019. "Joko Widodo between a rock and a hard place over terrorist Abu Bakar Ba'aysir's release". *ABC News.* Accessed 22 January 2019. www.abc.net.au/news/2019-01-23/joko-widodo-in-dilemma-after-touting-abu-bakar-bashir-release/10737900; Resty

Yuniar, 2019. "Radical cleric Abu Bakar Bashir will be free to 'preach hate', Australia warns Indonesia". *South China Morning Post.* Accessed 22 January 2019. www.scmp. com/news/asia/southeast-asia/article/2183155/radical-cleric-abu-bakar-bashir-will-be-free-preach-hate.

45 The Mujahedeen Indonesian Timor was a prominent one, as was the JAD, the Jemaah Islamiyah splinter organization, and the Abu Sayyaf Group in the Philippines. Likewise a range of Islamic insurgent commanders including Abu Jandall, Bahrun Naim, Chep Hernawan, and Bahrumsyah have each claimed the title of ISI Amir in Indonesia. SOURCES: Andrew Henshaw, 2015. *Transnational Macro-Narrative Decendancy in Violent Conflict: A Case Study of the Mujahidin Indonesia Timur in Central Sulawesi.* Sydney: Macquarie University Press; Joseph Liow, 2016. "ISIS reaches Indonesia: The terrorist group's prospects in Southeast Asia". *Brookings Institute.* Accessed 10 December 2018. www.brookings.edu/opinions/isis-reaches-indonesia-the-terrorist-groups-prospects-in-southeast-asia/.

46 Australian Government. 2019. *Population Clock. Bureau of Statistics.* Accessed 5 January 2019. www.abs.gov.au/ausstats/abs@.nsf/0/1647509ef7e25faaca2568a 900154b63?OpenDocument.

47 For an excellent history of Pancasila see: Benyamin Intan, 2006. "Public Religion and the Pancasila-based State of Indonesia: An Ethical and Sociological Analysis". *Journal of Islamic Studies* 18 (2): 278–281.

48 Abuza declared in 2007 that Jemaah Islamiyah had been neutralized as an immediate threat. Stillwell wrote it would be difficult for Jemaah Islamiyah to continue as an organization and that internal divisions meant it would not undertake complex operations again. He added, "The feebleness of its allies like al-Qaeda weakens Jemaah Islamiyah's ability to train and fund its operations, as well as operate successfully within Southeast Asia." Acharya made conflicting statements that Jemaah Islamiyah had completely disintegrated after Bali 2002, and then that it still presented a threat but remained fractured. SOURCES: Zachary Abuza, 2007. "Indonesia Neutralizes JI as Immediate Threat". *Terrorism Focus* 4 (19): 2–3; Chris Stillwell, 2015. "Terrorism in Southeast Asia: Jemaah Islamiyah". *The Globe.* 5 November. Accessed 16 March 2018. http://theglobegwu.com/2015/11/05/terrorism-in-southeast-asia-jemaah-islamiyah/; Arabinda Acharya, 2006. *The Bali Bombings: Impact on Indonesia and Southeast Asia.* Washington, D.C.: The Hudson Institute – Center for Eurasian Policy, Occasional Research Paper Series II (Islamism in Southeast Asia) No. 2.

49 MMI was only designated as a foreign terrorist organization in June 2017. SOURCE: Caleb Weiss, 2017. "U.S. designates Indonesian-based Jihadist Group". *Threat Matrix* 6 (2017).

50 According to Abuza, Saudi charities used to procure terror financing include the Saudi Al-Haramain and the International Islamic Relief Organization, and two Indonesian charities: Indonesian Al-Haramain, KOMPAK and the Medical Emergency Relief Charity. SOURCE: Zachary Abuza, 2009. "Jemaah Islamiyah Adopts the Hezbollah Model: Assessing Hezbollah's Influence". *Middle East Quarterly* Winter (2009): 15–26.

51 Just after his release in 2004 Abu Bakar Ba'asyir was re-arrested on 15 October for involvement in the 2002 Bali bombings and attacks on the Marriot Hotel Jakarta on 5 August 2003. Gunaratna claims that from his prison cell in 2003 during his 20-month incarceration, Ba'asyir was re-elected for his second term as Amir of MMI, reflecting his committed attention elsewhere. SOURCE: SMH, "Bashir gets 30 months' jail for Bali bomb plot". *Sydney Morning Herald.* Accessed 22 December 2018. www.smh.com.au/national/bashir-gets-30-months-jail-for-bali-bomb-plot-20050304-gdkuo7.html.

52 Dujana was believed to have revitalized Jemaah Islamiyah's operational capabilities and was a commander of Poso operations that incited violence between Muslims and Christians. He is also said to have been directly involved in the Australian Embassy attack in Jakarta in 2004 as well as other actions. Karnavian maintained that Adung "was arrested in 2004 in Solo for illegal weapons possession and for hiding the fugitives Dr Azahari Husin and Noorudin M. Top". Adung was sentenced to seven years in April 2005 but released in March 2009 after serving less than two years. SOURCES: Kathy Quiano, 2007. "Police Capture Asia Terror Leader". *CNN.* Accessed 21 December 2018. http://edition.cnn,com/2007/world/asiapct/06/12/indonesia.Terror/; M T. Karnavian, 2015. "Al-Jamaah al-Islamiyah: From Insurgency to Terrorism". *Insurgency and Terrorism Series* (2014): 39–75; ICG, 2010. *Indonesia: Jihad Surprise in Aceh. Crisis Group Asia Report No. 189.* Jakarta/Brussels: International Crisis Group.

53 Afterwards, he and Abu Dujana turned police informers in 2007 and gave evidence against Abu Bakar Ba'asyir. SOURCE: Detik News, 2007. "Zarkasi Alias Mbah Mulai Ungkap Jaringan Jemaah Islamiyah". *Voice of the Reader.* Accessed 19 December 2018. https://news.detik.com/berita/805011/zarkasi-alias-mbah-mulai-ung-kap-jaringan-ji.

54 It is very important to note here that Jemaah Islamiyah, like many other organizations involved in insurgency, and other forms of political violence, is a covert organization, not a clandestine one. Many scholars such as Sulastri, Tilly, Ruby, and Kilcullen, and others, frequently classify terrorism, terrorists, and insurgent organizations as clandestine. Sulastri for example writes "Jemaah Islamiyah is a clandestine Islamist group". With a declared political party how could this ever be? A covert organization, agent, or operation is secret only so long as it needs to be, i.e. until the attack occurs. This way it avoids disruption before reaching its end state. After the attack it is likely that some form of acknowledgement or credit will be claimed. In clandestine acts, the purpose is to never be discovered and when the results of a clandestine act, action, agent, or attack are known, that the perpetrators remain secret and undiscovered. This is the critical difference between the two. SOURCES: Sulastri Osman, 2010. "Jemaah Islamiyah: Of Kin and Kind". *Journal of Current Southeast Asian Affairs* 29 (2): 157–175; Charles Tilly, 2004. "Terror, Terrorism, Terrorists". *Sociological Theory* 22 (1): 5–13; Charles Ruby, 2002. "The Definition of Terrorism". *Analyses of Social Issues and Public Policy* 2 (1): 9–14; David Kilcullen, 2006. "Globalization and the Development of Indonesian Counterinsurgency Tactics". *Small Wars and Insurgencies* 17 (1) 44–64.

55 Boland and Fowler refer to these as "performance control loops" wherein different actors have responsibilities for unique functions. When these are smaller in size it can increase efficiency by avoiding wasted effort and defining individual action and responsibility. SOURCE: Tony Boland and Alan Fowler, 2000. "A Systems Perspective of Performance Management in Public Sector Organizations". *International Journal of Public Sector Management* 13 (5): 417–446.

56 New non-consanguine members are brought into the *ikhwan* – the fraternity of brotherhood, and work in *usrob* – literally, small family clusters. These represent a cellular structure in which operations are fostered by small darkened groups from across the Jemaah Islamiyah organization, run by commanders like Noorudin Top, Hambali, Gempur Angkoro, and Umar Patek as shown. SOURCES: Barry Desker, 2003. "The Jemaah Islamiyah (Jemaah Islamiyah) Phenomenon in Singapore". *Contemporary Southeast Asia – A Journal of International and Strategic Affairs* 25 (3): 489–507; Noor Huda Ismail and Susan Sim, 2016. "From prison to carnage in Jakarta: Predicting terrorist recidivism in Indonesia's prisons. Part 2". *Brookings Institute.* Accessed 22 May 2017. www.brookings.edu/opinions/predicting-terrorist-recidivism-in-indonesias-prisons/.

57 Jemaah Islamiyah's decentralized efficiency is further enabled by its ideological embedment in the regional jihadist spectrum, developed through its diffused kinship network. This means Jemaah Islamiyah has evolved to the point of developing multi-agent operational groups from different organizations under Jemaah Islamiyah's ideological and political flags, rather than a central Jemaah Islamiyah command and control group. Supporting this, Manyin *et al.* assert "the networks goal of developing indigenous jihadis meant that Jemaah Islamiyah members often have worked with and/ or created local groups outside of its control." SOURCE: Bruce Vaughn *et al.*, 2005. *Terrorism in Southeast Asia.* 2009. Washington, D.C.: Congressional Research Service.

58 This aligns with Jemaah Islamiyah's aims of parenting ongoing occurrences of deniable operations to meet its political aims, as outlined in the PUPJI manual, which envisages Jemaah Islamiyah as a Qoi'dah Aminah, or secure base with resilient insurgent military capabilities. SOURCE: Elena Pavlova, 2007. "From a Counter-Society to a Counter-State Movement: Jemaah Islamiyah According to PUPJI". *Studies in Conflict & Terrorism* 30 (9): 777–800.

59 SOURCES: Straits Times, 2016. "Timeline of previous bomb attacks in Indonesia". *East Asia.* Accessed 1 December 2018. www.straitstimes.com/asia/se-asia/timeline-of-previous-bomb-attacks-in-indonesia; Mapping Militant Organizations, 2018. "Jemaah Islamiyah". *Center for International Security and Cooperation.* Accessed 15 July 2018. https://cisac.fsi.stanford.edu/mappingmilitants/profiles/jemaah-islamiyah.

60 Senior Jemaah Islamiyah operations commander Al Ghozi worked closely with MILF explosives expert Saifullah "Mukhlas" Yunos in planning, preparing and closely directing the attack. In testimony they gave before state prosecutors they claim that they worked under the immediate direction of Jemaah Islamiyah leader Riduan Isamuddin, also known as Hambali, and Fais bin Aby Bakar Bafana. SOURCE: ABC News, 2003. "Jemaah Islamiyah Leaders 'Financed Philippines bombing'". Accessed 2 December 2018. www.abc.net.au/news/2003-06-18/ji-leaders-financed-philippines-bombing-court-hears/1872298.

61 Jemaah Islamiyah was proscribed by United Nations on 23 October 2002 under UNSCR 1267 as an entity related to al-Qaeda. This was updated in 2011 and 2015, paragraph 36 of Resolution 2161 (2014) listing an additional 28 Jemaah Islamiyah figures. SOURCES: Matt Cianflone *et al.*, 2007. *Anatomy of a Terrorist Attack: An In-Depth Investigation into the 2002 Bali, Indonesia Bombings.* Pittsburgh, Matthew B Ridgway Center for International Security Studies; UNSCR, "Security Council Committee Pursuant to Resolutions 1267". 2014.

62 SOURCE: University of Maryland. 2018. *Global Terrorism Database.* www.start. umd.edu/. Accessed 11 December 2018. www.start.umd.edu/gtd/search/.

63 Smith states that "family was stressed as the most fundamentally important part of Jemaah Islamiyah". SOURCE: Greg Smith, 2011. *The Bali Paradox: An Examination of Jemaah Islamiyah 1992–2002.* MacDill, Florida: Joint Special Operations University.

64 SOURCES: Peace Research Institute Oslo (PIRO). "Armed Conflict Dataset". Accessed 2 May 2017. www.prio.org/Data/Armed-Conflict/UCDP-PRIO/; Nils Gleditsch *et al.*, 2002. "Armed Conflict 1946–2001: A New Dataset". *Journal of Peace Research* 39 (5): 615–637.

65 Atran *et al.* state that the al-Mukmin, al-Islam and Lukman al-Hakiem madrassa "have been vital in furthering the mission of the most volatile terrorist groups, such as Jemaah Islamiyah, in efforts to attack America, Australia and other Western-related interests". SOURCE: Scott Atran *et al.*, 2008. "Radical Madrasas in Southeast Asia". *CTC Sentinel* 1 (3): 1–4.

66 Joint training camps and shared expertise across Indonesia, Sulawesi, Aceh, the Philippines, and of course Afghanistan and Pakistan, demonstrate this. SOURCE: Scott Atran and Justin Magouirka, 2008. "Jemaah Islamiyah's Radical Madrassah Networks". *Dynamics of Asymmetric Conflict: Pathways Toward Terrorism and Genocide* 1 (1): 25–41.

References

ABC News. 2003. "Jemaah Islamiyah Leaders 'Financed Philippines bombing'". Accessed 2 December 2018. www.abc.net.au/news/2003–06–18/ji-leaders-financed-philippines-bombing-court-hears/1872298.

Abuza, Zachary. 2003a. "Al-Qaeda in Southeast Asia: Exploring the Linkages". In *After Bali: The Threat of Terrorism in Southeast Asia*, edited by Kumar Ramakrishna and See Seng Tan, 133–160. Singapore and London: Institute of Defence and Strategic Studies.

Abuza, Zachary. 2003b. "Militant Islam in Southeast Asia". *Survival* 46 (3): 153–184.

Abuza, Zachary. 2004. *Strategic Asia 2003–2004. Fragility and Crisis – Special Studies Terrorism: The War on Terrorism in Southeast*. Seattle, WA: International Bureau of Asian Research, 334.

Abuza, Zachary. 2005. "Al-Qaida Comes to Southeast Asia". In *Terrorism and Political Violence in Southeast Asia: Transnational Challenges to States and Regional Stability*, edited by Paul J. Smith, 38–61. London: M.E. Sharpe.

Abuza, Zachary. 2006. "Abu Dujana: Jemaah Islamiyah's New al-Qaeda Linked Leader". *Terrorism Focus* 3 (13): 1.

Abuza, Zachary. 2007. "Indonesia Neutralizes JI as Immediate Threat". *Terrorism Focus* 4 (19): 2–3.

Abuza, Zachary. 2009. "Jemaah Islamiyah Adopts the Hezbollah Model: Assessing Hezbollah's Influence". *Middle East Quarterly* Winter (2009): 15–26.

Abuza, Zachary. 2011. "Borderlands, Terrorism, and Insurgency in Southeast Asia". In *Borderlands of Southeast Asia: Geopolitics, Terrorism, and Globalization*, edited by James Cladd, Sean McDonald, and Bruce Vaughn, 89–106. Washington, D.C.: Center For Strategic Resaerch: Institute for National Strategic Studies.

Acharya, Arabinda. 2006. *The Bali Bombings: Impact on Indonesia and Southeast Asia.* Washington, D.C.: The Hudson Institute – Center for Eurasian Policy, Occasional Research Paper Series II (Islamism in Southeast Asia), No. 2.

Ahmad, Abdul Razak. 2013. "The ASEAN Convention On Counter-Terrorism 2007". *Asia-Pacific Journal on Human Rights and the Law* 14 (1–2): 93–147.

AHRC. 2018. "INDONESIA: Weak Judicial System and Legal Aid". *Scoop News.* 10 March. Accessed 3 May 2018. www.scoop.co.nz/stories/WO1803/S00062/indonesia-weak-judicial-system-and-legal-aid.htm.

AP. 2007. "DNA Test Confirms Death of Philippine Separist Leader". *New York Times.* 21 January. Accessed 1 July 2018. www.nytimes.com/2007/01/21/world/asia/21filip.html.

Atran, Scott. 2005. "The Emir: An Interview with Abu Bakar Ba'asyir, Alleged Leader of the Southeast Asian Jemaah Islamiyah Organization". *Spotlight on Terrorism* (Jamestown Foundation) 3 (9): 1–4. https://jamestown.org/interview/the-emir-an-interview-with-abu-bakar-baasyir-alleged-leader-of-the-southeast-asian-jemaah-islamiyah-organization/.

Atran, Scott. 2009. "To Jihad and Back". *Foreign Policy.* Accessed 1 November 2005. https://jeannicod.ccsd.cnrs.fr/ijn_00000648.

Atran, Scott and Magouirka, Justin. 2008. "Jemaah Islamiyah's radical madrassah networks". *Dynamics of Asymmetric Conflict: Pathways toward terrorism and genocide* 1 (1): 25–41.

Australian Government. 2017. *Jemaah Islamiyah (JI).* Canberra: Australian National Security – Australian Government. Accessed 24 January 2018. www.nationalsecurity.gov.au/Listedterroristorganisations/Pages/JemaahIslamiyahJI.aspx.

Australian Government. 2019. *Population Clock. Bureau of Statistics.* Accessed 5 January 2019. www.abs.gov.au/ausstats/abs@.nsf/0/1647509ef7e25faaca2568a900154 b63?OpenDocument .

Ayling, Julie. 2009. "Criminal Organizations and Resilience". *International Journal of Law, Crime and Justice* 37 (1): 182–196.

Bacon, Tricia. 2017. "Why al-Qaida is still strong 16 years after 9/11". *The Conversation.* Accessed 28 September 2017. https://theconversation.com/why-al-qaida-is-still-strong-16-years-after-9-11-83403.

Barker, Anne. 2019. "Joko Widodo between a rock and a hard place over terrorist Abu Bakar Ba'aysir's release". *ABC News.* Accessed 22 January 2019. www.abc.net.au/ news/2019-01-23/joko-widodo-in-dilemma-after-touting-abu-bakar-bashir-release/10737900.

Bartolucci, Valentina and Corman, Steven. 2014. *The Narrative Landscape of al-Qaeda in the Islamic Maghreb Valentina .* Tempe, AZ: Center for Strategic Communication.

BBC. 2011. "Indonesia pressured over Ahmadiyah Muslim sect killings". *BBC World.* 8 February. Accessed 2 May 2018. www.bbc.com/news/world-asia-pacific-12389097.

Belford, Aubrey. 2010. "Rise and Fall of a Terror Cell". *The Diplomat.* Accessed 26 October 2018. https://thediplomat.com/2010/04/rise-and-fall-of-a-terror-cell/.

Berger, J. 2007. "Mohammed Jamal Khalifa: Life and Death Secrets". *IntelWire.* 31 January. Accessed 16 April 2018. http://news.intelwire.com/2007/01/mohammed-jamal-khalifa-life-and-death.html.

BIN. 2002. *Interrogation Report of Omar al-Faruq.* Jakarta: Badan Intelijen Negara (State Intelligence Agency) Indonesia.

Blomfield, Adrian. 2009. "Police foil plot to kill Indonesian president after raid on top terror suspect". *Telegraph.* 8 August. Accessed 28 April 2018. www.telegraph.co.uk/ news/worldnews/asia/indonesia/5994928/Police-foil-plot-to-kill-Indonesian-president-after-raid-on-top-terror-suspect.html.

Boland, Tony and Fowler, Alan. 2000. "A Systems Perspective of Performance Management in Public Sector Organizations". *International Journal of Public Sector Management* 13 (5): 417–446.

Bond, Christopher. 2005. *Indonesia and the Changing Front in the War on Terrorism.* Washington, D.C.: The Heritage Foundation.

Bonner, Raymond and Perlez, Jane. 2002. "Threats and Responses: Jakarta; Indonesia Links Muslim Group With Terrorism". *New York Times.* 17 October. Accessed 16 April 2018. www.nytimes.com/2002/10/17/world/threats-and-responses-jakarta-indonesia-links-muslim-group-with-terrorism.html.

Bonura, Carlo. 2010. "Geopolitical Articulations: Global Terrorism, Southern Thailand". In *International Relations and States of Exception: Margins, Peripheries, and Excluded Bodies*, edited by Shampa Biswas and Sheila Nair, 48–70. London and New York: Routledge.

BRIMOB, "Indonesian Police's Detachment 88". Accessed 14 April 2016. http:// indonesiaeliteforces.tripod.com/id37.html.

Buehler, Michael. 2016. "Islamist Movements after 1998: Mobilization and Influence". In *The Politics of Shari'a Law: Islamist Activists and the State in Democratizing Indonesia*, edited by Michael Buehler, 132–158. Cambridge: Cambridge University Press.

Butt, Simon. 2009. *Indonesian Terrorism Law and Criminal Process.* Camperdown: The University of Sydney Law School.

Calderoni, F., Brunetto, D., and Piccardi, C. 2017. "Communities in Criminal Networks: A Case Study". *Social Networks* 48 (1): 116–125.

Carter, Jeremy, Carter, David, Chermak, Steve, and McGarrell, Edmund. 2017. "Law Enforcement Fusion Centers: Cultivating an Information Sharing Environment while Safeguarding Privacy". *Journal of Police and Criminal Psychology* 32 (1): 11–27.

Catanese, Salvatore, De Meo, Pasguale, and Fiumar, Giacomo. 2016. "Resilience in Criminal Networks". *Journal of Physical, Mathematical, and Natural Sciences* 94 (2): 1–19.

CFR. 2005. *State Sponsors: Libya.* Washington, D.C.: Council on Foreign Relations.

Chau, Andrew. 2008. "Security Community and Southeast Asia: Australia, the U.S., and ASEAN's Counter-Terror Strategy". *Asian Survey* 48 (4): 626–649,

Chopra, Anuj. 2010. "Indonesia tries rehabilitation to wipe out extremism". *The National.* Accessed 11 September 2018. www.thenational.ae/world/asia/indonesia-tries-rehabilitation-to-wipe-out-extremism-1.590716.

Chun Wai, Wong and Zolkepli, Farik. 2014. "Dangerous and on the loose". The Star. 04 July. Accessed 3 April 2020. www.thestar.com.my/news/nation/2014/07/04/ most-wanted-and-not-dead-as-thought-fbi-has-put-out-a-rm16mil-bounty-on-malaysian-who-supplies-bomb.

Cianflone, Matt, Cull, Jason, Fisher, John, Holt, Dave, Krause, Amanda, Moore, Julie, Wadhwani, Anita, and Yancey, Jared. 2007. *Anatomy of a Terrorist Attack: An In-Depth Investigation into the 2002 Bali, Indonesia Bombings.* Pittsburgh, Matthew B Ridgway Center for International Security Studies.

Coles, Gregory. 2018. "What Do I Lack as a Woman? The Rhetoric of Megawati Sukarnoputri". *A Journal of History of Rhetoric* 36 (1): 58–91.

Collins, Nancy-Amelia. 2009. "Top Indonesian Terrorist's Wife Arrested in Philippines". *Voa News.* 31 October. Accessed 1 July 2018. www.voanews.com/a/a-13-2006-10-06-voa20/321323.html.

Comras, Victor. 2005. "Al Qaeda Finances and Funding to Affiliated Groups". *Strategic Insights* IV (1): 1–16.

Conboy, Ken. 2004. "The Provocateurs". In *The Second Front: Inside Asia's Most Dangerous Terrorist Network,* edited by Ken Conboy, 109–111. Jakarta, Singapore: Equinox Publishing.

Crossley, Nick, Edwards, Gemma, and Stevenson, Rachel. 2012. "Covert Social Movement Networks and the Secrecy-Efficency Trade Off: The Case of the UK Suffragettes (1906–1914)". *Social Netowrks* 34: 634–44.

Daskon, Chandima. 2010. "Cultural Resilience – The Roles of Cultural Traditions in Sustaining Rural Livelihoods: A Case Study from Rural Kandyan Villages in Central Sri Lanka". *Sustainability* 2: 1080–1100.

Davies, Ed. and Rondonuwu, Olivier. 2010. "U.S.-funded Detachment 88, elite of Indonesia security". Reuters. Accessed 14 April 2016. www.reuters.com/article/ us-indonesia-usa-security/u-s-funded-detachment-88-elite-of-indonesia-security-dUSTRE62H13F20100318.

Desker, Barry. 2003. "The Jemaah Islamiyah (Jemaah Islamiyah) Phenomenon in Singapore". *Contemporary Southeast Asia – A Journal of International and Strategic Affairs* 25 (3): 489–507.

Detik News. 2007. "Zarkasi Alias Mbah Mulai Ungkap Jaringan Jemaah Islamiyah". *Voice of the Reader.* Accessed 19 December 2018. https://news.detik.com/ berita/805011/zarkasi-alias-mbah-mulai-ungkap-jaringan-ji.

Djuhari, Lely. 2004. "Abu Bakar's arrest sparks more violence". *Sydney Morning Herald.* Accessed 4 May 2018. www.smh.com.au/articles/2004/05/02/1083224653686.html.

Eliason, Philip. 2010. "Yemen may foster new generation of Bashirs". *Sydney Morning Herald.* 23 August. Accessed 17 January 2018. www.smh.com.au/federal-politics/

political-opinion/yemen-may-foster-new-generation-of-bashirs-20100823-13hei. html.

Eliraz, Giora. 2004. *Islam in Indonesia: Modernism, Radicalism, and the Middle East Dimension.* First edition. Brighton and Portland: Sussex Academic Press.

Ellis-Petersen, Hannah and Lamb, Kate. 2018. "Surabaya blast: family of five carried out bomb attack on Indonesian police station". *The Guardian.* Accessed 16 May 2018.

Eti-Tofinga, Buriata, Douglas, Heather, and Singh, Gurmeet. 2017. "Influence of Evolving Culture on Leadership: A Study of Fijian Cooperatives". *European Business Review* 29 (5): 534–550.

Everton, Sean and Cunningham, Dan. 2013. "Detecting Significant Changes in Dark Networks". *Behavioral Sciences of Terrorism and Political Aggression* 5 (2): 94–114.

Fealy, Greg and Borgu, Aldo. 2005. *Local Jihad: Radical Islam and Terrorism in Indonesia.* Canberra: Australian Strategic Policy Institute.

Fitzpatrick, Stephen. 2010. "Abu Bakar Bashir's Son al-Qaeda's Propaganda Man". 5 June. Accessed 16 January 2018. www.theaustralian.com.au/news/world/abu-bakar-bashirs-son-al-qaidas-propaganda-man/news-story/fe2450cbc0d2f5ccf41d69baa0c0d349?sv=325c02894f36101098b4c7839abebf71.

Forbes, Mark. 2005. "Bali bomber killed in shootout, police believe". *Sydney Morning Herald.* 10 November. Accessed 14 April 2018. www.smh.com.au/news/world/bali-bomber-killed-in-shootout/2005/11/09/1131407706370.html.

Gacad, Romeo. 2010. *JI Assessments.* Accessed 19 April 2018. https://worldview.stratfor.com/article/indonesia-dismantling-another-militant-cell.

Galamas, Francisco. 2015. *The Militant Groups of Radical Ideology and Violent Nature Series Area: Indian Subcontinent and Southeast Asia.* Ceseden, Spain: Del Instituto Espanol de Estudios Estrategicos (IEEE).

Gerges, Fawaz. 2005. *The Rise of Trans-nationalist Jihadi's and the Far Enemy.* Cambridge, Cambridge University Press.

Gleditsch, Nils, Wallensteen, Peter, Eriksson, Mikael, Sollenberg, Margareta, and Strand, Harvard. 2002. "Armed Conflict 1946–2001: A New Dataset". *Journal of Peace Research* 39 (5): 615–637.

GMA. 2009. "Rizal Day Bombng Chronology". *GMA News.* 23 January. Accessed 20 January 2018. www.gmanetwork.com/news/news/content/145645/rizal-day-bombing-chronology/story/.

Gregory, Robert. 2015. "Political Independence, Operational Impartiality, and the Effectiveness of Anti-Corruption Agencies". *Asian Education and Development Studies* 4 (1): 125–142.

Griswold, Eliza. 2010. "Philippines: A Kidnapping". In *The Tenth Parallel: Dispatches from the Faultline Between Christianity and Islam*, edited by Eliza Griswold, 217. London: Penguin Books.

Halverson, Jeffry, Corman, Steven, and Goodall, Jamie. 2011. *Master Narratives of Islamist Extremism.* New York, Palgrave Macmillan.

Hariyadi, Mathias. 2007. "Several Jemaah Islamiyah Members Seized in Java". *Asia News.* 27 March. Accessed 4 January 2018. www.asianews.it/news-en/Several-Jemaah-Islamiyah-members-seized-in-Java-8838.html.

Hastings, Justin. 2010. "Territory and Transnational Terrorism: The Decline of Jemaah Islamiyah 1999–2009". In *No Man's Land: Globalization, Territory, and Clandestine Groups in Southeast Asia*, edited by Justin Hastings, 64–86. New York: Cornell University Press.

Helfstein, Scott and Wright, Dominick. 2011. "Success, Lethality, and Cell Structure Across the Dimensions of Al Qaeda". *Studies in Conflict & Terrorism* 34 (5): 367–382.

Henshaw, Andrew. 2015. *Transnational Macro-Narrative Decendancy in Violent Conflict: A Case Study of the Mujahidin Indonesia Timur in Central Sulawesi.* Sydney: Macquarie University Press.

Hoare, Daniel. 2005. *Gareth Evans downplays terrorist risk in Australia.* Accessed April 18, 2018. www.abc.net.au/worldtoday/content/2005/s1469369.htm.

Hassan, Muhammad and Mostarom, Tuty. 2011. *A Decade of Combating Radical Ideology: Learning From the Singapore Experience (2001–2011).* RSIS Monograph No. 20. 2011. Singapore: S. Rajaratnam School of International Studies.

Hwang, Julie. 2010. "Conclusions: Patterns of Mobilization". In *Peaceful Islamist Mobilization in the Muslim World.* New York: Palgrave Macmillan.

Hwang, Julie. 2012. "Terrorism in Perspective: An Assessment of 'Jihad Project' Trends in Indonesia". *Asia Pacific Issues* 104 (1): 1–12.

IBA. 2008. "Government and Politics". In *Indonesia Diplomatic Handbook*, edited by IBA, 103. Washington, D.C.: USA International Business Publications.

ICG. 2002. *Indonesia Backgrounder: How the Jemaah Islamiyah Terrorist Network Operates.* Jakarta/Brussels: International Crisis Group. Report 43.

ICG. 2003. *Jemaah Islamiyah In Southeast Asia: Damaged But Still Dangerous. ICG Asia Report No. 63.* Jakarta/Brussels: International Crisis Group. Accessed 1 January 2018. www.crisisgroup.org/asia/south-east-asia/indonesia/jemaah-islamiyah-south-east-asia-damaged-still-dangerous.

ICG. 2005. *Weakening Indonesia's Mujahidin Networks: Lessons from Maluku and Poso. Asia Report No. 103.* Jakarta/Brussels: International Crisis Group. Accessed 16 April 2018. www.crisisgroup.org/asia/south-east-asia/indonesia/weakening-indonesias-mujahidin-networks-lessons-maluku-and-poso.

ICG. 2008. *Indonesia: Implications of the Ahmadiyya Decree. Report No. 78.* International Crisis Group. Briefing 78 (Asia). Jakarta/Brussels: International Crisis Group.

ICG. 2010. *Indonesia: Jihad Surprise in Aceh. Crisis Group Asia Report No. 189.* Jakarta/Brussels: International Crisis Group.

Intan, Benyamin, "Public Religion and the Pancasila-based State of Indonesia: An Ethical and Sociological Analysis". *Journal of Islamic Studies* 18 (2): 278–281.

Ismail, Noor. 2006. "The Role of Kinship in Indonesia's Jemaah Islamiya". *Terrorism Monitor* 4 (11): 1–2.

Ismail, Noor. 2008. "Kinship and Radicalization Process in Jemaah Islamiyah's Transnational Terrorist Organization". In *Jihadi Terrorism and the Radicalization Challenge in Europe*, edited by Rik Coolsaet, 55–68. Farnham: Ashgate.

Ismail, Noor Huda and Sim, Susan. 2016. "From prison to carnage in Jakarta: Predicting terrorist recidivism in Indonesia's prisons. Part 2". *Brookings Institute.* Accessed 22 May 2017. www.brookings.edu/opinions/predicting-terrorist-recidivism-in-indonesias-prisons/.

Jeffry, Simon. 2004. "Profile: Jemaah Islamiyah". *The Guardian.* 10 September. Accessed 1 November 2018. www.theguardian.com/world/2004/sep/09/indonesia.australia.

Jones, Sidney. 2018. "Surabaya and the ISIS family". *Lowy Institute.* 15 May. Accessed 16 June 2018. www.lowyinstitute.org/the-interpreter/surabaya-and-isis-family.

Kalathil, J., Collier, B., Bhakta, R., Daniel, O., Joseph, D., and Trivedi, P. 2011. *Recovery and Resilience: African, African-Caribbean and South Asian Women's*

Narratives of Recovering from Mental Distress. London: Mental Health Foundation and Survivor Research.

Kamarulnizam, Abdullah. 2011. "Kumpulan Mujahidin Malaysia (KMM) and Jemaah Islamiyah (JI): The Links". *Journal of Policing, Intelligence and Counter-Terrorism* 4 (1): 29–46.

Karmini, Niniek. 2011. "Indonesian terror suspect went to meet bin Laden in Pakistan earlier this year". *Associated Press.* 4 May. Accessed 1 May 2018. www.thestar.com/news/world/2011/05/04/indonesian_terror_suspect_went_to_meet_bin_laden_in_pakistan_earlier_this_year.html.

Karnavian, M.T. 2015. "Al-Jamaah al-Islamiyah: From Insurgency to Terrorism". *Insurgency and Terrorism Series* (2014): 39–75

Kaur, Jasmeet. 2017. "Working of Jemaah Islamiya: A Radical Trajectory from 2000–2009". *Journal of Arts, Humanities and Social Science* 5 (9B): 1210–1219.

KBK/RSJ. 2010. "Slain JI Leader Dulmatin still alive – Marine Chief". *GMA News.* 9 February. Accessed 18 April 2018. www.gmanetwork.com/news/news/regions/183494/slain-ji-leader-dulmatin-still-alive-marine-chief/story/.

Kilcullen, David. 2006. "Globalization and the development of Indonesian Counterinsurgency Tactics". *Small Wars and Insurgencies* 17 (1) 44–64.

Kippe, Gregory. 2010. *Jemaah Islamiyah: re-evaluating the most dangerous terrorist threat in Southeast Asia.* Monterey, California: Naval Postgraduate School, December. Accessed 15 April 2018. https://calhoun.nps.edu/bitstream/handle/10945/5060/10Dec_Kippe.pdf?sequence=1.

Krasner, Stephen. 2012. "Talking Tough to Pakistan: How to End Islamabad's Defiance". *Journal of Foreign Affairs* 91 (1): 8796.

Kunkler, Mirjam and Stepan, Alfred. 2013. "Indonesian Government Approaches to Radical Islam". In *Democracy and Islam in Indonesia*, edited by Mirjam Kunkler and Alfred Stepan, 106–116. New York: Columbia University Press.

Larue, Patrick. 2017. "Judicial Responses to Counter-Terrorism Law after September 11". *Democracy and Security* 13 (1): 71–95.

Leow, Rachel. 2016. *Taming Babel: Language and the Making of Malaysia.* Cambridge, Cambridge University Press.

Liow, Joseph. 2016. "ISIS reaches Indonesia: The terrorist group's prospects in Southeast Asia". *Brookings Institute.* Accessed 10 December 2018. www.brookings.edu/opinions/isis-reaches-indonesia-the-terrorist-groups-prospects-in-southeast-asia/.

Lord, Jonathan. 2015. "Undercover Under Threat: Cover Identity, Clandestine Activity, and Covert Action in the Digital Age". *International Journal of Intelligence and Counterintelligence* 28 (4): 666–691.

Madjid, Dien and Wahyudi, Johan. 2018. "Local Resistance in Kerinci in the 20th Century". *Tawarihk – Journal of Historical Studies* 9 (2): 137–150.

Magouirk, Justin and Atran, Scott. 2008. "Jemaah Islamiyah's Radical Madrassah Networks". *Dynamics of Asymmetric Conflict* 1 (1): 25–41.

Mapping Militant Organizations, 2018. "Jemaah Islamiyah". *Center for International Security and Cooperation.* Accessed 15 July 2018. https://cisac.fsi.stanford.edu/mappingmilitants/profiles/jemaah-islamiyah.

Marks, Julie. 2018. "How SEAL Team Six Took Out Osama bin Laden". *History.* 24 May. Accessed 24 April 2018. www.history.com/news/osama-bin-laden-death-seal-team-six.

Mcguirk, Rod. 2010. "Bali bombing mastermind may be dead, officials say". *Washington Herald.* 9 March. Accessed 22 April 2018. www.heraldnet.com/news/bali-bombing-mastermind-may-be-dead-officials-say/.

Micchi, Ken. 2016. "Looking at Links and Nodes: How Jihadists in Indonesia Survived". *Journal of Asian Ethnology* 75 (1): 1535–1543.

Moore, Matthew. 2003a. "Evidence destroys conspiracy theories". *The Age.* 21 January. Accessed 6 May 2018. www.theage.com.au/articles/2003/01/20/1042911326415.html.

Moore, Matthew. 2003b. "Insider says Jemaah Islamiyah in Australia". *The Age.* Accessed 21 April 2016. www.theage.com.a/articles/2003/06/26/1056449367273. html.

Morfit, Michael. 1981. "Pancasila: The Indonesian State Ideology According to the New Order Government". *Asian Survey* 21 (8): 838–851.

Murdoch, Lindsay. 2007. "Captured JI Leader hints at more terror attacks". *Sydney Morning Herald.* 22 December. Accessed 16 April 2018. www.theage.com.au/news/world/captured-ji-leader-hints-at-more-terror-attacks/2007/12/21/1198175340531. html.

Mydans, Seth. 2002. "Singapore Details Terrorist Plot to Bomb U.S. Ships and Soldiers". *New York Times.* 11 January. Accessed 22 April 2018. www.nytimes.com/2002/01/11/international/singapore-details-terrorist-plot-to-bomb-us-ships-and-soldiers.html.

Mydans, Seth. 2003. "16 Die in Bombing in Southern Philippines: Rebels Deny Link". *New York Times.* Accessed 17 May 2019. www.nytimes.com/2003/04/03/world/16-die-in-bombing-in-southern-philippines-rebels-deny-link.html.

Nakashima, Ellen. 2002. "Megawati in the Middle". *Washington Post.* 12 December. Accessed 2 May 2018. www.washingtonpost.com/archive/politics/2002/12/12/megawati-in-the-middle/e2faa42b-33a1-491b-a856-0d3728860b89/?noredirect=on&utm_term=.120d9744a1b7.

Nash, Carolyn. 2018. "Saudi Arabia's Soft Power Strategy in Indonesia". *The Middle East Institute.* 3 April. Accessed 3 May 2018. www.mei.edu/content/map/saudi-arabias-soft-power-strategy-indonesia.

Nirmala, M. 2013. *Staying One Step Ahead of the Terrorists.* Accessed April 20, 2018. www.straitstimes.com/singapore/staying-one-step-ahead-of-terrorists.

Nisa, Eva 2018. "Female suicide bombers: how terrorist propaganda radicalises Indonesia women". Australian National University.

Noorhaidi, Hasan, Hendriks, Bertus, and Meijer, Janssen. 2012. "From 'Hard' to 'Soft' approaches". In *Counter-terrorism Strategies in Indonesia, Algeria and Saudi Arabia,* edited by Roel Meijer, 28–38. The Hague: Netherlands Institute of Internaitonal Relations.

Osman, Sulastri. 2010. "Jemaah Islamiyah: Of Kin and Kind". *Journal of Current Southeast Asian Affairs* 29 (2): 157–175.

Parameswaran, Prashanth, 2016. "Islamic State Attack in Indonesia?" *The Diplomat.* Accessed 25 March 2017. https://thediplomat.com/tag/indonesia-and-the-islamic-state/.

Pavlova, Elena. 2007. "From a Counter-Society to a Counter-State Movement: Jemaah Islamiyah According to PUPJI". *Studies in Conflict & Terrorism* 30 (9): 777–800.

Peace Research Institute Oslo (PIRO), "Armed Conflict Dataset". Accessed 2 May 2017. www.prio.org/Data/Armed -Conflict/UCDP-PRIO/.

Poushter, Josh. 2017. "In nations with significant Muslim populations, much disdain for ISIS". *Pew Research Centre.* 17 November. Accessed 6 May 2018. www.pewresearch. org/fact-tank/2015/11/17/in-nations-with-significant-muslim-populations-much-disdain-for-isis/.

Priyambodo. 2011. "Police arrest three wanted suspects in police attack in Palu". *Antara News.* 7 June. Accessed 27 April 2018. https://en.antaranews.com/news/72409/police-arrest-three-wanted-suspects-in-police-attack-in-palu.

Purdy, Susan. 1982/1983. "The Civil Religion Thesis as It Applies to a Pluralistic Society: Pancasila Democracy in Indonesia (1945–1965)". *Journal of International Affairs* 36 (2): 307–316.

Quiano, Kathy. 2007. "Police Capture Asia Terror Leader". *CNN.* Accessed 21 December 2018. http://edition.cnn.com/2007/world/asiapcf/06/12/indonesia.Terror/.

Quijano, Elaine, Hiscock, Geoff, Aglionby, John, and Ressa, Maria. 2002. "Bali terrorist blast kills at least 26". *CNN.* Accessed 26 September 2018. https://edition.cnn.com/2005/WORLD/asiapcf/10/01/bali.blasts/.

Ramakrishna, Kumar. 2009. "Radical Pathways: Understanding Muslim Radicalization in Indonesia". Santa Barbara: Praeger Security International.

Ramakrishna, Kumar. 2017. "The Growth of ISIS Extremism in Southeast Asia: Its Ideological and Cognitive Features – and Possible Policy Responses". *New England Journal of Public Policy* 29 (1): 1–6.

Realuyo, Celina and Stapleton, Scott. 2004. "Response to Bali: An International Success Story". *US Journal of Economic Perspectives* (1) (September): 13–18.

Reid, Anthony. 1974. *The Indonesian National Revolution 1945–1950.* Harlow, UK: Longman Publishing.

Rekhi, Shefali. 2013. *The Hidden Journey of a Singapore Detainee.* Accessed April 16, 2018. www.straitstimes.com/asia/the-hidden-journey-of-a-singapore-ji-detainee.

Ressa, Maria. 2013. "From Bin Laden to Facebook: 10 Days of Abduction, 10 Years of Terrorism". London: Imperial College Press.

Ressa, Maria. 2015. "Marwan's ties that bind: Ren-Ren Dongon". *Rappler News.* 4 February. Accessed 15 April 2018. www.rappler.com/newsbreak/in-depth/82889-marwan-ties-bind-ren-ren-dongon.

Ressa, Maria and Shubert, Atika and Chew, Amy. 2003. "Asia's most wanted in U.S. hands". *CNN.* Accessed 21 June 2018. http://edition.cnn.com/2003/WORLD/asiapcf/southeast/08/15/hambali.capture/.

Ridley, Nicholas. 2012. "They Haven't Gone Away You Know". In *Terrorist Financing: The Failure of Counter Measures*, edited by Nicholas Ridley, 137–177. Cheltenham, U.K.: Edward Elgar Publishing.

Riviere, Craig. 2016. *The Evolution of Jihadist-Salafism in Indonesia, Malaysia and the Philippines, and Its Impact on Security in Southeast Asia.* Canberra: Australian Defence College.

Rottenberg, Chris, 2012. *Jamaah Ansharut Tauhid (JAT): The Perpetual Threat.* Washington, D.C.: The Osgood Centre for International Studies.

Royds, David, Lewis, Simon, and Taylor, Amelia. 2005. "A case study in forensic chemistry: The Bali bombings". *Talanata* 67 (2): 262–268.

Ruby, Charles. 2002. "The Definition of Terrorism". *Analyses of Social Issues and Public Policy* 2 (1): 9–14.

Saiful, Ahmad, Bin, Rijal, Steckman, Laura, Arianti, V., Yasin, Nur, and Gunaratna, Rohan. 2016. "Women's Proactive Roles in Jihadism in Southeast Asia". *Counter Terrorist Trends and Analysis* 8 (5): 9–15.

Salleh, Mohamed and Hassan, Muhammad. 2009. "The Disconnection of Indonesia's Jemaah Islamiyah and al-Qaeda from the Afghan Jihad Experience". *Terrorism Monitor* 7 (39): 5–8.

Schmid, Alex. 2014. *Al-Qaeda's "Single Narrative" and Attempts to Develop Counter Narratives: The State of Knowledge.* The Hague, NL: International Centre for Counter-Terrorism the Hague.

Scott, Margaret. 2016. "Indonesia: the Saudis are coming". *Financial Review*. Accessed 5 March 2016. www.afr.com/news/world/asia/indonesia-the-saudis-are-coming-20161017-gs3u7j.

Shamasundari, Rebecca. 2017. "Embrace Pancasila in combating terrorism, hails Joko Widodo". *ASEAN Post*. 17 August. Accessed 6 May 2018. https://theaseanpost.com/article/embrace-pancasila-combating-terrorism-hails-joko-widodo.

Sherlock, Stephen. 2002. *The Bali Bombing: What It Means for Indonesia – Current Issues Brief No. 4*. Canberra: Australian Government Information and Research Services. Department of Foreign Affairs.

Siddiq, Taufiq. 2018. "Police to Review Abu Bakar Ba'asyir's House Arrest". *Tempo*. 2 March. Accessed 26 September 2018. https://en.tempo.co/read/916238/police-to-review-abu-bakar-baasyirs-house-arrest/full&view=ok.

Sim, Susan. 2013. *Leveraging Terrorist Dropouts to Counter Violent Extremism in Southeast Asia. Phase II, Volume II*. Doha: Qatar International Academy for Security Studies (QIASS).

Singh, Bilveer. 2016. *Revising Indonesia's Anti-Terrorism Laws*. Singapore: RSIS Rajaratnam School of International Studies. Report No. 57.

SMH, "Bashir gets 30 months' jail for Bali bomb plot". *Sydney Morning Herald*. Accessed 22 December 2018. www.smh.com.au/national/bashir-gets-30-months-jail-for-bali-bomb-plot-20050304-gdkuo7.html.

Smith, Greg. 2011. *The Bali Paradox: An Examination of Jemaah Islamiyah 1992–2002*. MacDill, Florida: Joint Special Operations University.

Stillwell, Chris. 2015. "Terrorism in Southeast Asia: Jemaah Islamiyah". *The Globe*. 5 November. Accessed 16 March 2018. http://theglobegwu.com/2015/11/05/terrorism-in-southeast-asia-jemaah-islamiyah/.

Straits Times, 2016. "Timeline of previous bomb attacks in Indonesia". *East Asia*. Accessed 1 December 2018. www.straitstimes.com/asia/se-asia/timeline-of-previous-bomb-attacks-in-indonesia.

Suriyanto. 2016. "Habis Santoso Terbit Bahrun Naim". *CNN Indonesia*. 28 December. Accessed 25 September 2018. www.cnnindonesia.com/nasional/20161228081318-12-182538/habis-santoso-terbit-bahrun-naim.

Syafputri, Ella. 2011. "Densus 88 arrests suspected terrorists cell member in Pemalang". *Antara News*. 11 June. Accessed 27 April 2018. https://en.antaranews.com/news/72777/densus-88-arrests-suspected-terrorist-cell-member-in-pemalang.

Synovitz, Ron. 2002. "Indonesia: Conspiracy Theorists Blame U.S. Agents For Bali Blasts". *Radio Free Europe*. 17 October. Accessed 6 May 2018. www.rferl.org/a/1101109.html.

Tan, Andrew. 2013. "Terrorism in Southeast Asia". In *East and South-East Asia: International Relations and Security Perspectives*, edited by Andrew Tan, 235–243. London and New York: Routledge.

Tan, See Seng and Nasu, Hitoshi. 2016. "ASEAN and the Development of Counter-Terrorism Law and Policy in Southeast Asia". *Counter-Terrorism Law and Policy in Southeast Asia* 39 (3): 1219–1237.

Taufiqurrohman, Muh. 2015. "The Road to ISIS: How Indonesian Jihadists Travel to Iraq and Syria". *Counter Terrorist Trends and Analyses* 7 (4): 17–25.

Thompson, Neil. 2017. "Islam and Identity Politics in Indonesia". *The Diplomat*. 17 November. Accessed 6 May 2018. https://thediplomat.com/2017/11/islam-and-identity-politics-in-indonesia/.

Tilly, Charles. 2004. "Terror, Terrorism, Terrorists". *Sociological Theory* 22 (1): 5–13.

Toohey, Paul. 2014. "Paradise for terrorists: 36 Bali bombers that killed 92 Australians are walkinjg free". *Daily Telegraph*. 4 May. Accessed 4 May 2018. www.dailytelegraph. com.au/news/nsw/paradise-for-terrorists-36-bali-bombers-that-killed-92-australians-are-walking-free/news-story/475b6709a01cbe186bbcd3abbf494d35.

Ulla, Fionna. 2016. "Indonesian Parties in a Deep Dilemma: The Case of the Golkar". *Perspectives* 2016 (35): 1–7.

UN. 2015. *Security Council Committee Pursuant to Resolutions 1267 (1989) (1999) (2011) and 2253 (2015) Concerning ISIL (Da'esh) al-Qaeda and Associated Individual Groups Undertaking Entities. QDe.092 Jemaah Islamiyah.* United Nations Security Council. Accessed 22 April 217. www.un.org/sc/suborg/en/sanctions/1267/aq_sanctions_list/summaries/entity/jemaah-islamiyah.

University of Maryland. 2018. *Global Terrorism Database*. www.start.umd.edu/. Accessed 11 December 2018. www.start.umd.edu/gtd/search/.

UNODC. 2017–2020. *Country Programme 2017–2020: Making Indonesia safer from crime, drugs and terrorism.* New York: United Nations Office on Drugs and Crime.

U.S. State Department. 2002. *Patterns of Global Terrorism 2002.* Washington, D.C.: Department of State Publications. Office of the Secretary of State, 23–25.

Utusan. 2001. "Indonesian police say bomb suspect trained in Afghanistan". *Utusan Wolrd News.* 25 September. Accessed 18 January 2018. http://ww1.utusan.com.my/utusan/info. asp?y=2001&dt=0925&pub=Utusan_Express&sec=World&pg=wo_01.htm.

Varagur, Krithika. 2017. "Saudi Arabia Quietly Spreads Its Brand of Puritanical Islam in Indonesia". *VOA News.* 17 January. Accessed 3 May 2018. www.voanews. com/a/saudi-arabia-quietly-spreads-its-brand-of-puritanical-islam-in-indonesia-/3679 287.html.

Vaughn, Bruce, Chanlett-Avery, Emma, Dolven, Ben, Manyin, Mark, and Martin, Michael. 2005. *Terrorism in Southeast Asia.* 2009. Washington, D.C.: Congressional Research Service.

Von Lampe, Klaus and Johansen, Per Ole. 2003. "Criminal networks and Trust". *Third Annual Meeting of the European Society of Criminology.* Helsinki: European Society of Criminology. 159–184.

Walsh, Froma. 2015. "A Familial Resileince Framework: Principles and Applicaitons". In *Sympozium Rodinné Resilience*, edited by Martina Friedlova and Martin Lecbych, 11–31. Olomouc: Univerzita Palackého.

Ward, Ken. 2011. *Indonesian justice strikes a blow against radical Islam with Bashir verdict.* Accessed 5 May 2018. www.smh.com.au/federal-politics/political-opinion/indonesian-justice-strikes-a-blow-against-radical-islam-with-bashir-verdict-20110616-1g5yj.html.

Wardhana, Wishnu and Wira Usaha, Panca. 2016. "Political Corruption Indonesia: Former Minister Dahlan Iskan Arrested". *Indonesia Investments.* 28 October. Accessed 3 May 2018. www.indonesia-investments.com/news/todays-headlines/political-corruption-indonesia-former-minister-dahlan-iskan-arrested/item7312?

Warneryd, Karl. 2014. *The Economics of Conflict: Theory and Empirical Evidence.* First edition. Cambridge: MIT Press.

Weatherbee, Donald. 1985. "Indonesia in 1984: Pancasila, Politics, and Power". *Asian Survey* 25 (2): 187–197.

Weiss, Caleb. 2017. "U.S. designates Indonesian-based jihadist group". *Threat Matrix* 6 (2017).

Whitaker, Beth. 2007. "Exporting the Patriot Act? Democracy and the 'War on Terror' in the Third World". *Third World Quarterly* 28 (5): 1017–1032.

Williams, Clive. 2015. "How has terrorism risk changed in Indonesia since the Bali bombings". *Sydney Morning Herald.* 2 October. Accessed 2 May 2018. www.smh. com.au/opinion/the-ides-of-october-in-bali-20151001-gjz1xf.html.

Winter, Charlie. 2015. *The Virtual 'Caliphate': Understanding Islamic State's Propaganda Strategy.* Report. London: Quilliam Foundation.

Yew, Lee Kuan. 2002. *Al-Qaeda's Southeast Asian Footholds.* Accessed April 16, 2018. www.forbes.com/global/2002/0401/014.html#1f3a899b7ee6.

Yunanto, Sri and Damayanti, Angel. 2017. "The Root Causes and Nexus of Militant Islamic Movements in Indonesia: Case Studies of Darul Islam and Jemaah Islamiyah". *Journal of Asia-Pacific Studies* 1 (2017): 1–39.

Yuniar, Resty. 2019. "Radical cleric Abu Bakar Bashir will be free to 'preach hate', Australia warns Indonesia". *South China Morning Post.* Accessed 22 January 2019. www.scmp.com/news/asia/southeast-asia/article/2183155/radical-cleric-abu-bakar-bashir-will-be-free-preach-hate.

Yuvienco, Dolores. 2005. "Circular Letter-Jemaah Islamiyah". Bangko Sentral Ng Pilipinas. Available at: www.bsp.gov.ph/regulations/regulations.asp?id=1829.

Zahra, Shaker. 2005. "Entrepreneurial Risk Taking in Family Firms". *Family Business Review* 18 (1): 23–40.

Zahra, Laela. 2011. "Terrorist Kutai Planner of Terror in Palu and Cirebon". *Inilahcom.* 14 June. Accessed 27 April 2018. https://nasional.inilah.com/read/detail/1604272/teroris-kutai-otak-teror-palu-dan-cirebon.

Zenn, Jacob. 2011. "Indonesia's 'Ghost Birds' Tackle Islamist Terrorists: A Profile of Densus 88". *Terrorism Monitor* 9 (32). Accessed 25 April 2016. https://jamestown.org/program/indonesias-ghost-birds-tackle-islamist-terrorists-a-profile-of-densus-88/.

6   Abu Sayyaf

The Abu Sayyaf Group is perhaps best known as a hardened criminal enterprise engaged in kidnap-for-ransom (K&R). The audacious raid on the Malaysian tourist resort on Sipadan Island on 24 April 2000 stunned the Western world, netted 21 captives and a ransom bounty of between 20 and 30 million U.S. dollars (Taylor 2017a). However, Abu Sayyaf has been waging a bloody insurgency in the Southern Philippines since 1989 with the goal of establishing an Islamic State. What became Abu Sayyaf started as a faction of the Moro National Liberation Front (MNLF) called the Mujahedeen Commando Freedom Fighters (MCFF), under the leadership of Abdurajak Ustadz Janjalani.[1] In 1991, Janjalani split away from the MNLF and with help from Mohammad Jamal Khalifa, the brother-in-law of al-Qaeda Amir Osama bin Laden, renamed his organization the Abu Sayyaf, meaning *Father of the Swordsman.*[2]

This chapter examines Abu Sayyaf as a meritocratic organization. The Abu Sayyaf Group, like the MNLF and Moro Islamic Liberation Front (MILF), draws largely from the Moro peoples of the Southern Philippines, but the Abu Sayyaf has its own distinct meritocratic leadership and recruitment systems.[3] While it has had some familial leaders, they were not chronological and they did not take office due to nepotism or inheritance. Khadaffy Janjalani for instance, the younger brother of Abdurajak Janjalani, became Amir in 2004 but only after the death of Ghalib Andang, who in turn had replaced Abdurajak. Equally, Khadaffy Janjalani had to contest the leadership position with others by competing on a meritocratic basis. Following Khadaffy was Abu Sulaiman in 2006 until he was killed in 2007 when Radullan Sahiron was elected to the Amir position. Therefore, while the origins of Abu Sayyaf are set broadly in the Moro ethnic base, as are the MILF, MNLF, and Bangsamoro Islamic Freedom Fighters (BIFF), Abu Sayyaf has fewer restrictions, and its internal promotion and leadership structure make it quantifiable as a meritocratic organization.

Abu Sayyaf is the pair to the familial structured Jemaah Islamiyah examined in the previous chapter. Comparing the organizations allows for many important variables to be held relatively constant. Abu Sayyaf and Jemaah Islamiyah are powerful insurgent actors with an extensive cooperative relationship, actively sharing training facilities and sanctuaries in their respective countries. Both have connections to the Afghanistan anti-Soviet jihad, and strong legacy connections to al-Qaeda, the Haqqani Network, and Lashkar-e-Taiba. The close relationships Abu Sayyaf has with Jemaah Islamiyah means that it has confronted similar external pressures, principally national and international counterinsurgency and counter-terrorism efforts over the recent decades. Consequently, Abu Sayyaf's meritocracy and Jemaah Islamiyah's familial structure is one of the main differences between the two organizations, making them well suited for a comparison of resilience.

This chapter is divided into three sections. The first examines the Abu Sayyaf organizational structure. It discusses meritocratic leadership, command and control, and organizational morphology. The second section examines the external pressures exerted against Abu Sayyaf, particularly in the counterinsurgency and law-enforcement contexts. These include hard-power, direct-kinetic pressures from military and specialist police operations, and soft-power pressures from civil, social, legislative, and economic actions. The third section is an appraisal of Abu Sayyaf's resilience and endogenous and exogenous adaptation to shock from external pressures. It considers equally the strengths and weaknesses of meritocracy and how external pressures shaped Abu Sayyaf as forces of change, or of destruction. The concluding analysis follows and discusses the implications of the findings.

Background

Abu Sayyaf went through a period of change over several years before becoming a separate organization. This is not dissimilar to Lashkar-e-Taiba, which was examined in Chapter 4, though on a lesser scale for Abu Sayyaf. What would eventually become Abu Sayyaf emerged in the late 1980s in the Southern Philippines as a new faction in the long-running Moro insurgency.[4] The broader insurgent conflict had been ongoing since October 1972 when President Marcos declared martial law, triggering the conflict (Noble 1976).[5] Since that time it was being fought by the MNLF and the MILF, from which Janjalani later disengaged and formed the Mujahedeen Commando Freedom Fighters. Abdurajak Janjalani changed this into the Abu Sayyaf in 1991, which correlated with the formation of his political pursuit of an Islamic state in the Southern Philippines.

The organization gained immediate support from the global connections Janjalani was largely responsible for establishing. Highly educated in religious doctrine, Janjalani received his training in Saudi Arabia from 1981 to 1984, afterwards returning home to Basilan in the Philippines to preach. In 1987, he travelled to Pakistan to participate in the anti-Soviet jihad, and there he became known to al-Qaeda leader Osama bin Laden.[6] Janjalani and bin Laden fought together with elements of the MNLF and forged a close friendship (Taylor 2017b).

Janjalani's MNLF faction was named after Abdul Rasul Sayyaf (Abd al-Rab al-Rasul Sayyaf), the patron of the Haqqani hosted al-Qaeda camp where he lived and fought.[7] Camp Saddah on the Afghanistan-Pakistan border was the first Afghani base for training Southeast Asian fighters from 1985 to 1992, with its commander Abdul Rasul Sayyaf overseeing the training of the non-Afghan members (Maloney 2015). Besides Filipinos, there were jihadist fighters from Thailand, Malaysia, and Indonesia housed at Camp Saddah. This amalgamation of international insurgents created the framework for a powerful nexus of rebellion across the globe, particularly in Asia and Southeast Asia.[8]

In 1991, Janjalani declared that the strategic goal of the Abu Sayyaf was the creation of an Islamic state in the Southern Philippines. This was an important event because it bypassed the possibility of coming to terms with the government through autonomy, independence, or revolution, and set a broad goal that was more a personal aspiration, rather than one representative of the Moro people. This strongly indicates the meritocratic values of Abu Sayyaf taking priority over ethnically based considerations of family and kinship. It also possibly indicates that Janjalani was intent to do whatever it took to achieve his strategic ambitions. This opened the organization structurally to meritocracy and the recruitment of fighters, commanders, and leaders who could best support this vision. Likewise, the extensive insurgent partnership network Janjalani had access to at the highest levels reflects his willingness to accept help from all quarters, outside of any familial restrictions.

Another aspect of the Southern Philippines insurgency further supports the meritocratic structure of Abu Sayyaf. While ethnic tensions among the Moro people were present, and indeed well represented by the various insurgent factions, the conflict was not an ethnic one but a religious and sectarian one (Wright-Neville 2004). It was not about family and kinship but Christians versus Muslims. The migration of state-supported Christians into the Mindanao areas traditionally dominated by Muslims caused increasing tensions, as Muslims soon became the minority in several ancestral areas.

Abu Sayyaf's enigmatic style was born of this. Its formative period is between 1991 and 1995, during which it undertook a number of high-profile operations. In this period Abu Sayyaf grew reasonably well. Some of Janjalani's earliest successes include the recruitment of ten high-ranking MNLF officials. These include Ustadz Wahab Akbar, whom Janjalani had first met in Libya. In 1998, Akbar became Governor of Basilan and quickly became known as a self-professed dictator (Torres 2007). Another important gain was the recruitment of Amilhussin Jumaani, who was a co-founding leader of the Tableegh Jamaat, a 300,000-strong organization based in Marawi dedicated to countering Western Christian practices (Billington 1995). When Jumaani moved to Abu Sayyaf he became a senior figure alongside Janjalani. An additional MNLF commander to join was Abdul Ashmad. From 1991, Janjalani expanded the organization from its initial cadre of MNLF dissenters and the few hundred fighters he had to 600 by 1995, according to Richburg (1995).

However, controversy remains concerning how Abu Sayyaf functions internally. Its meritocracy invites members to display their strengths and to vie for leadership roles, but whether this occurs through formal processes is debatable.[9] Duenas (1994) re-produced an Intelligence Service of the Armed Forces of the Philippines (ISAFP) diagram of their purported understanding of the Abu

Sayyaf organizational structure, seen in Figure 6.1. The ISAFP portrays it as being an organization with a mature, formalized structure and a clear hierarchically chain of command, also indicating its operational areas and functions.

The ISAFP chart probably represents an aspirational structure of Abu Sayyaf, one that both Janjalani and the Philippine Armed Forces separately envisaged, rather than an accurate reflection of the organization on the ground. The basic utility of the structure and characteristics found in similar organizations are there, but a lack of deeper details suggest the chart may have been drawn up on the basis of known knowns of the time.[10] Mindanao State University Professor and Abu Sayyaf commander Octavio Dinampo (2007) did support it as being accurate, but not as a reflection of any formal realization.

It is more likely that Abu Sayyaf only achieved the formal development of an upper echelon of command and control, without detailing lower organizational functions. This is reflected in the joint conclusions that came out of the 1991 Talipao summit of leaders. Dinampo (2007) reports that while Abdurajak was Amir, the only other appointed leaders were: the Chief of Staff – Ruddah; Chairman for Lupah Sug – a man named Jurmail (Doc); Chairman for Basilan – Hector Janjalani, the brother of Abdurajak; and Abu Sayyaf Secretary-General – Dinampo himself.[11] The deliberately structured organization depicted in this

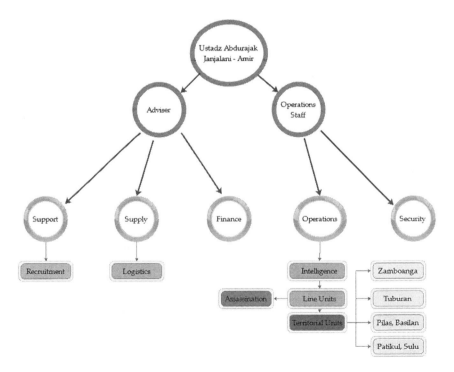

Figure 6.1 Organizational chart of Abu Sayyaf produced by the Intelligence Service of the Armed Forces of the Philippines.

arrangement, seen in Figure 6.2, suggests an organization with a formal chain of command and intent of achieving its goals, but with little structure at lower levels.

This structure held together for some years until external pressures began to squeeze. These pressures were a direct result of Abu Sayyaf's high operational tempo, busy with bombings, ambushing troops, kidnapping people, executing hostages, and terrorizing the Filipino Christians in Basilan and Mindanao. Major attacks include a grenade attack in Zamboanga and the bombing of a Christian missionary ship, the M/V Doulos, both in 1991 (GMA 2010). This made Abu Sayyaf an increasingly resilient threat the central government had little choice but to confront.

In 1995, Abu Sayyaf undertook one of its most audacious and provocative operations, attacking the Christian town of Ipil with a force of 200 heavily armed fighters. It inflicted significant damage on the town of 120.000 inhabitants, looting several banks, burning the commercial district to the ground, and killing 53 soldiers, police, and civilians and leaving many more wounded (Ramos 2000). An unintended consequence of this was that it deepened the political alienation of Abu Sayyaf. Turner (1995) writes that while the government was committed to striking a peace deal with the MILF, it was simultaneously committed to hunting down and destroying Abu Sayyaf because of its uncompromising pursuit of a violent insurgency. However, after Ipil, the group went into a darkened operational phase. This is probably because of the 1996 MNLF peace deal, which Abu Sayyaf did not support, in conjunction with later ongoing efforts to target it.[12]

This changed in 1998, a critical year for the Abu Sayyaf and for the Southern Philippines peace process as cracks began to appear. Bertrand (2000) claims that peace had all but been eroded because of failed transitional autonomous institutions due to mismanagement and corruption. MNLF failures to consolidate peace, a growing external discord outside of MNLF core supporters, and a lack

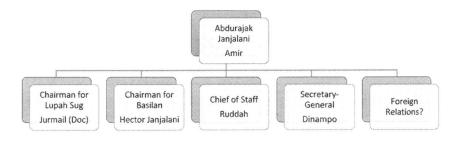

Figure 6.2 Abu Sayyaf actual organizational senior structure.

of land and property reforms as promised fuelled the breakdown. The other major event that year was the killing of Abu Sayyaf founder Amir Abdurajak Janjalani. The ramifications of this were perhaps the most significant shock it suffered from external pressures at any time, past or present. On 18 December 1998, special police raided a safe house in Lamitan on Basilan Island and killed Abdurajak, resulting in a severe splintering of Abu Sayyaf into two groups, one under the younger Khadaffy Janjalani, and the other under the command of Ghalib Andang.[13]

Khadaffy Janjalani did not succeed his brother by default, or by any form of familial leadership succession. Abu-Bakr's planned successor was Ustadz Ibrahim, former Secretary-General of the MNLF. However, Ibrahim was arrested just days before Abu-Bakr's slaying. That Khadaffy was not the arranged successor, coupled with the splintering of the group into factions, shows that meritocracy was the prevalent organizational structure in Abu Sayyaf. Likewise, Andang's faction was decidedly more about criminality and profiteering than a commitment to Moro liberation and independence. Figure 6.3 shows the group's structure after the demise of Abdurajak Janjalani. The left stream is the insurgent organization in Basilan, and the right the criminal Abu Sayyaf elements in Sulu.

Shortly afterwards, Andang's crime-for-profit faction ramped up its operations. In April 2000 Andang commanded his forces in a daring raid on the Malaysian tourist resort of Sabah that netted them 21 foreign hostages, a further three French journalists being captured in a subsequent raid in July. A year later they had been paid an estimated U.S.$10 to $25 million in ransom via Libyan authorities (Hookway 2000).[14] This was highly lucrative, not only for Abu

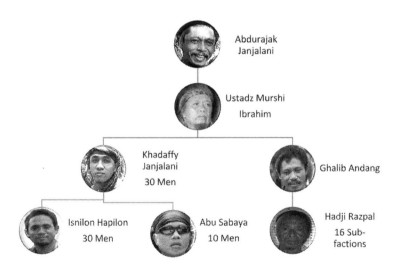

Figure 6.3 Abu Sayyaf structure post Janjalani, 1998.

Sayyaf, but because it pumped millions of dollars into the local economy, where corruption of police and military commanders helps feed demand for graft (Ugarte 2008).

The Andang group was identifiably more about profiteering than fighting an insurgency. The division also meant that Abu Sayyaf was not a close-knit organization, nor a likeminded one. Wadi critically states, "Abu Sayyaf is not a formal organization. It has no organizational structure. It is merely a jama'a [grouping], a loose, almost chaotic grouping of disenchanted Muslim youth. When the Abu Sayyaf is projected as a well-organized phalanx of Mujahedeen, this neat picture is provided by the Armed Forces of the Philippines (AFP)" (2003, 16). Andang's faction demonstrates this by working almost ad hoc and exclusively for the attainment of material rewards, and the organizational splintering that occurred validates Wadi to an extent. However, the Basilan Abu Sayyaf was certainly coordinated, effective, and lethal.

Likewise, the Abu Sayyaf mantle meant that both factions could cooperate when faced with common external threats, or to assist each other in fundraising. More so, both factions are equally based on meritocracy. Andang's Abu Sayyaf has a focus on merit-based status competition that supports gains, like kidnappings, whereas Khadaffy Janjalani's Abu Sayyaf was a meritocratic group with a focus on politics and unity.

Why not family?

The previous section establishes the basis of Abu Sayyaf meritocracy and describes broadly how meritocracy functions in it. This section delves deeper and examines the function of meritocracy in Abu Sayyaf versus familial organizations, and the associated strengths and weaknesses of them. Meritocracy in Abu Sayyaf has advantages and disadvantages. Meritocracy provides wider resource pools of expertise to draw from but with less security and higher vetting costs. Likewise, meritocracy can increase the contestation of command roles at all levels, leading to in-fighting, instability, and splintering. Familial recruitment therefore seems easier, cheaper, and more efficient, but limits external opportunities for professional commanders and experts.

At first glance this may seem surprising. Abu Sayyaf is derived from the ethnic Moro people of the Southern Philippines. Seemingly, this familial identity gives it exclusive kinship access to a focused resource base. However, others like the MNLF, MILF, and BIFF also compete for resources from this ethnic group. While it makes sense that kinship and family should play an important role in its organization, Abu Sayyaf is meritocratic. Abdurajak Janjalani's worldview is a part of this. Having travelled to Saudi Arabia for religious training, his global perspective may have influenced his ideas about organizations.

Likewise, his intimate involvement with other groups like al-Qaeda, the Islamic Movement of Uzbekistan (UIM), and the Jaish-e-Mohammed (JeM) may have imparted to him some benefits of meritocracy. More probably, however, it was the splintering from MNLF, and the very real need to recruit the most capable fighters and commanders available, irrespective of personal proximity. This certainly fits, as meritocracy allows Abu Sayyaf to recruit from a much broader base of potential members. Many are Moro and join to participate in the politics of Islamic insurgency that was most notable initiated by the MNLF in the 1970s, as discussed. However, dissatisfaction with MNLF peace agreements and failures to deliver on promises have driven militants to other groups. The failures of others may have therefore passively increased Abu Sayyaf's meritocratic recruitment. Still, why not recruit from kinship and family? It seems there are several further reasons for this, each that explain Abu Sayyaf's meritocracy.

First, the people of the Southern Philippines are not a homogeneous group. Deep sectarian tensions have existed for several decades and are common across Cotabato, Lanao, Sultan Kudarat, Sulu, Basilan, Tawi-Tawi, and the Zamboanga regions. Second, there is much intercommunal conflict across these areas that may make familial organization difficult. The Moro are a diverse group of families, clans, and tribes, making it an ethnographic melting pot in which familial and kinship lines are blurred, and division, conflicts, and feuds are rife (Reilly 2002).

Lara and Chapman (2009) contend that many inter- and intra-clan conflicts are highly persistent and are often never fully resolved, going through peaks and troughs of violence. When settlements remain elusive, the triggers of inter-familial blood-feuds are passed on to the next generation to exercise and so on. Adding to this is the mix of Islam with native cultural practices and mysticisms that often conflict. Therefore, endemic ethnic and familial clashes and lack of religious unity mean kinship associations can be turbulent and cause increased instability, more so than they offer advantages.[15]

In addition, Abu Sayyaf's international roots seem important, stemming from Abdurajak Janjalani's time in Saudi Arabia and in Afghanistan in Camp Saddah. There, he mixed with other Southeast Asian jihadists, Arabs, Pashtuns, and Afghans, including the camp's patron Abdul Rasul Sayyaf, who was one of Afghanistan's six most powerful warlords.[16] This provided him with international recruitment pools, resources, financing, and assistance from partners and affiliates. Complementing Filipinos, some Abu Sayyaf fighters are Indonesians, Malays and Thais. In addition, Abu Sayyaf has functioned as a gateway to MILF and other Moro insurgent groups like BIFF for foreign jihadists seeking training (na Thalang 2017). This reflects Abu Sayyaf's transnational nature in contrast to the relatively closed familial nature of MILF for example, meaning Abu Sayyaf is the go-to organization. This enables it to filter recruits both ways and pick from the best.

Another important aspect is that in the international standing of insurgent organizations, Abu Sayyaf is a merit-based actor and has been a regional partner of choice for al-Qaeda, and later of the Islamic State organization because of its demonstrated operational capabilities. Osama bin Laden was a powerful patron of Abu Sayyaf, helping to establish it as the Southeast Asian al-Qaeda leader (Zenn 2011). After bin Laden's death however, Abu Sayyaf easily integrated into the new jihadist reality, breaking from al-Qaeda, and turning to the Islamic State. Changing loyalties and pursuing niche insurgent markets does not mean that family and kinship have little part in Abu Sayyaf, but in terms of organizational structure, leadership, and function, it is firmly a meritocracy. Family is a vehicle of social capital and trust, particularly in the Moro membership base, but leadership and command and control are established through merit, often forcefully.

This meritocratic organizational structure is well suited to Abu Sayyaf and the insurgency it is fighting. Being religious and ideological rather than ethnic means the group can traverse familial and broader regional talent pools for fighters and commanders. Osama bin Laden's brother-in-law, Mohammed Jamal Khalifa, was a senior operational planner in Abu Sayyaf, and many al-Qaeda trainers have embedded with it to provide tactical and operational guidance.[17] As regards the criminal Abu Sayyaf elements, meritocracy has been similarly suitable. There is a highly focused body of analysis on these criminal factions, particularly the Sulu groups, which are decidedly more about profit than insurgency (Makarenko 2004; Salem 2016).

Likewise, each faction of the insurgents and the criminals has been able to trade-off the actions of the other. By either faction, the brutal treatment of civilian and military hostages has often overshadowed political actions, inciting terror and damaging the image of the Philippines Government. Abu Sayyaf favours killing captives by beheading, a common sentence given to hostages whose families do not pay the ransom demanded. However, while brutal, not all kidnappings and hostage executions have been about profiteering. In Table 6.1 are listed the beheadings of hostages from 2000 to 2018. Incidents on 3 August 2001; 11 July 2007; 28 July 2007; 2 February 2013; 29 August 2016; and 24 April 2017 relate to the execution of military personnel where no ransom had been asked for and the killings were extrajudicial. Unlike kidnap and ransom killings, those killings were carried out as part of the organization's insurgency, and support Abu Sayyaf political goals of weakening the appearance of the incumbent forces.

Meritocracy in command and control

From the previous sections we have developed a sound understanding of how Abu Sayyaf originated, the role of meritocracy in general, and how meritocracy was prioritized over familial organization. This section specifically analyses meritocracy in the senior leadership, particularly the retention of meritocracy during the splitting of the group. Unlike Jemaah Islamiyah, which fractured along decidedly familial lines, regrouping in kinship clusters and cells, splits in Abu Sayyaf see increased competition for leadership roles, and further subsequent factions emerging in competition when no single leader can cement power. The following analysis completes the first section and the holistic understanding of meritocracy from Abu Sayyaf's base to its highest levels.

Table 6.1 Abu Sayyaf hostage beheadings 2000–2006

Victims	Date	Incident details	Target	Type
Filipino Christian school children, teachers and a Catholic priest	19 April 2000	2 of 29 hostages held captive since 20 March 2000, mostly schoolchildren plus teachers, were beheaded.	Civilians	Insurgent
Filipino Christian villagers	3 August 2001	9 villagers beheaded after Abu Sayyaf seize 30 hostages from a Christian village on the island of Basilan.	Civilians	K&R
Jehovah's Witnesses	22 August 2000	2 Jehovah's Witnesses were beheaded and their heads dumped into a public market in the Southern Philippines. The heads were found in a bag with a note saying "infidels".	Civilians	Insurgent
Philippine Marines	7 July 2007	14 of 23 members of a Marines combat unit were beheaded in an encounter with Abu Sayyaf and MILF insurgents in Basilan.	Military	Insurgent
Doroteo Gonzales	17 May 2009	A farmer, Gonzales was kidnapped on 25 April and beheaded on 17 May after his family failed to pay a ransom.	Civilian	K&R
Gabriel Canizares	9 November 2009	Canizares was a teacher. His head was found at a petrol station in Jolo 3 weeks after being kidnapped. His body was found on 11 November 2009 in Patikul, Sulu. 6 other teachers also kidnapped that year were released unharmed.	Civilian	K&R
Forrest workers	11 June 2010	3 loggers near Maluso Town near Basilan were abducted and beheaded.	Civilians	K&R
Philippine Marines	28 July 2011	5 members of a 7-man Marine patrol were caught and beheaded by Abu Sayyaf in the jungle around Sulu.	Military	Insurgent
MNLF	2 February 2003	Abu Sayyaf beheaded 8 MNLF fighters after a dispute near Pakitul.	Insurgent	Insurgent
Bernard Then	17 November 2015	Kidnapped from a restaurant in Sandakan, Sabah on 15 May 2015. He was beheaded in Parang, Sulu when his ransom was not paid.	Civilian	K&R
John Ridsdel	25 April 2016	The Canadian national was kidnapped from a resort on Samal Island, Philippines on 21 September 2015. He and fellow captive Robert Hal1 were taken to Jolo and beheaded.	Civilian	K&R

Name	Date	Description		
Robert Hall	13 June 2016	Hall was also kidnapped from a resort on Samal Island, Philippines. He was beheaded with John Ridsdel.	Civilian	K&R
Patrick Almodovar	24 August 2016	A Filipino teenager, Almodovar was beheaded after a 1 million dollar (U.S.) bounty was not paid by his family.	Civilian	K&R
Philippine Army	29 August 2016	2 soldiers were beheaded and 15 killed in a firefight with Abu Sayyaf.	Military	Insurgent
Jurgen Kantner and Sabine Merz	27 February 2017	The German tourists were kidnapped from a yacht off Malaysia's Sabah coast in November 2016. Merz's body was found on the boat with a gunshot wound. A deadline for payment of 30 million pesos (566,900 – 600,000 Euro) was not met by 26 February and Kantner was beheaded.	Civilians	K&R
Noel Besconde	16 April 2016	A Filipino fisherman, he was held for a year and beheaded when he became sick.	Civilian	K&R
Anni Siraji	24 April 2017	Siraji was an MNLF member who joined the army. He was beheaded in retaliation for 3 Abu Sayyaf members killed in combat with the military.	Military	Insurgent
Hoang Trung Thong and Hoang Van Hai	4 July 2017	These Vietnamese sailors from the cargo ship *Royal Sixteen* were kidnapped in November 2016. They were beheaded in July 2017 after no ransom was paid.	Civilian	K&R
Forest workers	30 July 2017	7 Filipino loggers kidnapped on 20 July 2017 were found beheaded in separate towns in Basilan.	Civilians	K&R
Abdurahim Kituh and Nadzwa Bahitla	5 January 2018	Filipino husband and wife beheaded in village in Basilan.	Civilians	K&R

Note
K&R = Kidnap for ransom

After the death of its founder in 1998, Abu Sayyaf became rimated. It split into several factions but had only one core, or body, which remained committed to insurgency as the other factions pursued crime-for-profit activities. Among the various scattered factions, Adang's in particular earnt Abu Sayyaf the broad moniker of being a criminal gang rather than holy warriors or insurgents. Attwell writes that Abu Sayyaf depends heavily on criminal activities to fund their operations, "thereby morphing into a criminal-terrorist organization .... They frequently partner with transnational organized crime groups to smuggle a variety of illicit items, ranging from drugs, to guns, to people" (2017, 1).[18]

At a holistic organizational level Abu Sayyaf never recovered from the split, and has remained factionalized into two camps. Khadaffy Janjalani led the Basilan group and Andang the Sulu-based one until his capture by police in 2003.[19] After Andang, Hadji Razpal took command of his faction and continued to pursue criminal interests, the faction further splitting into an additional sixteen subgroups (Sunstar 2003).[20] In 2002, Abu Sayyaf Basilan's strength had deteriorated to about 70-plus members, further divided into 10 largely independent yet cooperative smaller groups. Khadaffy retained the majority of members with some 30 fighters under his direct command. Isnilon Hapilon, the future Amir, also commanded 30 men and led the security division. Abu Sabaya commanded the remaining members and supported Khadaffy. Each of these three command groups had sub-groups of roughly three to four men each.

This was an important time for Abu Sayyaf and is reflected in its engagement with other organizations. It was not kinship that facilitated its nexus activities but meritocracy, forged over years through combined involvement in global insurgency, jihad, and crime. For example, in 2003 insurgents from Malaysia and Indonesia asked for help in getting fighters into MILF camps in Mindanao for training (na Thalang 2017). Similarly, from 2004 there is evidence showing that elements of the Indonesian Jemaah Islamiyah were fully embedded into Abu Sayyaf activities in the Southern Philippines (O'Brien 2012).

This inter-organizational collaboration was strong, as was Abu Sayyaf's continued dislike of the MNLF. The Basilan group drew on its namesakes in Sulu to provide access to its MILF partners into the Tausig Sulu archipelago. This was in order for the MILF to begin usurping the MNLF elements there for control of the area and the people. This was an ethnic struggle that Abu Sayyaf had little vested interest in or kinship association, and was much more about benefiting from helping the MILF while weakening the MNLF.

Command and control was also dynamic during this period. Andang's death in prison saw the further deterioration of his faction into full banditry, and increased external pressures on Khadaffy and his groups by the Philippines military and international partners. This ultimately led to his demise in August 2006. Replacing Khadaffy was Abu Solaiman. The ascendance of Solaiman to Amir was once again firmly a meritocratic example. After Khadaffy, Solaiman (a.k.a. Jainal Antel Sali Jr.) was considered the most capable Abu Sayyaf commander (Jacinto 2007). He had been a priority target of Philippine and U.S. forces for some years with a U.S.$5 million bounty on his head. This was largely because it was his leadership and operational planning of the February 2004 Superferry 14 bombing, in conjunction with Jemaah Islamiyah, which enabled it to succeed. At the time, this attack was considered to be the second-worst terrorist attack in Southeast Asia with 116 civilians killed. Solaiman had proven his credentials, and was therefore deemed the best leader to take over.[21]

Abu Sayyaf suffered another serious blow less than six months later when Solaiman was killed in January 2007 (MacKinnin 2007). Khadaffy Janjalani and Abu Solaiman were highly cohesive leadership figures in the group, and after their passing, the splintering of Abu Sayyaf that had already started became inevitable. In Sulu, "Abu Sayyaf" became a broad moniker for criminal gangs with some form of past association with what was a feared insurgent organization. However, Solaiman's death opened the way for an infusion of new disaffected MNLF members, many of whom were increasingly unhappy about the terms of the MNLF peace deal. In March 2007, former MNLF commander Habier Malik defected to Abu Sayyaf, but the poor state of organizational affairs quickly saw hand-to-mouth criminal activities taking place rather than insurgent operations.

This began to change later in 2007 due to developing forces in the global geopolitical environment that had been manifesting since 2003. After al-Qaeda's global influence started to become usurped by ISIL, Abu Sayyaf began gravitating towards it. This began when Abdurajak Janjalani was still Amir, perhaps because he saw ISIL as a reflection of his own organization. During the development of ISIL when it transitioned away from al-Qaeda as the semi-autonomous al-Qaeda in Iraq, it was led by the ruthless Abu Musab al-Zarqawi, known for his extreme brutality (Michael 2007). However, Abu Sayyaf was already widely feared for its beheadings and particularly cruel treatment of its victims long before ISIL began using similar tactics.

When Isnilon Hapilon took command of Solaiman's faction, he re-orientated the group back to insurgency and the ardent pursuit of an Islamic state, all the while sustaining the group with criminal activities and occupying it with acts of terror.[22] In January of 2016, Hapilon sent a video to ISIL Amir Abu Bakar al-Baghdadi pledging his organization's allegiance (Chalk 2016). ISIL acknowledged and accepted this on 14 February 2016 via its al-Furat media wing. This marked Abu Sayyaf's membership in the ISIL nexus and re-invigorated the Southern Philippines insurgency. It also marks the revivification of external pressures, as discussed in the next section.

As for meritocracy, the Solaiman faction's development and role in the splintering of Abu Sayyaf suggest it is critically linked to the resilience of leadership, particularly because only the strongest leaders have emerged at the apex, and only the most capable of those have consolidated stray elements back into the insurgent core. Likewise, the bandit nature of Abu Sayyaf in Sulu has seen only the most successful criminal leaders take command positions. These elements are depicted in Table 6.2. Succinctly, this section has examined meritocracy under these terms and exposed the benefits and detriments. Overall, meritocracy has been a powerful driver of resilience though analysis does show that some of

Table 6.2 Effects of meritocratic setup on organization – Abu Sayyaf

Structural dynamics	Organizational effect
Meritocratic organization	Open recruitment unfettered by class or ethnicity.
	Highly integrated with criminal networks.
	Internal security vulnerabilities.
	High contestation of leadership, causing instability therein.
Command and control	Loyalty personality-driven, resulting in splintering.
	Coordination across factions.
Resources	Extensive crime for profit in territorial areas.
	Strong support from corrupt officials and police.
	International support from Libya, al-Qaeda, and then ISIL.
Strategic behaviour	Crime for profit with little focus on insurgency.
	Less compartmentalization of damages.
	Burden-sharing.
	Daily and tactical operations support long-term prosperity.

those same benefits led to weaknesses under other conditions, such as a loss of cohesion and unity, and ongoing contestation of command, making the organization susceptible to external pressures.

External pressures

Similarly to Jemaah Islamiyah, Abu Sayyaf experiences external pressures from domestic actors and incumbents, as well as regional actors like ASEAN, and international actors like the U.S. It has also gone through cycles of high activity and darkening. A notable point of comparison is that, like Jemaah Islamiyah, external pressures on Abu Sayyaf increased dramatically from 2000. While the Philippines Government had already been fighting the MILF, and having come to failed terms with the MNLF, Abu Sayyaf remained a primary concern of the state, excluded from amnesties and peace processes. Likewise, Abu Sayyaf has been ardent in its hostile refusal of coming to accommodations with the central authority, echoing the bone of contention many militants had with the MNLF agreement (May 2001). Adding to this has been a tense international security landscape, particularly so after the 9/11 2001 al-Qaeda attacks in the United States because any affiliates were thereafter considered equal targets in the War on Terror.[23]

Rivera (2012) states that the Arroyo Government in the Philippines saw the changing geopolitical environment as an opportunity to cash in and gain some much-needed international funding, training, and assistance. Riding on his "no compromise with terror" agenda, President Bush announced in 2003 in the Philippines that the U.S. would modernize and reform the Philippines military and drastically increase defence cooperation (Bush 2003).[24] When President Arroyo later visited the U.S. and reaffirmed her staunch support for the war in Afghanistan she was rewarded with U.S.$92.2 million of military aid, about

10 per cent of the military's budget, and 600 U.S. troops including 130 Special Forces as advisers that stayed until 2014.[25]

Operation "Balikatan" (Shoulder-to-Shoulder) was the first major Philippine-U.S. operation to target Abu Sayyaf. U.S. Special Forces troops deployed into the field with their Filipino colleagues and were cleared to engage the enemy in self-defence. U.S. troops were actively involved in hunting Abu Sayyaf from Sulu in hostage-rescue attempts, and several of its members have been killed in combat with U.S. soldiers (Bale 2010). Some in Mindanao, both Christian and Muslim, welcomed the presence of U.S. military assistance in the hope that it would end the violence. According to Morada (2003), there was also some high-level support. The Sultan of Sulu, Esmail Kiram, was a prominent supporter of U.S.-Philippine joint exercises, and won over Parouk Hussin, the governor of the Autonomous Region in Muslim Mindanao (ARRM), who initially opposed foreign troops there (2003).

In the initial stages, Balikatan was not without controversy however. While public support was important for effectively countering Abu Sayyaf there were problems between the Americans and the Filippinos. Manila's desires revolved around training and equipping their forces whereas the U.S. was eager to engage Abu Sayyaf in the field, much like it had done with the Taliban in Afghanistan. Further issues pertained to terminology. The U.S. insisted these actions were operations, whereas Philippine officials wanted them called exercises. Likewise, the U.S. would not yield to its forces coming under Filipino command, so a dual command structure had to be created, causing conflicts and miscommunictions (Morada 2003).

Despite these setbacks, Operation Balikatan was effective in restricting Abu Sayyaf activities. Robinson *et al.* state that over a 14-year period the joint operation was able to "substantially reduce the transnational terrorist threat in the Southern Philippines" (2016, xi). This limited Abu Sayyaf's freedom of movement and increased community sentiments against it. Hammerberg and Faber (2017) contend that joint operations also reduced Abu Sayyaf's access to funding, and to resources such as recruitment. They cite more succinctly that attacks were reduced by 56 per cent from 2001 to 2011 (see Figure 6.4), while Abu Sayyaf numbers were reduced from 2,000 down to about 430.[26]

Among those killed in clashes with the military was Amir Khadaffy Janjalani in 2006. Shortly afterwards in January 2007, senior Abu Sayyaf Sulu commander Jainal Antel Sali (a.k.a. Solaiman, Abu Sulayman, or "The Engineer") was killed in a major clash with Filipino Special Forces on the island of Jolo.[27] The combination of these losses was extremely damaging to Abu Sayyaf and drastically weakened the organization. In particular, these killings only deepened divides and internal meritocratic power struggles within the group. Operationally this resulted in an increase in kidnappings and other criminal activities for sustenance, but an inverse reduction in insurgent actions.[28]

However, while this caused several issues such as shrinking manpower and limitations of movement and mobility, Abu Sayyaf was able to undertake a number of bombings in response during 2009. There were nine bomb attacks

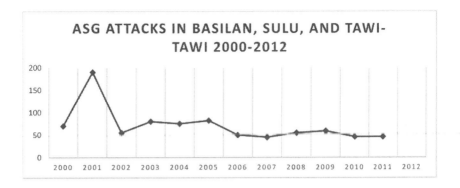

Figure 6.4 Abu Sayyaf attacks in Southern Philippines, 2000–2012.

that year of varying sizes and importance. Six civilians were killed in a bomb attack in Zamboanga, and in Jolo another bomb planted by Abu Sayyaf killed two U.S. forces members.[29] In July of 2009 a further 12 bombs were found on a ferryboat, the Lucena, but were disarmed before they could sink the ship. According to Ozaeta (2009), this foiled attack demonstrated that Abu Sayyaf retained the intent to target and severely damage the maritime infrastructure in the Southern Philippines, as well as sowing terror.[30] Conversely, the start of 2010 saw a significant drop in activities, which Montlake (2010) attributes to the effectiveness of direct kinetic, intelligence-led external pressures.

Another particularly significant blow to Abu Sayyaf came in 2010 with the slaying of its new Amir, Albader Parad. Parad was a high-profile commander who, along with five Abu Sayyaf fighters, died in a firefight with Philippine Marines near Maimbung. His death severely damaged Abu Sayyaf (GMA 2010). In fact, it has been the extent of damage to the Abu Sayyaf leadership that has probably been the greatest type of external pressure the organization has suffered. This seems to be more of chance than design, reflecting Abu Sayyaf's meritocracy because its most senior leaders are often in the field with fighters, commanding tactical actions as much as securing their own positions.

After Jainal Antel Sali was killed, Radullan Sahiron was the highest-ranked Abu Sayyaf leader, but he has not been seen since being wounded in a shootout with Filipino forces in 2008. In fact, Sahiron's wounding led to a surge in attempted kidnappings of doctors and nurses in Zamboanga city. During the same period, Abu Sayyaf suffered responding incumbent retributive pressures that did not let up and continued to whittle away its command and control and senior leadership. After Parad's death, Philippine Lieutenant-General Ben Dolorfino said "there are no young leaders emerging.... There is no such coordination among all the groups" (Abuza 2010, 12). Marine Commandant Major-General Juancho Sabban added "the Basilan group has no contact with the Sulu group or with the Tawi-Tawi group. In effect, we have isolated each group and eventually, piece by piece we will be able to neutralize these groups" (Abuza 2010, 11).

As external pressures continued, Abu Sayyaf was on the back-foot and by 2016 Philippine forces succeeded in killing Puruji (Furuji) Indama, the commander charged with the beheading of ten Filipino Marines in July 2007, and for a 2010 massacre of civilians in Basilan (SMH 2007).[31] The leadership decapitations and overall weakening of Abu Sayyaf through attrition and from restrictions in mobility and communications degraded it significantly. Those same pressures constrained its criminal operations as well, and the days of asking for, and sometimes receiving, multi-million dollar ransoms were gone. This was very detrimental, particularly with regard to recruitment and the replacement of lost fighters and leaders.

Unlike Jemaah Islamiyah that recruits through family, the financial and vocational rewards for joining Abu Sayyaf were decaying in line with its restricted operational mobility. This was compounded by further losses of much of its subject matter and operational experts who were killed off due to police and military actions. Abu Sayyaf explosives trainer Abdulbasit Usman is a good example. On 14 January 2010, Pakistani authorities announced the U.S. had killed Usman in Waziristan (Shah 2010). It is unclear what Usman was doing at the Haqqani Network compound where he and a dozen others were killed by a U.S. drone. It is possible that external pressures at home forced Usman out of the Philippines, or that he was there independently or as an envoy. Either way, his loss was another blow. Conversely, it demonstrates that Abu Sayyaf still retained its long-established global insurgent networks, and while external pressures on it were acute, it was still involved in insurgency at domestic and international levels.[32]

Taken together, these external pressures suggest that there is an association between hard-power pressures and the vulnerability of meritocratic organizations. First, damage sustained by Abu Sayyaf reduced is leadership and numbers, and therefore its cohesion, direction, operational capacity, and, in particular, communications and intra-organizational coordination. This is similar to a doom-loop scenario where organizations get into self-reinforcing spirals that can become increasingly damaging (Skipton 2013). Compared to Jemaah Islamiyah, which faced very similar pressures over the same period, Abu Sayyaf weakened considerably in comparison. Jemaah Islamiyah was able to lay low and draw from its extensive kinship base to support it during darkened phases. Abu Sayyaf was not. While it had ethnic roots, Abu Sayyaf did not enjoy advantage from them nearly as much. Likewise, the group's meritocratic nature changed its structural and operational efficiencies in line with external pressures as the organization took damage and contracted, forcing it to further decentralize.

Another result of strong external pressures was for Abu Sayyaf to largely disengage from insurgency. Instead, it reverted to criminality because it could attract recruits with the proceeds through the payment of salaries, and importantly, it was often in the violent and brutal criminal world that most of Abu Sayyaf's leaders thrived, and where leaders established their names.[33] Therefore, criminality was important for Abu Sayyaf's meritocracy beyond profiteering. Likewise, the insurgency probably could not have been sustained without all the benefits the criminal-insurgent nexus brought.

This demonstrates the other key result of direct kinetic, hard-power pressures on meritocratic organizations, and that is the structural organizational changes that result from them. In the Indonesian example Jemaah Islamiyah contracted, reinforced, went dark, and hid, but it always maintained its orientation to insurgency. It had enduring and comprehensive familial networks and relationships to sustain it, and when not possible to work covertly it operated overtly through phoenixed and seemingly legitimate political organizations, and vice versa. Abu Sayyaf lacked this and instead scattered, splintering into geographical fiefdoms of criminality, and was only intermittently drawn back together sporadically by charismatic and powerful leaders if and when they emerged.

Soft-power pressures

This section examines external pressures short of hard-power, direct kinetic and military methods. As defined in Chapter 1, soft-power pressures include activities to arrest, degrade, and delegitimize insurgency. These are critically important because efforts against Abu Sayyaf did not occur in a vacuum of direct kinetic efforts alone. Likewise, a strong range of external pressures against the insurgency were underway prior to U.S. participation from 2001. The Philippines Government has decades of experience combating the MNLF, MILF, and BIFF, as well as the New Peoples Communist Army (NPA) in insurgency, employing a mixture of police and military special operations, and social, civil, legislative, and political initiatives.[34]

However, the type and extent of soft-power pressures and their effectiveness have oscillated in direct correlation to political tides. Ferrer (2005) tells us that incumbent state responses to the Moro insurgency during the Marcos Presidency primarily revolved around the use of force as a mainstay of policy, while soft-power methods were secondary. These included penetrating insurgent organizations, co-opting and developing members, offering amnesties, and enticing people away from insurgency by promising (but not necessarily delivering) social development programmes.[35]

Failures to deliver tangible social reforms and to address, or initially determine, grievances and root causes, coupled with the blanket use of force in some cases meant that soft-power pressures in the infancy of the insurgency through the 1960s, 1970s, and 1980s were weak (Overholt 1986).[36] Although the Abu Sayyaf was not then in existence, this is highly relevant because it established a mandate to address insurgency with force and the entrenchment of deception and insincerity into soft-power pressures and political solutions. While this changed considerably during the Aquino Period between 1986 and 1992, discussed next, the legacy that Marcos established was never far from the surface.

When Aquino came to power, military solutions were put on the backburner in favour of dialogue and engagement. Aquino began talks very quickly with

MNLF leader Nur Misuari. Dismissing protocol in an attempt to demonstrate his government's resolve to finding peace, Aquino and Nur Misuari met in person. This led to a halt in hostilities and the commencement of the Tripoli agreement.[37] Under this agreement, the MNLF abandoned its goal of total independence in exchange for autonomy, to be enacted by the constitutional autonomy legislation for Mindanao (Rood 2012).

The relevance to Abu Sayyaf is apparent for several reasons. First, while very different from Marcos, the efforts of the Aquino Government melded together to form the new duality of dealing with future insurgency in the Southern Philippines. The Marcos mandate of total war and the Aquino mandate of dialogue and engagement led to the development of constitutional change. Ultimately, those changes were then used as the benchmark for future dealings, but by refusing to participate, Abu Sayyaf set itself outside of the political solutions Aquino implemented, and firmly in the Marcos era sandbox of solution-seeking through hard power.

There was a further downside. While Aquino and his successor President Ramos sought autonomy, and recognized the Muslim Moro concerns on ethnic and sectarian grounds, Abu Sayyaf continued to demand an Islamic state with no compromise under other terms. As the central government's aim was about assuaging the concerns of Muslims, Abu Sayyaf effectively removed itself as a part of the community, and instead established itself as an organization with a political purpose that did not reflect the majority. Likewise, Abu Sayyaf's intensive criminal activities during these times created angry opposition in some segments of the population who tired of the violence it propagated.

This further evidences Abu Sayyaf as a meritocratic organization because members pursued self-interest over communal or kinship ones. However, it also shows that meritocracy was blinded to the option of accepting soft-power responses from the incumbent government as an easier means of dealing with it, over a determined ideology of fighting at all costs. This placed Abu Sayyaf in what was essentially a three-way crossfire. As extensive hard-power pressures took a heavy toll, soft-power pressures were having a twofold effect.

On one level, by addressing broad social grievances there was a reduction in the causes of societal conflict. Second, by increasing community satisfaction through civic development, peace efforts inversely reduced support for organizations, including Abu Sayyaf. Unfortunately however, momentum stalled as it had in the past as the Aquino Government failed to fully achieve many of its initiatives, leaving the Tripoli Agreement fractured after implementation. While this represents a failed opportunity to secure tangible gains against the insurgents, it did set a framework for President Ramos to build upon.[38]

On 2 September 1996, the MNLF signed a peace agreement with the Ramos Government.[39] The agreement had important soft-power ramifications for Abu Sayyaf because it set up a local Muslim administrative body, the Southern Philippines Council for Peace and Development (SPCPD), which was succeeded by the Regional Autonomous Government (RGA) in September 1999. The RGA governed 14 provinces and nine cities in a Special Zone of Peace and Development (SZOPAD).[40] Effectively, this meant that Abu Sayyaf would be in direct conflict with a local Muslim government, rather than the central Catholic government.

On 11 September 1996, MNLF leader Nur Misuari was elected as the Governor of the Autonomous Region of Muslim Mindanao unopposed, and appointed Chairman of the SPCPD. In addition, Misuari was also promoted as the presiding officer of the SZOPAD. This was a well-considered strategy by President Ramos. Rivera writes that "it was believed that placing Misuari in both positions, the peace settlement would gain wide acceptance among the Moros and demonstrate to the non-Muslim community that autonomy would benefit all groups" (Rivera 2012, 98).[41]

While not as effective as envisaged, it was an obstacle for Abu Sayyaf as many MNLF forces were integrated into new roles, and much of its leadership into the apparatus of government in the region. MNLF's agreement with the central government saw its top-tier leaders appointed to positions of significant power in the bureaucracies and offices of the newly established SPCPD, and the ARMM. Likewise, there was extensive opportunity for MNLF fighters to join the army and Philippine National Police Forces, including in specialist units carrying out, for example, intelligence and technical operations. In all, over 5,200 MNLF members joined the military and 1,250 the Philippine National Police (Hall 2009).

This situation should have presented a range of issues for Abu Sayyaf. First, former MNLF leaders now had the power and authority to suppress the Abu Sayyaf. Second, the transformed MNLF administration gained significant law enforcement, community, social, and political capabilities to support its hard-power capabilities, all supported by the central government. However, lack of follow-through meant that yet again, potential gains were never fully realized. When Joseph Estrada replaced Ramos, serving as president from 1998 to 2001, attention was turned to reigning in the MILF. President Ramos acknowledged MILF forces, camps, and areas of operations and initiated infrastructure projects and significant development in MILF territories as a sign of goodwill and Manila's commitment to peace. Initially this went well and presented another significant soft-power pressure on Abu Sayyaf as its affiliates gravitated to the new government, forcing Abu Sayyaf to become increasingly violent and as a result, alienist.

In March 2003, Abu Sayyaf took 53 hostages including a priest, teachers, and students from Basilan, a Moro ethnic enclave. On 20 April, the birthday of President Estrada, the bandits beheaded two of the male hostages as a "sinister gift" to the President (Garcia 2018). This prompted a heavy response from Manila that instigated a significant military direct kinetic response.[42] Conversely, when President Gloria Macapagal Arroyo came into power the counterinsurgency approach oscillated back. Arroyo immediately implemented a ceasefire and re-commenced peace talks. These alternating approaches distinctly demonstrate the oscillation of external pressures with political tides.

Following this, MILF Amir Hashim Salamat renounced the insurgent struggle in a public display, on 23 June 2003 as a measure to cement the peace agreement with the government. This was not a superficial undertaking and as a speech act it conveyed a strong message. Salamat said "to stress this point, I hereby reiterate our condemnation and abhorrence of terrorist tendencies", adding that the MILF saw terrorism being against Islam (Swaak-Goldman and Nybondas 2006, 302). This had significant implications for Abu Sayyaf as it effectively closed their access to MILF camps, limited operational cooperation, and distanced a long-time and important ally.[43]

The year 2003 also marked the start of the joint Filipino-U.S. Operation Balikatan that came to be known by the Americans as Operation Enduring Freedom-Philippines (Hall 2010). While the hard-power pressures on Abu Sayyaf have been reviewed in the earlier sections of this chapter, Operation Balikatan had many soft-power successes also. One particular focus was building solutions that could more permanently degrade insurgent material and combative capabilities. Stentiford (2018) reports that the U.S. strongly engaged with their Filipino partners and redoubled efforts to address historical economic and social issues feeding the insurgency, actively investing in socio-economic development and eliminating chronic law-enforcement corruption.[44]

These efforts worked in concert with broader defence reforms and international assistance in the military, law-enforcement, and civil development spheres including health, infrastructure, and education. Conjointly they gave the Philippines Government capabilities that increasingly reduced the fundamental issues in the South that had fuelled insurgent politics for decades. Similarly, the end of the Siege of Marawi placed significant strain on these groups. The fragments of Abu Sayyaf retreated and have not been able to rebuild an active status on Mindanao as at 2020, and its organizational coherence has been significantly degraded.[45]

Summary of external pressures

Overall, it seems that external pressures of each type have been effective, even though they were disproportionate, oscillating, reactive, and poorly supported. Likewise, a clear lack of strategic foresight by incumbent authorities has contributed to Abu Sayyaf's resilience rather than degrading it. The meritocratic structure of Abu Sayyaf certainly seems to be a part of its weaknesses, yet also of its strengths. Not only is attaining senior positions in the organization highly competitive, but also when leaders are lost there is a propensity for inter-organizational groups to splinter between the next-lowest leadership candidates, rather than draw together and remain cohesive. On the other hand, the impressive profiteering Abu Sayyaf has enjoyed from its kidnap and criminal enterprises has made it an attractive employer, something seen in other meritocratic organizations. The lack of restrictions on joining and the means of attaining power through utility have proven that meritocracy is the bedrock of its organization. How well Abu Sayyaf has adapted within this structure in direct contrast to the damage it suffered is examined in the next section.

Abu Sayyaf resilience

We will now review Abu Sayyaf's resilience and adaptation to shocks from external pressures. The role of its meritocratic structure is a central focus of doing so. This is important because Abu Sayyaf has been repeatedly declared as damaged, depleted, and severely fractured (Sunstar 2003; Abuza 2005), yet it has remained resilient, resurfacing and undertaking increasingly deadly operations. This has occurred at least three times. Abu Sayyaf first went dark from 1995 to 1998 after the signing of the Tripoli agreement between the central government and the MNLF. The second occasion was at the time of the MILF peace accord in 2003. The third was after the siege of Marawi when President Duterte declared all-out war on Abu Sayyaf. Each time it went dark, the security environment and the nature of external pressures was highly unfavourable to the operations of the insurgent and the criminal-based factions alike.

During these periods of darkening Abu Sayyaf reorganized, frequently splintering with new subgroups emerging, sometimes melding back together with others or forming loose coalitions because of pre-existing social capital and trust relationships. It is interesting that the meritocratic structure of Abu Sayyaf has been the primary conduit for fragmenting and splintering, but also seems potentially to be one of the organization's greatest resilience mechanisms. Although meritocracy resulted in a fragmentation-like effect where groups continually split into smaller ones, the highly decentralized nature of splits along meritocratic lines made Abu Sayyaf much harder to target by incumbent and U.S. forces, compared to one homogeneous organization that may reside in one place.

Although unintended, this decentralization means that even if some of the factions and subgroups were eliminated there would always be other Abu Sayyaf factions to continue the fight. Conversely, Abuza (2005) suggests that there is a deliberate logic to such factionalism, asserting that it is caused by generational issues because the younger members are dissatisfied with the lack of progress by the older leaders in establishing the caliphate. As a theory this can be partially supported by Bacon (2018), who found that inter-organizational conflicts exacerbate tensions that can cause splintering, but there is no evidence that this is in any way intentional, or by strategic design. Rather, Abu Sayyaf's decentralization appears to have, initially at least, come about by chance, with the benefits only being realized much later.

It is also apparent from examination of Abu Sayyaf that decentralization, brought about by external pressures, has been a fertile landscape for meritocracy. The major factions of Abu Sayyaf in Basilan and Sulu each have strong merit-based leadership structures and organizational morphologies. Among the Basilan insurgents, charismatic leaders when they manifested, such as Khadaffy Janjalani and Isnilon Hapilon, refreshed the organization's commitment to insurgency, violent jihad, and the establishment of an Islamic caliphate. In Sulu and other locations, criminal Abu Sayyaf networks were led by the most daring and ruthless members such as Ghalib Andang and Alhabsy Misaya. In each case it is meritocracy, not family or kinship, that dictates entry and positioning, the polar opposite to Jemaah Islamiyah. The Moro kinship canvas was simply an ethnographic backdrop rather than a critical element of resilience, of gaining inputs, or of insurgency capabilities and efficiency.

Another interesting facet of Abu Sayyaf resilience across both sides of the organization are perceptions of martyrdom versus longevity. The minimal use of suicide bombers lends strong credence to the politics of insurgency, rather than to an extremist religious theology, or willingness to sacrifice for family. Basra and Neumann (2016) refer to this as the profit-versus-ideology dichotomy. Certainly, the criminal networks of Abu Sayyaf have significant and vested interests in staying alive and enjoying the spoils of their crimes. This is in stark contrast to Jemaah Islamiyah, which uses suicide bombings and attacks extensively in its operations. Almost all of Abu Sayyaf's operations have been planned with extraction routes, and bombing operations like Superferry 14 were conducted remotely with no Abu Sayyaf casualties.

Likewise, a tactical analysis of its insurgent operations shows the clear employment of survivalist infantry and small-unit tactics. Abu Sayyaf forces tend to employ fighting withdrawals and tactical retreats rather than stand, fight, and die strategies. This was particularly evident in Marawi to which the vast majority of surviving Abu Sayyaf insurgent forces escaped, perhaps with some covert assistance from military and police elements secured with loot worth U.S.$40 million (Franco 2017).[46] Abu Sayyaf Amir Isnilon Hapilon was himself killed while trying to flee, rather than making a heroic last stand as the leader of the Mujahedeen.

This suggest that the resilience architecture of Abu Sayyaf is centred around individual and organizational survival at all costs. While Jemaah Islamiyah is very willing to blow up fighters in mass-casualty suicide operations, Abu Sayyaf is not. This, along with the contrast of political versus religious ideology, is one of the greatest differences between the two. Therefore, a durable survivalist mentality is at the heart of Abu Sayyaf resilience. This has permeated its criminal activities, driving them and sustaining its insurgent operations. Abuza (2005) writes that Abu Sayyaf, flush with funds, has three significant sources of strength. These are, first, improved capabilities, technology, and the capacity to undertake operations; second, the pursuit of encouraging sectarian violence between Muslims and Christians; and third, its ability to recruit from across society and develop agents that pass under the radar.

If Abuza is correct, and we ignore other factors of necessity common to insurgency in general, Abu Sayyaf should be more formidable, and at least more active outside of its principal heartland, but there is no data to support this. Additionally, its highly decentralized nature and organizational distribution across Sulu, Basilan, and Mindanao provide it with critically favourable operational areas it tends not to stray from, a primary determinant of insurgency success, the importance of which Galula (1964) has asserted. With regard to the stated strengths, all organizations need funding, arms, technology, and a purpose. Likewise, sectarianism is widespread in insurgency across the world and is not unique in any way to the Abu Sayyaf. Likewise, the analysis presented in this chapter shows that Abu Sayyaf's meritocracy enables it to recruit foreign nationals and members with few or no previous affiliations. This strongly suggests that it is meritocracy that is a key enabler of its potency.

This is evident in the short time from 2017 to 2018 when Abu Sayyaf undertook three major operations. In conjunction with its close partners the Maute Group, 63 civilians were killed in 2017 in Abu Sayyaf attacks (Dudley 2018). This was also a period of intensive operational planning. In conjunction with Jemaah Islamiyah, Abu Sayyaf planned a massive operation to target the closing ceremony of the Southeast Asian Games in Kuala Lumpur (Chew 2019). Overall, 46 Sayyaf fighters were captured, foiling the plot, and 35 Jemaah Islamiyah members. Although it did not succeed, the attack planning demonstrates significant resilience and operational capacity and efficiency. Following this in 2018, Abu Sayyaf detonated a car bomb in the Philippine city of Basilan, killing multiple soldiers and civilians (Villamor 2018).

Leading on from this, ongoing inherent failures to develop, employ, and maintain sustained and balanced external pressures, both hard and soft, despite significant international assistance to the Philippines Government, have allowed Abu Sayyaf to regroup and revitalize. Chronic failures to follow up on tactical wins and leverage advantages when they have occurred have contributed to its survival. Adding to Abu Sayyaf's sources of strengths, corruption and assistance from local authorities and their collusion in criminal activities is more about individual profiteering than a grand strategic design.[47] Figure 6.5 depicts Abu Sayyaf's criminal fundraising operations between 2011 and 2016, showing a high tempo of kidnapping activity during the period. In 2017 Abu Sayyaf shifted tactics

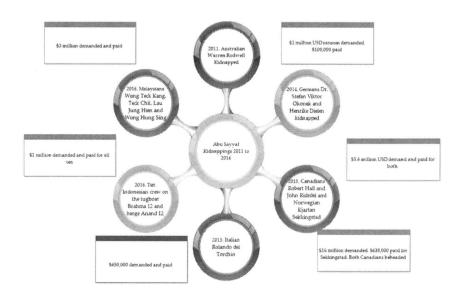

Figure 6.5 Abu Sayyaf kidnap and ransom activity, 2011–2016.

from land-based targets to seaborne, with 17 attacks against shipping traffic resulting in 65 hostages being taken from six different countries (Abuza 2017). The year 2018 was relatively quiet with no new kidnappings and only ongoing management of extant captives. In October of 2019 Abu Sayyaf kidnapped Allan Arthur Hyrons, a British businessman, and his Filipino wife from Zamboanga in the Southern Philippines (Gutierrez 2019). Most recently, in January of 2020, eight Indonesian fishermen were abducted off the coast of Sulu.

This is reflected in the macro-counterinsurgency approach taken to combat it. Oscillating political fortitude and opinion in Manila has been a strong factor in the application of pressure on Abu Sayyaf, and the Southern insurgency as a whole. Each incoming administration has practically reversed the initiatives of the previous one, alternating between states of all-out war against it to offering olive branches and diplomacy. This has afforded Abu Sayyaf time to rest and recover, and despite the seriously fractured nature of the organization, there is ample evidence from the analysis in this chapter that various factions have been highly cognisant of this, and used it to their advantage. Succinctly, Abu Sayyaf has demonstrated significant organizational resilience and it is likely to continue doing so.

Conclusion

Hammerberg and Faber state that "Abu Sayyaf has regained strength and influence in the Southern Philippines in the years after the majority of U.S. Special Operations Forces departed. Abu Sayyaf's resurgence is also linked to affiliation to ISIL" (2017, 21). This is an excellent summary of the resilience of Abu Sayyaf and the importance of meritocracy to its continuing survival. Operating outside of familial and kinship contracts, it continues to recruit from a wide talent pool domestically and internationally. Its extensive and successful criminal activities, including financing from insurgency such as the sacking of Marawi, have yielded it tens of millions of U.S. dollars with which it entices talented recruits. Therefore, meritocracy and affluence make Abu Sayyaf an employer of choice, not only for fighting for the insurgency, but on socio-economic levels in the poorer areas of the Southern Philippines where criminality is most profitable.

Additionally, external pressures on Abu Sayyaf have contributed significantly to its resilience, rather than detracting from or degrading it. The successive killings of powerful leaders such as Abu-Bakr Janjalani, Khadaffy Janjalani, Isnilon Hapilon, Ghalib Andang, and Radullan Sahiron have decentralized the organization, but rather than destroying it, this has resulted in a diffused and networked yet extremely potent insurgency. Interestingly, while hard-power pressures have resulted in the deaths of many of its most important leaders and commanders, as a strategy this has not been nearly as effective as similar approaches with Jemaah Islamiyah and other insurgent groups that have been considerably weakened, or forced into operational dark phases by leadership decapitation.

Abu Sayyaf's meritocracy is central to this as it is more capable of effectively recovering from leadership losses. The ability for lower ranks to assert leadership and assume higher command roles, unimpeded by rules and boundaries as are in place in familial organizations, means it is easier for Abu Sayyaf to replace leaders from a large pool of members eager to establish themselves. Meritocracy in Abu Sayyaf appears to make it more adaptive and resilient to external pressures over time by limiting damage to specific cells, sub-groups, and factions. Likewise, this retards the spread of damage across organizational arms.

In direct contrast to Jemaah Islamiyah, it has been soft-power pressures that have been most effective against Abu Sayyaf compared to the results of hard-power pressures. Infrastructure, civic development, and the improvement in standards of living have turned away some deep-rooted support for Abu Sayyaf among local communities (East 2013). Likewise, new infrastructure has assisted government forces accessing previously difficult operating environments. Last, with the decline of the ISIL organization in Syria and Iraq, some gloss has worn off the appeal of an Islamic caliphate. Abu Sayyaf will probably remain fixed on prioritizing criminal gains over insurgency, but the appearance of new and effective leaders who can fight their way up the meritocracy ladder may change this. It has been demonstrated time and again that Abu Sayyaf is an organization that rewards talented leaders and those able to thrust themselves to the forefront of leadership and command.

Notes

1 The MCFF, known in Arabic as *al-Harakatul Islamia*, was a breakaway group from the MNLF formed by Janjalani until its name change in 1991 after Janjalani returned from Afghanistan. The Moro National Liberation Front was founded in 1972 by Nur Misuari. It was the largest of the Muslim secessionist movements and at its peak it enjoyed considerable state sponsorship from the Libyan and Malaysian Governments, in particular from the governor of Sabah, Tun Mustapha. In 1976, the Libyan Government brokered a peace accord between the GRP and MNLF, but it was poorly implemented and fighting quickly resumed. In 1978, a faction led by Salamat Hashim broke away from Misuari, whom they accused of being too secular. The offshoot was formally founded as the Moro Islamic Liberation Front (MILF) in 1984. SOURCES: Moshe Yegar, 2002. "Part Three: The Moro Muslims". In *Between Integration and Succession: The Muslim Communities of the Southern Philippines, Southern Thailand, and Western Burma/Myanmar*. Lanham, Boulder, New York, and London: Lexington Books; Zachary Abuza, 2005. *Balik-Terrorism: The Return of the Abu Sayyaf*. Carlisle: Strategic Studies Institute, Army War College

2 Via Mohammad Jamal Khalifa, al-Qaeda channelled funds to Janjalani from pro-Islamist donors via international charitable fronts until 1995. SOURCE: Jeffrey Bale, 2010. *The Abu Sayyaf Group in its Philippine and International Contexts*. Middlebury, Vermont: Middlebury Institute of International Studies at Monterey.

3 Schiavo-Campo and Judd (2005) put it that the term "Moro" was a Spanish word for Filipino Muslims, and came from a Spanish terms used in reference to Muslim Arabs in Spain and Africa. It was therefore not a Filipino word in origin, but was adopted by them and is in common use. SOURCE: Salvatore Schiavo-Campo and Mary Judd, 2005. "The Mindanao Conflict in the Philippines: Roots, Costs, and Potential Peace Dividends". *Social Development Papers: Conflict Prevention and Reconstruction* 24 (2): 1–23.

4 Fellman states that Southern Philippines insurgent groups have historically revolted in response to what they consider a usurpation of Moro territory by Christian immigrants. A second point of contention is a perceived lack of political representation in the national government. Successive failures by other organizations emboldened Abu Sayyaf to become increasingly violent in pursuit of their objectives. SOURCE: Zack Fellman, 2015. "Abu Sayyaf Group". *AQAM Futures Project Case Study Series, Case Study Number 5* (Nov. 2011): Center for Strategic and International Studies.

5 McKenna asserts that for many of the Muslims in Mindanao the insurgency actually began hundreds of years before the Marcos declaration, and it was the commencement of Spanish colonialism in the sixteenth century and their consolidation of conquest in the Philippines that sparked the anti-colonial wars. According to Majul, the primary purpose of the Spanish Legazpi expedition was about converting the Moros to Catholicism. SOURCES: Thomas McKenna, 1998. *Muslim Rulers and Rebels: Everyday Politics and Armed Separatism in the Southern Philippines.* Berkeley CA, Oxford: University of California Press; Cesar Majul, 1988. "The Moro Struggle in the Philippines". *Third World Quarterly* 10 (2): 897–922.

6 This relationship also gave Abu Sayyaf other advantages. Osama bin Laden sent Wali Khan Amin Shah, his close friend, to the Philippines to help Janjalani recruit, organize, and establish the Abu Sayyaf, managing large deliveries of weapons via Victor Blout, a Tajik weapons dealer who also supplied al-Qaeda and the Taliban. SOURCE: Donald McNeil, 2002. "Belgium Seeks Arms Deals with Suspected al-Qaeda Ties". *New York Times,* 27 February, 2002, 54.

7 Abdul Rasul Sayyaf also knew and taught Riduan Isamuddin (a.k.a. Hambali, the military leader of Jemaah Islamiyah). Fellman, "Abu Sayyaf Group". 2011.

8 In the seven years of operations, some 360 Indonesians went through training there, establishing the fighting capabilities of many Southeast Asian terror organizations. SOURCE: Justin Hastings,. 2010. *No Man's Land: Globalization, Territory, and Clandestine Groups in Southeast Asia.* Ithaca and London: Cornell University Press.

9 Walton *et al.* call this "affirmative meritocracy" where leadership is pursued and attained, rather than being qualities that are recognized and rewarded. Similarly, Bunker states that pure meritocracies where leaders are selected do not exist; rather, potential leaders aggressively leverage their strengths to obtain their positions. They cite the case of Osama bin Laden as an excellent example of this. SOURCES: Gregory Walton, *et al.* 2013. "Affirmative Meritocracy". *Social Issues and Policy Review* 7 (1): 1–35; Robert Bunker, 2010. "Leadership and OPFOR Networks". *Advancing Policing Leadership; Lessons Learned and Preferable Futures* 6: 122–137.

10 This term comes from a famous speech given by U.S. Secretary of Defense Donald Rumsfeld in 2002 in his response to questions at a Defense Department news briefing in February of that year. Secretary Rumsfeld said: "as we know, there are known knowns – there are things we know we know. We also know there are known unknowns; that is to say, we know there are some things we do not know. But there are also unknown unknowns – the ones we don't know we don't know." SOURCE: U.S. Department of Defense. 2002. "DoD News Briefing Secretary Rumsfeld and Gen Meyers". February 12. Accessed 1 December 2018. http://archive.defense.gov/Transcripts/Transcript.aspx?TranscriptID =2636.

11 There is very little further information about the actual identity of Jurmail (Doc), but he is likely to have been drawn from the ten senior MNLF commanders lured into the Abu Sayyaf. Ruddah for example is most probably Radulan Sahiron, a former senior MNLF officer regarded as one of MNLF's fiercest warriors. SOURCE: Victor Taylor, 2017b. "Evolution of the Abu Sayyaf Group: Part 1". *The Mackenzie Institute.* 21 April. Accessed May 1, 2017. http://mackenzieinstitute.com/evolution-abu-sayyaf-part-1/.

12 Nur Misuari represented the MNLF as the sole voice of the Moro people, which isolated other groups like the MILF, and of course Abu Sayyaf. Publicly, the peace deal signed in Manila in 1996 enjoyed initial public support, but that soon deteriorated. SOURCE: S.P. Harish, 2006. "GRP-MILF Peace Process: The Quest for International and Domestic Legitimacy". *IDDS Commentaries, Southeast Asia and ASEAN*. Accessed 24 October 2018. www.rsis.edu.sg/rsis-publication/idss/760-the-grp-milf-peace-process-t/#.XrAOD5lS9PZ.

13 Andang also had the fearsome moniker of "Commander Robot", a title gained through his cold, callous treatment of prisoners. SOURCE: The Star Online. 2003. "Command Robot Captured". *ASEAN News*. Accessed 13 December 2018. www.the-star.com.my/news/regional/2003/12/08/commander-robot-captured/.

14 Another raid of a Palawan resort in May 2001 netted fifty foreign hostages and other kidnappings a further 140, including Westerners, schoolchildren, and priests. SOURCE: Zachary Abuza, 2010. "The Philippines Chips Away at the Abu Sayyaf Group's Strength". *CTC Sentinel* 3 (4): 11–13.

15 Kreuzer observes that much of the ethnic violence in the Southern Philippines comes from cultural traditions that often pre-date and over-rule Islamic teachings, making them contradictory to Islam. Strict clan thinking and codes of honour demand precedent, and this creates further conflicts with Islamic religious authorities, ideologues, and particularly militants. SOURCE: Peter Kreuzer, 2005. *Political Clans and Violence in the Southern Philippines*. Oslo: Peace Research Institute (PIRO).

16 Zia-Zarifi states that the apex of power in Afghanistan consists of several major warlords, each with a significant geographic, ethnic, and political base of support. Besides Abdul Rasul Sayyaf, others include General Atta and General Dostum in the north, Ismail Khan in the west, Gul Agha Shirzai in the south, Abdul Rasul Sayyaf in the centre, and, the most powerful, Marshall Fahim, the senior vice president and minister of defence. SOURCE: Sam Zia-Zarifi, 2004. "Losing the Peace in Afghanistan". *Human Rights Watch*. Accessed 12 February 2018. www.hrw.org/wr2k45/5.htm.

17 Mohammed Jamal Khalifa was also closely involved with financing and supporting Abu Sayyaf's Indonesia partner organization, Jemaah Islamiyah, and was a primary financing conduit to the group. SOURCE: Aurel Croissant and Daniel Barlow, 2007. "Following the Money Trail: Terrorist Financing and Government Responses in Southeast Asia". *Studies in Conflict and Terrorism* 30 (2): 131–156.

18 Hesterman puts it that all organizations need money to survive, which is true. He wrote "the lifeblood of any nefarious organization is money". Therefore, most organization would engage in criminal activity to support themselves. In the Andang case, it is more about the group's activities supporting the acquisition of wealth. SOURCE: Jennifer Hesterman, 2013. *The Terrorist-Criminal Nexus: An Alliance of International Drug Cartels, Organized Crime, and Terror Groups*. Boca Raton: CRC Press.

19 Andang was later killed in a prison riot at Camp Bagong Diwa prison in southeastern Manila when Andang on other Abu Sayyaf commanders, including Alhamser Limbong (a.k.a. Commander Kosovo) and Nadjmi Sabdulla (a.k.a. Commander Global), tried to break out. Three hundred special police stormed the prison killing Andang and 21 other prisoners. SOURCE: SMH, "Commander Robot among 23 killed in prison siege". *Sydney Morning Herald*. Accessed 3 December 2018. www.smh.com.au/world/commander-robot-among-23-killed-in-prison-siege-20050316-gdkxli.html.

20 For an excellent discussion of the Sulu-based criminal Abu Sayyaf see: Salem Allan Jones. 2016. "Nexus of Crime and Terrorism: The Case of the Abu Sayyaf Group". Monterey: Naval Postgraduate School.

21 Khadaffy and Janjalani's other brother, Hector, was not considered for leadership. Although incarcerated in Bilibid prison, he we was a senior Abu Sayyaf leader but he

did not possess the strong leadership credentials necessary. SOURCE: Eduardo Ugarte, 2008. "The Phenomenon of Kidnapping in the Southern Philippines: An overview". *Journal of South East Asia Research* 16 (3): 293–341.

22 The May 2017 siege of Marawi is a keystone example. Abu Sayyaf and BIFF fighters in conjunction with the Maute Group took control of Marawi, a lakeside city and important economic centre in Mindanao, the second-largest Island in the Philippines. The siege lasted for five months before Abu Sayyaf and its forces retreated. Marawi was the most significant urban warfare to occur since the Battle of Manila in World War II. SOURCE: ICG, 2018. "Philippines: Addressing Islamist Militancy after the Battle for Marawi". *International Crisis Group: Commentary Asia.* Accessed 12 January 2019. www.crisisgroup.org/asia/south-east-asia/philippines/philippines-addressing-islamist-militancy-after-battle-marawi.

23 The War on Terror, initiated by President Bush, is a multidimensional military campaign with extremely broad scope to engage threats globally. SOURCES: Mary Habeck, 2007. *Knowing the Enemy: Jihadist Ideology and the War on Terror.* New Haven: Yale University Press; Ian Lustick, 2006. *Trapped in the War on Terror.* Philadelphia: University of Pennsylvania Press.

24 Abu Sayyaf and al-Qaeda have been designated Foreign Terrorist Organizations since 1993 when al-Qaeda bomb maker Ramzi Ahmed had undertaken significant planning and operational activity in Manila when organizing the 1993 World Trade Centre Attacks in New York. Abu Sayyaf has continued to be listed every year since then on the State Department terror list. SOURCES: Vali Nasr, 2000. "International Politics, Domestic Imperatives, and Identity Mobilization: Sectarianism in Pakistan, 1979–1998". *Journal of Comparative Politics* 32 (2): 171–190; Paul Pillar, 2001. *Terrorism and U.S. Foreign Policy.* Washington, D.C.: Brookings Institution Press.

25 President Bush gave U.S.$100 million in military assistance to the Philippines in 2002. This included a C-130 transport plane and 16,000 pounds of military hardware. On 20 December, the U.S. Army sent 30 sniper rifles, 25 81mm mortars, and 350 M-203 grenade launchers. Philippine officials said the equipment package would also include eight UH-1 "Huey" helicopters, Cyclone-class patrol boats, and 30,000 M-16 infantry rifles with 120,000 magazines. Other items on their wish list are twelve AH-1 "Cobra" attack helicopters and an unmanned reconnaissance plane, or "drone". In mid-January, the first contingent of a scheduled 650 U.S. troops arrived in the Philippines to train with and advise Philippine forces in their campaign against Abu Sayyaf. SOURCES: George Bush, 2001. "Joint Statement between the United States of America and the Republic of the Philippines". *The White House, Office of the Press Secretary.* 20 September 2001. Accessed 20 November 2019. https://georgewbush-whitehouse.archives.gov/news/releases/2001/11/20011120-13.html; Human Rights Watch, 2002. "Changes to U.S. Military Assistance After September 11". *Dangerous Dealings* 14 (1): 11–12.

26 Created using ESOC data. Attack data are for all threat groups in Basilan, Sulu, and Tawi-Tawi provinces between 2000 and 2012. The total number of attacks in these three provinces declined from 73 in 2000 to 32 in 2012. SOURCE: Empirical Studies of Conflict, 2018. "Philippines". Princeton University. Accessed 2 March 2018. https://esoc.princeton.edu/.

27 Solaiman "Sali" was born in Basilan and was a prominent figure in Abu Sayyaf. He acted as a spokesman during his career with the group and is regarded as the highest-ranking Abu Sayyaf leader to be killed by U.S.-backed forces in the area. He had a U.S.-imposed U.S.$5 million bounty on his head. SOURCE: Al Jacinto, 2007. "Senior Abu Sayyaf Leader Abu Solaiman Shot Dead". *Arab News.* 1 January. Accessed 22 March 2017. www.arabnews.com/node/293358.

28 From June 2008 Abu Sayyaf kidnapped Filipina journalist Ces Drilon and a cameraman, then three Red Cross workers followed by two Chinese fishermen in November

2009. It also kidnapped several Filipinos and beheaded a schoolteacher. SOURCES: Carlos Conde, 2008. "Abu Sayyaf Free Kidnapped News Crew in Philippines". *The New York Times*. Accessed 29 December 2018. www.nytimes.com/2008/06/19/world/asia/19filip.html; Mananghava, James. 2009. "Abu Sayyaf behead Sulu Principal". *Phil Star Global*. Accessed 5 May 2019. www.philstar.com/headlines/2009/11/10/521710/abus-behead-sulu-principal.

29 Espejo (2013) writes that Abu Sayyaf has killed over 300 civilians in just 12 years in its bombing campaign. SOURCE: Edwin Espejo, 2013. "Mindanao bombs: over 300 killed in 12 years". Rappler News. Accessed 31 December 2018. www.rapplercom/nation/35493-mindanao-bombs-300-killed-12-years.

30 Herbert Burns (2005) asserts that Abu Sayyaf targets ferries because they are the most vulnerable types of vessels and their purpose is the mass movement of people, making them attractive terrorist targets. Likewise, the high-tempo operations of ferries precludes many security options for bomb-sweeping and other basic security arrangements. SOURCE: Rupert Herbert-Burns, 2005. "Terrorism in the Early 21st Century Maritime Domain". In *The Best of Times, The Worst of Times: Maritime Security in the Asia Pacific*, eds. Joshua Ho and Catherine Raymond. Singapore: Worldwide Scientific, 155–177.

31 Beheading military personnel is common for Abu Sayyaf. On 10 July 2007, three years earlier, Abu Sayyaf beheaded fourteen AFP Marines, and in 2011 a further five. SOURCES: Jolo Malig, 2011. "Al'Barka: How Villagers Killed Marines, Special Forces Troops". *ABS-CBN News*. Accessed 15 June 2019. https://news.abs-cbn.com/-depth/10/19/11/al-barka-how-villagers-killed-marines-special-forces-troops; D.J. Yap and Julie Alipala, 2011. "5 Marines beheaded by Abu Sayyaf; Aquino Mad". *The Inquirer*. Accessed 15 October 2018. https://newsinfo.inquirer.net/33101/5-marines-beheaded-by-abu-sayyaf-aquino-mad.

32 Other examples include Jemaah Islamiyah master bomb-makers Dulmatin and Umar Patek, both of whom were forced out of Indonesia because of external pressures and sought refuge with Abu Sayyaf in Sulu where they hid from Indonesian authorities. SOURCE: Abuza, "The Philippines Chips Away at the Abu Sayyaf Group's Strength". 11–13.

33 In 2006, a Public Employment Services Office (PESO) in Guihulngan, Philippines referenced that Abu Sayyaf recruiters promised prospective new members a monthly salary of P20,000. SOURCE: GMA. 2006. "Aby Sayyaf scouting for recruits in Visayas towns". *GMA News*. Accessed 31 December 2018. www.gmanetwork.com/news/news/nation/25039/abu-sayyaf-scouting-for-recruits-in-visayas-towns/story/.

34 The Communist insurgency in the Philippines dates back to the 1960s and the New People's Army continues to be a serious insurgent threat. Likewise, against the backdrop of the Cold War, U.S. President Nixon and the CIA were also deeply concerned about communism in Asia as they fought their war in Vietnam. For excellent resources on the NPA see: Fedor Alexander Mediansky and Dianne Court, 1984. *The Soviet Union in Southeast Asia*. Canberra: Strategic and Defence Studies Centre, Australian National University; Justus Van Der Kroef, 1973. "Communism and Reform in the Philippines". *Journal of Public Affairs* 46 (1): 29–58.

35 Marcos was an authoritarian president who ruled in the Philippines from 1972 to 1986, when he was removed from power in a military coup by long-time ally Juan Ponce-Enrile with the popular backing of the people. SOURCE: Albert Celoza, 1997. *Ferdinand Marcos and the Philippines: The Political Economy of Authoritarianism*. Westport: Greenwood Publishing Group.

36 This included the Marcos Period (1972 to 1986) during which President Marcos had a firm policy of Total War against the insurgency in the Southern Philippines. This was a full-blown conventional fight in which MNLF took control of Mindanao and Jolo. According to Ricardo (2003), MNLF engaged and bogged down over 50 battalions of

the Armed Forces of the Philippines for several years. In this period up to 60,000 people died and more than 200,000 took refuge in neighbouring states. SOURCE: David Ricardo. 2003. *The Causes and Prospect of The Southern Philippines Secessionist Movement*. Monterey: Naval Postgraduate School.

37 The Tripoli Agreement halted the conflict and started the process for autonomy, commencing in 1987, but the MNLF soon abandoned it. The MNLF wanted far more than Aquino was willing to offer, seeking 14 southern provinces under their control rather than the five on offer by the government. Coupled with frequent low-intensity contacts between forces, the MNLF lost faith. The government went ahead with constitutional changes, such as the Autonomous Region of Muslim Mindanao (ARMM) that was created in February 1987, but this exacerbated tensions rather than soothing them. SOURCES: Ronald May, 1990. "Ethnic Separatism in Southeast Asia". *Pacific Viewpoint* 31 (2): 28–59; Federico Magdalena, 1997. "The Peace Process in Mindanao: Problems and Prospects". *Journal of Southeast Asian Affairs* 1991: 245–259.

38 Aquino's government suffered from conflicts in civilian and executive-military relations and agreement on how to deal with the insurgency. Powerful military members caused political instability and the executive branch was destabilized by successive coup attempts and plots. Unable to exercise full control over the military, many insurgent groups found reason to abandon peace efforts and return to a state of war. Contributing to the weaknesses in soft power initiatives, many substantive and meaningful reforms to address Muslim grievances were blocked in Congress as political power actors pursued their own agendas, often in line with powerful military figures. SOURCE: Noel Morada and Christopher Collier, 2001. "The Philippines: State versus Society". In *Asian Security Practice Manual and Ideational Influences*, ed. Muthiah Alagappa. California, Stanford University Press.

39 Official government figures report that the government had spent U.S.$2.78 billion in the 26-year conflict with the Moros. Of the 100,000 recorded casualties, half were Moro with government forces accounting for 30 per cent and civilians the remaining 20 per cent of casualties. SOURCE: UNHCR 2004, *Minorities at Risk Project*. United Nations. Accessed 15 October 2018. www.refworld.org/publisher,MARP,,VEN,,,0.html.

40 The 14 provinces spanned Abu Sayyaf territories and bases of operation. These areas included Davao del Sur, Basilan, Cotabato, Lanao, Lanao del Norte, Palawan, Maguindanao, Palawan, Sarangani, Sulu, South Cotabato, Sultan Kudarat, Tawi-Tawi, Zamboanga del Sur, and Zamboanga del Norte. SOURCE: Rizal Buendia, 2004. "The GRP-MILF Peace Talks: Quo Vadis?" *Journal of Southeast Asian Affairs* 2004 (2004): 205–221.

41 It was also hoped that Nur Misuari's appointment would calm international concerns and attract investment into the region by ASEAN member nations. SOURCE: Eliseo Mercado, 2001. "Social-Cultural Cleavages and the Peace Process in the Southern Philippines". In *Social Cohesion and Conflict Prevention in Asia: Managing Diversity Through Development*, eds. Nat Colletta *et al.*, Washington, D.C.: The World Bank, 418–427.

42 The AFP attacked an Abu Sayyaf mountain base of operations with artillery and gunships killing at least 12 Abu Sayyaf members. Clashes between MILF and government AFP forces also resulted in heavy casualties. In response, President Estrada declared "all-out war" on MILF and Abu Sayyaf, storming 50 MILF camps, killing MILF fighters, and dispersing the rest. SOURCES: Ronald May, 2001. "Muslim Mindanao: Four Years after the Peace Agreement". *Journal of Southeast Asian Affairs* 1 (1): 263–275; Nathan Gilbert Quimpo, 2000. "Back to War in Mindanao: The Weaknesses of a Power-Based Approach to Conflict". *Philippine Political Science Journal* 21 (44): 118–121.

43 In July 2003, President Arroyo signed the ceasefire agreement with MILF and opened further peace talks to take place in Malaysia. As a gesture of goodwill, the

government agreed to drop all arrest warrants of MILF leaders. President Arroyo stated, "As we address the roots of rebellion and secession, I am confident that we shall also effectively isolate and marginalize the dwindling terrorist cells in Mindanao and across our seas in the region." SOURCE: Republic of the Philippines, 2003. "The President's Day". *Official Gazette of the Republic of the Philippines*. Accessed 15 August 2018. www.officialgazette.gov.ph/2003/05/17/the-presidents-day-may-17-2003/.

44 Eckert reports that 2006 was a good example in which joint operations resulted in the establishment of 10 wells, the building and renovation of 19 schools, 5 community centres, 5 road projects, and 5 water-distribution centres in Jolo alone. SOURCE: William Eckert, 2006. "Defeating the Idea: Unconventional Warfare in the Southern Philippines". *Special Warfare: The Professional Bulletin of the John F. Kennedy Special Warfare Center & School* 19 (6): 15–22.

45 According to Hart, since Marawi ended, the Abu Sayyaf has been hounded by the military, which has consistently attacked its hideouts and forced the group onto the back foot. Small Abu Sayyaf groups have returned to crime to raise funds. SOURCE: Michael Hart, 2018. "A Year After Marawi, What's Left of ISIS in the Philippines?" *The Diplomat*. Accessed 12 June 2019. https://thediplomat.com/2018/10/a-year-after-marawi-whats-left-of-isis-in-the-philippines/.

46 The July 2018 suicide attack was carried out by the Moroccan Abu Kathir al-Maghribi, who had a personal grievance against security forces. SOURCE: GMA, 2018. "Lorenzana says Moroccan national eyed in Basilan blast". *GMA News*. Accessed 13 November 2018. www.gmanetwork.com/news/news/nation/663642/lorenzana-says-moroccan-national-eyed-in-basilan-blast/story/.

47 Warren Rodwell (see Figure 6.5) was kidnapped from his home in Ipil by four men dressed in police uniforms. Three were Abu Sayyaf, but the fourth was Jun Malban, a policeman. Malban is also the cousin of Abu Sayyaf leader Khair Mundos. East states that areas where Abu Sayyaf operate are well known as being frontier lands dominated by corrupt police, politicians, and powerful warlords. SOURCES: Agency France-Presse, 2015. "Philippines policeman arrested over kidnap of Australian Warren Rodwell". *The Guardian*. Accessed 30 May 2019. www.theguardian.com/world/2015/may/19/philippines-policeman-arrested-over-kidnap-of-australian-warren-rodwell2015; Robert East, 2016. *472 Days Captive of the Abu Sayyaf*. Newcastle, UK: Cambridge Scholars Publishing.

References

Abuza, Zachary. 2005. *Balik-Terrorism: The Return of the Abu Sayyaf*. Carlisle: Strategic Studies Institute, Army War College.

Abuza, Zachary. 2010. "The Philippines Chips Away at the Abu Sayyaf Group's Strength". *CTC Sentinel* 3 (4): 11–13.

Abuza, Zachary. 2017. "Why Vietnam Must Fight the Islamic State Terror Threat". *The Diplomat*. 3 August. Accessed 5 April 2020. https://thediplomat.com/2017/08/why-vietnam-must-fight-the-islamic-state-terror-threat/

Agency France-Presse, 2015. "Philippines policeman arrested over kidnap of Australian Warren Rodwell". *The Guardian*. Accessed 30 May 2019. www.theguardian.com/world/2015/may/19/philippines-policeman-arrested-over-kidnap-of-australian-warren-rodwell2015

Attwell, Rob. 2017. "Criminals With a Cause: The Crime-Terror Nexus in the Southern Philippines". *The Diplomat*. 11 April. Accessed 15 June 2017. https://thediplomat.com/2017/04/criminals-with-a-cause-the-crime-terror-nexus-in-the-southern-philippines/.

Bacon, Tricia. 2018. "A Theory of Alliance hubs and Alliance Formation". In *Why Terrorist Groups Form International Alliances*, edited by Tricia Bacon, 27–63. Philadelphia: University of Pennsylvania Press.

Bale, Jeffrey. 2010. *The Abu Sayyaf Group in its Philippine and International Contexts.* Middlebury, Vermont: Middlebury Institute of International Studies at Monterey.

Basra, Rajan and Neumann, Peter. 2016. "Criminal Pasts, Terrorist Futures: European Jihadists and the New Crime-Terror Nexus". *Perspectives on Terrorism* 10 (6): 25–40.

Bertrand, Jacques. 2000. "Peace and Conflict in the Southern Philippines: Why the 1996 Peace Agreement Is Fragile". *Pacific Affairs* 73 (1): 37–54.

Billington, Gail. 1995. "Afghani-Linked Terror in the Philippines". *Executive Intelligence Review* 13 (10): 33–36.

Buendia, Rizal. 2004. "The GRP-MILF Peace Talks: Quo Vadis?" *Journal of Southeast Asian Affairs* 2004 (2004): 205–221.

Bunker, Robert. 2010. "Leadership and OPFOR Networks". *Advancing Policing Leadership; Lessons Learned and Preferable Futures* 6: 122–137.

Bush, George W. 2003. "Remarks by the President to the Philippine Congress". Manila: United States Department of State.

Celoza, Albert. 1997. *Ferdinand Marcos and the Philippines: The Political Economy of Authoritarianism*. Westport: Greenwood Publishing Group.

Chalk, Peter. 2016. "The Islamic State in the Philippines: A Looming Shadow in Southeast Asia?" *CTC Sentinel* 9 (3): 10–14.

Chew, Amy. 2019. "Islamic State 'wolf pack' in Malaysia planned wave of terror attacks, police say after detaining four suspects in sting operation". *South China Morning Post.* 13 May. Accessed 5 July 2019. www.scmp.com/news/asia/southeast-asia/article/3010061/islamic-state-wolf-pack-malaysia-planned-wave-terror.

Conde, Carlos. 2008. "Abu Sayyaf Free Kidnapped News Crew in Philippines". 2008; Mananghava, "Abu Sayyaf behead Sulu Principal". *The New York Times.* Accessed 29 December 2018. www.nytimes.com/2008/06/19/world/asia/19filip.html.

Croissant, Aurel and Barlow, Daniel. 2007. "Following the Money Trail: Terrorist Financing and Government Responses in Southeast Asia". *Studies in Conflict and Terrorism* 30 (2): 131–156.

Dinampo, Octavio. 2007. "A Last Extended Interview with Janjalani". *Philippine Daily Inquirer*, 22 January: 1.

Dudley, Dominic. 2018. "The Deadliest Terrorist Groups In The World". *Forbes.* 5 December. Accessed 16 December 2018. www.forbes.com/sites/dominicdudley/2018/12/05/deadliest-terrorist-groups-in-the-world/#6cabed472b3e.

Duenas, M. 1994. "Servants of Allah or Terrorists?" *Philippines Free Press*, 22 January: 10.

East, Robert. 2013. "The Turning Point and the Death of Abu Sayyaf". In *Terror Truncated: The Decline of the Abu Sayyaf Group from the Crucial Year 2002*, edited by Robert East, 23–35. Newcastle: Cambridge Scholars Publishing.

East, Robert. 2016. *472 Days Captive of the Abu Sayyaf*. Newcastle, UK: Cambridge Scholars Publishing.

Eckert, William. 2006. "Defeating the Idea: Unconventional Warfare in the Southern Philippines". *Special Warfare: The Professional Bulletin of the John F. Kennedy Special Warfare Center & School* 19 (6): 15.

Espejo, Edwin. 2013. "Mindanao bombs: over 300 killed in 12 years". *Rappler.* Accessed 31 December 2018. www.rapplercom/nation/35493-mindanao-bombs-300-killed-12-years.

Empirical Studies of Conflict. 2018. "Philippines". Princeton university. Accessed 2 March 2018. https://esoc.princeton.edu/.

Fellman, Zack. 2015. "Abu Sayyaf Group". *AQAM Futures Project Case Study Series, Case Study Number 5* (Nov. 2011): Center for Strategic and International Studies.

Ferrer, Miriam. 2005. "The Moro and the Cordillera Conflicts in the Philippines". In *Ethnic Conflicts in Southeast Asia*, edited by Kusuma Snitwongse and Willard Thompson, 109–151. Bangkok: ISIS Institute for International and Security Studies.

Franco, Joseph. 2017. "Assessing the Feasibility of a 'Wilayah Mindanao'". *Perspectives on Terrorism* 11 (4): 29–38.

Galula, D. 1964. "The Prerequisites for a Successful Insurgency". In *Counterinsurgency Warfare: Theory and Practice*, edited by F. Praeger, 13–31. New York: Praeger.

Garcia, Teofilo. 2018. "Abu Sayyaf man linked to mass kidnap in Basilan". *Republic of the Philippines, Philippines News Agency.* 10 March. Accessed 5 June 2018. www.pna.gov.ph/articles/1028182.

GMA. 2006. "Aby Sayyaf scouting for recruits in Visayas towns". *GMA News.* Accessed 31 December 2018. www.gmanetwork.com/news/news/nation/25039/abu-sayyaf-scouting-for-recruits-in-visayas-towns/story/.

GMA. 2010. "AFP Expects new ASG leader to emerge". *GMA News.* 23 February. Accessed 11 December 2017. www.gmanetwork.com/news/news/regions/184539/afp-expects-new-abu-sayyaf-leader-to-emerge/story/?related.

GMA, 2018 "Lorenzana says Moroccan national eyed in Basilan blast". *GMA News.* Accessed 13 November 2018. www.gmanetwork.com/news/news/nation/663642/lorenzana-says-moroccan-national-eyed-in-basilan-blast/story/.

Gutierrez, Jason. 2019. "British Man and Filipino Woman Abducted in Philippines". *The New York Times.* 5 October. Accessed 4 April 2020. www.nytimes.com/2019/10/05/world/asia/philippines-kidnapping-british-man-militants.html.

Habeck, Mary. 2007. *Knowing the Enemy: Jihadist Ideology and the War on Terror.* New Haven: Yale University Press.

Hall, Rosalie. 2009. "From Rebels to Soldiers: An Analysis of the Philippine and East Timorese Policy Integrating Former Moro National Liberation Front (Mnlf) and Falintil Combatants into the Armed Forces". Toronto: APSA 2009 Toronto Meeting Paper.

Hall, Rosalie. 2010. "Boots on Unstable Ground: Democratic Governance of the Armed Forces under post 9/11 US-Philippine Military Relations". *Asia-Pacific Social Science Review* 10 (2): 25–41.

Hammerberg, Kathleen and Faber, Pamela. 2017. *Abu Sayyaf Group (ASG): An Al-Qaeda Associate Case Study.* Arlington. Center for Naval Analyses (CNA).

Harish, S.P. 2006. "GRP-MILF Peace Process: The Quest for International and Domestic Legitimacy". *IDSS Commentaries, Southeast Asia and ASEAN.* Accessed 24 October 2018. www.rsis.edu.sg/rsis-publication/idss/760-the-grp-milf-peace-process-t/#.XrAOD5l-S9PZ.

Hart, Michael. 2018. "A Year After Marawi, What's Left of ISIS in the Philippines?" *The Diplomat.* Accessed 12 June 2019. https://thediplomat.com/2018/10/a-year-after-marawi-whats-left-of-isis-in-the-philippines/.

Hastings, Justin. 2010. *No Man's Land: Globalization, Territory, and Clandestine Groups in Southeast Asia.* Ithaca and London: Cornell University Press.

Hedman, Eva-Lotta. 2006. "The Philippines in 2005: Old Dynamics, New Conjuncture". *Asian Survey* 46 (1): 187–193.

Herbert-Burns, Rupert. 2005. "Terrorism in the Early 21st Century Maritime Domain". In *The Best of Times, The Worst of Times: Maritime Security in the Asia*

Pacific, edited by Joshua Ho and Catherine Raymond, 155–177. Singapore: Worldwide Scientific.

Hesterman, Jennifer. 2013. *The Terrorist-Criminal Nexus: An Alliance of International Drug Cartels, Organized Crime, and Terror Groups*. Boca Raton, CRC Press.

Hookway, James. 2000. "Philippine Rebels Gree Five Hostages for $5 Million Ransom from Libya". *The Wall Street Journal.* 28 August. Accessed 15 July 2017. www.wsj.com/articles/SB967364748866013168.

Human Rights Watch. 2002. "Changes to U.S. Military Assistance After September 11". *Dangerous Dealings* 14 (1): 11–12.

ICG, 2018. "Philippines: Addressing Islamist Militancy after the Battle for Marawi". *International Crisis Group: Commentary Asia.* Accessed 12 January 2019. www.crisisgroup.org/asia/south-east-asia/philippines/philippines-addressing-islamist-militancy-after-battle-marawi.

Jacinto, Al. 2007. "Senior Abu Sayyaf Leader Abu Solaiman Shot Dead". *Arab News.* 1 January. Accessed 22 March 2017. www.arabnews.com/node/293358.

Jones, Salem Allan. 2016. *Nexus of Crime and Terrorism: The Case of the Abu Sayyaf Group*. Monterey: Naval Postgraduate School.

Kreuzer, Peter. 2005. *Political Clans and Violence in the Southern Philippines.* Oslo: Peace Research Institute (PIRO).

Lara, Francisco and Chapman, Phil. 2009. *Inclusive Peace in Muslim Mindanao: Revisiting the Dynamics of Conflict and Exclusion.* London: International Alert.

Lustick, Ian. 2006. *Trapped in the War on Terror.* Philadelphia: University of Pennsylvania Press.

MacKinnin, Ian. 2007. "Philippine Military Kills Abu Sayyaf Leader". *The Guardian.* 18 January. Accessed 16 August 2017. www.theguardian.com/world/2007/jan/17/alqaida.terrorism.

Magdalena, Federico. 1997. "The Peace Process in Mindanao: Problems and Prospects". *Journal of Southeast Asian Affairs* 1991: 245–259.

Majul, Cesar. 1988. "The Moro Struggle in the Philippines". *Third World Quarterly* 10 (2): 897–922.

Makarenko, Tamara. 2004. "The Crime–Terror Continuum: Tracing the Interplay between Transnational Organised Crime and Terrorism". *Global Crime* 6 (1): 129–145.

Malig, Jolo. 2011. "Al'Barka: How Villagers Killed Marines, Special Forces Troops". *ABS-CBN News.* Accessed 15 June 2019. https://news.abs-cbn.com/-depth/10/19/11/al-barka-how-villagers-killed-marines-special-forces-troops.

Maloney, Sean. 2015. "Army of darkness: The jihadist training system in Pakistan and Afghanistan, 1996–2001". *Small Wars & Insurgencies* 26 (3): 518–541.

Mananghava, James. 2009. "Abu Sayyaf behead Sulu Principal". *Phil Star Global.* Accessed 5 May 2019. www.philstar.com/headlines/2009/11/10/521710/abus-behead-sulu-principal.

May, Ronald. 1990. "Ethnic Separatism in Southeast Asia". *Pacific Viewpoint* 31 (2): 28–59.

May, Ronald. 2001. "Muslim Mindanao: Four Years After the Peace Agreement". *Journal of Southeast Asian Affairs* 1 (1): 263–275.

McKenna, Thomas. 1998. *Muslim Rulers and Rebels: Everyday Politics and Armed Separatism in the Southern Philippines.* Berkeley, LA; Oxford: University of California Press.

McNeil, Donald. 2002. "Belgium Seeks Arms Deals with Suspected al-Qaeda Ties". *New York Times,* 27 February, 54.

Mediansky, Fedor Alexander and Court, Dianne. 1984. *The Soviet Union in Southeast Asia*. Canberra, Strategic and Defence Studies Centre: Australian National University.

Mercado, Eliseo. 2001. "Social-Cultural Cleavages and the Peace Process in the Southern Philippines". In *Social Cohesion and Conflict Prevention in Asia: Managing Diversity Through Development*, edited by Nat Colletta, Teck Ghee Lim, and Anita Kelles-Viitanen, 418–427. Washington, D.C.: The World Bank.

Michael, George. 2007. "The Legend and Legacy of Abu Musab al-Zarqawi". *Journal of Defence Studies* 7 (3): 338–357.

Montlake, Simon. 2010. "Philippines Kills Abu Sayyaf Most Wanted Albader Parad". *Christian Science Monitor*. 22 February. Accessed 25 June 2017. www.csmonitor.com/World/Asia-Pacific/2010/0222/Philippines-kills-Abu-Sayyaf-most-wanted-Albader-Parad.

Morada, Noel. 2003. "Philippine-American Security Relations After 11 September: Exploring the Mutuality of Interests in the Fight Against International Terrorism". In *Southeast Asian Affairs*, edited by Chin Kin Wah and Daljit Singh, 228–238. Singapore: Institute of South East Asian Studies.

na Thalang, Chanintira. 2017. "Malaysia's Role in Two South-East Asian Insurgencies: 'An Honest Broker'?" *Australian Journal of International Affairs* 71 (4): 389–404.

Nasr, Vali. 2000. "International Politics, Domestic Imperatives, and Identity Mobilization: Sectarianism in Pakistan, 1979–1998". *Journal of Comparative Politics* 32 (2): 171–190.

Noble, Lela. 1976. "The Moro National Liberation Front in the Philippines". *Journal of Pacific Affairs* 49 (3): 405–424.

O'Brien, McKenzie. 2012. "Fluctuations Between Crime and Terror: The Case of Abu Sayyaf's Kidnapping Activities". *Terrorism and Political Violence* 24 (2): 320–336.

Overholt, William. 1986. "The Rise and Fall of Ferdinand Marcos". *Asian Survey* 26 (11): 1137–1163.

Ozaeta, Arnell. 2009. "12 Bombs Found on Lucena Ferry". *Philippine Star*, 27 July: 1.

Pillar, Paul. 2001. *Terrorism and U.S. Foreign Policy*. Washington, D.C.: Brookings Institution Press.

Quimpo, Nathan Gilbert. 2000. "Back to War in Mindanao: The Weaknesses of a Power-Based Approach to Conflict". *Philippine Political Science Journal* 21 (44): 118–121.

Ramos, Fidel V. 2000. "Erap: Reform or Resign: Hindsights and Insights into E-Mindanao Peace and Development". Kusog, Mindanao: Prospects of Recovery and Reconstruction in the Light of the Recurring War and National Economic and Leadership Crisis Conference.

Reilly, Benjamin. 2002. "Internal Conflict and Regional Security in Asia and the Pacific". *Pacifica Review: Peace, Security & Global Change* 14 (1): 7–21.

Republic of the Philippines. 2003. "The President's Day". *Official Gazette of the Republic of the Philippines*. Accessed 15 August 2018. www.officialgazette.gov.ph/2003/05/17/the-presidents-day-may-17-2003.

Ricardo, David. 2003. *The Causes and Prospect of The Southern Philippines Secessionist Movement*. Monterey: Naval Postgraduate School.

Richburg, Keith. 1995. "Spoilers of Peace". *Washington Post*, 25 May: 33.

Rivera, Carla. 2012. *Philippines Cooperation on Terrorism: The Fight Against The Abu Sayyaf Group Since 9/11*. Washington, D.C.: Georgetown University Press.

Robinson, Linda, Johnston, Patrick, and Oak, Gillian. 2016. *U.S. Special Operations Forces in the Philippines, 2001–2014*. Santa Monica: RAND.

Rood, Steve. 2012. "Interlocking Autonomy: Manila and Muslim Mindanao". In *Autonomy and Armed Separation in South and Souteast Asia*, edited by Michelle Ann Miller, 256–278. Singapore: ISEAS – Institute of Southeast Asian Studies.

Salem, Allan Jones. 2016. *Nexus of crime and terrorism: the case of the Abu Sayyaf Group*. Thesis. Monterey, CA: Naval Postgraduate School.

Schiavo-Campo, Salvatore and Judd, Mary. 2005. "The Mindanao Conflict in the Philippines: roots, costs, and potential peace dividends". *Social Development Papers: Conflict Prevention and Reconstruction* 24 (2): 1–23.

Shah, Pir. 2010. "Drone Reportedly Killed Filippino in Pakistan". *The New York Times*. 21 January. Accessed 5 January 2017. www.nytimes.com/2010/01/22/world/asia/22pstan.html.

Skipton, Leonard. 2013. "The History and Current Status of Organizational and Systems Change". In *The Wiley-Blackwell Handbook of the Psychology of Leadership, Change, and Organizational Development*, edited by Leonard Skipton, Rachel Lewis, Arthur Freedman, and Jonathan Passmore, 237–266. New Jersey: John Wiley & Sons.

SMH, 2005. "Commander Robot among 23 killed in prison siege". *Sydney Morning Herald*. Accessed 3 December 2018. www.smh.com.au/world/commander-robot-among-23-killed-in-prison-siege-20050316-gdkxli.html.

SMH. 2007. "Militants kill 14 Philippine marines, behead 10: military". *Sydney Morning Herald*. 11 July. Accessed 17 November 2017. www.smh.com.au/world/militants-kill-14-philippine-marines-behead-10-military-20070711-n73.html.

Stentiford, Barry. 2018. *Success in the Shadows Operation Enduring Freedom – Philippines and the Global War on Terror, 2002–2015*. Leavenworth: Combat Studies Institute Press.

Sunstar. 2003. "Commander Robot's Capture Big Blow to Abu Sayyaf". *The Sun Star*. 8 December. Accessed 18 February 2017. www.sunstar.com.ph/static/net/2003/12/08/commander.robot.s.capture.big.blow.to.abu.sayyaf.html.

Swaak-Goldman, Olivia and Nybondas, Maria. 2006. "International Criminal Courts Roundup". In *Yearbook of International Humanitarian Law, Volume 6*, edited by Timothy McCormack, 292–318. The Hague: T.M.C. Asser Press.

Taylor, Victor. 2017a. "Terrorist Activities of the Abu Sayyaf". *The Mackenzie Institute*. 14 March. Accessed 5 May 2018. http://mackenzieinstitute.com/terrorist-activities-abu-sayyaf/.

Taylor, Victor. 2017b. "Evolution of the Abu Sayyaf Group: Part 1". *The Mackenzie Institute*. 21 April. Accessed 1 May 2017. http://mackenzieinstitute.com/evolution-abu-sayyaf-part-1/.

The Star Online. 2003. "Command Robot Captured". *ASEAN News*. Accessed 13 December 2018. www.thestar.com.my/news/regional/2003/12/08/commander-robot-captured/.

Torres, Jose. 2007. "Wahab Akbar: The Terror of Basilan". *GMA NEws*. 14 November. Accessed 15 June 2017. www.gmanetwork.com/news/news/specialreports/68626/wahab-akbar-the-terror-of-basilan/story/.

Turner, Mark. 1995. "Terrorism and Secession in the Southern Philippines: The Rise of the Abu Sayaff". *Contemporary Southeast Asia* 17 (1): 1–19.

Ugarte, Eduardo. 2008. "The Phenomenon of Kidnapping in the Southern Philippines: An overview". *Journal of South East Asia Research* 16 (3): 293–341.

UNHCR. 2004. *Minorities at Risk Project*. United Nations. Accessed 15 October 2018. www.refworld.org/publisher,MARP,,VEN,,,0.html.

U.S. Department of Defense. 2002. "DoD News Briefing Secretary Rumsfeld and Gen Meyers". February 12. Accessed 1 December 2018. http://archive.defense.gov/ Transcripts/Transcript.aspx?TranscriptID=2636.

Van Der Kroef, Justus. 1973. "Communism and Reform in the Philippines". *Journal of Public Affairs* 46 (1): 29–58.

Villamor, Felipe. 2018. "Philippine Bombing Kills 10, Showing Insurgents Remain a Problem". *New York Times*. 30 July. Accessed 16 December 2018. www.nytimes. com/2018/07/30/world/asia/philippines-bombing-abu-sayyaf.html.

Wadi, J.M. 2003. "They've come this far". *Newsbreak* January–June (1): 16–19.

Walton, Gregory and Spencer, Steven and Erman, Sam. 2013. "Affirmative Meritocracy". *Social Issues and Policy Review* 7 (1): 1–35.

Wright-Neville, David. 2004. "Dangerous Dynamics: Activists, Militants and Terrorists in Southeast Asia". *The Pacific Review* 17 (1): 27–46.

Yap, D.J. and Alipala, Julie. 2011. "5 Marines beheaded by Abu Sayyaf; Aquino Mad". *The Inquirer*. Accessed 15 October 2018. https://newsinfo.inquirer.net/33101/5-marines-beheaded-by-abu-sayyaf-aquino-mad.

Yegar, Moshe. 2002. "Part Three: The Moro Muslims". In *Between Integration and Succession: The Muslim Communities of the Southern Philippines, Southern Thailand, and Western Burma/Myanmar*. Lanham, Boulder, New York, and London: Lexington Books.

Zia-Zarifi, Sam. 2004. "Losing the Peace in Afghanistan". *Human Rights Watch*. Accessed 12 February 2018. www.hrw.org/wr2k45/5.htm.

Zenn, Jacob. 2011. "Demise of Philippine's Abu Sayyaf Terrorist Group Begins in Abbottabad". *Terrorism Monitor* 9 (21): 4–6.

7 Findings

This book began by pointing to the paucity of theory on the relationship between resilience and the structures of insurgent organizations. The role of organizational structure, either familial or meritocratic, in maintaining ongoing operational and political perpetuity was this book's primary focus. The book therefore looked into the question of how familial and meritocratic structures affect organizational resilience in response to an incumbent's counterinsurgency strategies. The explicit type and vigour of application of external pressures cannot be completely controlled as a variable, but the book has been able to hold it relatively constant by pair selection across the case studies, meaning that the most significant change has occurred in the area of interest, being the resilience of meritocratic versus familial structures.[1]

This book found that social trust is the primary means of organizational efficiency, which in turn is the major predicator of insurgent resilience. Social capital and trust function differently between familial and meritocratic organizations because there are different socio-economic values and different person-to-person transaction needs in familial versus meritocratic organizations. The different nature of the functions of social capital and trust in organizations help them respond to external pressures in different ways. This occurred in the case studies, while the variable of external pressures was relatively constant and stable.

For example, the Haqqani Network and Lashkar-e-Taiba both faced comparable pressures from the United States, Afghan National Government, and the International Assistance Force. In Pair Two, Indonesia, the Philippines, Australia, the U.S., Singapore and Malaysia were all active against Jemaah Islamiyah and the Abu Sayyaf Group consistently. Therefore, analysis of the variables against the case studies shows variation between pairs but similarities between the organizations within each pair. As a result, the most significant differences between organizations is how social capital and trust function differently in familial organizations compared to meritocratic ones, and in turn how the efficiency benefits translate into resilience between the two types.

As external pressures were relatively constant, this difference stands out as the notable variance that can explain insurgent resilience. This is particularly apparent because across all organizations there were commonalities of application and synchronicity by incumbents in their application of hard- and soft-power pressures. This allowed insurgent organizations to remain resilient as well as enabling them to become stronger in some instances. Figure 7.1 shows social capital and trust levels across the case studies over time, from the 1970s through to 2019, while Figure 7.2 shows organizational resilience behaviour over the same period and across the three phases of insurgency. This provides insight into how each case study developed, matured, and continues to function.

LeT is somewhat enigmatic in that it was subjected to severe external pressures in Jammu and Kashmir, its most active operational areas, but its core apex leadership and insurgency systematics have been securely ensconced in Pakistan, making it highly resilient. Therefore, the results of the data reflect its holistic values across those areas and at home.

It is evident that social capital and trust are high at inception for the familial organizations and lower for the meritocracies. When they mature and develop the capabilities to challenge incumbents, familial insurgencies have remained unchanged, whereas the meritocratic organizations increased in social capital and trust as they matured. However, after periods of sustained conflict, familial organizations show reduction, specifically because as time goes by, eternal pressures in particular have reduced familial core command and control and the kinship resource pools that have sustained them. This contrasts with meritocracies that have maintained their trajectories and continued to increase in social capital and trust strength over time.

The chart of organizational resilience shows a strikingly similar set of organizational trajectories as social capital and trust. This validates the key findings that maintaining social capital and trust is the primary mechanism of organizational efficiency, and in turn resilience. For the Haqqani Network, which sits on the lower cusp of retaining high resilience, its trajectory is firmly in the downward

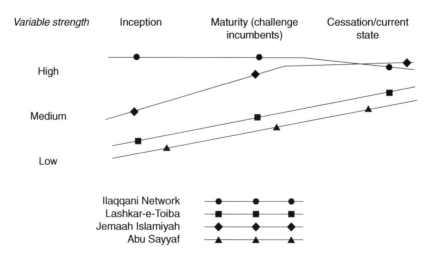

Figure 7.1 Social capital and trust through phases of insurgency.

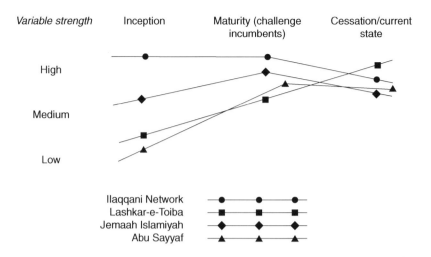

Figure 7.2 Organizational resilience through phases of insurgency.

direction. Direct kinetic losses have reduced and squeezed its consanguine kinship group considerably, and unless it has time to recover, over a period of years, even decades, its future as a familial organization is uncertain. This would not necessarily see the end of its insurgency however, as it could transform and adopt more meritocratic behaviour by necessity.[2]

Jemaah Islamiyah also had a pronounced change from its peak of operational strength in the late 2000s, which is supported by the data of its attack chronology that shows an enduring period of darkness. Likewise, changes in the global insurgent landscape have seen it become less of an operational organization at the street level, and more of an incubator and nursery of others. Next, Lashkar-e-Taiba has steadily strengthened throughout is life span. Significant support and sponsorship from its host Pakistan has allowed it openly to recruit from all sections of society and all countries, and its expansive social services and education systems have become highly effective at developing social capital and trust across many levels of society and government.[3] While Pakistan remains adversarial towards India, something that is unlikely to change, LeT should continue with its trend into the near future.

Last, Abu Sayyaf demonstrated the most significant rise to maturity of the meritocratic organizations. Thriving in its environment, it leveraged connections and networks to rapidly recruit the most hardened and vicious fighters as commanders, and attracted recruits from across the multi-ethnic base of the Southern Philippines to become the most effective and deadly insurgent purveyor of terrorism in the region. When organizational unity was disrupted with the slaying of founding Amir Abdurajak Janjalani, it split, but rather than be destroyed the two factions that had emerged continued to function with relative efficiency. Despite repeated attempts by the central authority to wipe it out, at times with all-out war approaches, it continues to be a challenging concern to regional security. Indeed, President Duterte's declaration of Martial Law in the Southern Philippines, which ended on 31 December 2019, achieved few if any tangible gains against Abu Sayyaf (Temby 2019).

Collectively this data is interesting because it shows distinct changes over time in the case study organizations, as well as between them as a result. This is valuable because it can be translated into greater understanding of which types of external pressures have the greatest effects, both individually against specific insurgent groups, against specific insurgent types, and more broadly against insurgency as a collective congregation. For example, during the start-up phase of insurgency, LeT and Abu Sayyaf were far more vulnerable to hard-power external pressures, and they possessed lower capacities to resist them, had they manifested, but these pressures at the time were minimal.

Conversely, the Haqqani Network and Jemaah Islamiyah were very resilient to hard-power external pressures, due to instant access to wide resource bases, and to security conditions in their home countries at the time. Those same conditions, being somewhat tolerant in the case of Jemaah Islamiyah and Abu Sayyaf, and actually supportive in the Haqqani Network and LeT, explain the lack of application hard-power pressures. Next, it is also evident that social capital and trust capacities were significantly different during inception, with familial organizations having high capacity at commencement of insurgency but meritocracies having much less.

This changed over time however, with social capital and trust becoming roughly equal in each organizational type at the middle maturity phases. At later stages, social capital and trust in the meritocratic case studies surpassed those in the familial ones. This is due to the decline of familial and kinship groups and the decay of immediate resources for them, whereas the meritocratic organizations were able to continue to build resources. Interestingly, Jemaah Islamiyah, which shared an ability similar to that of meritocracies to expand its resource base through new kinship additions, declined somewhat in this regard largely because of the significant changes to its structure, which became diffused and holacratic and contributed to compartmentalization rather than cohesion, which is more accommodating of social capital unity.

In regard to soft-power pressures, LeT and Jemaah Islamiyah largely experienced few issues. For LeT this was because it was comfortably ensconced inside Pakistan. For Jemaah Islamiyah it was probably due to the strong cross-generational nationalist Darul Islam sentiments interwoven through the community, particularly within some sections of the political elite. This is in contrast to the Haqqani Network and Abu Sayyaf. In Afghanistan, the enduring international effort against the insurgency became a stage for the furthering of broader geo-strategic ambitions of India, Russia, China, Pakistan, and the U.S. In particular, China and Russia were able to exert political and economic influence on Pakistan to pay heed to their interests, while the U.S. and India made strong in-roads with civic development and pecuniary initiatives in Afghanistan that pressured the Haqqani Network. For Abu Sayyaf, its ardent rejection of any sort of political solution-seeking marked it as a priority enemy of the government, which with its close partner the U.S., undertook a range of development programmes that slowly matured into measurable gains.

If the trends evident in the findings here continue, it is possible that the familial case study organizations would continue to decline as resources and familial talent pools shrank because of external pressures. Likewise, meritocracies, so long as they can remain resilient, could continue to strengthen and surpass their familial counterparts. This is a particular concern for the Haqqani Network, which suffered ongoing leadership decay since 2004, mostly due to technology advancements and the favourable operating environment of Afghanistan for U.S. drone warfare en masse. This has proved particularly effective at reducing Haqqani advantages of geography, mobility, and the external support that it enjoyed almost unfettered for decades. This form of kinetic pressure is one of the greatest risks the Haqqani Network faced, and only its ability to move somewhat freely within its own tribal lands and easily integrate into other areas has thus far enabled the survival of the top-tier leadership.

In fact, leadership is equally important to all the case studies. While some of the organizations examined have had extremely stable leadership, such as LeT and the Haqqani Network, Jemaah Islamiyah and Abu Sayyaf have had dynamic leaderships. In Jemaah Islamiyah, the highly diffused and holacratic structure meant that leadership losses were compartmentalized and damage was confined to specific cells. This contrasts with the Abu Sayyaf because its structure became fixed into two distinct arms of the organization, making it more detectable and susceptible. While each recovered, it affected them in different ways. The familial Jemaah Islamiyah demonstrated a considerable period of inactivity between 2009 and 2016, probably as a result of this, while Abu Sayyaf remains irreparably fractured into two wings but has maintained its operational tempo.

Further contrasts exist between the case study pairs in terms of soft-power damage. The Haqqani Network and LeT are both extremely resilient to low-risk political isolation and social rejection, whereas Jemaah Islamiyah and Abu Sayyaf are at greater risk of damage and are less resilient. This is possibly a result of the levels of operational maturity across the organizations. Analysing the results from a longitudinal basis helps to explain these findings. A significant commonality across each case study is change over time, and particularly the ability of organizations to adapt in *response* to external pressures in different ways. As per the modified Holling model presented in Chapter 2, organizational disruption due to external pressures offers the greatest opportunity for efficient change. As Schoon (2006) demonstrates, resilience derives from outcomes rather than processes, stressing it is a characteristic that occurs only after exposure to disruption.

The evidence from the case studies supports this, and can be seen in the results of external pressures on insurgent organizations. From the early 2000s onwards, each exhibited significant change. When the former ally of the U.S. gave shelter to al-Qaeda, the Haqqani Network was targeted continuously with hard-power pressures, particularly from 2004, exerted by the combined international forces engaged in the conflict. This resulted in it changing its methods from direct engagement it once undertook, such as the complete sacking of cities, to asymmetric warfare, ambushes, and shock tactics. Similarly, when LeT relocated to Pakistan it began operations in Jammu and Kashmir, but its 2001 attack on the Indian Parliament marked the start of its ongoing strikes into the heart of India.

In Pair Two, both Jemaah Islamiyah and Abu Sayyaf suffered their most significant damage during this same period, but rather than decay, they were able to adapt and respond positively to become stronger as a result. The dismantling of Jemaah Islamiyah's Mantiqi structure and the complete destruction of Mantiqi I in Singapore resulted in it adopting a new and more resilient structure with additional focus and reinforcement through family. Likewise, when Abu Sayyaf splintered it became more resilient, as a result making it harder to target, and its new cellular nature gave it significant security advantages. Therefore, disruption was the catalyst of change in each organization, but in contrasting ways because how each remains resilient is due to the specific means by which social capital and trust function.

The role of social capital

As organizational type is a structural variable, this book has included social capital and trust to examine the non-structural operational variable of organizational function and efficiency. This has proven important for addressing the unpredictability of structure as a singular determinant of organizational resilience at the outset. It has been established that in familial organizations, members usually work for the good of the group with holistic long-term survival being most important. Tilly (2004) established that members in meritocracies create benefit for the organization primarily for the attainment of personal gain, and by being part of a successful team. Therefore, in familial groups social capital and trust are used to help others and facilitate group advancement and development, whereas in meritocracies social capital and trust are used by individual members to help the organization through self-advancement. Levi and Stoker's (2000, 476) assertion that "trust is relational" reflects this.

Consequently, the differences between the outward and sharing versus an inward and individualistic use of social capital and trust in family organizations and meritocracies are highly important. As found, social capital and trust in familial versus meritocratic organizations possess different socio-economic values and efficiencies. These are representable as security-efficiency/security-vulnerability trade-offs. The levels of trade-off organizations accept are mostly organic and bound to their structure and type, and considerably influence their resilience to external pressures. This also goes some way to understanding how familial organizations make up for some limitations pertaining to recruitment and promotion restrictions, and how meritocratic organizations counter-balance structural vulnerabilities and internal security weaknesses.

Figure 7.3 shows how the relationship between organizational type and social capital and trust influences success requirements differently. For example, in the

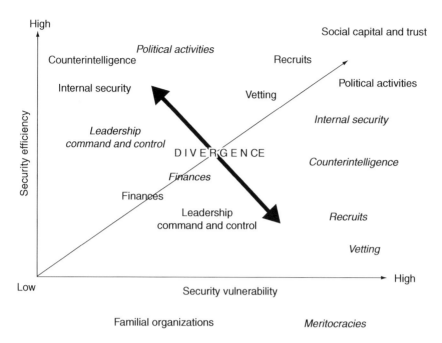

Figure 7.3 Security efficiency – vulnerability matrix.

familial organizations, leadership and command and control have been at risk of becoming less efficient because of limitations of drawing leaders from a restricted family base. This is apparent in the Haqqani Network case study because it is restricted by tribal and clan boundaries. In contrast, Jemaah Islamiyah added new kinship connections through marriage, in theory enabling it to continue to expand unrestricted. However, while these organizations differ in this context, leadership replacement is still an issue. In Jemaah Islamiyah, ongoing losses of senior leaders have seen control pushed further down the hierarchy where experienced commanders are increasingly absent. The significant operational gap between the second JW Marriot and Ritz-Carlton Jakarta attacks in July 2009 and the attacks in central Jakarta in January 2016 (Tomsa 2016) is probably a reflection of the result of organizational damage to senior leadership and the time needed to rebuild capabilities.

There are offsets to such risks, however. Recruitment and vetting were higher in efficiency in familial organizations because of pre-existing social capital and trust exchanges that provide kinship screening, whereas in meritocracies vetting needed to be far more extensive and potentially invasive. Sinno (2008) states that during the Afghan anti-Soviet war, Jalaluddin Haqqani and other Mujahedeen were highly effective at mobilizing the rural population through clan and kinship links, which proved very successful at quickly coordinating field commanders in battle. The ethnic tapestry of Afghanistan is weaved together with clan and tribal threads. Consequently, Shapiro and Siegel (2007) have found that kinship, and other endogamic ties, are critically important to the ability to organize, and to be secure and resilient because of the social capital and trust benefits that kinship reinforces. This was particularly evident in the Iraq example after 2001 where family and kinship ties constituted the architecture of the insurgency (ICG 2006). Ensly and Pearson's argument supports this, stating that kinship results in "higher cohesion, potency, task conflict, and shared strategic consensus than those ... with less 'familiness'" (2005, 267).

In contrast, the meritocracies had advantages in accessing wider recruitment resource bases, but many candidates had unknown qualities, and had to prove themselves or go through lengthy vetting processes so organizations could be sure they were getting only the most capable and suitable in their ranks. Recruits in LeT had to follow the *corporate* culture to avoid agency issues and internal conflicts. From Chapter 4 it is evident that Lashkar-e-Taiba has developed significant indoctrination, training, and development programmes for its recruits for this exact purpose, particularly for its aspiring leaders (Copland 2005).

Therefore which is most resilient, familial or meritocratic organizations? The findings suggest that both types have equally powerful resilience potential, although the case studies oscillate in vulnerabilities to different risks, making organizational structure less relevant as the answer than other factors. For example, how specific organizations manifest their own organic resilience in their individual security environments, particularly through the nuances of their internal uses of social capital and trust, seems to be far more predictive of resilience than structure alone.

Likewise, it is evident that time is a factor. At commencement, familial organizations had greater resilience because they had readymade low-cost resources, whereas meritocracies had to grow to the point at which they could effectively and efficiently collect resources in sufficient quantity and quality to start challenging incumbents. Over the longer term however, familial organizations become restricted by the limitations of kinship boundaries on resources pools. A partial exception to this was Jemaah Islamiyah, but it remains restricted to the resources that can be gathered from over time, meaning it must keep adding more new connections that will take time to mature so long as they are not destroyed first.

Summary of results

The results of the book establish the importance of social capital and trust in organizational resilience. The significance of these findings began with their in-depth examination in Chapter 2. There, evidence that social capital and trust can provide efficiency, security, and legitimization-enhancing benefits in each organizational type was established, and then tested in the case studies. The book also found that in kinship groups it can strengthen and reinforce political, ideological, and religious norms and beliefs, cement in-group cohesion, and delineate group trust-based efficiency boundaries.[4] Conversely, socio-economic social capital exchange describes how actors become governed by rules in meritocratic organizations that support cohesion, and individual adaptation that shapes organizational culture and efficiency (Tilly 2004), which is evident in the case studies. However, social capital and trust can come with significant risk, particularly in regard to operational and strategic divergence within organizations that can rupture and fragment organizational cohesion and unity.

This is a particular concern for meritocracies when decentralized nodes develop autonomy and independence from central leadership over time and break into independent entities. This occurred in LeT to some extent and in Jemaah Islamiyah in greater frequency. In Abu Sayyaf, however, it directly resulted in irreparable organizational splitting. Thus, diffused organizations can present an increased efficiency risk because of disconnection between top-tier leaders and mid-level commanders and fighters. However, decentralized groups enjoy low-cost structures, flexibility, and redundancy, which promote efficiency and resilience. This is also demonstrated in Jemaah Islamiyah and the Abu Sayyaf, the former a familial organization and the latter a meritocracy.

Therefore, the comparative case studies broadly support the argument advanced in the introduction that organizational structures are not what directly results in resilience. Rather, it is the way in which different organizational structures experience, facilitate, and enable social capital and trust and their relevance to organizational efficiency, including insurgency systematics, that most directly affects an organization's resilience. Meritocratic organizations in particular pass through various stages of internal social capital and trust as members become fully enmeshed and indoctrinated, or, drift away. Borum (2011a, 2011b), for example, demonstrated that entry into meritocracies requires extensive indoctrination, and ongoing growth through connections development to add layers of screening and security. Alternatively, agency issues can cause others to become disassociated.

In the Lashkar-e-Taiba example, Rassler *et al.* (2013) maintained that LeT is careful not to recruit from the Ahl-e-Hadith Islamic tradition, even though this is its theological basis and one with strong roots to the current organization. Fair (2014) writes this is because LeT's ideology is derived from Ahl-e-Hadith traditions, but it fears they may compromise and influence its organizational culture, moving it away from its declared goals. In familial organizations social capital is usually facilitated organically, economically, and internally which gives them efficiency bonuses. For example, the Haqqani Network is able to draw on organic tribal and broad clan ties to quickly muster resources that support it in times of need, such as leveraging the Taliban's extensive resource capabilities, or al-Qaida's finical networks as Dressler (2010) remarks. Similarly, the practice of inter-group marriage in Jemaah Islamiyah enabled it to create organic consanguine ties to powerful regional groups such as the MILF, Ring Baten and Abu Sayyaf, providing correspondingly important intra-organizational support and assistance for joint operations and shared facilities.

In meritocratic organizations social capital is generated by professionalization and utilitarianism, and developed both externally and internally as they seek to recruit suitable new leaders and develop existing ones. LeT, for example, leverages its ties to the Pakistani ISI to employ the most capable intelligence and military officers as training staff (Shafiq 2007). Last, in Abu Sayyaf, the highly criminalized and completive nature of its meritocracy demonstrates the strong presence of self-interest in individual development, wherein only and most capable commanders rise to leadership positions. Morselli *et al.* (2006) refer to this as the consistent need for covert organizations to seek ongoing network efficiencies and the balancing of organizational security with risk and reward.

The comparative evidence therefore supports the argument that changing the values of social capital and trust can influence the organizational efficiency of insurgent organizations and as a consequence their organizational resilience. As Table 7.1 demonstrates, significant changes in organizational resilience correlate with adjustments to organizational efficiency. These changes have traditionally occurred through extant incumbent external pressures of hard and soft types, as anticipated by the theory and examined extensively. Reductions in organizational efficiency reduced resilience relatively quickly and effectively in every instance it occurred, except in cases when insurgent resilience was largely derived from external patrons. In those instances, mainly in LeT and to a lesser extent the Haqqani Network, efficiency reduction did manifest, but to a lesser degree due to external ISI support and assistance.

From the data we can infer that a divergence of social capital and trust values, away from organizational efficiency, means a reduction in organizational resilience in numerous ways. For familial organizations, a decrease in family leaders and commanders reduces the primary social capital and trust group, sometimes shifting it from close consanguine family to less-connected extended kin. While social capital and trust remain organic in these situations, it can be weaker. The Haqqani Network is at significant risk of this whereas for Jemaah Islamiyah the risk lies more in the reduction of strategic cohesion, as leadership is pushed onto less-experienced familial leaders and holistic unity and coordination become more diffused.

The case studies find that meritocratic organizations seem to suffer less from leadership losses because this offers new opportunities for junior leaders. Utilizing social capital exchange, aspiring leaders offer new capabilities, ideas, and enthusiasm. When a leadership position becomes available, lower-level members can compete for it on a basis of their intelligence, leadership aptitude, military effectiveness, or ideological/religious zeal. Another interesting finding is the effect of restricting mobility and communications. Familial organizations have to increase their reliance on lesser-connected or non-familial members when they are forcefully entrenched, this thereby having an adverse effect on efficiency due to higher social capital transaction costs. Meritocracies do not have the same problem because social capital and trust economics remain the same, therefore providing a comparative efficiency dividend.

Next, the research shows that familial organizations are far more resilient to counterintelligence risks, such as family members being developed by intelligence services or penetrated by adversarial agents. They are also more likely to

Table 7.1 External pressure effects per organizational type

	Type of pressure	Familial org. effects	Duration	Social capital and trust divergence	Meritocratic org. effects	Duration	Social capital and trust divergence
Eliminate senior leadership	Hard	Reduce family control	Long	Yes	New leaders rise	Short	No
Degrade command and control	Hard	Expand familial inclusion	Short	No	Disruption	Short	Yes
Remove influencers and power nodes	Hard+soft	Disruption	Medium	Yes	Structural damage	Long	Yes
Restrict mobility and communications	Hard+soft	Isolation	Short–medium	No	Isolation	Short–medium	No
Incumbent concessions	Soft	Unlikely due to unity	Short	No	Possible	Short–long	Yes
Destroy insurgent infrastructure	Hard	Pressure on familial territories	Short–long	No	Possible relocation	Short–medium	No
Covert recruitment of senior insiders	Soft	Unlikely	Short	No	Medium	Short–long	Yes
Smear campaigns against leadership	Soft	Low effectiveness	Short	No	High	Short–long	Yes
Pressure insurgent family members	Hard+soft	Low	Short–medium	No	Medium	Short–long	Yes
Political recognition for renouncement	Soft	Possible	Short–long	No	Medium	Short–medium	Yes
Limited amnesties	Soft	Possible	Short–long	No	Medium	Short–medium	Yes

resist incumbent concessions and offerings because approval by the majority of family leaders would be needed, therefore reducing the risks of splintering and dispersion. This has been especially apparent in both familial case studies. Siraj Haqqani's appointment as the second-in-command of the Taliban illustrates the unity among the principal Afghan insurgents well. In Jemaah Islamiyah, the changes in structural morphology from formal and hierarchical to diffused and holacratic increased security through decentralization, and to its low-cost structures, which were flexible and redundant.

Conversely, in meritocratic organizations counterintelligence risks are much higher, and concessions, amnesties, and political accommodations are more likely to create internal conflict and competitive in-group factions as leaders seek the best result for their individual situations. Equally, such organizations are far more susceptible to intelligence penetrations. Open recruitment offers opportunities for incumbent intelligence services to embed agents at the bottom rungs of organizations and work their way up, gaining increasing trust as they rise through the ranks. Arquilla and Ronfeldt stated, for example, that in meritocracies, a critical vulnerability is that they have "more difficulty instilling, and enforcing, a sense of personal identity with loyalty to the network" (2001, 9). This might create the ideal atmosphere for enemy agents to thrive.

The importance of efficiency in organizations

Organizational efficiency determines resilience over structure in every example, particularly as some organizations such as Jemaah Islamiyah and Abu Sayyaf Group, familial and meritocratic respectively, significantly changed their structures over time. In Jemaah Islamiyah, the organizational structure completely collapsed but familial assemblages maintained efficiency, with demonstrated ongoing operational capability for a considerable period before going dark in 2009. In Abu Sayyaf, the integrated meritocratic structure fractured into two distinct and geographically separated factions with several sub-factions emerging. However, the operational tempo of attacks and kidnappings continued concurrently as the structural disintegration took place.

In Lashkar-e-Taiba it was evident that the organization was extremely susceptible to international external pressures, but damage did not manifest due to its insulation inside Pakistan. Subsequent localized pressures in Jammu and Kashmir did have results, and LeT operations there could have been destroyed if not for continued support by the Pakistani State. Despite kinetic damage outside of Pakistan, LeT maintained efficient operational actions as well as continuing to act in the political interests of the Pakistani State in contest with anti-state Deobandi groups.

This experience is distinctly different from that of the Haqqani Network, which was extensively targeted, and suffered significant hard-power-derived damage to its structure. This resulted in substantial leadership losses but with little tangible reductions in organizational efficiency. As a result, hard- and soft-power external pressures in both examples affected insurgent structures but had a less-direct effect on organizational efficiency. The impact of state patronage on insurgent organizations in the context of the organizational efficiency/resilience paradigm, and the relationship of family versus meritocracy, is an area of research that would further contribute to security studies in this area. However, as a generality of familial organizations this is only true if insurgent conflicts are won quickly, as the longer they endure, the less-resilient familial insurgencies seemingly become.

More broadly these findings provide strong evidence that familial organizations, like the Haqqani Network and Jemaah Islamiyah, may suffer structural degradation and change, but the familial employment of social capital and trust across kinship networks means that organizational efficiency is maintainable. In the meritocratic examples of Lashkar-e-Taiba and Abu Sayyaf Group, social capital and trust significantly contributed to maintaining organizational efficiency across professional risk-and-reward operational endeavours, at times fostering cooperation for mutual benefit. In contrast, meritocracies are at far greater risk of being extinguished in the early and middle phases of conflict, but will generally increase in resilience the longer insurgency lasts.

Future directions

John Le Beau (2008), a former Cavalry officer and Senior Operations office at the CIA Clandestine Services division said that "it is prudent to note that neither insurgency nor the strategy and tactics required to combat it represent new phenomena". Kalyvas and Balcells (2010) observe that insurgency has been a significant dimension of international conflicts since the Cold War. Applying the same COIN approaches to new insurgent conflicts is producing few, if any new outcomes. This book has found that external pressures, which are the primary methods incumbents have used to fight insurgency over time, have overall failed to reduce insurgent resilience effectively. This is mostly due to failures to recognize and consequently attempt to degrade organizational efficiency over organizational structures, which are the primary targets of extant methods.

This creates a paradox in current approaches that may actually be encouraging the development of insurgent resilience, particularly as organizations adapt in new ways to well-established counterinsurgency practices. As the findings here suggest, further research into organizational type, efficiency, and resilience is needed. This could be achieved in a number of ways. For example, analysis of incumbent counterinsurgency rationale, particularly the use of external pressures and the targeting logic and selection they use may help to clarify where, how, and with what pressures insurgent efficiencies could be better degraded. Elsewhere, work on disrupting adaptation capacities as per the Holling model may also yield valuable insights. Finally, a deeper examination of soft-power pressures on resilience and the development of conflict circumvention initiatives may also yield benefits equally to familial and meritocratic organizations alike.

In addition to the summary and critique of the findings, this book has offered a modest attempt to discern how familial versus meritocratic insurgent organizations maintain resilience, the importance of their familial versus merito-cratic governance structures, the links to social capital and trust, and the critical importance of organizational efficiency. Having done so, I now offer a new and nuanced way to move forward using a strategic counterintelligence doctrine, one intended specifically to manipulate non-traditional vulnerabilities and asymmet-rically exploit strengths through the intelligence-led use of clandestine influence. A summary of the doctrine is presented in Part III. As established by the results of the comparative case research, organizational efficiency is more relative to resilience than organizational structure, and is developed and used within the complex constructs of social capital and trust. This suggests they may be highly malleable.

Notes

1 The paired case study method also provided the additional control for external pres-sures because the external pressures each case study pair experienced were similar. While variations did occur they have been allowed for, and integrity has been main-tained as changes were not significant or especially unique, and any variation has been discussed in the case studies and documented throughout. Likewise, the most apparent variation, where it did occur, was between case study pairs and not between the organizations in specific pairs, which was relatively stable. This was expected as the incumbents and the conflict and geo-security environments of Pair One and Pair Two are different, whereas for the organizations in those pairs they are similar.

2 It must be noted, however, that changing geo-security circumstances in Afghanistan in late 2019, such as foreign troop drawdowns, or fresh rounds of peace talks between the U.S., Taliban/Haqqani, and the incumbent government, would probably provide the Haqqani Network with the time and operational space it needs to return to peak strength.

3 With significant pressure from the international community, Pakistan in late 2019 stated that LeT Amir Hafiz Saeed would be prosecuted for terror financing. The Anti-Terrorism Court (ATC) in Lahore is pursuing charges against Saeed and other senior officers. However, these charges are levelled at specific individuals and not at the LeT/JuD organizations, meaning they will remain intact, operational, and well supported by the ISI. SOURCE: Press Trust of India. "JuD chief Hafiz Saeed to face trial for terror financing charges on December 7". *India Today*. Accessed 20 November 2019. www.indiatoday.in/world/story/jud-chief-hafiz-saeed-to-face-trial-for-terror-financing-charges-on-december-7–1624032–2019–12–01.

4 See: Abdulkader Sinno, 2008. *Organizations at War in Afghanistan and Beyond*. Ithaca: Cornell University Press; Paul Adler and Seok-Woo Kwon, 2002. "Social Capital: Prospects for a New Concept". *The Academy of Management Review* 27 (1): 14–40; Armando Salvatore and Mark LeVine, 2005. "The Overlapping Dimensions of the Civic and the Public". In *Religion, Social Practice, and Contested Hegemonies: Reconstructing the Public Sphere in Muslim Majority Societies*, eds. Armando Salvatore and Mark LeVine. New York: Palgrave Macmillan, 29–56; Richard Emerson, 1976. "Social Exchange Theory". *Annual Review of Sociology* 2 (1): 335–362.

References

Adler, Paul and Kwon, Seok-Woo. 2002. "Social Capital: Prospects for a New Concept". *The Academy of Management Review* 27 (1): 14–40.

Arquilla, John and Ronfeldt, David. 2001. "Networks, Netwars, and the Fight for the Future". *Journal of the Internet* 6 (10): 1–19. https://firstmonday.org/ojs/index.php/fm/article/view/889/798.

Borum, Randy. 2011a. "Radicalization into Violent Extremism I: A Review of Social Science Theories". *Journal of Strategic Security* 4 (4): 7–36.

Borum, Randy. 2011b. "Radicalization into Violent Extremism II: A Review of Conceptual Models and Empirical Research". *Journal of Strategic Security* 4 (4): 37–62.

Copland, S. 2005. *Psychological Profiling of Terrorists: A Case Study of the Bali Bombers and Jemaah Islamiyah.* Canberra: Department of Foreign Affairs and Trade: Counter-Terrorism Branch.

Dressler, Jeffry. 2010. *Afghanistan Report No. 6 – The Haqqani Network: From Pakistan to Afghanistan.* Washington, D.C.: Institute for the Study of War.

Emerson, Richard. 1976. "Social Exchange Theory". *Annual Review of Sociology* 2 (1): 335–362.

Ensley, Michael and Pearson, Allison. 2005. "An Exploratory Comparison of the Behavioral Dynamics of Top Management Teams in Family and Nonfamily New Ventures: Cohesion, Conflict, Potency, and Consensus". *Journal of Entrepreneurship Theory and Practice* 29 (3): 267–284.

Fair, Christine. 2014. "Insights from a Database of Lashkar-e-Taiba and Hizb-ul-Mujahideen Militants". *Journal of Strategic Studies* 37 (2): 259–290.

ICG. 2006. *In Their Own Words: Reading the Iraqi Insurgency.* Amman and Brussels: International Crisis Group.

Kalyvas, Stathis and Balcells, Laia. 2010. "International System and Technologies of Rebellion: How the End of the Cold War Shaped Internal Conflict". *American Political Science Review* 104 (3): 415–429.

Le Beau, John J. 2008. "The Renaissance of Insurgency and Counter-Insurgency: Examining Twenty-First Century Insurgencies and Government Responses". *Connections* 7 (1): 154–166.

Levi, Margaret and Stoker, Laura. 2000. "Political Trust and Trustworthiness". *Annual Review of Political Science* 3 (1): 475–507.

Morselli, Carlo, Giguère, Cynthia, and Petit, Katia. 2006. "The Efficiency/Security Trade-Off in Criminal Networks". *Social Networks* 29 (1): 143–153.

Press Trust of India, "JuD chief Hafiz Saeed to face trial for terror financing charges on December 7". *India Today.* Accessed 20 November 2019. www.indiatoday.in/world/story/jud-chief-hafiz-saeed-to-face-trial-for-terror-financing-charges-on-december-7-1624032-2019-12-01.

Rassler, D., Fair, C., Chosh, A., Jamal, A, and Shoeb, N. 2013. *The Fighters of Lashkar-e-Taiba: Recruitment, Training, Development and Death.* West Point, NY: CTC – Combating Terrorism Center.

Salvatore, Armando and LeVine, Mark. 2005. "The Overlapping Dimensions of the Civic and the Public". In *Religion, Social Practice, and Contested Hegemonies: Reconstructing the Public Sphere in Muslim Majority Societies*, edited by Armando Salvatore and Mark LeVine, 29–56. New York: Palgrave Macmillan.

Schoon, Ingrid. 2006. *Risk and Resilience: Adaptations in Changing Times.* First edition. Cambridge: Cambridge University Press.

Shafiq, A. 2007. "The Jihad Within". *Herald (Karachi, Pakistan)*, 1 April: 92–93.

Shapiro, Jacob and Siegel, David. 2007. "Underfunding in Terrorist Organizations". *International Studies Quarterly* 51 (1): 405–429.

Sinno, Abdulkader. 2008. *Organizations at War in Afghanistan and Beyond.* Ithaca: Cornell University Press.

Temby, Quinton. 2019. "Cells, Factions and Suicide Operatives: The Fragmentation of Militant Islamism in the Philippines Post-Marawi". *Contemporary Southeast Asia: A Journal of International and Strategic Affairs* 41 (1): 114–137.

Tilly, Charles. 2004. "Trust and Rule". *Journal of Theory and Society* 33 (1): 1–30.

Tomsa, Dirk. 2016. "The Jakarta Terror Attack and Its Implications for Indonesian and Regional Security". *Perspective* 5 (2016): 1–8.

Part III

A new approach

8 Strategic counterintelligence

This chapter expands on the core findings of the research by testing how the manipulation of organizational resilience variables can be achieved with a strategic counterintelligence doctrine by using hypothetical modelling.[1] The purpose of building this knowledge is in order that new methodologies can be developed to counter, degrade, and destroy insurgent resilience to make organizations critically susceptible to other forms of external pressures. This is important because as discussed in the Introduction, insurgencies are increasing globally, not decreasing. It is also significant because it demonstrates that extant methods are not containing insurgency, and per contra strongly suggests that new approaches can make viable contributions.

The book has thoroughly established that organizational resilience is achieved through prioritizing organizational efficiency over organizational type and structure. This is not to say that type and structure are less important however, as diffused holacratic organizations have demonstrated greater resilience than those organizations with formal hierarchical structures. One apparent exception to this are organizations that enjoy significant state support. In addition, organizational type remains important because social capital and trust have different socio-economic values in familial versus meritocratic organizations. In contrast, while this can offer challenges to traditional COIN approaches, these same differences offer new opportunities for a strategic counterintelligence doctrine. This is because they provide access that is more dynamic to the most critical agents of organizational resilience, being people, because without people organizations do not exist.

Using the data and findings from the research presented in this book, this chapter introduces a model of strategic counterintelligence and describes how it can be used to mitigate the efficiencies of insurgency, manipulate operational capabilities, and degrade organizational resilience by influencing resilience variables. Strategic counterintelligence is holistic, non-linear, and works against broad tactical as well as conceptual insurgency threats phenomenologically. It is these macro aspirations of strategic counterintelligence that set it aside. The role of social capital and trust in the resilience of insurgent organizations is of particular interest because it fulfils the requirements of access to groups and networks for intelligence-led exploitation. Likewise, it is how people interact with each other that determines the efficiencies those interactions produce.

The chapter is presented in three sections. The first provides a brief understanding of what strategic counterintelligence is, how it differs from other intelligence methods and doctrines, and what the potential outcomes could be for a successful strategic counterintelligence mission. The second section drills down into the details and discusses how practitioners might employ strategic counterintelligence to achieve in-theatre tactical and operational outcomes, as well as fulfilling broader national-level geo-security requirements. In doing so, it draws extensively on the findings of the book, and uses the examples of the Haqqani Network and the Abu Sayyaf Group for the hypothetical modelling. The third section discusses the implications for the future and the developmental needs for strategic counterintelligence to successfully erode, degrade, and manipulate insurgent organizational resilience, as a tool of conflict reduction.

Section 1: defining the doctrine

Before postulating how the resilience of insurgency can be degraded and influenced via strategic counterintelligence, it is necessary first to understand the importance of strategic intelligence processes and delineate analysis from counterintelligence.[2] To begin, intelligence analysis at the strategic level forms the basis of creating strategies to achieve critical outcomes. This involves developing nuanced intelligence collection and analysis schemes to address information gaps and populate target models, being the area of interest to be understood. This also encompasses anticipating and planning for future needs, future gaps, and potential new information requirements moving forward.

However, rather than being a plan, strategic intelligence is the logic that drives the plan and informs practitioners and consumers about how to achieve it (Heidenrich 2007). While this is applicable to strategic counterintelligence, strategic intelligence in the traditional sense is the opposite side of the coin. America's foremost scholar and practitioner of strategic intelligence, the late Sherman Kent of the CIA, described it as the information requirements an actor has in order to "know about the future state of other separate sovereign states, the course of action they are likely to initiate themselves, and the courses of action they are likely to take up in response to some outside stimulus" (1966, 39). This is not limited to states as it is equally applicable to organizations, groups, and other collectives with either formal structures or ad hoc and diffused ones. Perhaps most importantly however, it identifies strategic intelligence as being defensive.

On the opposite side is strategic counterintelligence, which is offensively dynamic, going further to get behind adversarial *counterintelligence screens* and actively ingrain into the responses, capabilities, and intentions of adversarial entities through covert manipulation and clandestine influence.[3] Rather than being a powerful tool of knowing, strategic counterintelligence is a tool of influencing and changing outcomes with the lightest of touches. *Ipso facto*, there are three means by which this occurs. These are: (1) to diminish the relevance of insurgent organizational strengths; (2) to isolate insurgent efficiencies and strengths from necessary supports; (3) to weaken insurgent organizational efficiencies by exploiting systemic resilience vulnerabilities.

On the surface this appears to be a standard approach of insurgent warfare. Indeed, strategic counterintelligence shares many commonalities. The key variances are the means of delivery and the non-linear nature of this doctrine. Strategic counterintelligence exploits the resilience mechanisms and efficiencies of insurgent organizations through internal changes to create influence and control from the inside out, rather than from the outside in as in traditional approaches. The benefits come not only from control and from mitigation, but from knowing the likelihood of adversarial actions through covert and clandestine influencing, thereby gaining the ability to tailor specify response propositions to them. Succinctly, strategic intelligence can assist in clearing the fog of war while strategic counterintelligence controls the other side of it, providing greater benefit and considerably increased mitigation potential.

This can be understood as knowledge gaps. These gaps can be periods of observation where incumbents are waiting to see the results or effects of their actions, and in turn the ramifications for, and the reactions of, insurgents. During these periods, incumbents have little if any oversight, understanding, or direct knowledge of what is occurring in insurgent organizations beyond analysis of their external behaviours. Conversely, strategic counterintelligence not only has coverage of these gaps, but also actively influences organizational behaviours in them. Figure 8.1 shows the knowledge gaps strategic counterintelligence covers.

This demonstrates that capability positioning in strategic counterintelligence is the means of gaining access to adversarial entities, and there are numerous ways this is achieved. Extant intelligence development and penetration vectors, for example, may be employed to exploit gaps that are already available to practitioners. Many of these come from existing counterintelligence and human source intelligence operations.[4] Other vectors can be tailored to specifically

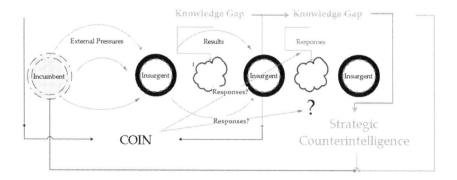

Figure 8.1 The Strategic Counterintelligence gap.

exploit security, financial, political, personal, motivational, and professional susceptibilities. Practitioners can select actors to target directly as agents, or use indirect means through family and friends, acquaintances, or peripheral yet important influence actors, stakeholders, suppliers, controllers, supporters, and donors. This can be achieved with additional tradecraft practices such as technical exploitations, cyber operations, Signals Intelligence, Information Warfare, and many more, as discussed in the following sections.

What becomes immediately apparent is the multi-faceted nature of diverse capabilities offered through the strategic counterintelligence mission. First, it is a multi-force endeavour requiring a range of assets, intelligence capabilities and tradecrafts, collection pathways, and delivery vectors.[5] Likewise, strategic counterintelligence is also scalable, meaning it can be a significant undertaking from the highest levels and complexities of state; or, it can be conducted from the lowest levels using only organic capabilities and small-group cellular assets. It can therefore be thought of as a continuum that is equally relevant for every level of operation. It is one where multiple mission-sets overlap and support each other to "layer" intelligence exploitation efforts and to maximize value, thereby contributing to the holistic intelligence-led influencing mission.

As a generality, the techniques, methods, and intelligence tradecraft employed in strategic counterintelligence are not necessarily new per se, but their application, particularly in concert with a focus on clandestine influence and manipulation, make them unique when employed in a considered doctrine. These critical facets of strategic counterintelligence make it highly appealing, particularly to policy-makers and practitioners because it opens up a range of tangible options outside of expensive hard- and soft-power pressures.[6]

At macro strategic through to tactical levels, strategic counterintelligence does not replace them. Rather, it complements them and maximizes their effectiveness by making insurgent organizations more malleable and susceptible. By working internally and manipulating human-based resilience drivers, strategic counterintelligence can erode an organization's capacity to resist external pressures, thereby leading it down new paths of de-escalation, conflict avoidance, collapse, or ultimate decay; whereas intelligence collection, strategic intelligence, and counterintelligence are about collection and defence – knowing and understanding, strategic counterintelligence is about changing the very nature of how insurgents perceive their environments by influencing their decision-making processes. This is the key difference.

Conceptually this could be achieved in a number of ways. The research shows that different organizational structures and organizational types have different counterintelligence vulnerabilities and strengths, particularly because of how social capital and trust function in each and generate efficiencies. Covert and clandestine control and influence over of adversarial decision-making processes consists of three distinct operational approaches: (1) Direct access; (2) Indirect influence; (3) Environmental control and manipulation. While it is possible that these intelligence-led undertakings occur as singular strategic counterintelligence missions, it is more likely they will be layered and employed cooperatively to work interactively with one another. These are discussed below.

Operational approaches

Direct access

Direct Access pertains to the direct development and manipulation of human sources inside insurgent decision-making centres. This includes targeting and developing organizational members directly as agents of influence, and by the clandestine manipulation of organizational members to influence their behaviours, perceptions, and decision-making. At this point there is little difference between existing penetration operations and those of the strategic counterintelligence type. Indeed, the methods and tradecraft are very similar. However, after the penetration has taken place, things change. In traditional operations, penetrations funnel intelligence out to provide incumbents with the opportunity to understand what may be happening. In strategic counterintelligence, influence is injected to actively shape choice and behaviour, and to control future actions and movement.

In direct development approaches of both types, the target member is probably aware that they are being recruited by the intelligence services, unless there is a need to disguise such links with the employment of suitable operational cover.[7] In the case of clandestine manipulation operations, the target is probably unaware of their selection. Likewise, Direct Access can be employed to develop existing members of an organization or to penetrate an organization with new members that develop access and integrate into command structures over time. Direct development methods are classic counterintelligence techniques while clandestine manipulation is not.

For example, in the strategic counterintelligence context, organizational members that have been developed would be active at both collecting intelligence and the seeding of new intelligence, influence, and control into their organizations. This is new, and in contrast to being passive collectors under traditional counterintelligence operations. Targets under clandestine manipulation would be influenced to act in specific ways because of situational shaping by covert means, such as manipulating their social media inputs, altering their surrounding social, financial, material, and familial dynamics, or by applying distracting pressures to other facets of the daily routine.

Because Direct Access centres on developing the deepest level of intelligence penetration and coverage of organizations, it faces a range of issues, yet also opportunities. This is because human source development is not black and white or a matter of singular focus or conceptual consideration. This means that intelligence practitioners must be working several steps ahead of each and every action they take. For example, an overt approach to a carefully selected member of a target organization would follow established tradecraft practices and may be successful. However, the possibilities for the target approached to harden in response to development and tasking efforts should be anticipated at the outset, and at every increment along the way. Rather than losing access because of this, it should be viewed as a positive way to introduce new influence dynamics and be proceeded with nonetheless. Insurgency tends to be non-cosmopolitan; therefore, it is possible to leverage insurgent insularity to manipulate their external prisms of understanding of the world around them.[8]

On the other hand, a target organization member who has become resistant or hostile to further contact and tasking could be influenced to restrict his movements and activities, as well as communications and associations if, for example, he knows that incumbent intelligence forces are at a particular place, or in a particular area for fear of running into them.[9] He may likewise begin to dread any association with incumbent forces for fear of compromise and accusations of guilt by association. These advantages can contribute to overt and covert manipulation, as well as indirect access to other members.

The tradecraft and methodology of Direct Access in strategic counterintelligence has much in common with traditional counterintelligence penetrations of organizations, particularly in terms of operational security, access opportunities, vulnerabilities to development, and intelligence exploitation. These are critical foundational considerations, particularly in modelling because similarly to incumbent intelligence services, insurgent organizations also devote considerable effort to studying the intelligence, security, and military forces working against them. Time and experience in the examples of the case studies demonstrates the exceptional capabilities of those organizations to respond

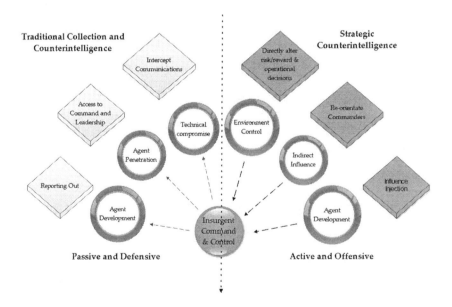

Figure 8.2 Traditional vs. strategic counterintelligence.

dynamically, and to adapt their security practices and tradecraft accordingly. Figure 8.2 illustrates difference between traditional counterintelligence penetration and strategic counterintelligence exploitation.

It is clear that strategic counterintelligence has additional requirements for Direct Access human source development operations. In order to affect insurgent decision-making, selected targets need to interact dynamically rather than just being covert collectors. This makes selection harder and more complex, and potentially makes successful development directly, or covertly, longer in duration, but much more effective. Operations can effectively target insurgents in logistics, command and control, operations, financing, records and information management, recruitment, security, bodyguards, servants, intelligence officers, pay officers, communications officers, and more. Non-member familial relations such as wives, children, cousins, and siblings can also be used for accessing insurgent commanders.

Indirect influence

Indirect Influence builds manifestly on Direct Access operations. It is likewise multifaceted. Indirect Influence is the practice of manipulating the intelligence products and intelligence processes insurgent decision-makers use to make assessments and judgements, accomplished by influencing their understanding of threats, risks, and rewards.[10] Indirect Influence differs from covert influence used in Direct Access operations because rather than targeting people, it targets intangibles. If there are limited approaches or risk-prohibitive reasons as to why decision-makers cannot be covertly prejudiced, Indirect Influence can be established by influencing the "intelligence traffic" on their immediate information networks from advisers, friends, stakeholders, supporters, patrons, affiliates, colleagues, and family. "Traffic" refers to the intelligence product and information exchanged between people.

Manipulating the human elements would be achieved with Direct Access operations. Therefore, the tailored employment of deception and obfuscation operations to confuse and disrupt the clarity of understanding, and the insurgent's sense of risk to particular courses of action are examples of this. Indirect Influence is powerful because deception is an integral component of military and political conflict, and as Caddell argues, is "intrinsic to all human interaction" (2004, 1). Correlated with the inherent human factor in insurgent organizational resilience, this strongly suggests that strategic counterintelligence is likely to be extremely effective in this form.

Indirect Influence employs deception that is misleading and actively makes intelligence, and intelligence assessments, distorted to present alternative scenarios. Therefore, by layering Indirect Influence over Direct Access operations, intentionally derived deceptive information can yield benefits to incumbent intelligence practitioners by influencing insurgents to act in self-detrimental ways, including inaction. To embed and mature Indirect Access and the introduction of new traffic into insurgent intelligence information networks, several inherent fundamental dynamics exist that make target actors vulnerable. Spellman *et al.* find that "parallel constraint satisfaction" (1993, 147) is a strong mechanism to influence attitudinal changes that can cause flow-on effects throughout information networks. Work by Kunda and Thagard (1996) supports the viability of this approach because once new traffic is covertly introduced into information networks, its sharing is relatively automatic and requires little conscious inference of validity, making it extremely effective.

Likewise, the phenomenon of "cognitive dissonance" (Maikovich 2005, 373) is also relevant because it influences actors to ignore information that does not conform to pre-existing theories and ways of thinking. Therefore, when traffic is tailored to reflect these conditions it can create what Caddell (2004) refers to as "inertia of rest", where actors remain committed to certain assumptions even if there is evidence to the contrary. Hence, a strength of Indirect Influence is that the effective use of clandestine influence leverages the ability to exploit the pre-existing cognitive assumptions of target actors. In Figure 8.3 are depicted the types of Indirect Access operations employable by strategic counterintelligence practitioners. This includes means and methods of manipulating information input streams, contesting current and projected situational understanding, creating ambiguity, casting doubt on trusted sources, and compromising insurgent partnerships and relationships.

When represented visually it is apparent that significant vectors exist for Indirect Influence to take place. These are not singular approaches but are highly developed, overlapping, and have strong durational potential. Moreover, the

Figure 8.3 Indirect Access operations.

range of vectors suggests that because so many avenues exist, it is extremely difficult to guard against, predict, or identify the means and approaches incumbent strategic counterintelligence practitioners may employ to achieve their goals.

Environmental control and manipulation

Environmental Control and Manipulation is somewhat removed from the first two approaches. It focuses on changing the operational environments around insurgent command structures at informational, social, political, and physical levels in order to affect and shift the identity-based, instrumental, and relational motivations of organizations into synchronicity with the strategic counterintelligence mission. Once more, operational layering to build on existing gains provides a force-multiplier effect.[11] Environmental Control and Manipulation can be achieved through psychological warfare, human intelligence operations, electronic warfare, cyber warfare, and economic-information warfare. Collectively these form part of an information warfare strategy that includes deception and propaganda, and tangible changes in physical spaces by the alteration of data and assets at localized and at macro levels.

Environmental operations are an element of a larger whole, and a means by which strategic counterintelligence is tied to broader COIN warfare such as external pressures, as well as battlefield containment and segregation operations. Imagine for instance a major engagement between incumbent security forces and insurgent fighters, one in which an order is given for insurgent forces to retreat at a time it is likely they may be gaining a battlefield advantage. Efforts to do this in traditional COIN warfare could come from deceptive communications broadcast in the open for the enemy to hear, or from battlefield psychological operations (PSYOPS), or by the clever use of tactical stratagems.[12] The problem is the likelihood of insurgent commanders suspecting a falsity of opportunity. However, what if such an order come from internal command and control, and from a senior insurgent officer making a well-considered tactical assessment based on reliable information from a trusted adviser, who himself used well-vetted and established intelligence sources? In such an example it is not a choice about deception, but of normal tactical decision-making as a result of how insurgent commanders perceive their operational environments.

The difference is that when decisions are made in the absence of ambiguity and doubt, they are far stronger. Several prominent scholars (Creed and Miles 2006; Markova and Gillespie 2008; Dunning and Fetchenhauer 2012) observe that people trust information from trusted sources far more than they do new information quickly presented to them. Henderson and Gilding refer to this as "hyper-personal communication" (2004, 487). This is an inherent human characteristic that strategic counterintelligence plays upon by understanding the needs of insurgents over the desired outcomes of the incumbent. Proceeding from this internal vantage point provides a conduit of influence and manipulation.

Understanding the social capital and trust pathways in insurgent organizations is a critical element of all operational approaches. Therefore, when information is passed on and decisions made based on how people interpret their surroundings, it is more believable than coming across advantageous information by chance. As Direct Access and Indirect Influence efforts mature, the strategic aspects of these components converge as layering and support, and strengthen Environmental Control and Manipulation efforts.

A primary means of successfully achieving this is the correlation of environmental manipulation operations with actual conditions, but rather than changing the ground, the strategic counterintelligence practitioner aims to change how insurgents perceive it and in turn how they interact with the environment on the ground. Figure 8.4 demonstrates how insurgent operations can be manipulated by influencing decisions about the environment they interact with, noting that environmental data is absorbed into the insurgent organization through the access already established by Direct Access and Indirect Influence operations.

Put simply, strategic counterintelligence actively operates behind the adversary's counterintelligence security screens and protections, going beyond strategic intelligence efforts that are passive and only seek to find, not to change. Caddell states, "a fundamental dichotomy to be found in the confusing world is the division of deception into 'active' and 'passive' categories" (2004, 6). Strategic counterintelligence diffuses this ambiguity and sets a clear pathway to achieve active influencing and manipulation of organizational resilience from

Figure 8.4 Environmental control and manipulation.

inside insurgent organizations themselves, where resilience mechanisms are far more malleable, thereby creating influence and filling the knowledge gap.

Outcomes of the strategic counterintelligence mission

The desired end-state of the strategic counterintelligence mission is the total degradation of threat from insurgent organizations. This can come about through the effective material destruction of their organizational structures, capabilities, and efficiencies or by ownership of control and influence in decision-making and risk considerations, reducing insurgent effectiveness to a point that it is untenable. A third outcome also exists, which consists in a careful balancing act of mitigating the insurgent threat to acceptable levels while simultaneously allowing organizations to function. In the practice of counterintelligence this is perhaps the most advantageous outcome because organizational continuance provides ongoing intelligence exploitation opportunities, as well as openings to expand areas of clandestine influence beyond the original target organization.

This is particularly relevant as the evidence produced throughout this book shows that a potent and extremely mature and complex nexus exists. This nexus includes each of the case study organizations as well as powerful state patrons such as Pakistan, Libya, Malaysia, and Saudi Arabia. Equally, affiliate networks encompassing al-Qaeda, ISIL, the Taliban, multiple UJC member organizations and many other groups in the global jihadist insurgency network are a part of it.[13] Figure 8.5 succinctly shows the three primary outcomes.

The inter-personal socio-economics between these nexus actors, supported by the findings of the study, demonstrate the importance of social capital and trust in organization-to-organization and person-to-person exchanges. This suggests that one of the most critical dangers to the resilience of insurgent organizations is insider threats. Bunn and Sagan (2016) categorically state that the consequences of insider threats for organizational security and efficiency are staggering.[14] Extant data on the ramifications of insider threats in terrorist and insurgent organizations is difficult to determine, largely due to the secrecy of such operations.

However, several highly prominent inverse examples exist, demonstrating the critical danger of malicious insiders. Kim Philby and the Cambridge-Five crippled British anti-Soviet intelligence efforts for years (McComas 2015). The CIA's Aldrich Ames' and FBI's Robert Hanssen's double agentry for the KGB nullified Western intelligence operations for decades (Cherkashin and Feifer 2005). More recently, the Edward Snowden and Bradley/Chelsea Manning leaks degraded the FIVE EYE's intelligence capabilities and resulted in the collapse of significant numbers of allied intelligence programmes and operations (Walsh and Miller 2016). Individually and conjointly, these examples demonstrate just how damaging and effective insider-influenced and -controlled intelligence assets are.

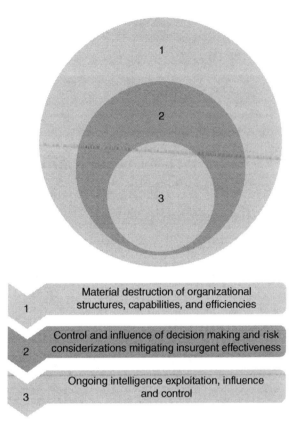

Figure 8.5 The primary outcomes of the strategic counterintelligence mission set.

Section 2: introduction

This section presents a bespoke model of the application of strategic counterintelligence. It employs data and findings from the book case studies, and offers a multi-agent model utilizing a familial insurgency, namely the Haqqani Network in Afghanistan, and a meritocratic insurgency represented by the Abu Sayyaf Group in the Southern Philippines. The model is presented in phases, reflecting the stages of the strategic counterintelligence mission. It commences with Direct Access, then Indirect Influence, and finally Environmental Control and Manipulation. The model shows the nuances of delivering strategic counterintelligence missions against a familial insurgent organization and a meritocratic one. From a diagnostic perspective, assessment of the manipulation of resilience variables provides an excellent framework for evaluating specific means and nuanced influence methods related to degrading insurgent organizational efficiency, and ultimately their resilience. This delivers additional validation of the research findings and of the effectiveness of the strategic counterintelligence doctrine to disrupt organizational resilience.

Phase one – direct access

Phase one of the modelling commences with Direct Access operations. Analysis of the Haqqani Network insurgency shows that there are several key decision-making bodies, or Shura councils, responsible for strategic, operational and tactical direction, risk management, and organizational governance.[15] These Shura represent a highly attractive point of access for intelligence exploitation that is scalable, meaning they can be equally targeted with the spectrum of mission types.

The majority of members of each Shura are eligible for Direct Access operations of overt development (including agent development under operational cover), and by covert influence. While it is extremely unlikely that the most senior organizational leaders, such as Siraj Haqqani, Anas Haqqani, Taj Mir Jawad and the like could overtly be developed as agents, they are susceptible to covert influencing and to overt overtures from the Afghan National Government, the U.S., and other international actors including perhaps Russia, Pakistan, or India.[16] While such approaches would be political rather than part of a strategic counterintelligence doctrine, they could certainly be well supported by Direct Access operations and the development and influence of associates.

Beyond this powerful apex group there is an array of other leaders, commanders, and managers that would be susceptible to Direct Access. The multi-agent and cooperative nature of the various Shura councils offers the means to do so. Figure 8.6 provides a summary of Direct Access vectors for the Haqqani Network Shura structure. Though brief, it demonstrates that Direct Access can also be achieved by developing agents directly adjacent to the target actors. People with direct connection to target actors who have daily interactions with them, and who are well placed to report out intelligence information as well as

Figure 8.6 Direct Access operations – Haqqani Network.

inject influence and deliver some modicums of stimulus or guidance, are also highly desirable.

Abu Sayyaf similarly has many access points. The splintered, multi-agent, and meritocratic nature of Abu Sayyaf's organizational factions mean that material gains are a strong incentive to members. This is equally apparent in its insurgent factions as well, a fact made apparent in the example of the siege of Marawi that netted tens of millions of dollars. Therefore, Abu Sayyaf's reliance on crime and insurgency-for-profit represents a scalable continuum for intelligence exploitation. Equally, all members are potentially vulnerable to Direct Access operations by developing them as human source agents, or by covertly influencing efforts. Likewise, the potential for fast vertical ascension means that initial efforts can target lower-level members with less security awareness, therefore making access easier. Some obvious Direct Access vectors for the Abu Sayyaf are shown in Figure 8.7.

These parallel examples show that the methodology remains constant, but the means alters between organizations as they reflect familial and meritocratic structures in turn. Likewise, while there are many commonalities there are also noticeable differences, such as leveraging the strong social capital and trust bonds in the familial example of the Haqqani Network, compared to leveraging the strong material and economic desires in the meritocratic example of the Abu Sayyaf. It is interesting to note that if these approaches were reversed and Direct Access was attempted via familial means in the Abu Sayyaf, and through material and economic ones in the Haqqani Network, intelligence penetrations might well occur, but they would be more susceptible to failure, compromise, and liabilities because they go against the grains of the respective conduits of organizational efficiencies present in both examples.

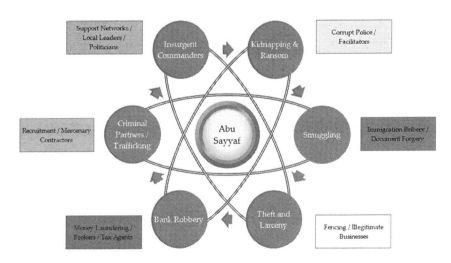

Figure 8.7 Direct Access operations – Abu Sayyaf.

This is because material acquisition is not the primary concern of family organizations in which the security of the family and the retention of familial control is more the central focus. Similarly, in meritocratic organizations, focusing on familial social capital economics over material and professional social capital exchange is not the norm. The consequences of not realizing this and tailoring methods inappropriately may result in unwanted attention to access attempts, and restricted approaches because familial socio-economics do not fit the specific culture and operational synchronicity of organizational structures in meritocracies.

Phase two: indirect influence

Evidence found in the case study research shows that many insurgent organizations have specific and determined characteristics. These drive and reinforce internal security efforts as well as enabling understanding of the counterintelligence risks from incumbent security forces. These present obstacles but also opportunities. While successfully introducing traffic that misleads is a good outcome, simply causing ambiguity and mistrust of intelligence information, in principle, is also a positive result.

There are a number of ways this can happen at the organizational level, including considerations of technical exploitation, social, social-media, exogenous supporters and population resources, justice systems (showing favourable or highly prejudicial treatment to solicit responses), economic changes like contract procurement avenues, and a raft of others. With regard to the Haqqani Network, there are many levers to pull to create access and influence, as well as to support environmental shaping. One readily accessible avenue is through its front companies that have secured hundreds of millions of U.S. dollars' worth of contracts from the Afghan and U.S. Governments. This example shows that profitability is important as it directly supports insurgent operations. It is therefore probably considered to be vital and suggests that threats to resource streams would invoke substantial organizational responses. As a result, correctly deployed Indirect Influence operations may actively shape operational activity by accessing the Haqqani Network through its resource collection agencies.

Additional advantages deriving from this method exist because businesses are likely to be softer target groups, and their counterintelligence strengths are probably less than those organizational areas directly involved in warfighting and broader insurgency. Therefore, businesses and front companies are more susceptible while remaining powerful and important organizational assets. Figure 8.8 highlights Indirect Access vectors for the Haqqani Network using businesses and front companies as the contextual prism.

In the Abu Sayyaf example there are also a multitude of access points. Both organizations maintain well-established and sophisticated networks of closely associated partner actors in the military, police, politics, other public life vocations (religion and public service), and of course partnered criminal gangs and international smuggling networks. Each of these can be used as entry vectors to develop influence injection and covert manipulations, and to extract intelligence through direct development. Bright *et al.* (2017) conducted studies of criminal

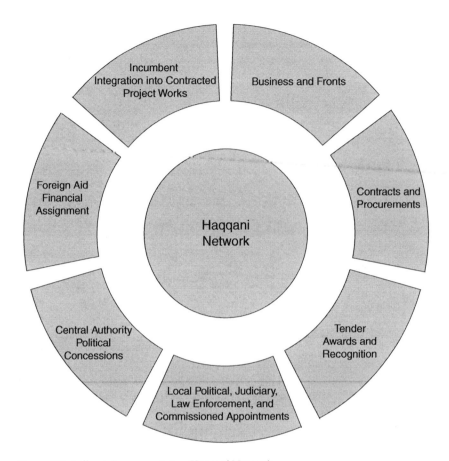

Figure 8.8 Indirect Access vectors – Haqqani Network.

networks and found overwhelmingly that the most important links in a network's success are those actors bound by strong social capital and human capital relationships. Targeting these therefore makes sense. Figure 8.9 illustrates several operational vectors of Indirect Influence for the Abu Sayyaf.

While the examples for both the Haqqani Network and Abu Sayyaf are by no means comprehensive, they do show that a plethora of vectors exists, and this list is only limited by imagination. Likewise, each vector probably has a similar array of sub-vectors, meaning that as with the broader strategic counterintelligence doctrine, approaches can be layered, multi-faceted, and mutually supportive as the capability is evolved.

Phase three: environmental control and manipulation

Developing and deploying an information warfare strategy to support Environmental Control and Manipulation is complex. Because it is a non-linear undertaking,

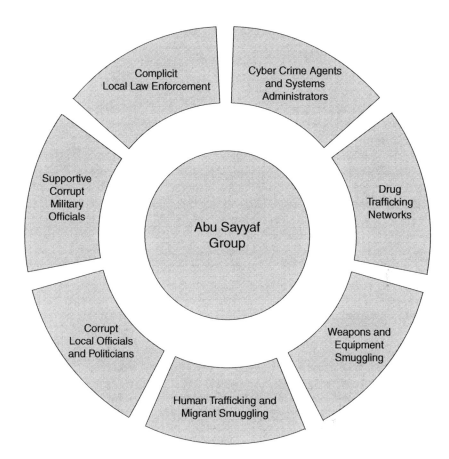

Figure 8.9 Indirect Access vectors – Abu Sayyaf.

controlling the insurgency environment is not about destroying forces or assets, but is about controlling options and choices by creating dilemmas, as well as presenting potential solutions to them. Those solutions are disadvantageous for insurgents and advantageous for incumbents while appearing to be the other way around. Dilemmas can be created in an ad-hoc fashion, drawing from the daily interactions of insurgents and their environments, or they can be developed around elaborate empirical and compliance measures to induce action and reaction.

In other terms, Environmental Control and Manipulation can include elaborately patterned dilemmas as well as the distinct absence of patterned dilemma activity. As Kasfir notes, the dilemmas faced by insurgent organizations may "constrict or even subvert their public commitments, or even their private principles they value" (2002, 2). Two major dilemma types in conflict theatres are avoidance and engagement (Walzer 2016). As with other paradoxes, when these dilemmas arise insurgents must make risk assessments and selections. If they engage they risk avoiding another conflict they may be better placed to win; if they avoid, they may be forced to engage elsewhere at greater cost.

When reinforced by the layering effect, and particularly the Indirect Influence-derived traffic that correlates to new environmental conditions, dilemmas can be presented without ambiguity. As a result, insurgent command and control would see an environment that is supported by the intelligence information that comes across its own internal networks. This adds validity and reinforces decision-making in a manipulated reality, increasing the potential that a new reality will be accepted and even normalized. When combined, the holistic layers of strategic counterintelligence that includes and supports this mission type are very powerful.

Besides physical characteristics of the battlefield, such as terrain and mobility infrastructure, it is information systems, communications, civil and social infrastructure, the projection of hard-power force delivery assets, and manipulation of political circumstance and tides that incumbent forces would use for control and manipulation. Largely, these exist as extant hard- and soft-power pressures. The theatre of war is replete with material properties that can be exploited and manoeuvred, but information warfare requires an additional component. Luckily, that component is in abundance. As the research has found, organizational social capital, efficiency, and ultimately, resilience require people and how they interact with each other more so than any other variables. As a result, the non-linear nature of strategic counterintelligence focuses on perceptions over tangibles.

Showcasing this non-linear nature, Henshaw's Loop, or "H-Loop" (Figure 8.10) presented below, demonstrates that manipulation of human and technical resilience vulnerabilities can have a range of effects on insurgent organizational robustness and longevity. Operations, training, recruitment, financing and the capacity for insurgents to continue to work at ongoing functional levels effectively can all be manipulated directly. Likewise, the development and presentation of dilemmas and nuanced possible solutions that are surreptitiously presented, and supported by multiple layers of veracity, make the clandestine influencing of insurgent risk/reward decision-making achievable. This can impact insurgent warfare strategies, operational planning, command and control intentions, organizational and cellular modus operandi, communications culture, and the retention and expansion of membership bases, all leading to the degradation of resilience.

Outcomes of the modelling

The modelling is comprised of three units, concurrent with the three phases of the strategic counterintelligence mission schema. These are not sequential but per se, can be undertaken in any order or combination. This is achievable because as the modelling has depicted, they are overlapping, non-linear, and complementary. Importantly, each level provides increased access and effectiveness for the next, but the model also works in reverse from the macro strategic

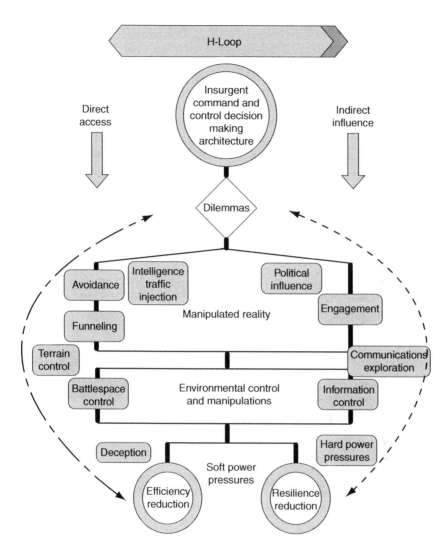

Figure 8.10 Henshaw's Loop of Organizational Manipulation.

level to the middle operations level, and down once more to the intimate tactical level. This multi-directional capability is the solutions-based strategic element of the doctrine. The three phases of the doctrine form the plan, providing the minutiae and architecture of how the strategy is achieved.

Likewise, the modelling is developed from the findings of the research. It reflects the conclusions that insurgent organizational resilience is a result of organizational efficiency. The purveyors of this are people, each interacting with others using social capital and trust. People, and the interactions between them, become central aspects of any future strategic counterintelligence programme.

The combat theatre is densely populated with a significant range of these actors. Incumbents and insurgents, like criminals, police, politicians, and state and social institutions play important and central roles in the continuance or abatement of conflicts. Other groups like civilians are either caught between the contesting sides or are a direct part of one or the other. In addition, where there is war there is profit as criminals, corrupt officials and security forces, transnational networks, and neighbouring states can each have strong self-interests. Each and every one of these is a potential vector of intelligence exploitation.

The modelling also tells us that within this continuum information flows between actors and between levels, rising and descending between the tactical and the strategic in cycles. The synergy of the strategic counterintelligence toolset utilizes this, creating control by manipulating the sources of information and the channels through which information moves. Using layering, this removes ambiguity and negative information effects because it exploits the existing information architecture of the insurgent battle-space. For example, Direct Access targets the sources and methods of intelligence that insurgent organizations use. Indirect Influence targets the intelligence product, or traffic, that insurgent command and control consumes. Environmental Control and Manipulation supports insurgent assessments and further influences insurgent choices by clandestinely presenting dilemmas, as depicted in the H-Loop.

Additionally, the modelling generates two further findings of interest. First, while people may be the most important single characteristic of any organization, because without them organizations would not exist, they do not in and of themselves represent a variable of resilience. Without rules, structures, goals, means, and methods, people cannot form organizations to achieve political outcomes. This is supported by Katz and Kahn, who find that the "interdependent behaviour of many people in their supportive and complementary actions takes on a form or structure which needs to be conceptualized at a more appropriate stage" (1996, 17). That stage is institutionalized as organizations.

In turn, there is no singular resilience variable that represents a generalizable Achilles heel. The research has clearly determined that organizational efficiency is the greatest determinant of organizational resilience, but it is not a singular dynamic that can be targeted. Rather, many drivers of resilience must be targeted together using the human dimension as the means of both access and manipulation. This means that a non-linear, multilateral approach is required to attack multiple manifestations of organizational resilience simultaneously.

Secondly, when organizational resilience begins to decay through the erosion of efficiency, the misdirection and manipulation of direction, and the destruction of tangible material capabilities in concert, insurgent organizations become extremely susceptible to extant hard- and soft-power pressures. This is a result of reducing internal strengths and increasing internal weaknesses, making it progressively difficult for organizations to address, counter, or mitigate damage they sustain from traditional COIN and CT treatments. Regardless of being vertical or horizontal, holacratic, hierarchical or diffused, organizational steering comes from leaders as the primary decision-makers. This presents the conclusion that it is how people interact with each other as organizational members, dictated by social capital and trust, that is the greatest strength, and therefore the most accessible vulnerability.

Section 3: the future

This section discusses the implications for the future of the strategic counterintelligence doctrine and the developmental needs for it to successfully erode, degrade, and manipulate insurgent organizational resilience as a tool of conflict reduction. Strategic Counterintelligence is the covert and clandestine ownership of insurgent decision-making processes to achieve a desired endstate. It offers a highly effective array of tangible methods for orchestrating the manipulation of insurgent organizational resilience variables. These have been identified and examined extensively throughout the book, and tested here briefly in the modelling.

Strategic counterintelligence is not a replacement option for COIN, counterterrorism, or other forms of warfare as practised today. Rather, it offers an additional means of enhancing them now and in the future. Additionally, strategic counterintelligence may offer significant value in the formative stages of domestic unrest, political instability, and ultimately civil war. This is because it is during the initial phases of insurgency in the organizing and guerrilla periods that it is most vulnerable (Tse-Tung 1961; Leites and Wolf 1970; Kalyanaraman 2003).[17]

In order to successfully build and mature strategic counterintelligence as an intelligence-led doctrine of counterinsurgent warfare, it first needs to be understood. This comes initially from knowing what it is and understanding how it functions. This chapter, and indeed this book, establishes the development of that knowledge. Next, new learning is needed for intelligence and operational practitioners, not to advance new methodologies per se, but to reconfigure and redeploy existing ones. Using prevailing operational approaches, capabilities and methods and layering them has the potential to deliver new proficiencies and outcomes. Likewise, changing the mindset from active defence, present in counterintelligence and intelligence collection, to offensive clandestine manipulation and covert control will take time.

However, before strategic counterintelligence can be practised, the target environments and theatres of conflict need to be more deeply understood from the vectors of organizational resilience. In particular, the organizations being worked against must be understood in terms of how they are susceptible. This book has presented an extensive study of the resilience of insurgent organizations, something applicable to terrorism as well as many other groups, collectives, and institutions. In short, strategic counterintelligence doctrine goes beyond prevalent intelligence collection methods that, while effective at providing a comprehensive exogenous overview of adversarial capabilities and intentions, do not provide access or means of endogenous regulation.

To change this, intelligence practitioners and policy-makers in particular need to develop a strategic mindset, looking years if not decades ahead. This will be difficult. Increasingly intelligence has become an "on-demand" product, fostering the urgency of tactical thinking to produce immediate results. As a consequence, strategic processes are often pushed to the background. Well-crafted intelligence collections and counterintelligence operations are finely honed, producing compartmentalized and detailed intelligence products. However, strategic counterintelligence is much less amenable to compartmentalization. The macro perspectives of theatre, national, and indeed geopolitical security realities are intertwined with a plethora of issues, actors, and competitive adversarial interests. As civil wars current and past clearly demonstrate, the challenges of insurgent conflicts are profoundly complex and durational, and attempts to address them with on-demand and near real-time tactical intelligence systems have been unable to deliver the longevity of outcomes needed.

Strategic counterintelligence doctrine offers a bespoke means to address insurgency holistically, and fight to win the war by working inside insurgent organizations themselves, rather than fighting small tactical battles against them from the outside in the hope of achieving compounding gains. Importantly, strategic counterintelligence is not a competitive doctrine, it does not replace existing methods, nor does it detract from them. Rather, it is supporting, complementary, and force-multiplying. Strategic counterintelligence therefore needs to be measured both in holistic terms, and in terms of the covert influence and clandestine manipulation capabilities it casts over the protracted duration of insurgencies in civil wars.

From theory to practice

This chapter has identified ways strategic counterintelligence can access insurgent organizations to manipulate their resilience with covert control and clandestine influence. However, what has been discussed here is but a fraction of the myriad of choices and methods available. Of those, most are not new and are practised in different forms or for different purposes. This is an important contributing factor as the tools, capabilities, practitioners, and assets are all present. What remains is the need for advocates to champion the doctrine. This is about changing perceptions and encouraging collaboration rather than competition or rivalry. Extant intelligence operations provide the product for the ever-hungry consumers of tactical intelligence of the here and now. Contrarily, strategic counterintelligence leads the tactical operations towards the end goal, rather than tactical operations steering hopefully towards one. Strategic counterintelligence is therefore the pull towards the desired end state rather than a push through the fog of war.

In order to operationalize the doctrine, five stages are required. First, the goals must be clearly understood, particularly the various outcomes the goals actually represent. For example, the goal of degrading insurgent resilience is a matter of accessing and influencing organizational variables that contribute to it.

This enables the understanding of operational tasks in real terms. Next, goals need to be translated down into the major phases of the strategic counterintelligence mission. This means breaking down and grouping approaches into goal-aligned programmes reflected in the Direct Access, Indirect Influence, and Environmental Control and Manipulation layers. This also allows greater understanding, which results in better task management and tracking.

Third, available assets and capabilities should be mapped and clearly correlated to layering assignments to understand how the strategic counterintelligence mission can accomplish its goals. This requires knowing the full extent of available resources from COIN agencies, systems, and assets and which ones can be re-tasked. The fourth step of operationalization is defining accountabilities. This would usually be done by setting timeframes. This is possible for activities that are much closer to the tactical end of the operational spectrum, but are likely to be somewhat looser towards the strategic end. They are critical however, because it is difficult to accomplish key outcomes in the absence of measurement. Therefore other metrics can be used in place of linear measurements of time. These include gains against insurgent territorial access or control, reductions in attacks, and increases in political solutions versus conflict options and the like.

Last, the combination of these processes needs to be executed at the individual mission level, with larger operational programmes being divided into chunks, or mission-sets. This allows for them to be tasked, resourced, managed and executed efficiently, including their interdependencies with other mission-sets as layering occurs. Being the area of interface with insurgents in the conflict environment, this is perhaps the most critical area where attention is needed. Steven Feld observers that tactical planning must be able to "delineate to the maximum extent possible the timelines, dependency relationships, resource allocations and costs" (2018, 2). This will be particularly important across all operational areas to reduce operational collisions and friction.

Conclusion

Every insurgent organization in war is on a trajectory to its default future. That future is not a result of passivity, but, rather, it comes about through planned actions, strategic design, and daily operations. The goals of strategic counterintelligence are to influence that default future and change the trajectory of insurgent organizations to make them weaker and less resilient as they move forward. These invisible rails of organizational trajectory are determined by strategic navigational forces, and are most critical when complex junctions of choice and intersections of decision arrive. The more mature, efficient, and resilient organizations are, the more likely it is their strategic navigation will be robust and able to recover from externally derived damage.

Hard-power and soft-power pressures are the means incumbents and other actors use to create junctions and therefore opportunities to damage insurgents. Some of these are the resources, recruits, mobility conditions, and partnerships organizations need, making them logical targets. It is in this external environment that COIN efforts reside. However, intersections of decision are internal and organizationally individual and unique. Variables of behaviour, social capital and trust exchange, intelligence analysis, promotion, organizational structures, hierarchies, command and control positioning, operational mindsets, informal networks, vested interests and more are all internal functions, ensconced securely within organizations that are often not accessible from the outside.

As a direct result, the bespoke strategic counterintelligence doctrine presented in this book embeds inside insurgent organizations and utilizes the strengths and weaknesses they possess as identified in the case study research. The strategic signatures of an organization's trajectory, and particularly the unique internal intersection decision-making that occurs, present the opportunities needed to influence organizational choices at various points along their axis of travel. This is not sudden or dramatic, but subtle and elusive. Many insurgent organizations share similar conditions, threats, and external pressures and therefore a similar strategic axis, but it is how they perceive their environments and make internal choices when dilemmas arise that dictates what their future will be.

This internal realm is highly susceptible and malleable to strategic counterintelligence because internal choices are reflected in organizational operations and how they move forward. Likewise, an insurgent organization's strategic signature can be shaped and funnelled in ways such that it becomes self-limiting, where decisions can compound to increasingly result in fewer choices and greater degradation of resilience variables. If organizations can be influenced and manipulated to follow certain paths over time, rather than forge their own, they can be defeated.

In closing, success at defeating insurgents in the long term, and their use of terrorism as a tool-set in the short term, can be achieved by eroding organizational resilience, but this requires clarity, purpose, and commitment. Achieving success necessitates that the people using strategic counterintelligence, from the policy-makers to operational commanders, and on to the tactical practitioners, all have the right level of understanding and incentives to execute the doctrine. Those that do understand what is being done, and how and why, will ultimately contribute to a better understanding of insurgent organizational resilience, and critically, how to defeat it. This brings hope to ending the ever-fought wars.

Notes

1 Modelling has become a well-accepted method of testing ideas and validating theories and research agendas. Granger and Teräsvirta find that modelling is particularly useful when focused on non-linear, dynamic, and multivariate relationships. Succar contends that modelling allows for the systematic investigation of divergent fields, components, and the delineation of boundaries. Similarly, Lockett *et al.* assert that modelling hierarchical processes, as are found in command and control orientated organizations, is effective at understanding group decision-making processes.

SOURCES: Clive Granger and Timo Terasvirta, 1993. "Modelling Non-Linear Economic Relationships". *Journal of Applied Econometrics* 9 (4): 479–480; Bilal Succar, 2009. "Building Information Modelling Framework: A Research and Delivery Foundation for Industry Stakeholders". *Automation in Construction* 18 (3): 357–375; Geoff Lockett, *et al.*, 1987. "Modelling a Research Portfolio Using AHP: A Group Decision Process". *Journal of Mathematical Modelling* 8 (1987): 142–148.

2 Strategic counterintelligence is just as applicable to terrorism as it is to insurgencies. However, as established comprehensively in the book there are distinct differences between terrorist groups and insurgent organizations. Strategic counterintelligence treatments against terrorist groups at home are driven to achieve the same mission outcomes, but have a far greater focus on actionable intelligence as terrorism attack planning is far more dynamic, and takes place over far shorter timeframes of months, weeks, days, and even hours. Insurgency on the other hand takes place over months, years, and even decades. SOURCE: Author comments; Seth Jones, 2008. "Defeating Terrorist Groups". *Testimony presented before the House Armed Services Committee, Subcommittee on Terrorism and Unconventional Threats and Capabilities.* Santa Monica: RAND.

3 Counterintelligence screens are referred to as the efforts and means used to protect from adversarial intelligence development of oneself and one's organization.

4 Human Source intelligence is geared to directly targeting adversarial insurgent decision-making infrastructure through a range of collection and assessment methodologies. Extant counterintelligence operations also provide a strong basis for developing the strategic dimension, using existing technical, analytical, investigative, agent-based collection and other methods. SOURCES: Vic Catano and Jeffery Gauger, 2017. "Information Fusion: Intelligence Centres and Intelligence Analysis". In *Information Sharing in Military Operations*, eds. Irina Goldenberg *et al.* Switzerland: Springer, 17–34; Robert Clark, 2016. "A Network View: A Target-Centric Approach". In *Intelligence Analysis: A Target-Centric Approach*, ed. Robert Clark. Singapore: Sage, 358–376; Nicholas Eftimiades, 1994. *Chinese Intelligence Operations: Espionage Damage Assessment Branch, US Defence Intelligence Agency.* Newberry Park: Frank Cass and Co. Ltd.

5 SIGINT is signals intelligence; GEOINT is geospatial intelligence based on satellite data; HUMINT is human-source intelligence derived from agents; SOCMINT refers to social media information collection and analysis; IMINT is imagery intelligence. COMINT is communications intelligence and ELINT is non-communications electromagnetic emissions intelligence. See: Lock Johnson, 2007. *Handbook of Intelligence Studies*. Abington and New York: Taylor & Francis.

6 Afghanistan is a shining example. Neta Crawford, Co-Director at the Costs of War Project at Brown University, puts the cost of the U.S. war in Afghanistan at U.S.$2 trillion since 2001. Crawford also forecasts an additional $7.9 trillion in future spending on veterans' services. The Watson Institute puts this figure higher at U.S.$4.8 trillion while Harvard economist Lina Blimes costs the war efforts at between U.S.$4 and $6 trillion. SOURCES: Charles Koch Foundation, "The true costs of the Afghan war, America's longest and most invisible war". *News Letters.* Accessed 10 December 2018. https://bigthink.com/charles-koch-foundation/the-true-costs-of-the-afghan-war-americas-longest-and-most-invisible-war; Neta Crawford, 2016. *Update on the Human Costs of War for Afghanistan and Pakistan, 2001 to mid-2016.* Paper, Boston: Washington Institute of International & Public Affairs. Accessed 5 February 2020. https://watson.brown.edu/costsofwar/files/cow/imce/papers/2016/War%20in%20Afghanistan%20and%20Pakistan%20UPDATE_FINAL_corrected%20date.pdf; Mark Thompson, 2015. "The True Cost of the Afghanistan War May Surprise You". *Time: Politics and Military.* Accessed 22 December 2018. http://time.com/3651697/afghanistan-war-cost/.

7 Operational cover has many forms. It can consist of commercial cover, which in the context of terrorism or insurgency can include criminal networks, smugglers, and other enablers including donors and supporters. Or, cover can be official but most probably under false-flag terms, meaning that intelligence officers would present themselves as officers of intelligence services from countries other than their own. Therefore cover is critical to conceal the actual hands of intelligence operations to protect their activities and goals. SOURCES: John Sano, 2015. "The Changing Shape of HUMINT". *AFIO's Intelligencer Journal* 21 (3): 77–80; Harvey McCadden, 1995. "Cover in Unconventional Operations". *Center for the Study of Intelligence* 5 (3): 1–4.

8 This is potentially more likely to occur in meritocratic insurgencies where there can be more avenues to create divisions in operational control because of the different personal goals of command actors. This offers opportunities to the strategic counterintelligence practitioner to foster ambiguity and instability in command structures by seeding legitimacy issue, consequences, and the moral standing of advocates. SOURCE: Charles Beitz, 1989. "Covert Intervention as a Moral Problem". *Journal of Ethics and International Affairs* 3 (1): 49–50.

9 Crous observes that in a law-enforcement context, intelligence tasking is about directing human source agents to obtain information and knowledge about specific activities so law enforcement can disrupt criminal activities. This mirrors traditional counterintelligence human source operations, but with a different focus of collecting even more information to enable intelligence agencies to monitor over the long term, rather than necessarily disrupt over the shorter term. In the strategic counterintelligence context, human source agents would also inject false intelligence, influence decision-making, and obfuscate risk analysis decision-making processes. SOURCES: Charl Crous, 2009. "Human Intelligence Sources: Challenges in Policy Development". *Security Challenges* 5 (3): 117–127; Michelle Van Cleave, 2007. *Counterintelligence and National Strategy*. Washington, D.C.: National Defense University.

10 Intelligence product refers to information that has been analysed into a tangible product that informs decision-makers and provides a deeper understanding and interpretation of activities relevant to their operational needs. Intelligence processes are phases of analytical research and assessment that provide deeper understanding of issues to develop strategies to respond and adapt to changing situations. SOURCE: Johnson, *Handbook of Intelligence Studies*, 2007.

11 A force-multiplier is an element that enhances the capabilities or the effectiveness of military units and assets beyond conventional levels. For example, a smaller Special Forces task force attached to a regular infantry company is a force-multiplier because it enhances the scope of operations able to be undertaken. Likewise, the utilization of new technologies and the inclusion of hardware absent elsewhere in the battlespace are also examples of force-multipliers. SOURCES: Blaise Cronin and Holly Crawford, 1999. "Information Warfare: Its Application in Military and Civilian Contexts". *The Information Society: An International Journal* 15 (4): 257–263; Henry Bartlett *et al.*, "The Art of Strategy and Force Planning". *Naval War College Review* 48 (2): 114–126.

12 Bernstein remarks that battlefield psychological operations (PSYOPS) employ political warfare characteristics and are directed at influencing an adversary's mind over their physical conditions. SOURCE: Alvin Bernstein, 1989. "Political Strategies in Coercive Diplomacy and Limited War". In *Political Warfare and Psychological Operations: Rethinking the US Approach*, eds. Frank Barnett and Carnes Lord. New York: National Strategy Information Center, 145.

13 As described in Chapter 4, the UJC, or United Jihad Council, is a conglomerate of 13 organizations including Al Mansoorian, Army of Madinah, the Falah-i-Insaniat Foundation, Islamic Jamaat ud Dawa, Tehreek-e-Tahafuz Qibla Awal, Paasban-e-Kashmir, Movement for Safeguarding the First Centre of Prayer, and Paasban-i-Ahle-Hadith.

14 One of the most successful examples of successful counterinsurgency intelligence operations is the near-complete penetration of Indonesian Komando Jihad. Commanded by the Intelligence Chief Murtopo, over 180 insurgents from Darul Islam and Jemaah Islamiyah were netted in the operation. SOURCES: James Cotton, 2001. "Part of the Indonesian World: Lessons in East Timor Policy-Making, 1974–76". *Australian Journal of International Affairs* 55 (1): 119–131; Martin Van Bruinessen, 2018. "Genealogies of Islamic Radicalism in Post-Suharto Indonesia". *South East Asia Research* 10 (2): 117–154; George Friedman, 2016. "The Cycle of Terrorism: Identifying Terrorists Requires a Shift in Intelligence Methods". *Indian Strategic Studies* 3 (2016). Accessed 5 October 2019. http://strategicstudyindia.blogspot.com/2016_03_25_archive.html.

15 As established in Chapter 3, command and control positions in the Haqqani Network are extensively connected via kinship. While all senior middle-level and senior leaders, managers, and commanders are potential intelligence targets, the scope is limited here to the most senior leaders for brevity.

16 In the case of Anas Haqqani, who has been held in custody for several years, investigators were unable to gain any intelligence of value from him. However, one team in 2017 observed that Anas always carried a book of poetry with him. Before this, no other investigator had bothered to ask Anas about it. The new team developed extensive dialogue with Anas about poetry and as a result, they were able to glean vital intelligence information from him. SOURCE: Provided to the author by a confidential source who had direct access to Anas Haqqani.

17 Fearon and Laitin observe that in many instances, insurgencies during their infancy splutter along at very low levels of intensity for some time, and only later flare suddenly into significant conflict when conditions are ripe. This can occur over years or decades. SOURCE: James Fearon and David Laitin, 2003. "Ethnicity, Insurgency, and Civil War". *The American Political Science Review* 97 (1): 75–90.

References

Bartlett, Henry, Holman, Paul, and Somes, Timothy. "The Art of Strategy and Force Planning". *Naval War College Review* 48 (2): 114–126.

Beitz, Charles. 1989. "Covert Intervention as a Moral Problem". *Journal of Ethics and International Affairs* 3 (1): 49–50.

Berstein, Alvin. 1989. "Political Strategies in Coercive Diplomacy and Limited War". In *Political Warfare and Psychological Operations: Rethinking the US Approach*, edited by Frank Barnett and Carnes Lord, 145. New York, National Strategy Information Center.

Bright, David, Greenhill, Catherine, Britz, Thomas, Ritter, Alison, and Morselli, Carlo. 2017. "Criminal Network Vulnerabilities and Adaptations". *Journal of Global Crime* 18 (4): 424–441.

Bunn, Matthew and Sagan, Scott. 2016. "Introduction". In *Insider Threats*, edited by Matthew Bunn and Scott Sagan, 1–10. New York: Cornell Univeristy Press.

Caddell, Joseph. 2004. "Deception 101 – Primer on Deception". *Conference on Strategic Deception in Modern Democracies: Ethical, Legal, and Policy Challenges.* North Carolina: U.S. Army War College, the U.S. Naval Academy, and the Triangle Institute of Security Studies. 1–26.

Catano, Vic and Gauger, Jeffery. 2017. "Information Fusion: Intelligence Centres and Intelligence Analysis". In *Information Sharing in Military Operations*, edited by Irina Goldenberg, Joseph Soeters, and Waylon Dean, 17–34. Switzerland: Springer.

Charles Koch Foundation. "The true costs of the Afghan war, America's longest and most invisible war". *News Letters.* Accessed 10 December 2018. https://bigthink.com/charles-koch-foundation/the-true-costs-of-the-afghan-war-americas-longest-and-most-invisible-war.

Cherkashin, Victor and Feifer, Gregory. 2005. *Spy Handler: Memoir of a KGB Officer – The True Story of the Man Who Recruited Robert Hanssen and Aldrich Ames.* Cambridge: Basic Books.

Clark, Robert. 2016. "A Network View: A Target-Centric Approach". In *Intelligence Analysis: A Target-Centric Approach,* edited by Robert Clark, 358–376. Singapore: Sage.

Cotton, James. 2001. "Part of the Indonesian World: Lessons in East Timor Policy-Making, 1974–76". *Australian Journal of International Affairs* 55 (1): 119–131.

Crawford, Neta. 2016. *Update on the Human Costs of War for Afghanistan and Pakistan, 2001 to mid-2016.* Paper, Boston: Washington Institute of International & Public Affairs. Accessed 5 February 2020. https://watson.brown.edu/costsofwar/files/cow/imce/papers/2016/War%20in%20Afghanistan%20and%20Pakistan%20UPDATE_FINAL_corrected%20date.pdf

Creed, Douglas and Miles, Raymond. 2006. "Trust in Organizations: A Conceptual Framework Linking Organizational Forms, Managerial Philosophies, and the Opportunity Costs of Controls". In *Trust in Organizations: Frontiers of Theory and Researchv,* edited by Roderick Kramer and Tom Tyler, 16–38. London and New Delhi: Sage.

Cronin, Blaise and Crawford, Holly. 1999. "Information Warfare: Its Application in Military and Civilian Contexts". *The Information Society: An International Journal* 15 (4): 257–263.

Crous, Charl. 2009. "Human Intelligence Sources: Challenges in Policy Development". *Security Challenges* 5 (3): 117–127.

Dunning, David, Fetchenhauer, Detlef, and Schlösser, Thomas. 2012. "Trust as a Social and Emotional Act: Non-economic Considerations in Trust Behavior". *Journal of Economic Psycho0logy* 33 (3): 686–694.

Eftimiades, Nicholas. 1994. *Chinese Intelligence Operations: Espionage Damage Assessment Branch, US Defence Intelligence Agency.* Newberry Park, Frank Cass and Co. Ltd.

Fearon, James and Laitin, David. 2003. "Ethnicity, Insurgency, and Civil War". *The American Political Science Review* 97 (1): 75–90.

Feld, Steven. 2018. "The 10 Essentials of Operational Planning You Need to Know". *Greater Phenix.* 24 September. Accessed 1 January 2019. https://greaterphoenix.score.org/blog/10-essentials-operational-planning-you-need-know-part-1.

Franco, Joseph. 2017. "Assessing the Feasibility of a 'Wilayah Mindanao'". *Perspectives on Terrorism* 11 (4): 29–38.

Friedman, George. 2016. "The Cycle of Terrorism: Identifying Terrorists Requires a Shift in Intelligence Methods". *Indian Strategic Studies* 3 (2016). Accessed 5 October 2019. http://strategicstudyindia.blogspot.com/2016_03_25_archive.html.

Granger, Clive and Terasvirta, Timo. 1993. "Modelling Non-Linear Economic Relationships". *Journal of Applied Econometrics* 9 (4): 479–480.

Heidenrich, John. 2007. "The State of Strategic Intelligence". *Studies in Intelligence* 51 (2): 1–15.

Henderson, Samantha and Gilding, Michael. 2004. "'I've Never Clicked This Much with Anyone in My Life': Trust and Hyperpersonal Communication in Online Friendships". *Journal of New Media & Society* 6 (4): 487–506.

Johnson, Lock. 2007. *Handbook of Intelligence Studies.* Abington and New York: Taylor & Francis.

Jones, Seth. 2008. "Defeating Terrorist Groups". *Testimony presented before the House Armed Services Committee, Subcommittee on Terrorism and Unconventional Threats and Capabilities.* Santa Monica: RAND.

Kalyanaraman, S. 2003. "Conceptualisations on Guerrilla Warfare". *Strategic Analysis* 27 (2): 172–185.

Kasfir, Nelson. 2002. "Dilemmas of Popular Support in Guerrilla War: The National Resistance Army in Uganda, 1981–86". *LiCEP 6.* Los Angeles: University of California. 1–47.

Katz, Daniel and Kahn, Robert. 1996. "Organization and the Systems Concept". In *The Social Psychology of Organizations,* edited by Daniel Katz and Robert Kahn, 17–35. New York, Chichester, Brisbane, Toronto, Singapore: John Wiley and Sons.

Kent, Sherman. 1966. "Substantive Content: The Speculative-Evaluative Element". In *Strategic Intelligence for American World Policy,* edited by Sherman Kent, 39–68. Princeton: Princeton University Press.

Kunda, Ziva and Thagard, Paul. 1996. "Forming Impressions from Stereotypes, Traits, and Behaviors: A Parallel-Constraint-Satisfaction Theory". *Psychological Review* 103 (2): 284–308.

Leites, Nathan and Wolf, Charles Jr. 1970. *Rebellion and Authority: An Analytical Essay on Insurgent Conflicts.* Chicago: Markham.

Libicki, Martin. 1995. *What is Information Warfare?* Washington, D.C.: National Defense University.

Lockett, Geoff, Stratford, Mike, Cox, Barry, Yallup, Barrie Hetherington. 1987. "Modelling a Research Portfolio Using AHP: A Group Decision Process". *Journal of Mathematical Modelling* 8 (1987): 142–148.

Maikovich, Andrea Kohn. 2005. "A New Understanding of Terrorism Using Cognitive Dissonance Principles". *Journal for the Theory of Social Behaviour* 35 (4): 373–397.

Markova, Ivana and Gillispie, Alex. 2008. *Trust and Distrust: Sociocultural Perspectives.* Charlotte, NC: Information Age Publishing.

McCadden, Harvey. 1995. "Cover in Unconventional Operations". *Centre for the Study of Intelligence* 5 (3): 1–4.

McComas, Kyra. 2015. "The Shadow of Kim Philby: Deceit, Betrayal, and British Espionage Literature". *Historical Perspectives* 20 (8): 38–72.

Sano, John. 2015. "The Changing Shape of HUMINT". *AFIO's Intelligencer Journal* 21 (3): 77–80.

Spellman, Barbara, Ullman, Jodie, and Holyoak, Keith. 1993. "A Coherence Model of Cognitive Consistency: Dynamics of Attitude Change During the Persian Gulf War". *Journal of Scoial Issues* 49 (4): 147–165.

Succar, Bilal. 2009. "Building Information Modelling Framework: A Research and Delivery Foundation for Industry Stakeholders". *Automation in Construction* 18 (3): 357–375.

Thompson, Mark. 2015. "The True Cost of the Afghanistan War May Surprise You". *Time: Politics and Military.* Accessed 22 December 2018. http://time.com/3651697/afghanistan-war-cost/.

Tse-Tung, Mao. 1961. *Mao Tse-Tung on Guerrilla Warfare.* First edition. Westport: Prager.

Van Bruinessen, Martin. 2018. "Genealogies of Islamic Radicalism in Post-Suharto Indonesia". *South East Asia Research* 10 (2): 117–154.

Van Cleave, Michelle. 2007. *Counterintelligence and National Strategy*. Washington, D.C.: National Defense University.

Walsh, Patrick and Miller, Seumas. 2016. "Rethinking 'Five Eyes' Security Intelligence Collection Policies and Practice Post Snowden". *Intelligence and National Security* 31 (3): 345–368.

Walzer, Michael. 2016. "The Risk Dilemma". *Philosophia* 44 (2): 289–293.

Index